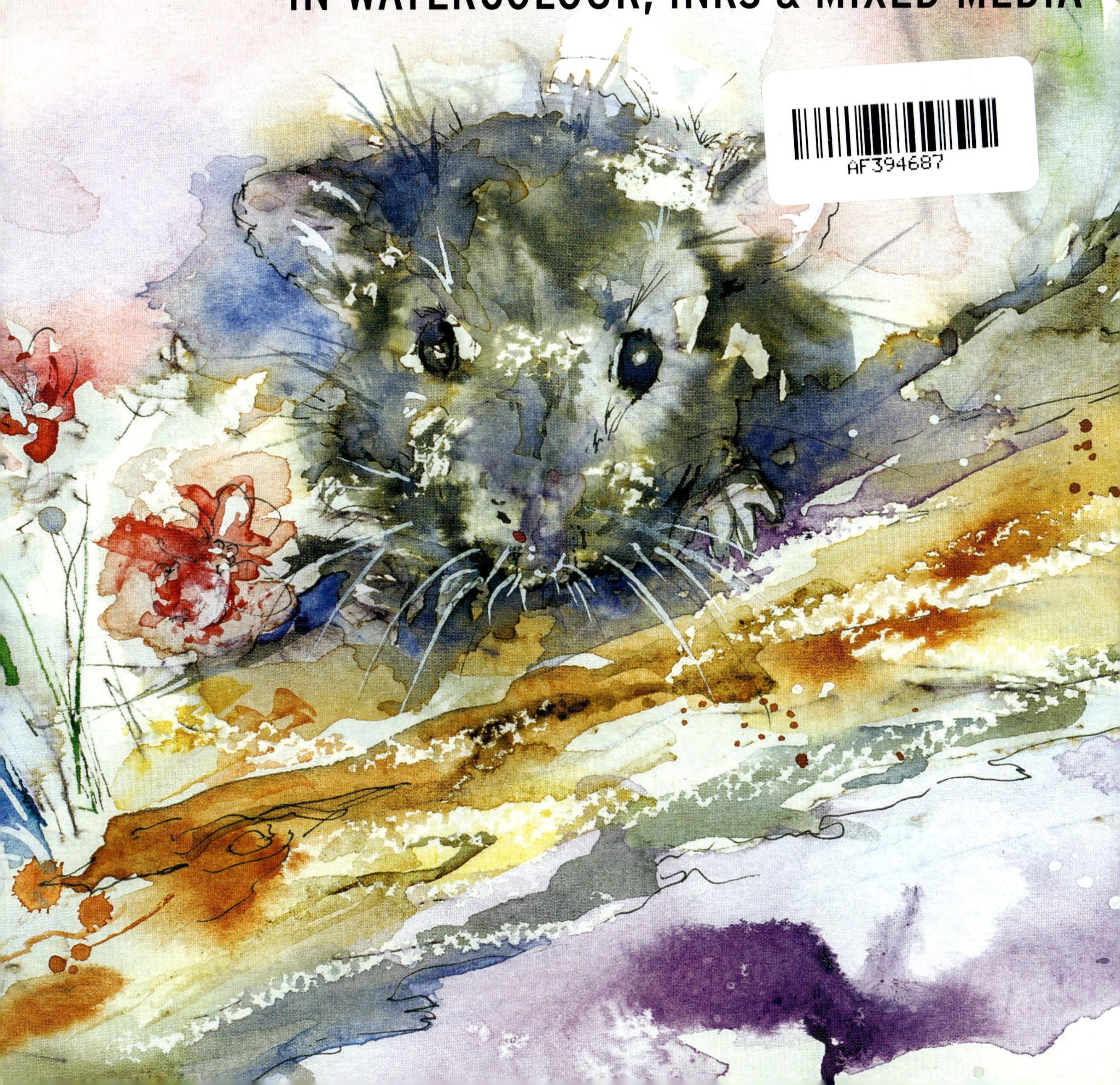

LOOSE AND LIVELY ANIMALS

IN WATERCOLOUR, INKS & MIXED MEDIA

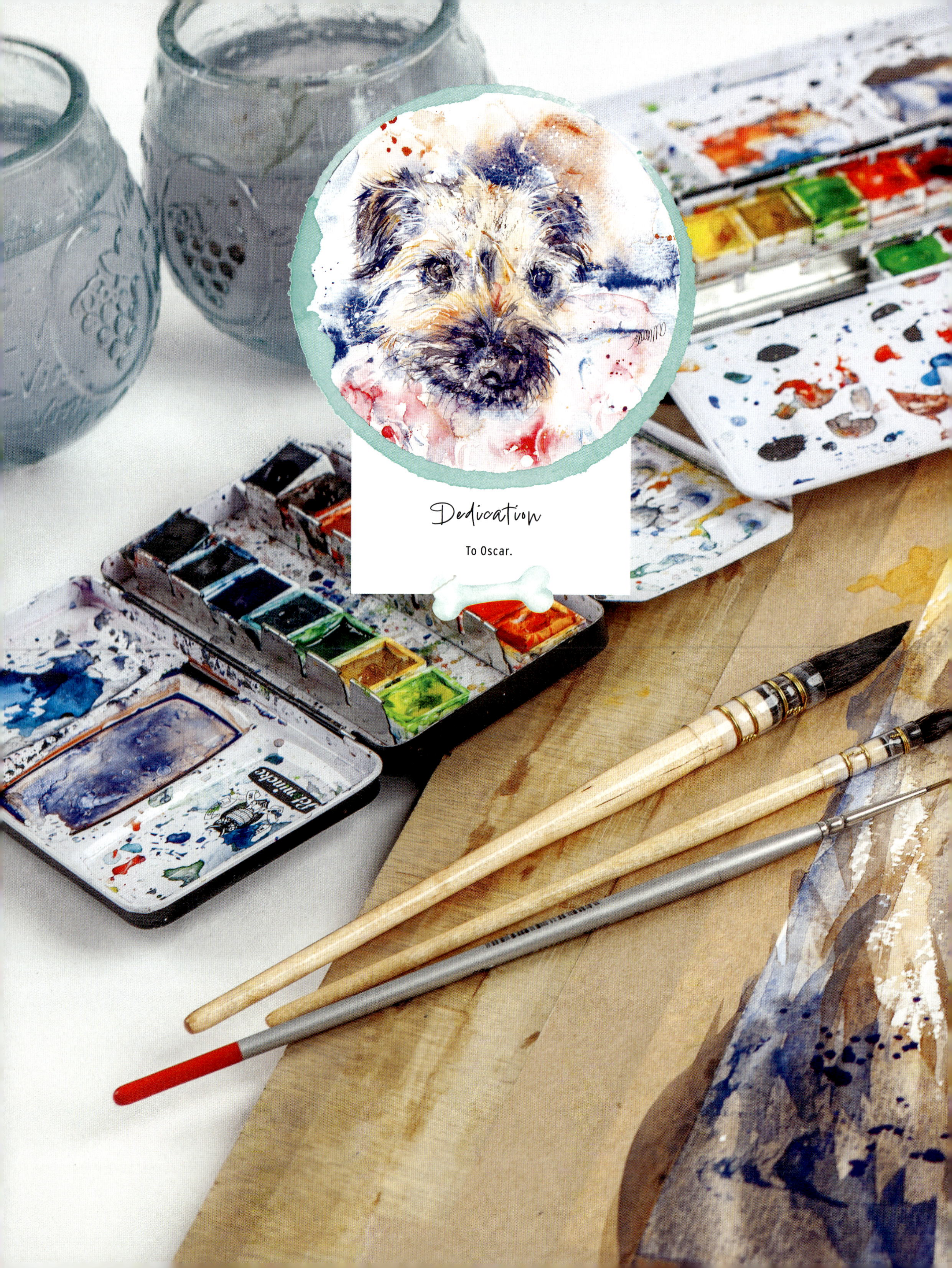
Dedication

To Oscar.

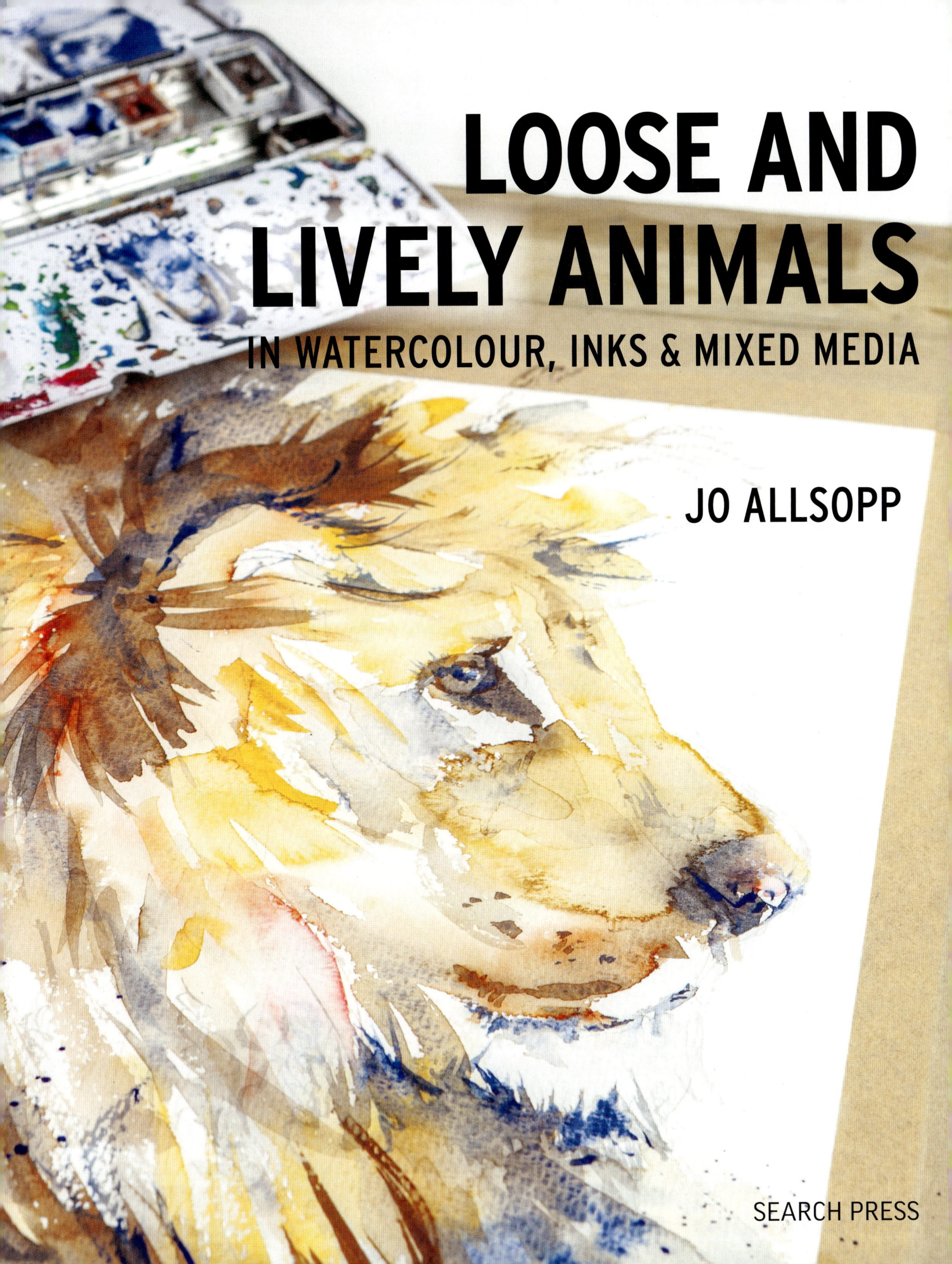

LOOSE AND LIVELY ANIMALS
IN WATERCOLOUR, INKS & MIXED MEDIA
JO ALLSOPP
SEARCH PRESS

Acknowledgements

I would dearly like to thank all who have encouraged and supported me on my own artistic adventure – and long may this continue – my family, close friends and particularly my editor, Edward Ralph, for his expertise and patience.
Many thanks too to all other departments within Search Press who have been involved, plus of course Mark Davison for his excellent studio photography. I must also give a huge thank you to everyone who permitted me use of their photography for the artworks within this book: Jorgie Allsopp, Martin Vaughan, Louise Roe, Iain Tall Photography, Holly Cannon, Coopers Dimension, Gina Rösner Photography, Don Barrick and Ady Shales.

First published in 2024

Search Press Limited
Wellwood, North Farm Road,
Tunbridge Wells, Kent TN2 3DR

Text copyright © Joanne Allsopp 2024

Photographs by Mark Davison at Search Press Studios, except for page 11, by Louise Roe; page 62, by Donald M. Barrick; pages 34 (t), 84, 92, 104 and 130 by Holly Cannon; pages 76 and 116 by Iain Tall; and pages 48 and 143, author's own.

Photographs and design copyright © Search Press Ltd. 2024

ISBN: 978-1-78221-995-8
ebook ISBN: 978-1-78126-988-6

Suppliers

If you have difficulty in obtaining any of the materials and equipment mentioned in this book, then please visit the Search Press website for details of suppliers: www.searchpress.com

You are invited to visit the author's website: www.sablestudiogallery.co.uk

You are invited to the Bookmarked online community for more ideas, inspiration and discussion. Membership of Bookmarked is free: www.bookmarkedhub.com

Cover:
Tiger
31 x 23cm (12½ x 9in)

Page 1:
Speedy
27 x 22cm (10½ x 8¾in)

In this painting of a little grey mouse, the colours I used for the background were not indicative at all of the reference picture I used. I decided he would look great with pinks and purples.

Opposite:
Hettie Hare
22 x 27cm (8¾ x 10½in)

I never tire of painting hares – they're a popular subject and never fail to attract comments.

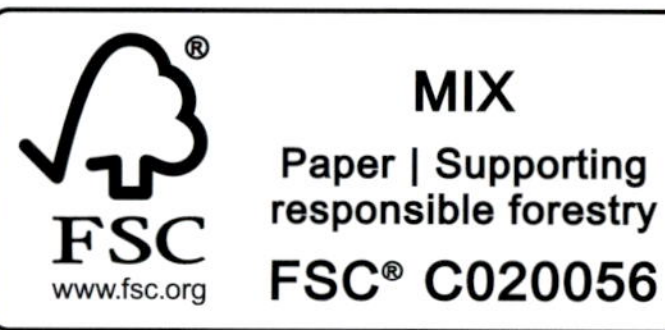

Contents

Introduction

Animals have been a constant source of inspiration for me. As a child I had pet hamsters and mice, and even hid a grass snake under my bed – though poor Fred swiftly disappeared when Mum found him as she swept!

You would always find me sketching and doodling. In school I preferred making my friends laugh to the more academic side, but remained drawn to the more creative and active classes. I have always been a creative and inquisitive being. I remember too that I loved writing little stories and poems and singing or humming along to songs. All of these things, I feel, were the 'arty' in me – and perhaps this is a familiar part of your own artistic journey?

After a successful career as a singer, I retrained as an adult tutor and began teaching the drawing and painting I so loved. It's this teaching that I have poured into this book. It is an invitation: I want to share with you my knowledge of – and enthusiasm for – both animals and colour; and to show you how to paint in my loose and lively style.

I would love for you to let yourself go and have some fun. Share some of this carefree energy with me in creating bright energetic paintings for us all to appreciate and admire. Let loose your inner creative on our very own little adventure… and now, follow me!

I've always adored bright colours. One of my favourite childhood toys was a kaleidoscope – painting means that I can make my own rainbow now.

Opposite:
Olwyn
24 x 31.5cm (9½ x 12½in)

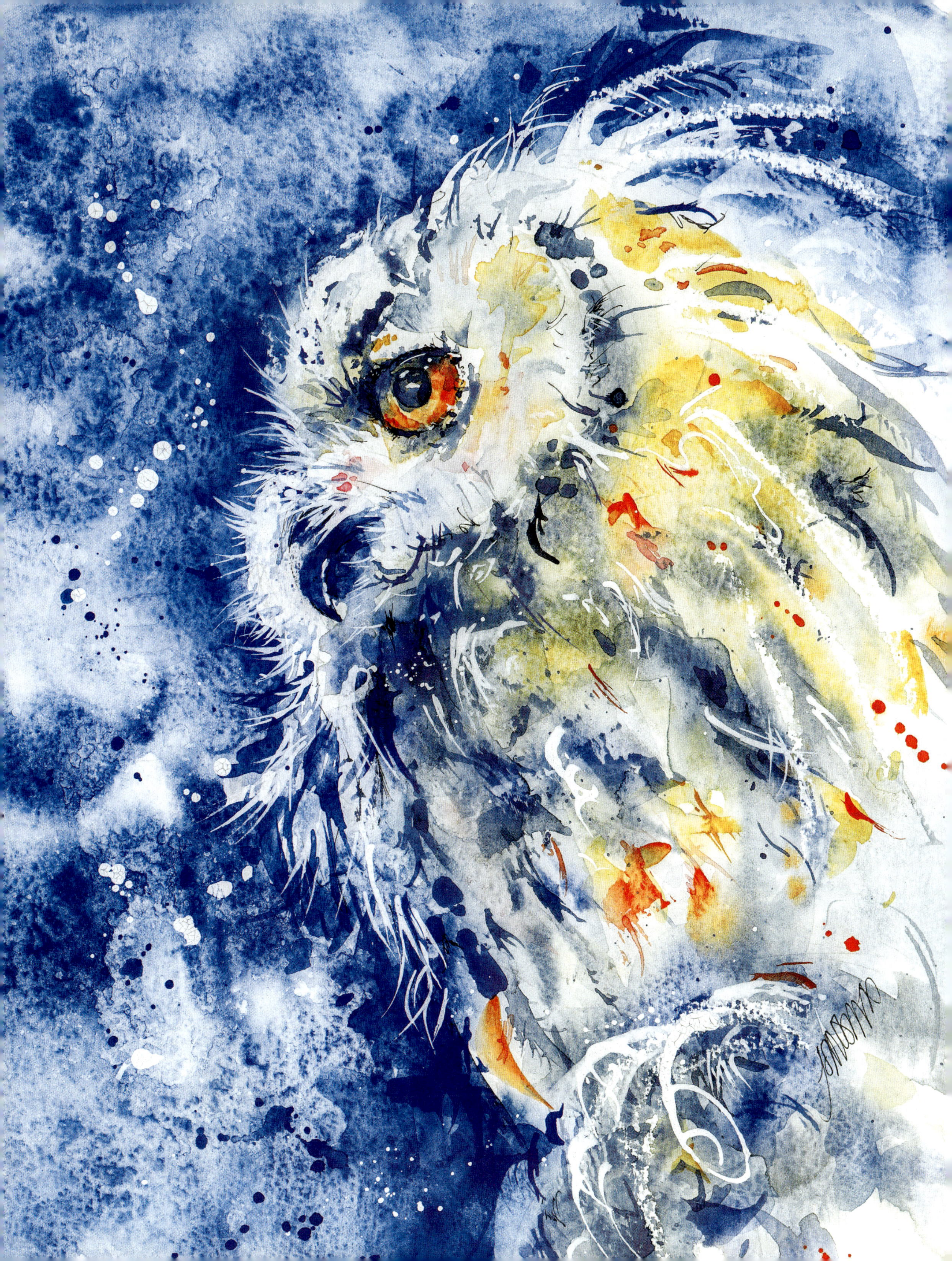

Inspiration and motivation

The following tips will help get you moving and thinking. If you want to loosen up your painting, start by loosening yourself up! You'll quickly find the ideas start to flow.

Fresh air Get outside and spend as much time as you can there. Look around to find all the potential painting subjects. Take photographs, scribble down ideas, make notes and create sketches outdoors. Breathing in fresh air will stimulate you and give you energy. Just as importantly, time spent outside will allow you space to contemplate your next creation.

Make space Surround yourself with things you love and find a creative space that you can dedicate to your art – and some valuable time for you. This does not have to be an elaborate studio. It could simply be a corner in one of your rooms.

Don't hoard Always use that best brush you've been hanging onto, that lovely paper you have stored away for something special, and do christen those paints. Using better quality materials will make it easier to get good results, and in turn that will encourage you to continue. Life is too short to say 'I will wait until I get better.'

Paint what you like When asked 'what shall I paint?', I always reply: 'something with meaning, something from the heart, something that makes you smile.' Always draw inspiration from a topic that really means something to you, that you enjoy, and that makes your heart sing. This might be a holiday, a special memory, a sport, a pet, a favourite flower, or a piece of music. Surround yourself with all these precious things as much as you can.

Work through failure When asked, 'what if it goes wrong?' or told 'I just want to throw it away', my advice is always the same: work with it, improve it, enhance it. This way you learn. If you throw your work in the bin, you can start to believe you are rubbish – and you are not! You just have to practise, practise and practise some more. If it is broken, try to fix it. You learn more from this than from giving in. I feel we can all improve in many things we do, we just have to want to. If you want to, you will – if you don't, then you won't.

Be kind to yourself We are often unnecessarily self-critical; it's time to be nice to yourself. Give yourself the opportunity now – today. You will get better with self-belief along with plenty of painting with passion. It is just a piece of paper, after all. Have fun splashing on it, and learn how it reacts with the paint, water and brush strokes that you apply.

Opposite:
King Leo
23 x 31cm (9 x 12in)

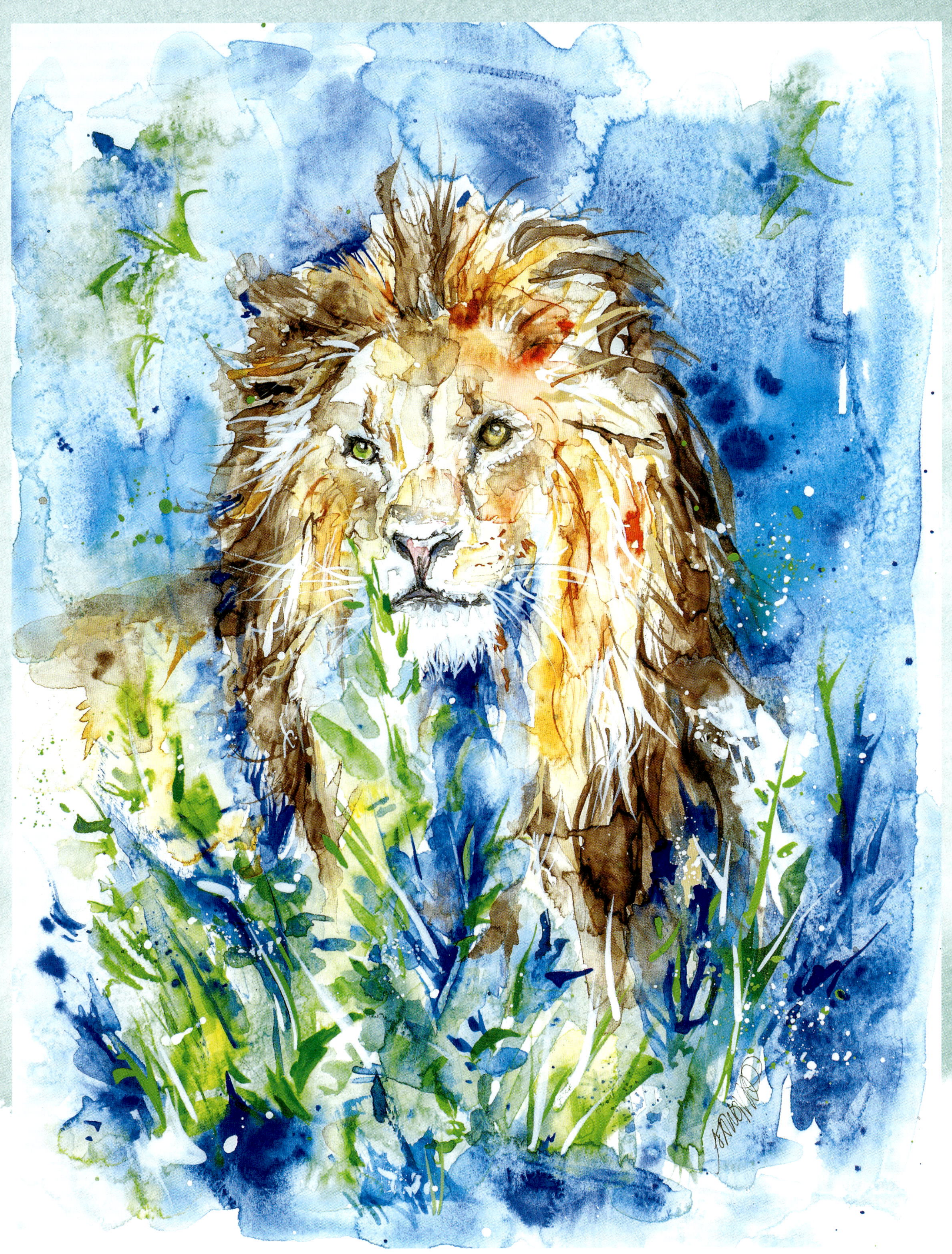

Reference material

Collecting photographs or creating an inspiration book to act as a visual resource will help with your animal artwork. Because you've picked your own favourite animals, the images will always appeal. Whether this is because of the colours, the texture or the vibrancy, I assure you that you'll never get tired of them: they'll resonate with you.

Photographs

When painting my animals, I usually work from photographs that I have taken, although I have often been gifted beautiful photographs by family and friends – another source of great reference material. I also work with professional photographers who have granted me permission to use their images for my artwork.

You can do all of the above, too. Don't be afraid to ask! Most people will be honoured that someone would love to reproduce their work to create art. The important thing is that you have permission from whoever took the photograph – this is particularly important if, like me, you sell your work.

Inspiration books

Over the past twenty years, I have compiled three inspiration books. These include my own photographs along with magazine cuttings and snippets. These aren't just of animals. They include homewares, fabrics, furniture, sculpture, pottery, and much more – anything that helps me feel positive and in the mood for painting. I love to look through these regularly and it is amazing how I never tire of these things.

You too can gather your favourites and get them out from time to time to look at and inspire you; you will be so glad you did.

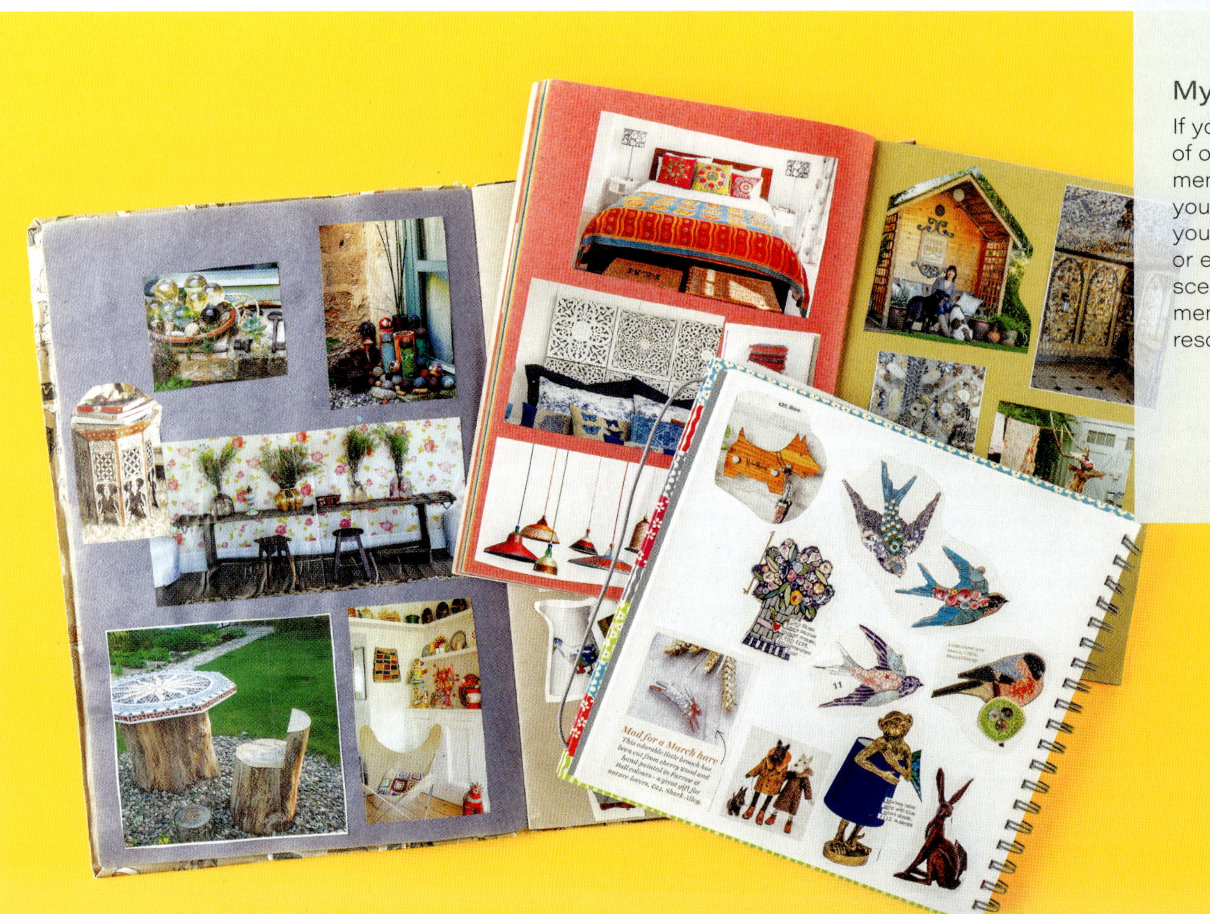

My inspiration books
If you are not a big collector of objects, try visiting a memorable place, play your favourite tunes, cook your most successful dish, or explore your favourite scents – experiences and memories are a valuable resource, too.

Your work area

I feel that it is absolutely imperative to have a designated space for painting: your own private sanctuary, with a storage area for your art materials, in which you can sit and delve into your artistic projects. As mentioned earlier, this does not have to be a full-blown studio. A corner of a room, or the nook under the stairs, is all you need.

However large or small your working space, it's important that you make it an enticing and inspiring space so that you can enjoy every moment there. You might place fresh flowers in a vase, a pot plant, some of your favourite photographs, or a mood board: anything that will help inspire you. Avoid it being too cluttered – clear space, clear mind and so forth – but do make it appealing.

Try, if you can, to find a space with lots of natural light, and where you can open a window to listen for birdsong and other sounds of nature. My garden has a water feature which really relaxes me, and if you don't have a garden, don't worry: you can buy some wonderful indoor water fountains these days. I don't know about you, but I just love to hear the sound of trickling water; it takes me to my happy place.

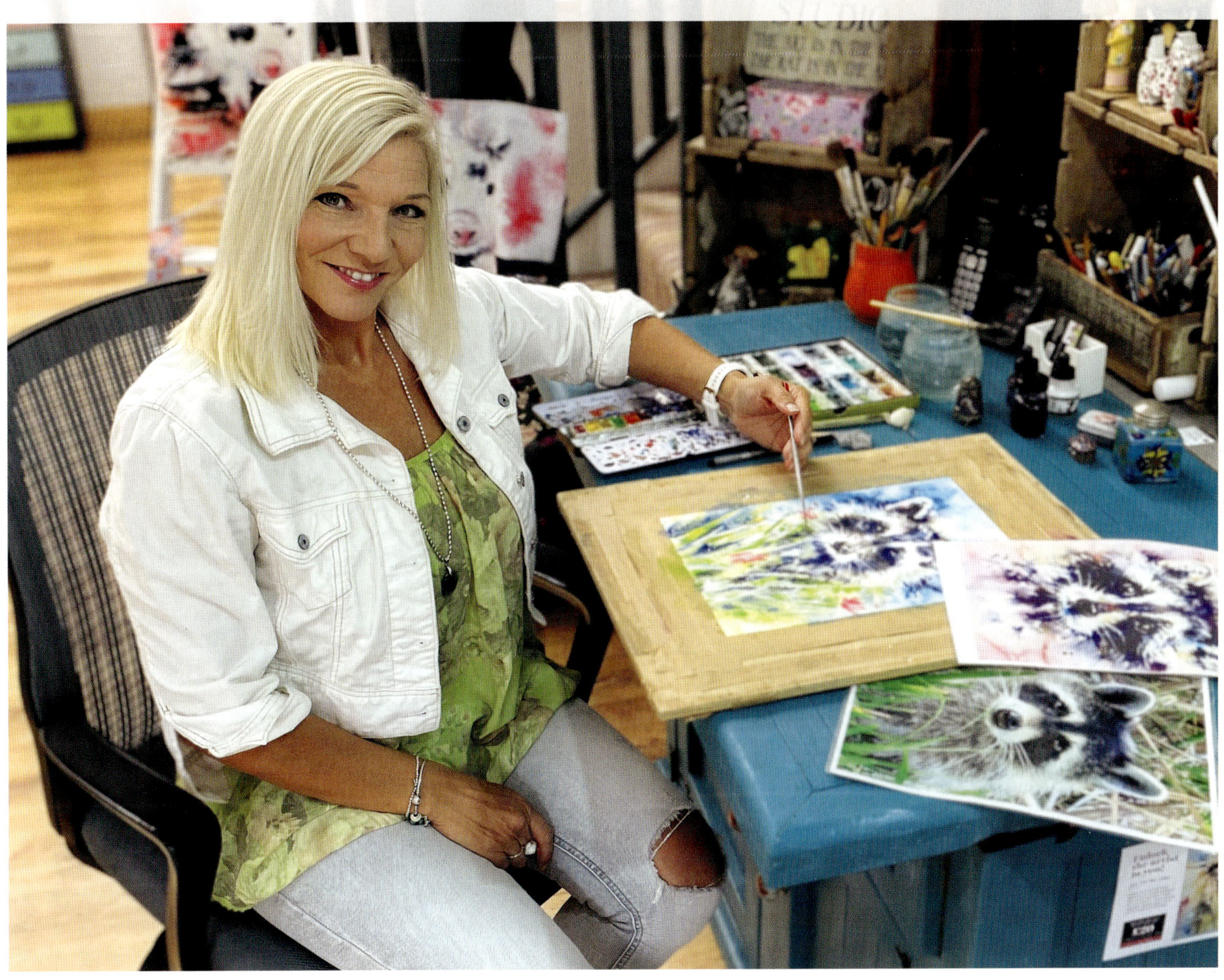

What inspires me

My nan used to liken me to a little squirrel because I would collect little stones, cute buttons, shells, leaves, broken pottery and 'diamonds' and squirrel them away in a box. I loved looking in her jewellery box at all her sparkly things and also admiring her glass cabinet of curios – I remember trying my hardest to colour a rough garden stone with felt tips so she would display my piece with her collection!

I dug my bare hands into the muddy stream where I lived and moulded the clay into shapes – mainly animals – and went on little adventures with friends, looking for mice, birds' nests, nuts, leaves and flowers to appreciate and study. It all provided me with so many ideas and so much inspiration.

Nature and wildlife continue to inspire me. On my regular walk with my beautiful border terrier Alfie, I'm lucky enough to enjoy canal towpaths on a daily basis, where I see so many of my favourite animals: water voles, fish, ducks, squirrels, hares, butterflies, bees... The excitement of catching a glimpse of these on a walk always fills me with enthusiasm and makes me to want to paint. Painting allows me to lock in the experience, giving me something to keep and remind me of these wonderful adventures. These experiences cost nothing but indeed mean everything. Nature is the most beautiful thing we have, and you cannot beat that for inspiration.

Both at home and in my gallery, alongside my brushes and art materials, I keep lovely things to look at on shelves: little knitted mice, a heart stone, a pretty salt pot, a bird's nest with faux eggs; all items that make me smile. Now and again, I move things around or swap and change these to keep it all fresh and interesting.

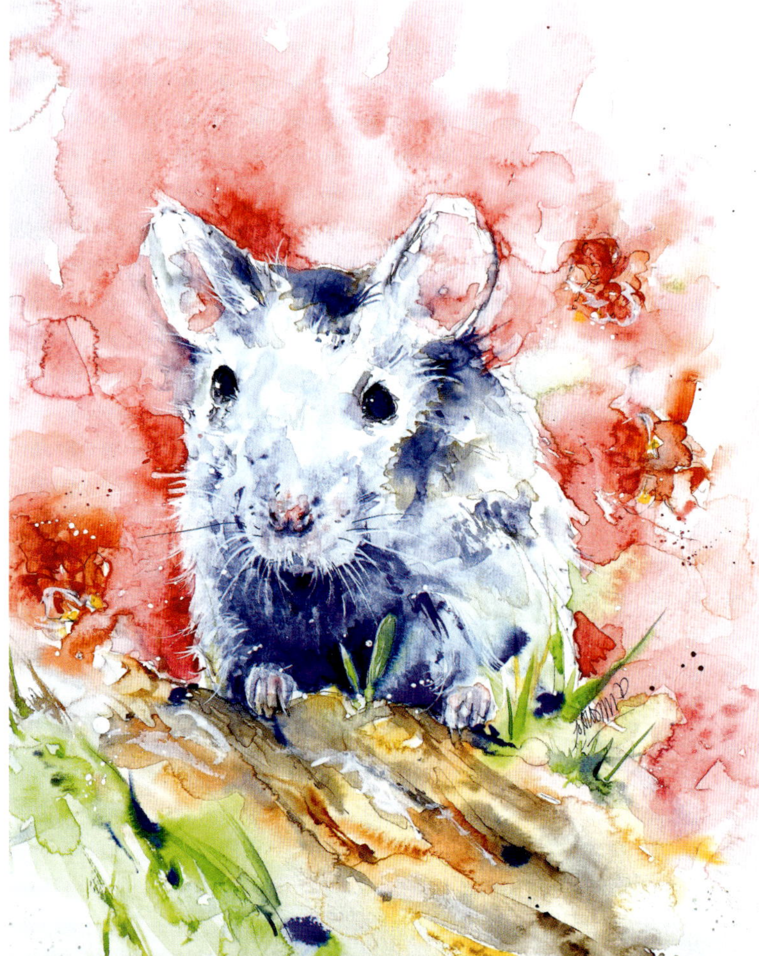

Ratty
26 x 36cm (10¼ x 14¼in)

Rats are really important to me. I have always loved little rodents and have quite a collection of ornaments of mice and rats: small ceramics, precious stones, Swarovski crystal – even knitted.

A not very nice boy at primary school gave me the nickname 'Ratty' – and also called my best friend 'Errol the hamster'! The name-calling was not pleasant at the time, but I'm rather fond of the nickname now, especially since I realised 'rat' is an anagram of 'art' – it is almost as though it was meant to be. My friend and I remained close, and today we affectionately sign off our messages to one another with these nicknames.

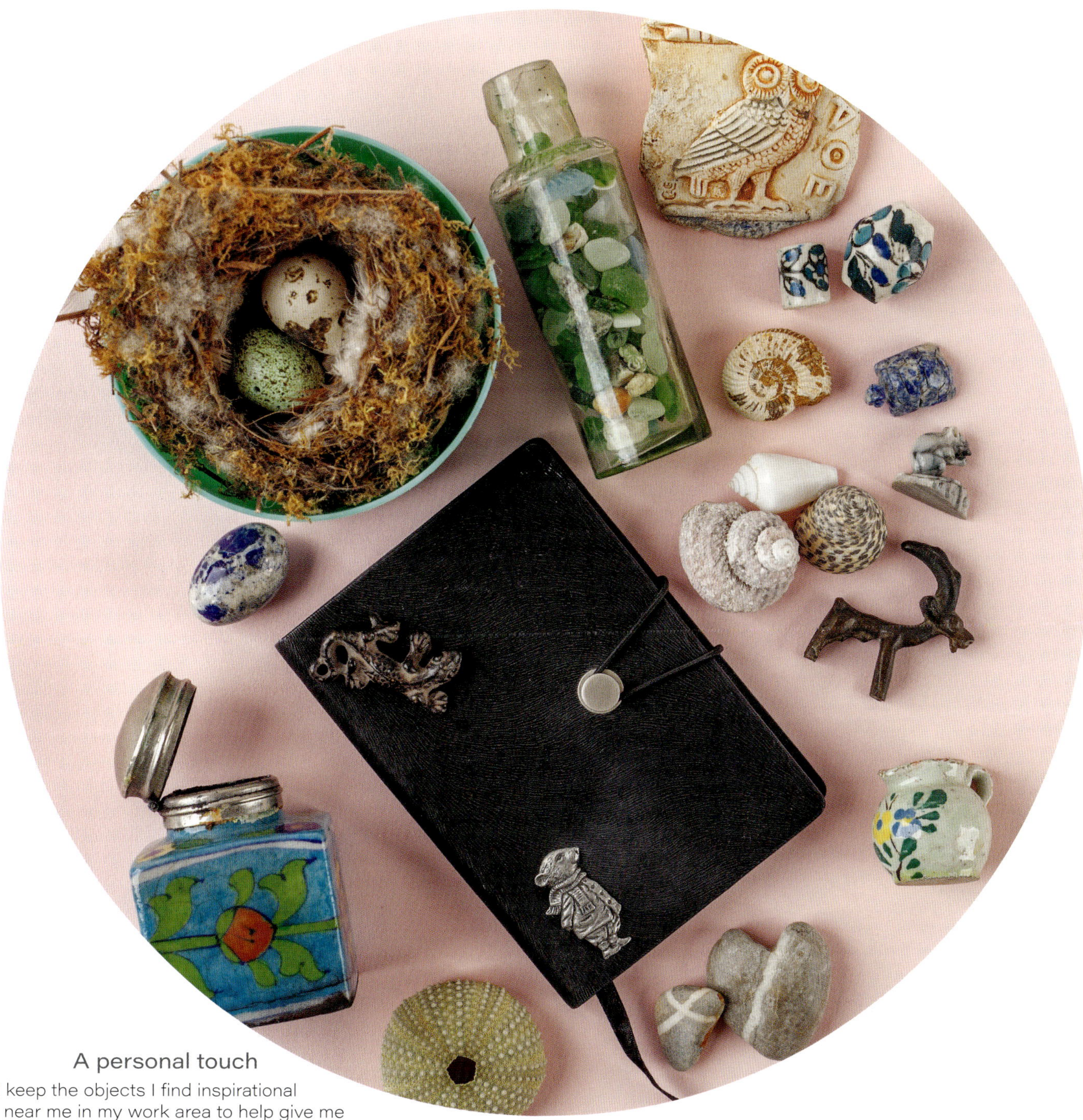

A personal touch

I keep the objects I find inspirational near me in my work area to help give me ideas. Having them around really works for me.

It's worth spending some time gathering together a box of your own favourite things – the physical equivalent to the inspiration books. These just need to be items which inspire you through their colour and texture, or simply because they make you feel good. These could include shells, feathers, fabrics, books, photographs, a nice stone, magazine cuttings, jewellery, ornaments, old toys – or perhaps a favourite song, poem or saying.

Minky

20 x 26.5cm (8 x 10½in)

The hairs in sable brushes come from the sable, or Siberian weasel – so what better tribute than to paint this animal using these wonderful tools?

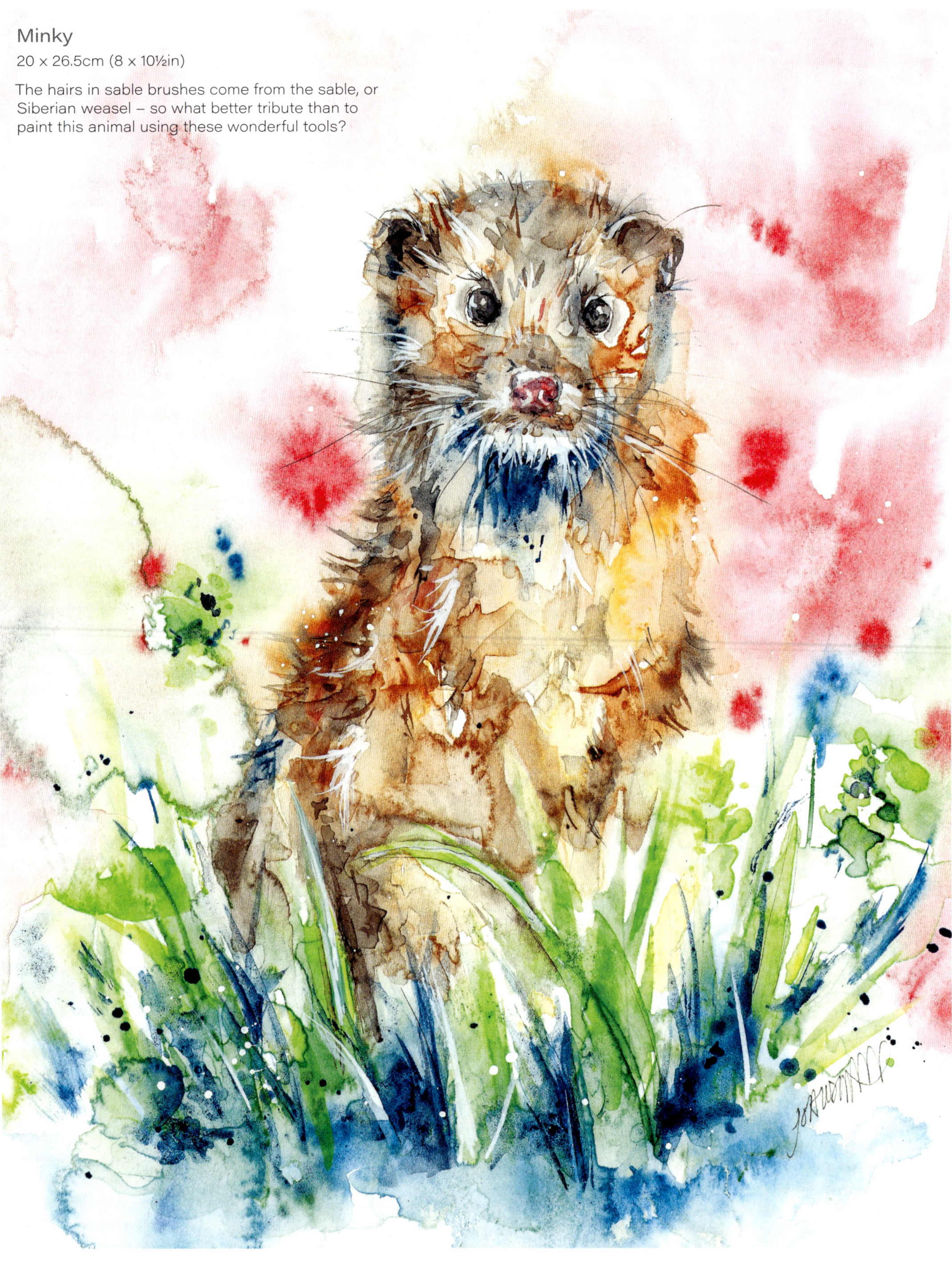

Let us loose!

You don't require lots of materials if you are just starting out with watercolours – just a few brushes, some watercolour paper and a handful of paints. It's important that they're of a reasonable quality to ensure the best results going forwards. If your budget won't stretch to high-end materials, don't worry. You can get great results with mid-range materials – just avoid the budget option. Better to buy less, but make sure it is of high quality.

You might ask family and friends for contributions towards your materials when asked what you would like for birthdays or other special occasions – it's lovely for them to know you're getting something you really want.

Over the next few pages I'll explain my own choices for these key tools, and explain what other useful extras you'll need.

Paintbrushes

Pure Kolinsky sable fur makes for elite paintbrushes. The soft, bouncy hairs spring back into shape, keep the perfect point, and hold water and paint beautifully without dripping out onto your work until you allow it. Indeed, I like them so much that I named my business, Sable Studio Gallery, after them! They can, unfortunately, also be hugely expensive. I find that squirrel-hair brushes offer some of the qualities of the sable at a much more affordable price – and so these are often my go-to brushes.

I mainly use just three brushes – two squirrel-hair rounds, and an SAA rigger (a very fine brush with long hairs) – which I affectionately name 'Daddy', 'Mummy' and 'Baby'. The large size 3 round is used for large washes (wet paint applied to an area), the middle size 0 is used for smaller areas and most details, and the rigger is used for final details and long lines.

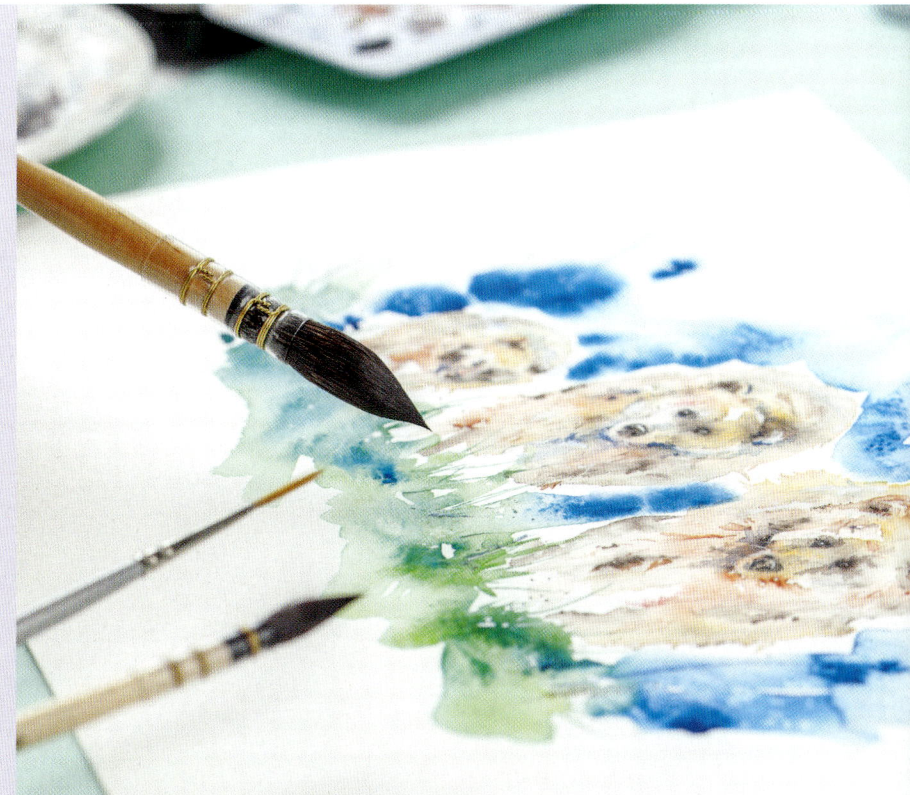

My brushes
Just like the three bears from Goldilocks, a set of Daddy, Mummy and Baby brushes is all you need. Shown here are a da Vinci Petit gris pur size 3 (Daddy), a da Vinci Petit gris pur size 0 (Mummy) and an SAA size 0 Small Rigger (Baby).

Watercolour paints

Watercolour paints are available in pans and tubes. I prefer to use pans as I find these so convenient – just wet and go – plus they are all contained in a handy tin that fits neatly in my bag. I find tubes a little fiddly: trying to squeeze out the correct amount is awkward, and I find the lids can sometimes become caked up and messy – but of course everyone has their favourite. Listed here is my preferred colour palette.

Yellow ochre Beautiful and delicate when watered down, but bold and with sufficient opacity to cover areas when undliuted, this is my 'golden' colour; my absolute favourite. I like it so much I even named a hamster 'Ochre' after this paint, as he had patches in exactly this wonderful colour.

Burnt sienna A rich, warm colour that I affectionately call my 'terracotta potter' as it reminds me of the colour of this kind of pot. I often drop touches of this into wet washes to create a warm burst of colour in animal fur.

Burnt umber This lovely deep strong brown creates a natural texture when mixed with French ultramarine. This combination is ideal for greys and blacks.

Rose madder Diluted with water, this pinky red is excellent for a warm rosy wash. Like many reds, on its own it is an aggressive, advancing colour – definitely there to be noticed! Mixed with French ultramarine, this makes beautiful purples too. I often put just a spot somewhere on my subject's head so that the eye is drawn to this area – see 'hot spots' on page 39 for more on this.

Vermilion A more vibrant red than rose madder, this can be used to shock. I use this both pure as a bold colour, and also to tinge my yellows to make them warmer and rich. Adding more vermilion will create a gorgeous orange.

Cobalt violet A lovely colour straight from the pan, this merges beautifully with French ultramarine and complements it perfectly. I opt for purples and blues as shadows for my animals (under the chin for example), as these are receding colours and so help to push things under, back and behind.

French ultramarine A perfect receding colour, French ultramarine is one of my favourite 'go-to' colours when I want to push something back: I often glaze areas like the rear leg of an animal to suggest it's slightly further away, for example. When used with less water, near the strength of pure pigment, this helps to make white whiskers (applied later with white ink) stand out as this dark paint provides a great contrast.

Vanadium yellow Another colour beautiful all on its own – it's so bright and cheerful. I also mix this with vermilion for a vibrant orange; with French ultramarine for an alternative green; or with May green for an even brighter green.

May green For leaves and grasses around my subject, I use this firstly on its own, and then add French ultramarine wet in wet to get darker tones. I also often combine it with yellow, as mentioned above.

Helio cerulean Another favourite of mine, helio cerulean is so bright that it really grabs your attention. I usually use it on its own for backgrounds, as I feel it looks beautiful just as is.

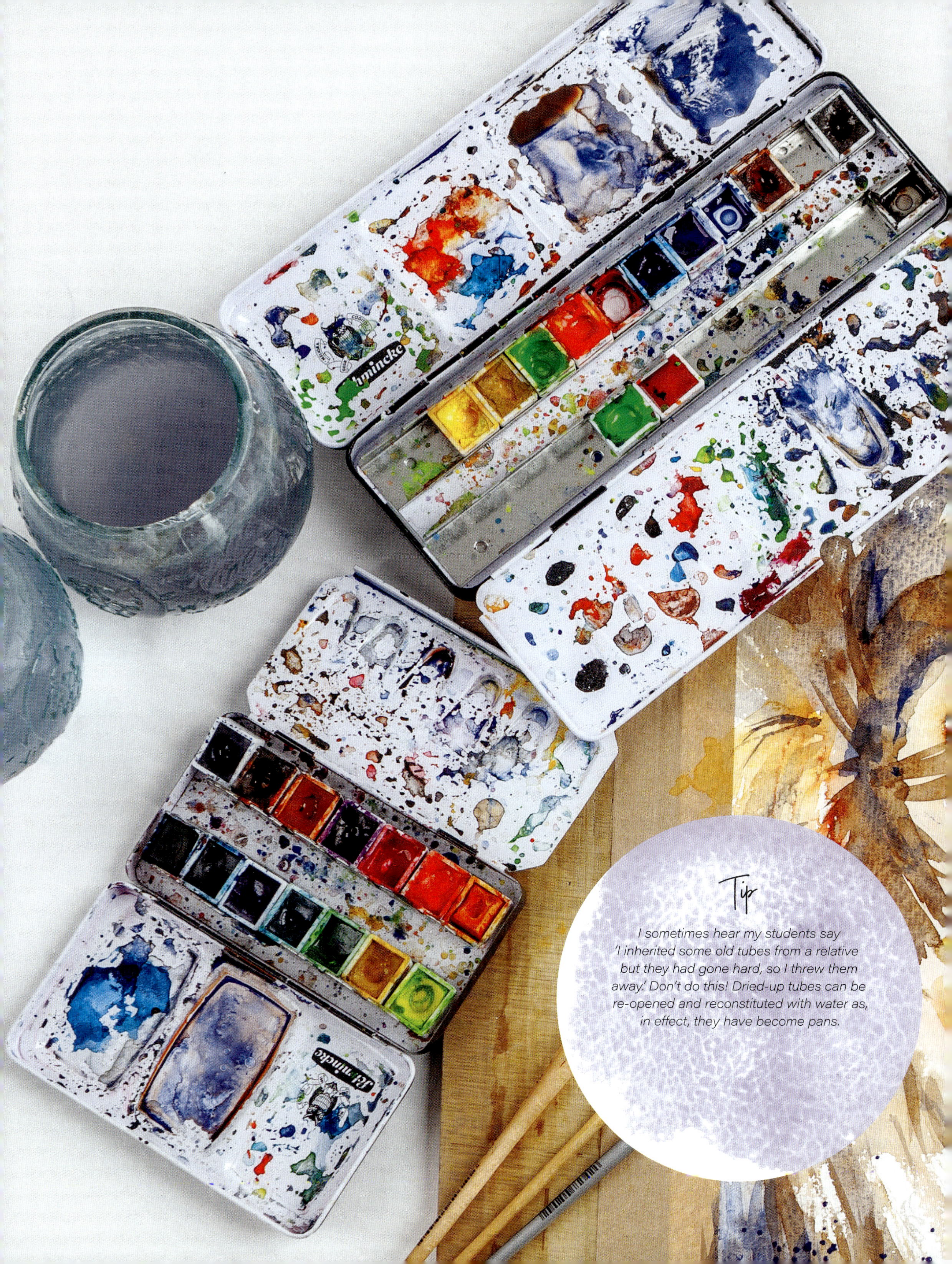
Tip

I sometimes hear my students say
'I inherited some old tubes from a relative
but they had gone hard, so I threw them
away.' Don't do this! Dried-up tubes can be
re-opened and reconstituted with water as,
in effect, they have become pans.

Paper

Watercolour paper is available with different surface textures, ranging from highly-textured Rough surfaces to smooth hot-pressed (HP) surfaces. In between these extremes are cold-pressed papers, also called CP or Not – short for 'not hot-pressed' – which has a subtle texture, or 'tooth'. I don't have a particular favourite surface texture. I will use all three, sometimes choosing a particular surface to suit the subject, but often simply on a whim. As you can see from the examples here, with the right techniques you can get good results with any subject on any paper.

The thing that is important is paper weight. Heavier papers are sturdier and resist cockling, which is where the paper curls and distorts as it gets wet, better than lighter-weight paper. Because I work so loosely – and due to the vast amounts of water and colour I throw at it! – I find whatever weight of paper I use inevitably cockles. For this reason, I almost always used gummed tape (see overleaf) to secure the paper firmly to a board, which keeps it in place. I do love the patterns that appear naturally from cockling paper, which is why I never pre-stretch it – I would rather embrace those cockles and let the paper stretch itself in the painting process.

Paper weight is measured in grams per square metre (gsm) or pounds per ream (lb). I recommend using a midweight paper; at least 300gsm (140lb). My personal favourite is St Cuthberts Mill Bockingford 300gsm (140lb), which works well with the techniques and materials I use.

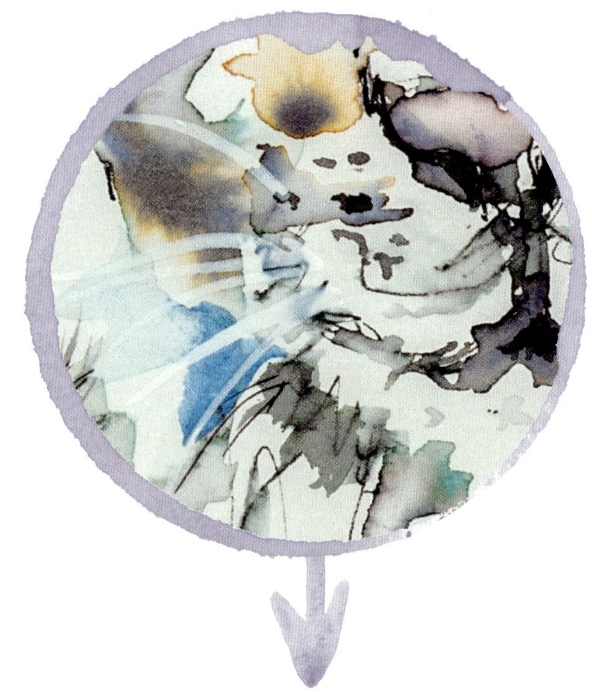

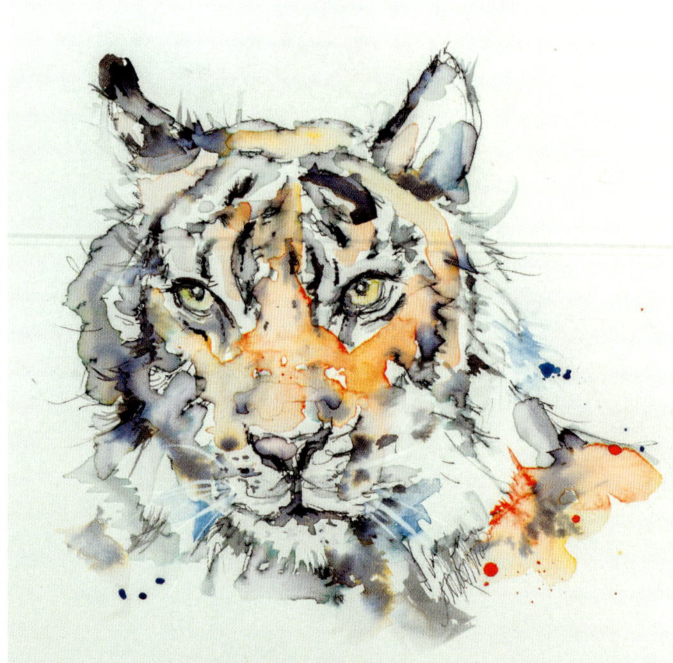

Smooth hot-pressed (HP) paper
This paper is smooth. WIth no evident 'tooth' (surface texture), this is perfect for anything requiring lots of detail, ideal for illustrative and botanical work. I personally love using salt on this surface (see pages 118–119), as it gives excellent results.

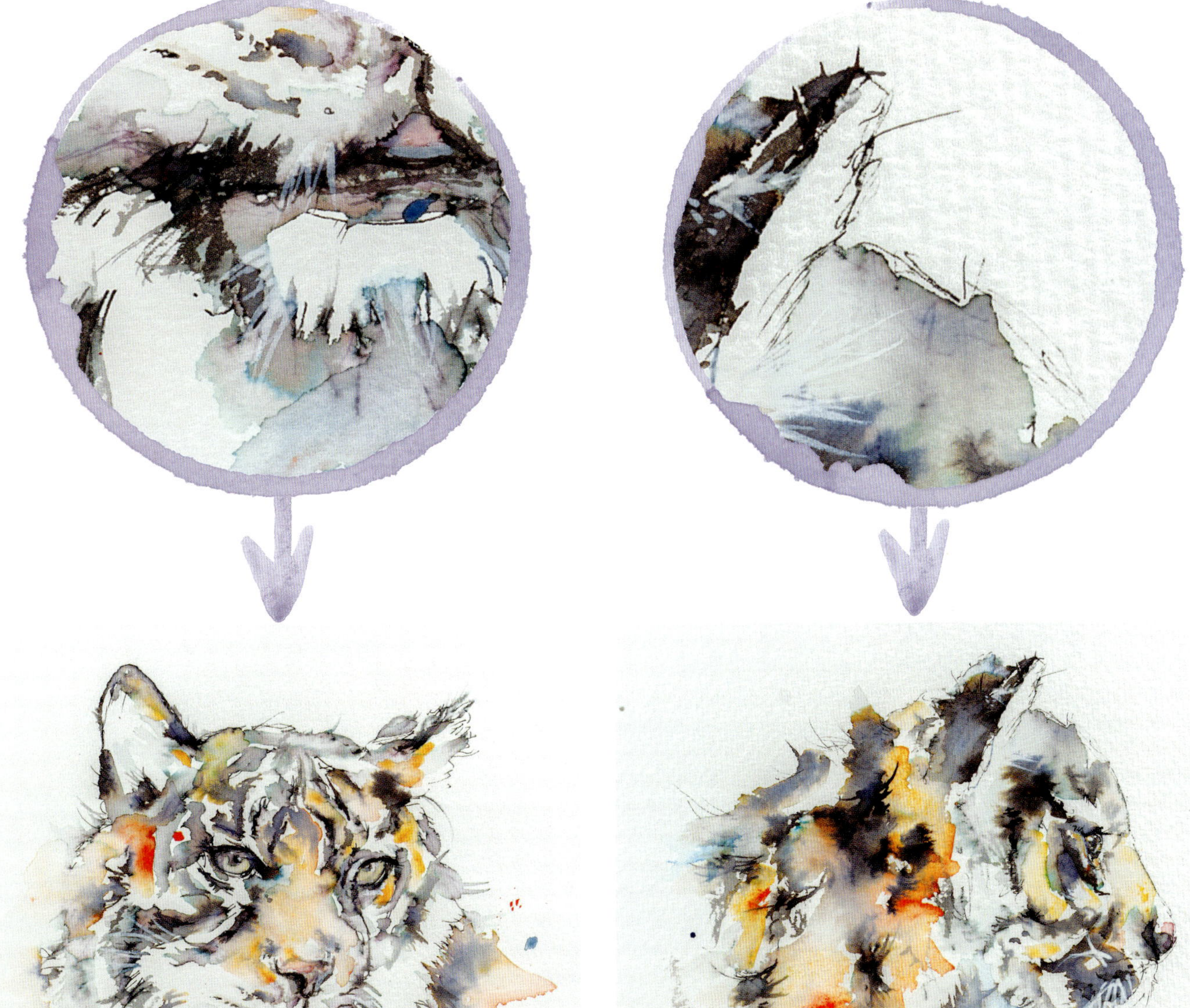

Not (CP) surface paper

The slightly textured surface of this paper means that this is suitable for most topics. It's the paper I would advise for those starting out, as I feel this is middle of the road, neither too smooth nor too rough. This surface allows for a fair amount of detail, and can also emulate texture when required.

Rough paper

Exactly as it sounds, Rough paper has an evident textured surface and more pronounced indentations – great when you want to emphasize the texture of animals with coarser hair or fur, the thick skin of the elephant or rhinoceros, or the shell of a crab. Such subjects are far easier to emulate on this type of paper.

Left to right:
Tai, Thorn and Tigris

Other materials

Wax I love to use a piece of wax candle to reserve areas of white paper: the wax stops the paint from adhering to the paper. I never know exactly where it is and so I love the element of surprise (or sometimes shock!) They say a shock now and again is good for your health – I'll go with that.

Fineliner pen I sign each painting with a micron 005 archival water-resistant black pen. I also sometimes use this to strengthen my paintings.

HB pencil I use an HB pencil when sketching as it is light, easy to cover with paint, and easy to erase.

Kneadable putty eraser I prefer a putty eraser to a plastic one, as it does not leave bits all over the page. Putty erasers are also more gentle on the paper surface.

Board I work incredibly wet in wet, so having my paper secured to a sturdy board is my preferred way of working.

Scalpel You can use the very tip of a scalpel blade to add highlights, by carefully scratching the surface once all the paint has dried. This is called 'scratching out'.

Gummed tape This keeps my work securely on the board, even when I wash a painting (see pages 95–96). The tape stays put until I decide my painting is complete and can then be cut off the board with my scalpel.

Water pots I always advise that you have two pots: one to clean your brushes between washes, and the other to transfer clean water to the paper. I prefer these to be see-through so that I can ensure the water is clean.

Mixed media

The materials listed so far are those I use for pure watercolour work. Throughout the book we'll also look at materials, ideas and techniques for incorporating mixed media in your animal paintings. See page 90 for information on these materials.

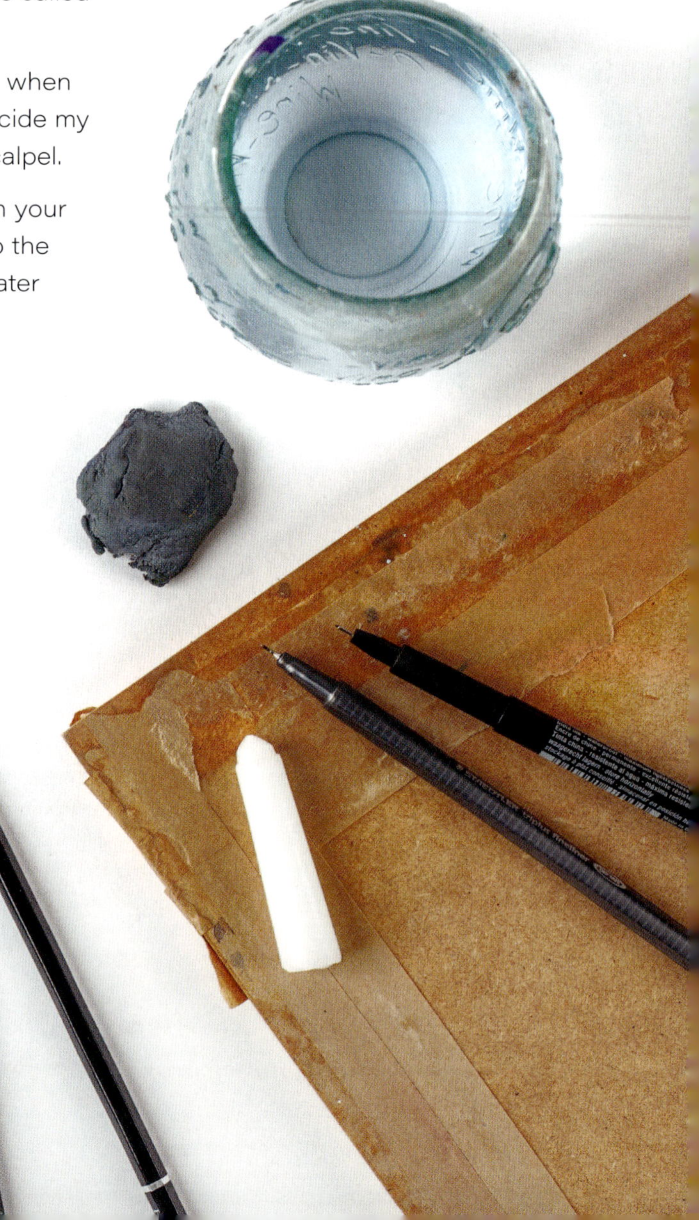

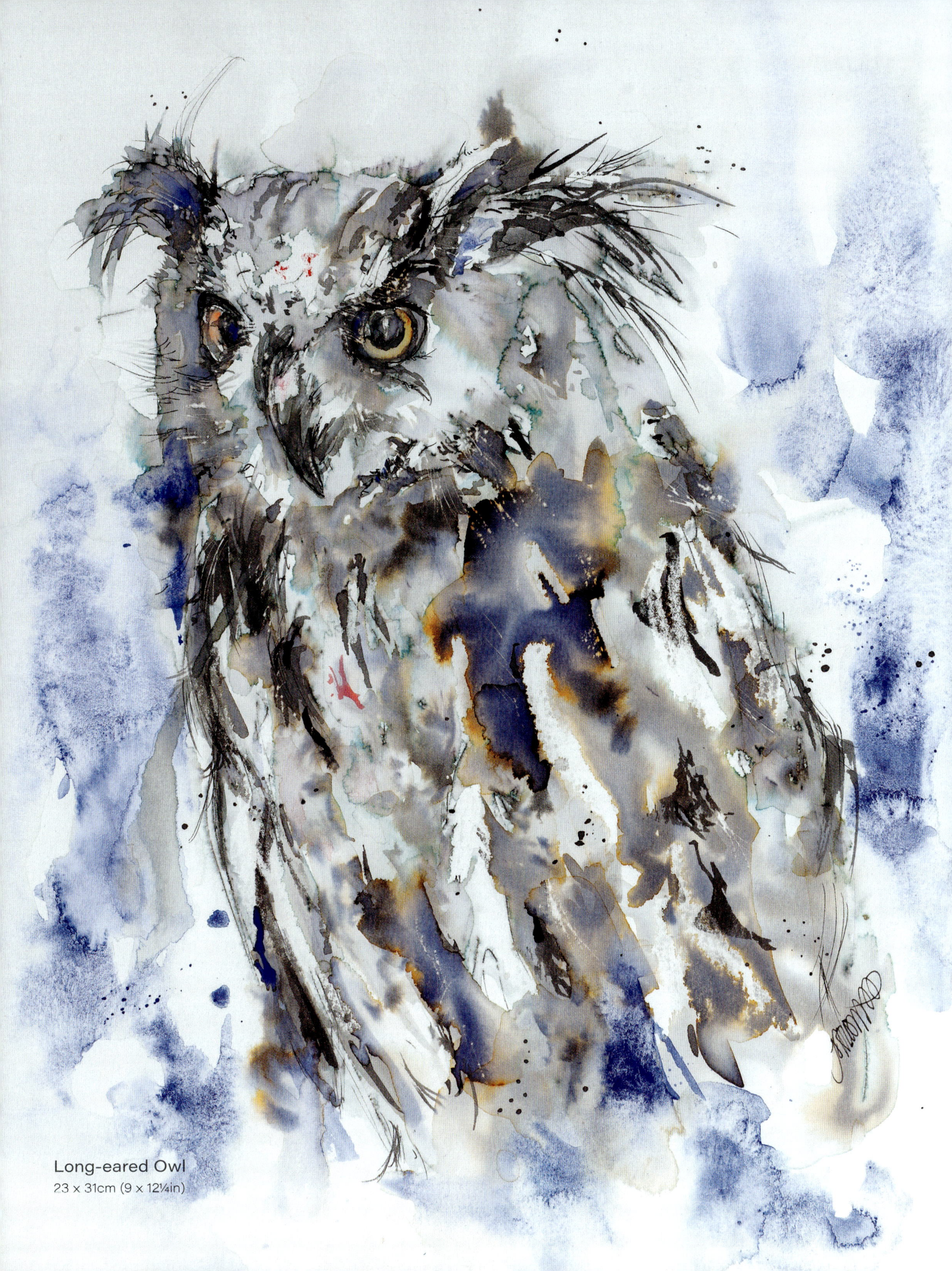

Long-eared Owl
23 x 31cm (9 x 12¼in)

Big is bold

It's possible to paint in a very detailed, almost photographic way, but deep in our heart of hearts, I think most of us realise that nothing is perfect – so there's always that urge to 'mess it up' a little!

It is exhilarating and exciting to work loosely with our brushes and paint – such carefree fun takes us back to our childhood, where nothing seemed to matter so much. I do find 'splashing around' most invigorating – give it a try and I'm sure you'll find it as freeing and enjoyable as I do.

Painting freely

People tell me that they can't paint loosely. This is because we're taught to hold a pen or pencil tightly, to give us control. We need to break that training and way of thinking, and get to hold that brush in a looser, freer way.

Whenever I'm asked, 'How can I stop my work looking too contrived and detailed?', my advice will always be: 'bigger paper, definitely a bigger brush, plus lots and lots of water!' To this advice I will add here: dare to be brave, be bold, bright and colourful.

The clue is in the word 'watercolours'. Don't be afraid to use lots of water with your paints – our paper can take it. Watercolours dry lighter than they appear, so dare to go brighter. Throw other media at it too – we don't have to be purists and we don't have to be perfect either.

The following pages give a variety of exercises to take you out of your comfort zone and loosen you up, as well as some things to bear in mind as you start painting. Don't worry about what animal to paint – you don't even need a subject just yet. The important thing is to practise the movements – and to enjoy yourself.

It doesn't matter how you get there, as long as you get there in the end.

Opposite:
Kingfisher
26 x 36cm (10¼ x 14¼in)

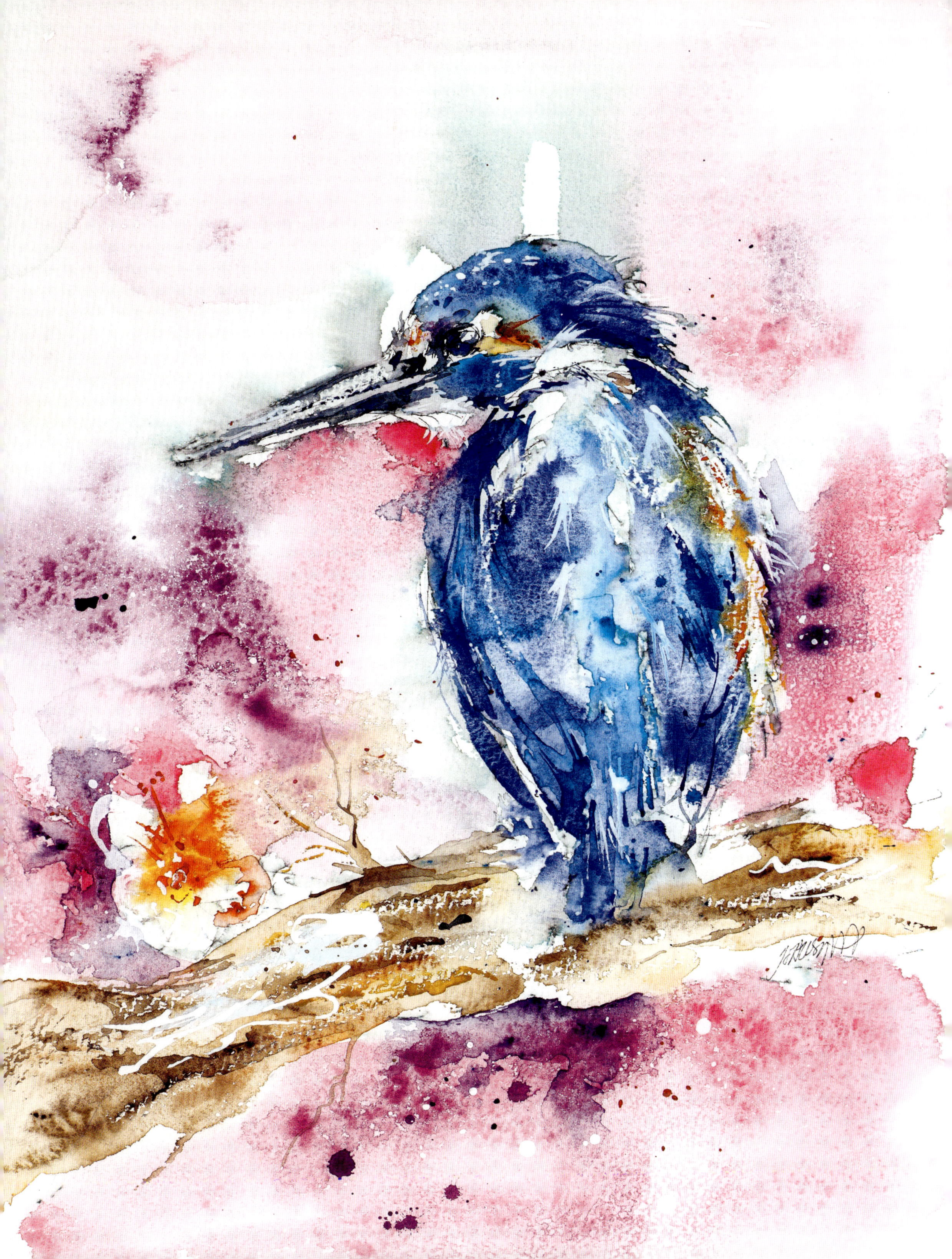

EXERCISE: USING YOUR NON-DOMINANT HAND

Try using your off-hand to try a little loose painting – it will inevitably appear looser, as we are not as competent with our non-dominant hand. In my case, I am left-handed, so swapping to my right results in looser results: I simply can't work stiffly right-handed!

Try a little painting with your non-writing hand and see how you hold the brush differently, how you push and pull the water and paint with a little more freedom and in a carefree way.

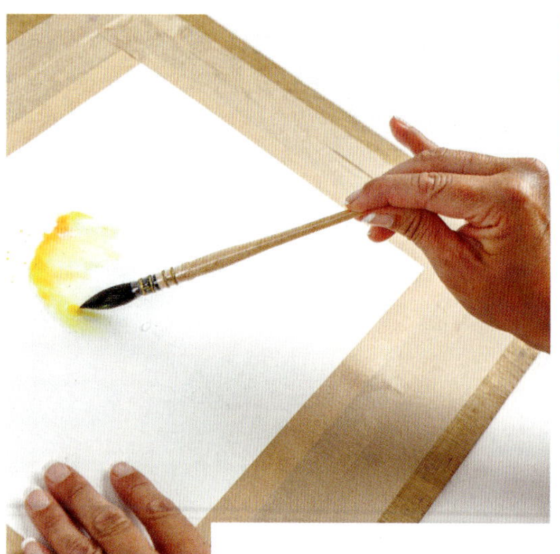

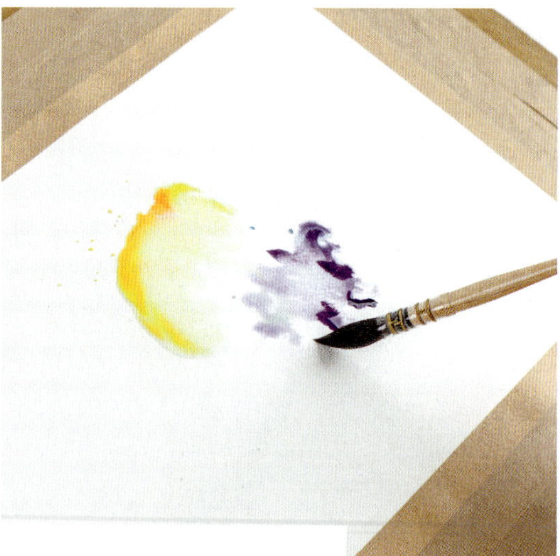

Using your non-dominant hand takes a little control away from you – it can seem a little scary, but try to enjoy it.

With less control, you're less able to lean into the temptation to work tightly, and small, and detailed. Instead, you're freed up to apply the paint without the pressure of doing 'your best work!'

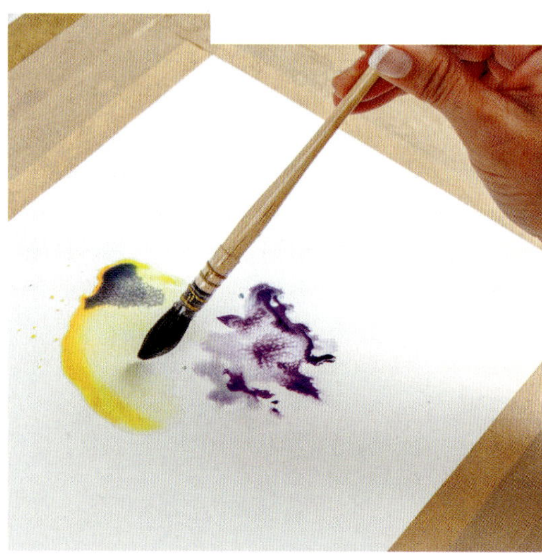

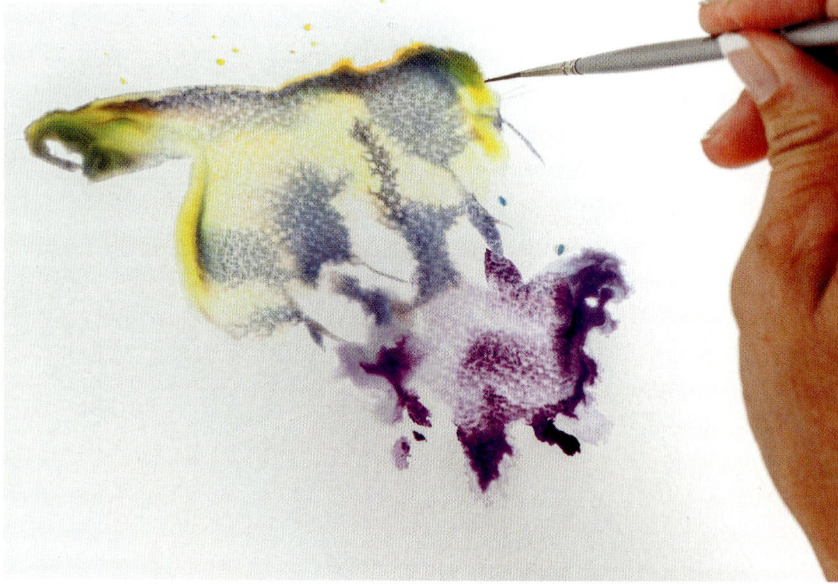

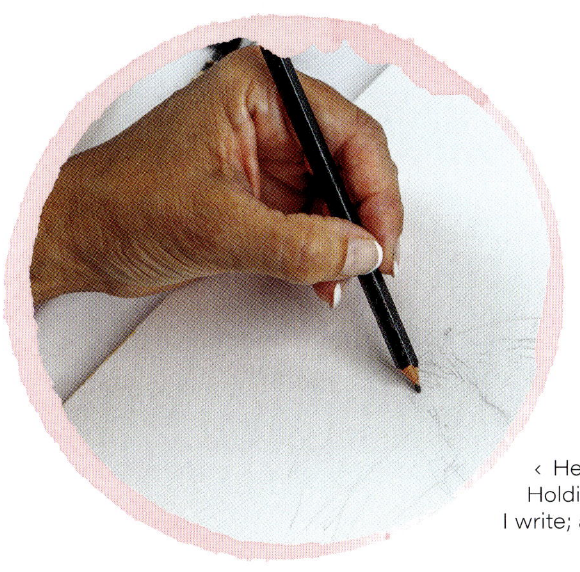

EXERCISE: HOLDING THE BRUSH AT THE END

Start a painting with a fully loaded big brush, held at the end of the brush handle, rather than close to the ferrule (the metal part that holds the hairs). Holding the end of the brush will stop you from being too precise in the first instance – we want to put energy into your art, and this simple trick really does help.

‹ Here's how I hold a pencil while making a sketch. Holding the pencil here is similar to how I hold it when I write; and it allows me lots of fine control.

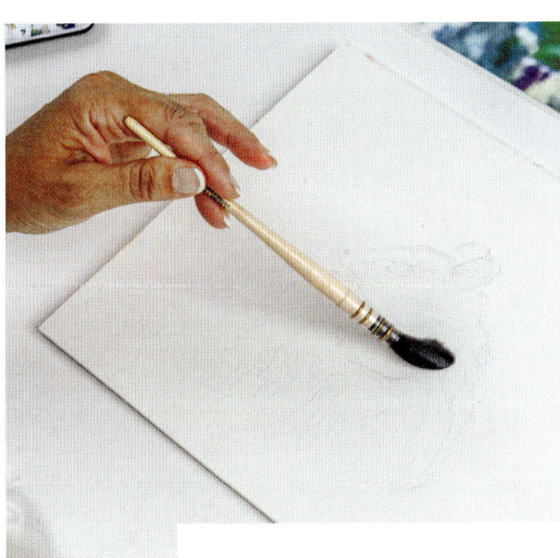

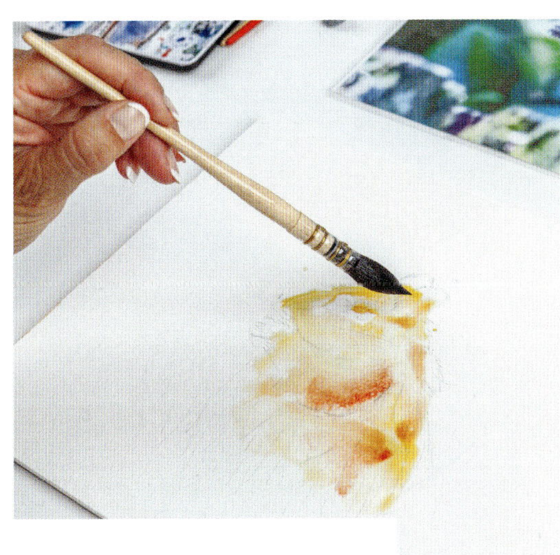

When you start to paint, hold the brush much further up the handle, near the end (see above). Any little movement you make with fingers or wrist will become a bigger, looser mark on the paper.

Later on, as you want more control, move back to something more like a pencil grip (see below).

Try to produce a simple painting without moving your fingers from the end of the handle.

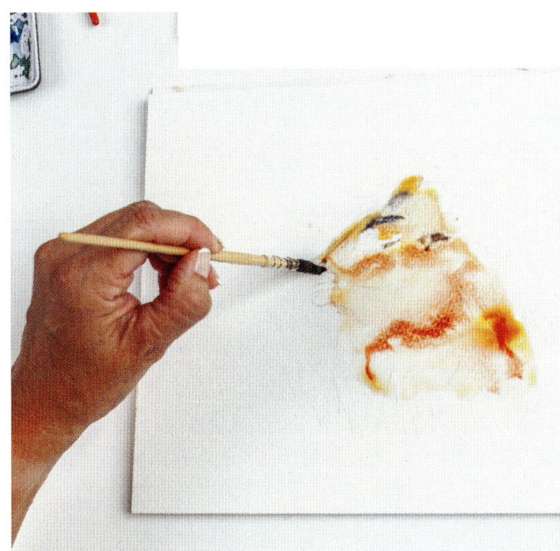

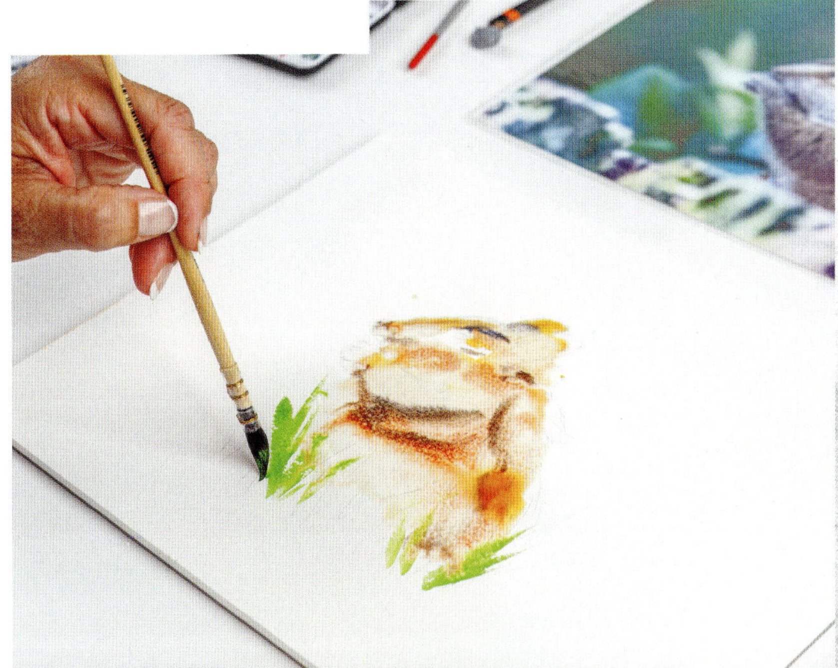

EXERCISE: USING YOUR WHOLE ARM

Stay free – avoid resting your wrist or elbow on the table as you paint to
help loosen up. This will allow you to move the brush using your whole arm,
including your shoulder, to pull the water and paint around. You'll find that
this ensures lively, bouncy shapes to get you started.

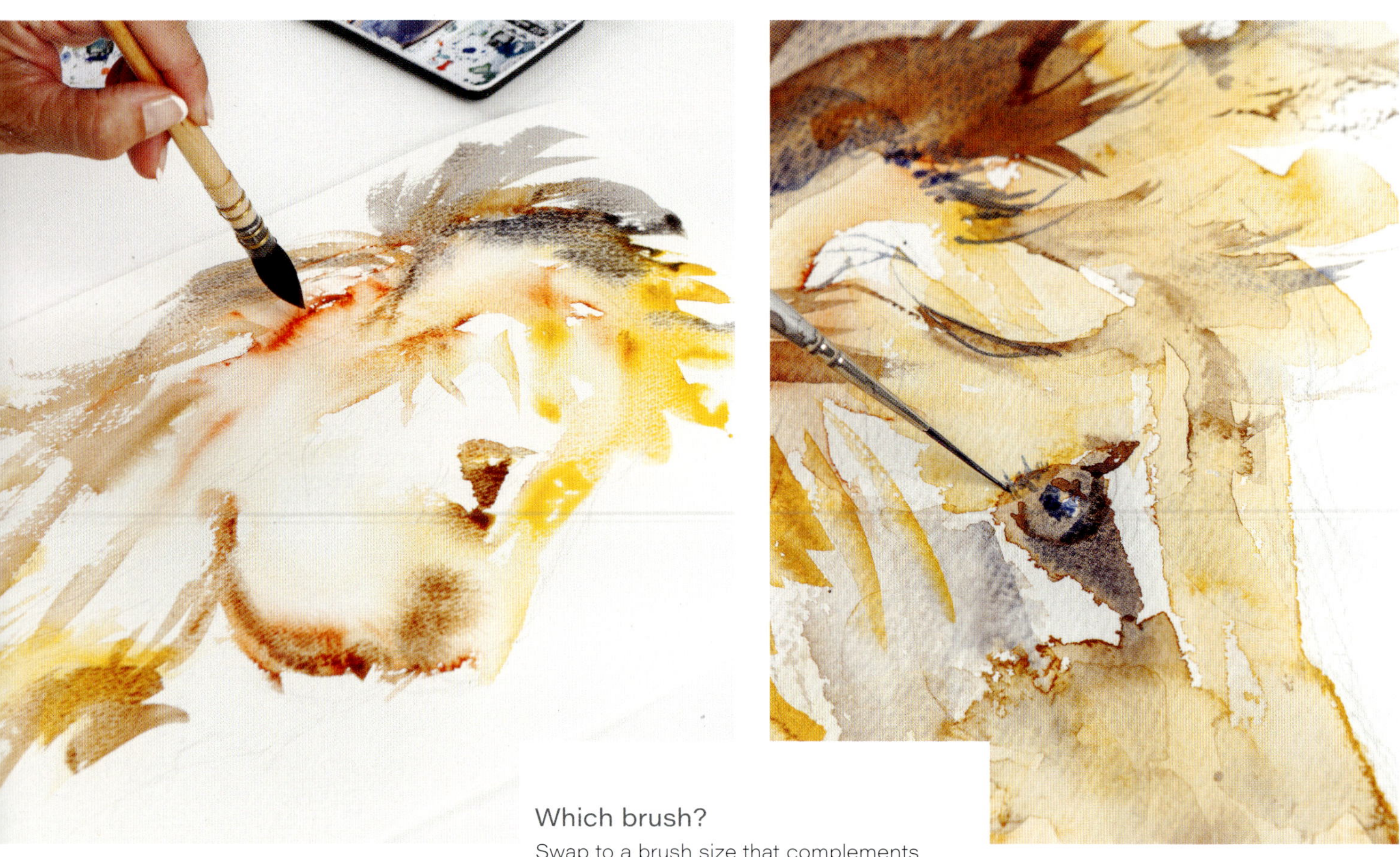

Which brush?

Swap to a brush size that complements
the movements you're making: big for bold
marks (see left), smaller to start applying
more depth and details, with the tiny rigger
(see right) reserved for the finishing touches.

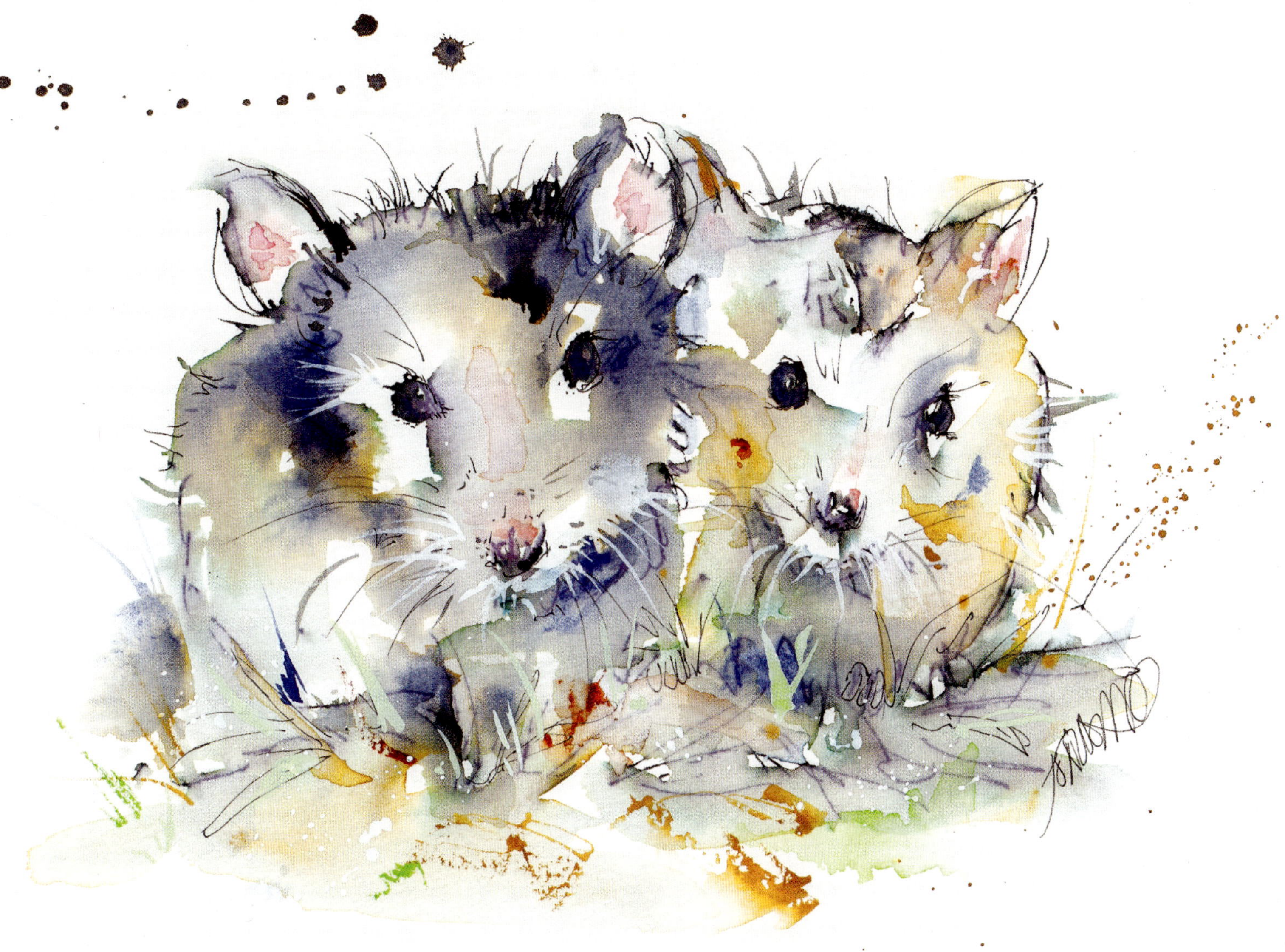

Inky and Ochre

22 x 20cm (8¾ x 8in)

Even small subjects can make a big impact, as you can see
from this painting of two of my little pets, Roborovski dwarf
hamsters lovingly named after some arty favourites of mine. You
can see the loose brushwork and spattering marks that I used
to apply the paint. You'll also spot the pen work that I used to
refine and rein in the looseness – a little goes a long way. You
can read more on using pen on page 56.

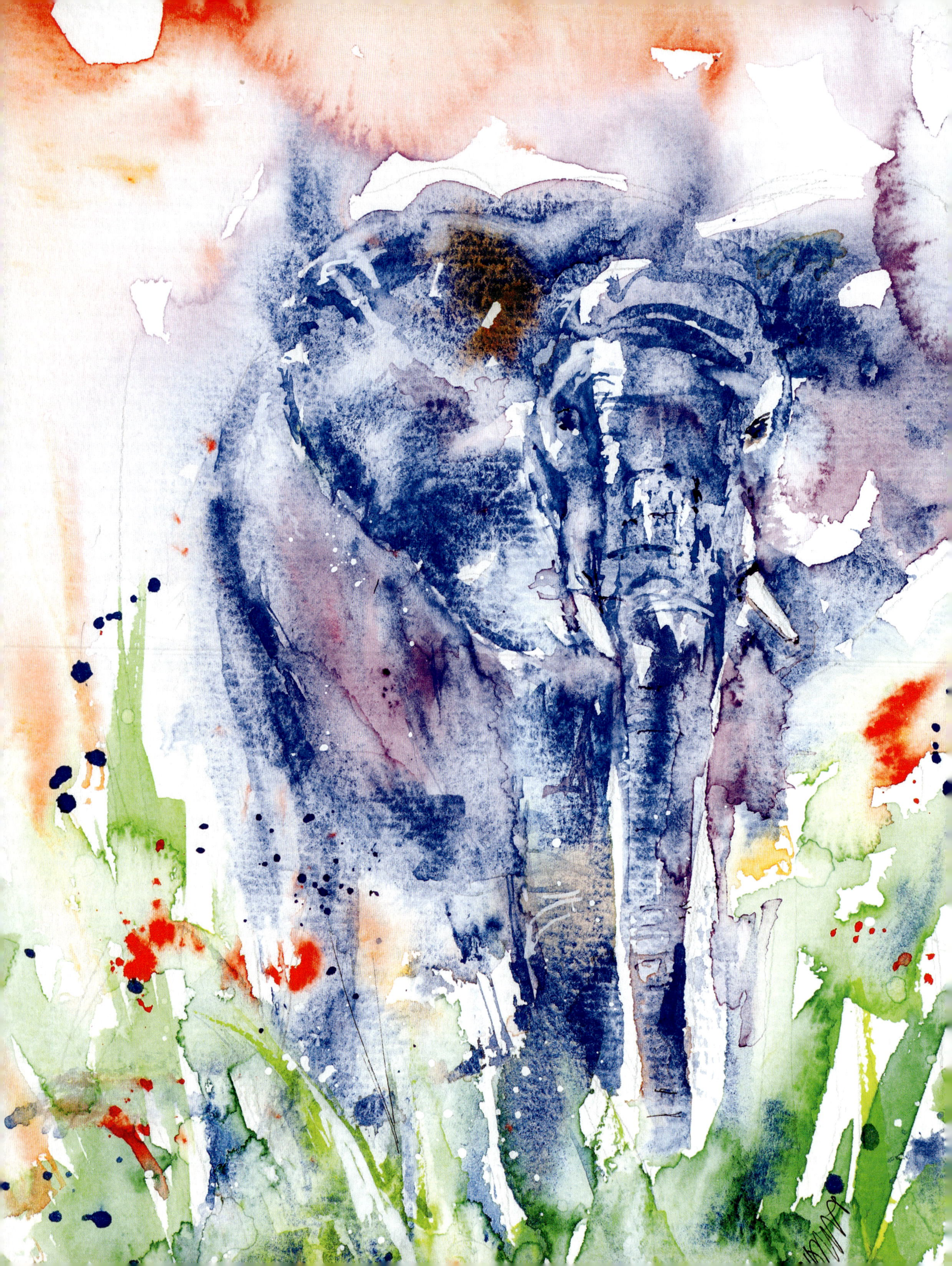

Getting started

When I set out to paint, I first ensure that whatever I choose as my subject is something I would enjoy painting – there is little point in painting something just for the sake of it. If it does not make you happy, then why do it? Painting subjects we like encourages us to make a good job of it, so as we move into the practicalities of painting, I suggest you pick a subject that lifts you: it will release all those feel-good hormones. Happy person, happy painting!

Securing your paper

First things first: secure your watercolour paper to a board using gummed brown tape (see right).

Alternatively, you could use a block of paper to keep things flat. This is a stack of watercolour paper sheets that are glued together at the edges. The glue at the edges will keep the paper flat while you work. Once you have finished and the painting has dried, you simply use a craft knife to cut the glue and release the top sheet of paper. There's a small gap in the gum.

Whether you choose to secure your paper with strips or use a block, you're now ready to move on to drawing. My way of working is explained overleaf.

Opposite:
Elephant
23 x 31cm (9 x 12¼in)

I loved the pose of this elephant in the reference picture, but the colours of both the animal and surroundings were very muted and grey. I used lots of colour to brighten up the whole scene completely – and the result is a much better reflection of how I felt about this wonderful creature than the rather dark photograph.

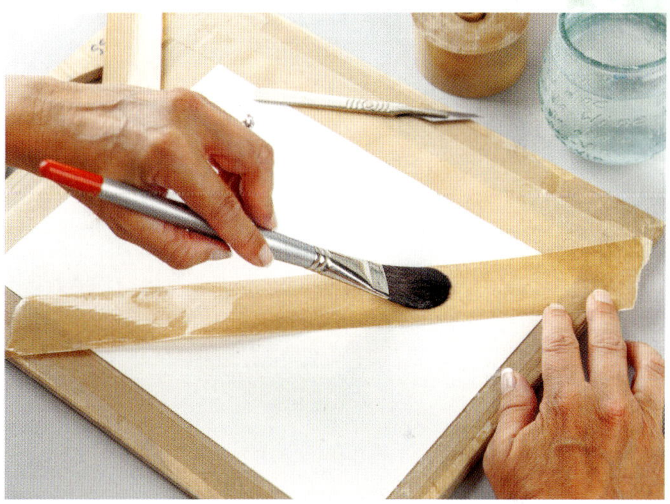

1 Wet strips of gummed paper with clean water and use them to secure your paper to the board.

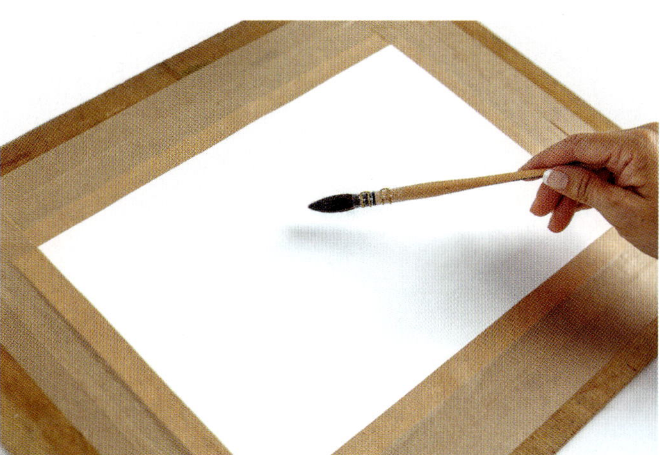

2 Once all the strips are in place, let everything dry before you start to draw.

My way of painting

This is a quick overview of the four stages of painting I use to ensure freshness and looseness in my artwork. You don't have to follow it exactly, but I find breaking things up like this helps me to identify and concentrate on the important elements, and to avoid overworking things towards the end.

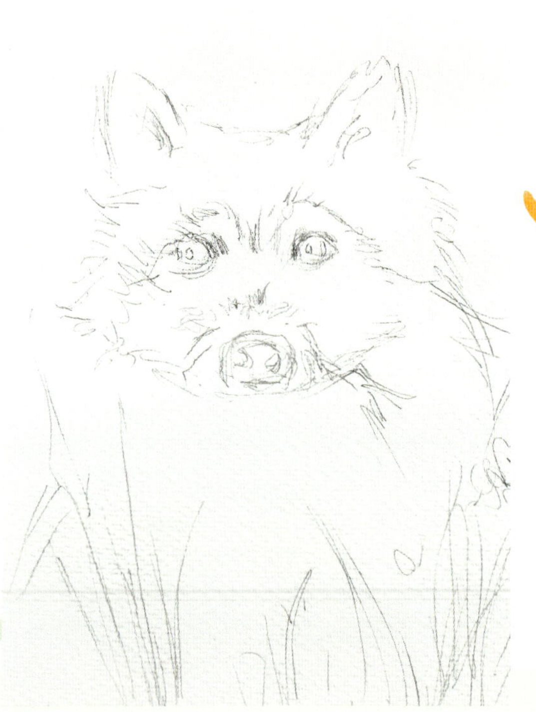

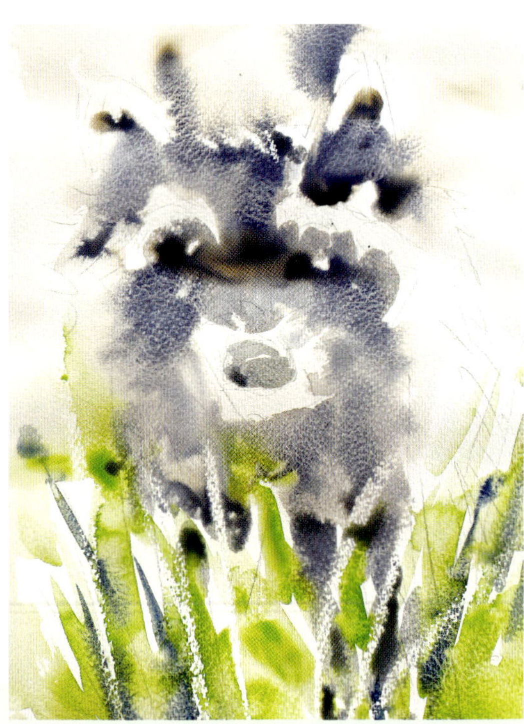

1 Loose sketch

With the paper secured, I start with a very loose, light sketch using a HB pencil, aiming to take no longer than five minutes. I prefer not to trace, nor scale up as I find this leads to the work becoming too precise and contrived. We'll look at drawing in more detail on the following pages.

Once I have my sketch, I often reserve any whites with wax (see page 115 for more ideas for wax resist) at this stage, unless I have decided to use negative painting (see page 138) for my highlights.

2 Loose washes

I usually begin with the subject. With my biggest brush, fully loaded with clean water, I wet the animal all over, before adding colours wet in wet. I allow them to mingle and merge quite freely at this stage as they will dry lighter, and can then be refined and strengthened.

I then add more water to the rest of the surface, drawing it up to my subject all the way around so the colour bleeds out to form a subtle background. This loosens the image and ensures the colours of the subject also appear in the background, which will help to unify the piece.

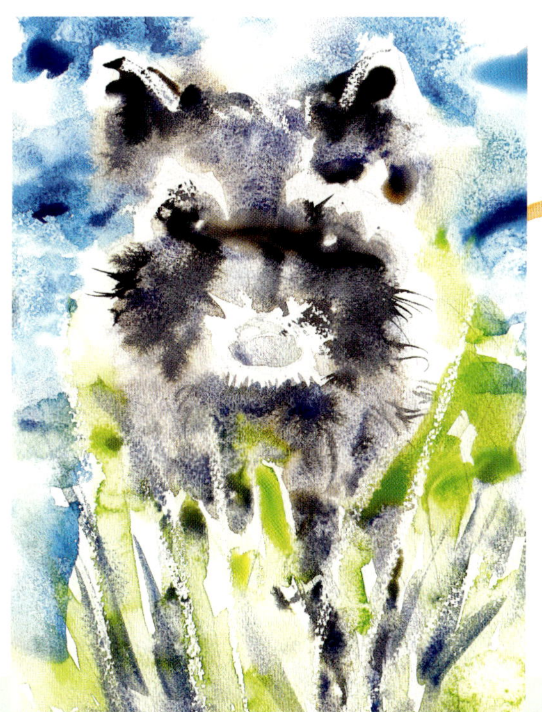

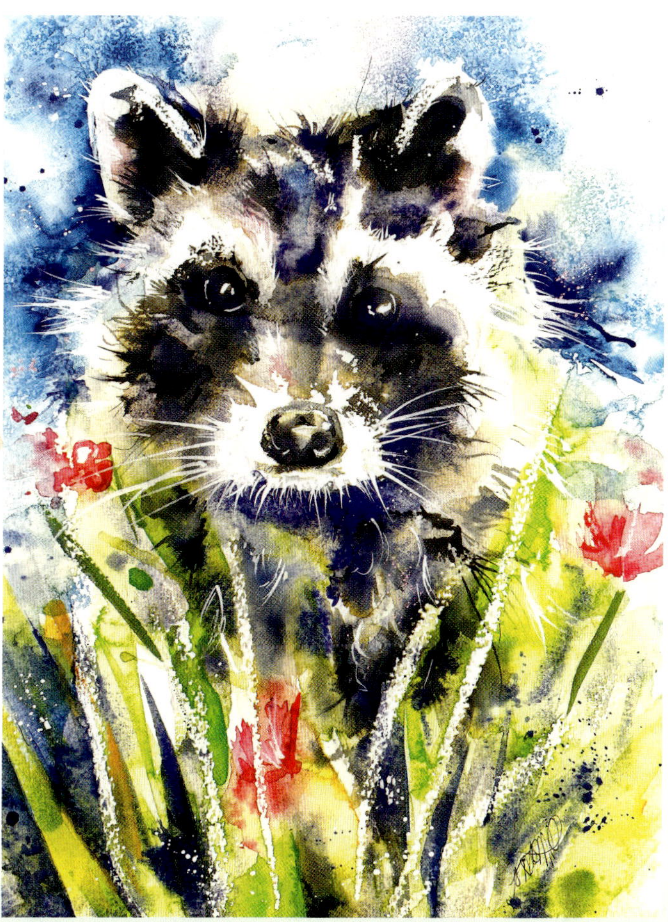

3 Strengthening enhancements

Strengthening the background comes next. The colours I use vary, but I tend towards brighter hues, knowing they dry quite a bit lighter – and I prefer vibrant colour. Sometimes at this stage I will use additives such as alcohol or salt, but I might instead simply drop more colour or water into an already drying wash to create blooms (sometimes called backruns) which I adore. One never knows how these may develop – it is all part of the excitement and fun for me.

The painting will continue to develop and later refinements can address issues. If it is not broken – do not try to fix it! Even if it is, we can try and sort this and learn in the process.

4 Fine details and closing in

Finally, I re-work the main subject to create more depth and detail. This is usually a continuation of my wet in wet painting from the previous stage, but sometimes I allow the whole painting to dry before further developing it. I favour using a rigger brush for these tiny details and sometimes add pen enhancements, spattering or ink, depending largely on my mood. My paintings are not normally rigidly planned, and are instead more of an organic process. I 'go with the flow' and continue with the painting until I feel it is finished, stopping occasionally to assess.

When asked, 'how do you know when a painting is finished?', my answer is always the same: 'When we are happy with what we see – not when other people are happy: just when we are.'

Sketching

Most of my paintings start with a sketch – a very quick and rough sketch. Of course, the sketch should resemble the animal and have the correct proportions (or thereabouts) – but there's no need to spend hours on this part. A loose, light sketch, just to give the idea of the subject, is all that's needed. The painting part is where you will bring the animal to life, working from big expressive marks down to finer details.

I tend to work from a reference photograph that has been blown up to the size I want for the painting and printed off. This means that you don't need to worry about scaling things up. After this, it's simply a case of drawing what you see.

A fast and expressive sketch will help to give your animal artworks liveliness. If the sketch is too detailed and tight, the painting is likely to follow suit. Therefore, try to work quickly where you can. This is especially important with the drawing stage – generally I spend just two to five minutes or so before I consider it complete.

I recommend you try and sketch for at least five minutes each day to build up your skills. Try not to extend beyond this if you wish to loosen up your painting; a detailed sketch will inevitably become a detailed painting. Remember: loose sketch, loose painting!

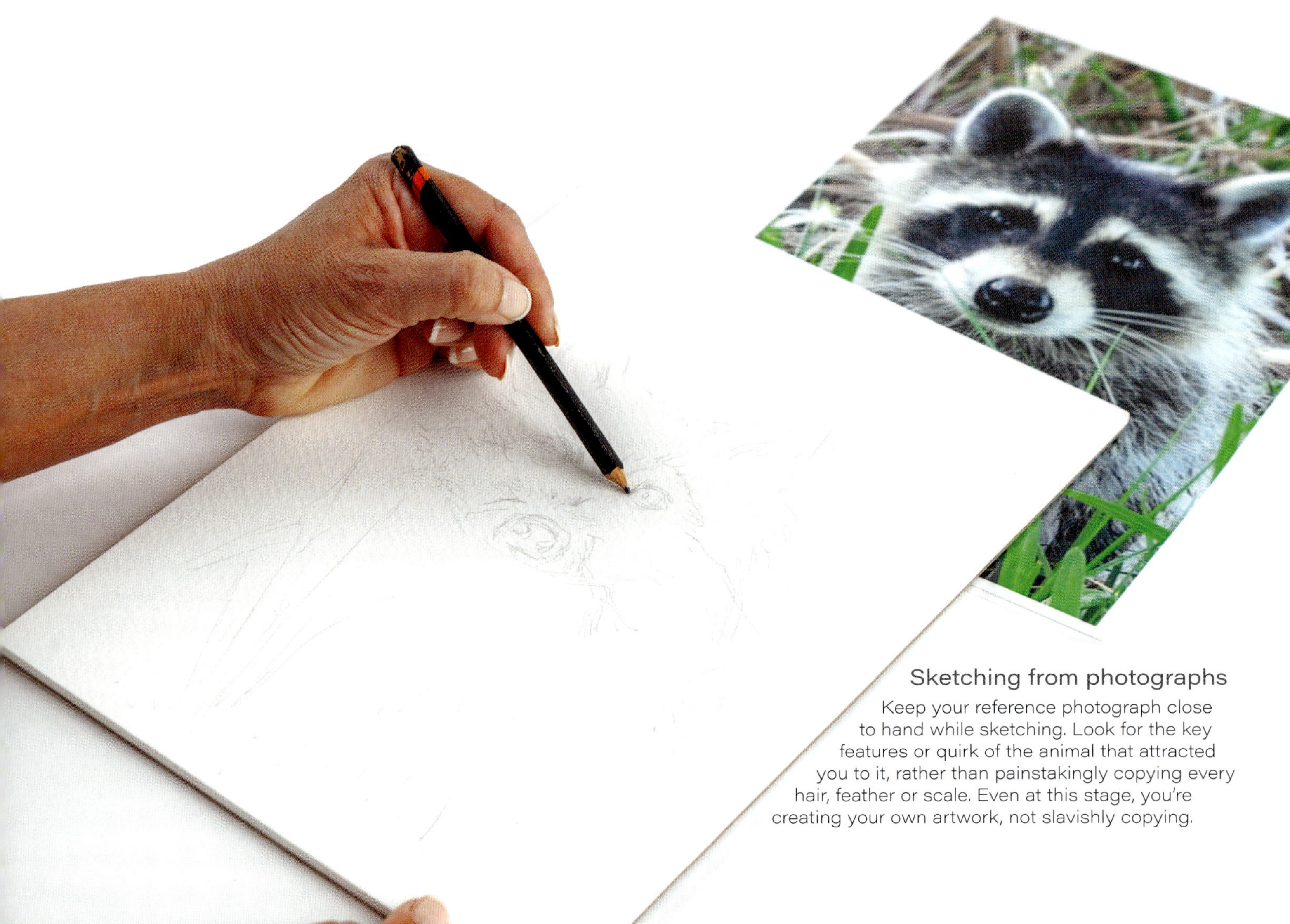

Sketching from photographs
Keep your reference photograph close to hand while sketching. Look for the key features or quirk of the animal that attracted you to it, rather than painstakingly copying every hair, feather or scale. Even at this stage, you're creating your own artwork, not slavishly copying.

Picking a suitable photograph

If you're taking your own photographs from which to sketch, make sure you take them of things you enjoy. It's more important to have something you're enthused about painting than anything else.

Try to get a clear photograph that shows as much of the animal as you can, but don't worry about it being professional quality – the choice of colours, background, in fact everything, is down to your artistic choice, so you don't need much more than an impression.

Sometimes I don't mind it being a 'bad shot' in technical terms – slightly out of focus, or too dark, or with part of the animal cropped out, for example – if the picture otherwise captures my imagination. If something's missing (the tip of an ear or tail, for example) from a shot, I look for other resource images to fill in the blanks while creating the sketch.

Top tips for sketching

Bear these key lessons in mind as you sketch, and you'll be on your way to sketch success!

- *One of my many sayings is 'draw what you see, not what you think you see'*
- *Refine, don't restart*
- *Changes you make while you sketch will create a sense of movement and make your animal seem more alive*
- *Make your first marks count*
- *Work from top to bottom*
- *Heads will help with proportions – how many heads can fit into the body?*
- *Continually refer to what you have already drawn*
- *Adjust and reassess*
- *Leave it loose*
- *Above all, remember that your sketch is not your painting.*

What should I use to sketch?

Mostly I sketch with an HB pencil, though sometimes I go straight in with a pen (see page 56 for more on this). If you choose to use a pencil, I encourage you not to erase the wrong marks until you have remedied them by working the right ones over the top. This is because it's daunting enough to start on a blank page – so there's no reason to return to it! Secondly, if we erase our mistakes, we are likely to put any new lines back in the same – still wrong – place. If we instead leave the marks, we can use them as reference points to ensure the new lines are correct before taking out the ones that are out of place.

Using a pen to sketch will help you to loosen up as it will mean you cannot erase or change things too much. This will force you instead to adapt and work with a piece. While there's nothing wrong with using a pencil, particularly when starting out, using a pen is valuable practice. Being forced to repair and work around our errors helps to build confidence – so when you return to pencil from pen work, you'll find it easier than it ever was.

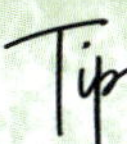

Tip

It's a myth that you can't remove pencil marks from a finished painting. It's easier, of course, if the marks aren't too heavy to begin with, and you've used a harder H pencil rather than an HB pencil.

Don't scrub backwards and forwards; instead, make repeated strokes in the same direction.

If you do decide to remove the pencil, it's important that the painting is completely dry.

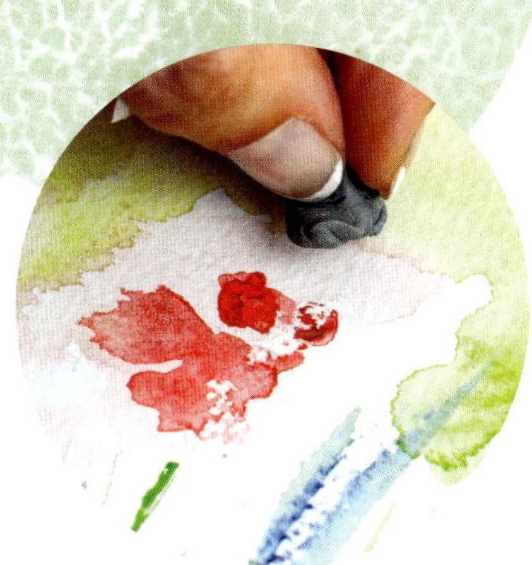

EXERCISE: MAKING A QUICK SKETCH

Try sketching along with me here, and you'll quickly pick up the keys to a simple but effective sketch. I'm demonstrating using a photograph of a bee, but the principles and techniques apply to any animal you wish to choose.

A good trick for getting the proportions right is to look for negative shapes. These are the shapes created by the gaps in between the actual objects – the triangular shape between the bee's body and wing, or the rectangular gap between the legs, for example, are negative shapes. Treat the negative shapes the same as the positive shapes and the whole animal will fit together like a jigsaw, and you won't over-emphasize areas like the eyes or other obvious features.

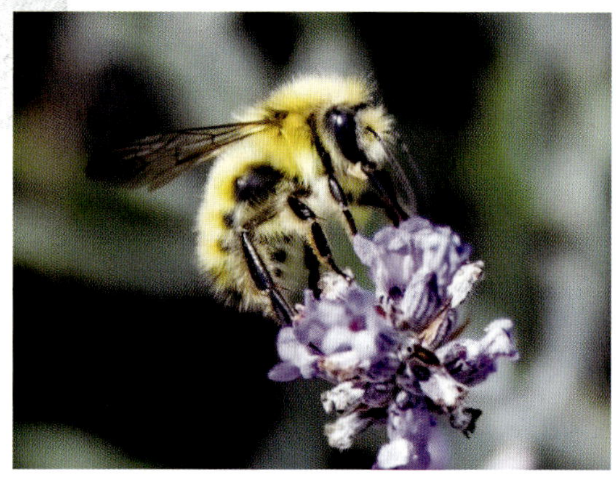

The source photograph.

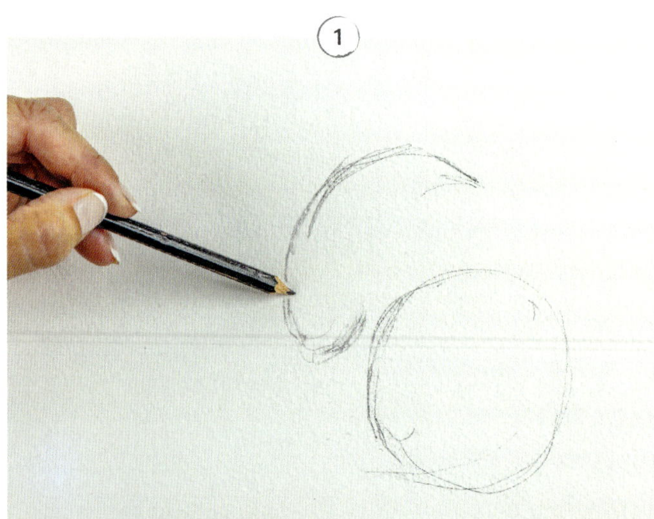

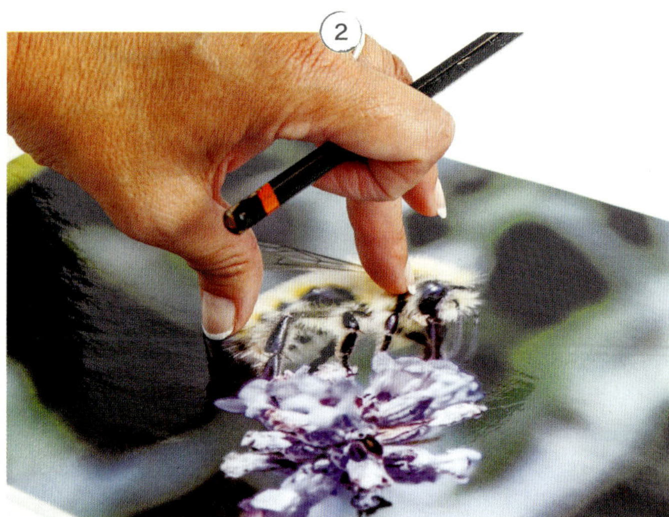

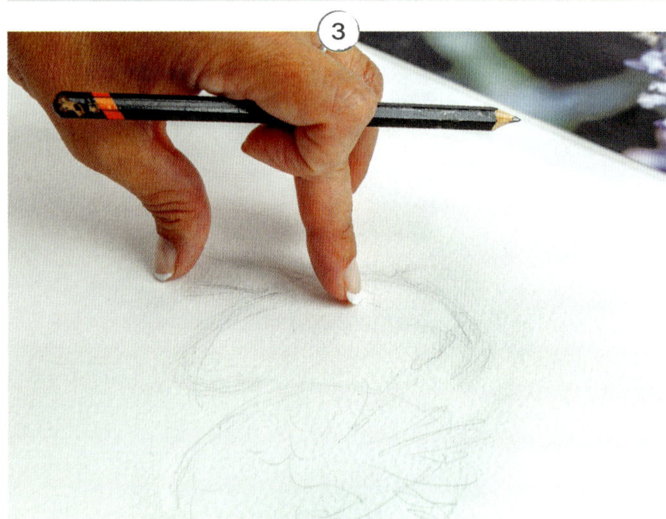

1 Use an HB pencil, because the marks it makes are light. Start wherever you like – for this, I'm using simple shapes for a bee on a flower. Work lightly and loosely – don't be tempted to rub out at this point. Instead, simply re-draw the line in the right place, using the wrong line to help guide you.

2 To quickly work out proportions, you can use your fingers to work out a distance – in this example, I want to see how far it is from the back of the bee to its head. Place your thumb on one point, then your finger on the other.

3 Keeping your fingers in the same position, move your hand and place it on the paper. It's a quick method, and doesn't need to be hugely precise.

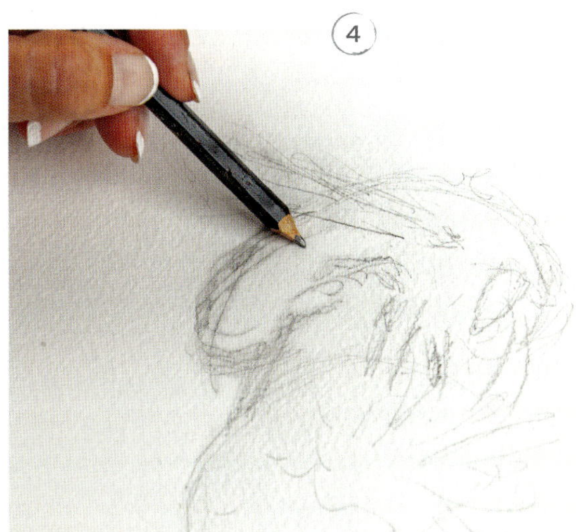

4 As you add more detail – such as the wing, here – use existing areas to help you with placement. Where on the animal's body does the feature sit? Which other features does it sit between, or above, or below?

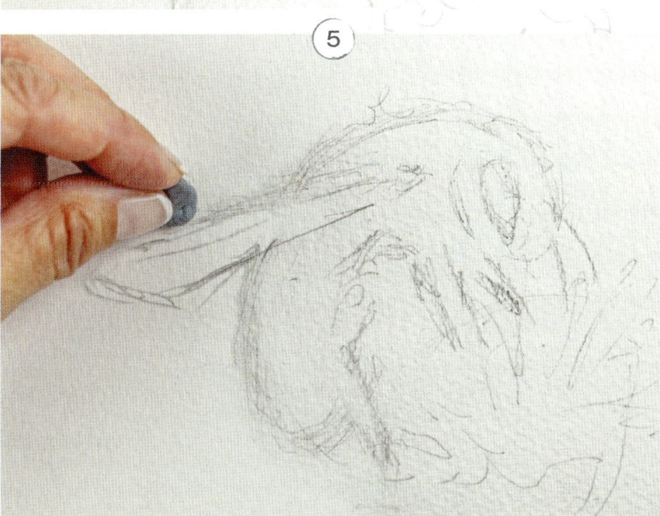

5 Use a putty eraser to remove any excess lines to simplify things, but don't over-tidy your work. Leave it loose.

The finished sketch.

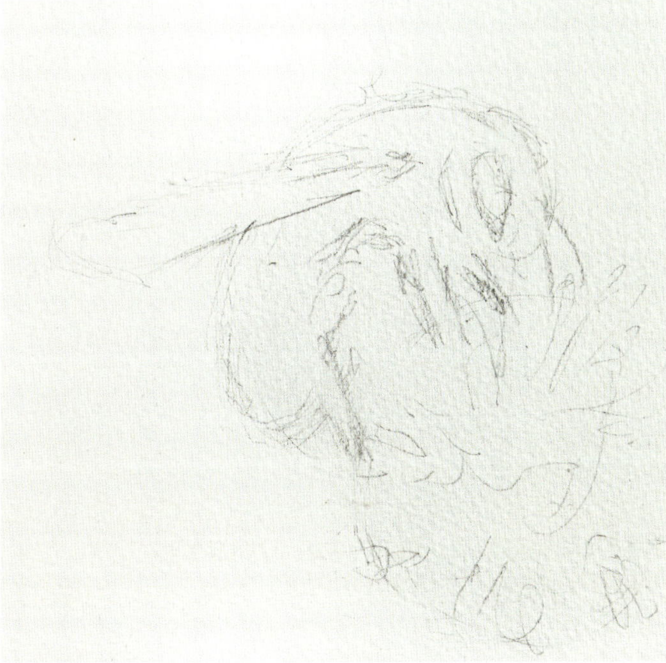

Composition

Composition is simply how the parts of a painting are arranged – where and how you place the animal on the page, and how you treat the background.

These two owls show how the choices you make can give very different results.

First decisions

After deciding which animal to paint, the next step is to work out how much of the animal to show. Sometimes I want to close in on a subject and paint just the head and shoulders, while at other times I want to show the whole animal in context, and so opt for the full body of the subject with a suggestion of grasses, flowers or sky in the background. In both cases I tend to keep the background very loose so the animal remains the star of the show.

Once I have decided on these basic elements, I search for a reference photograph that captures what I want to paint. Once permission has been granted by the photographer for me to be able to use the image, I follow the scene quite closely for my sketch.

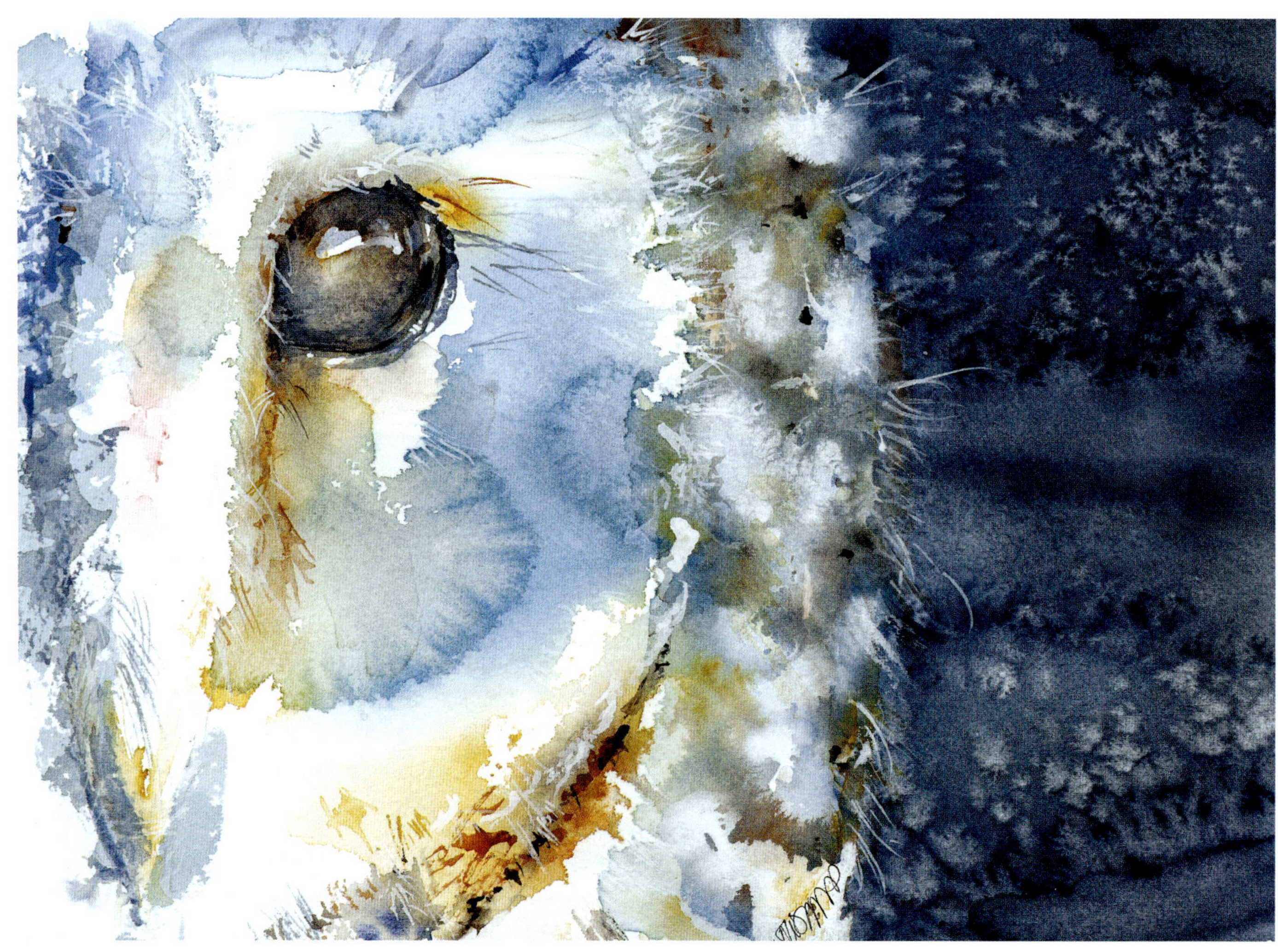

The Observer
33.5 x 23.5cm (13 x 9¼in)

While I draw what I see from my reference photographs, I will not necessarily paint what I see. Instead, I make adaptations as I please throughout the painting process. This is where I allow myself much more freedom to be responsive and creative, so the composition continues to evolve and be refined until the painting is finished.

While I avoid fussy, over-detailed backgrounds, I will often change background colours to become much brighter and livelier as I love colour so much. This helps to frame the animal, and gives the often muted natural colours more impact.

For example, the background on the close-up composition opposite, *The Observer*, was black on the photograph. I wanted the owl to be out on a starry night, and knew that the salt effect would perform particularly well against darker pigment. I decided to use a receding blue, as I wanted a sense of coldness and darkness without the oppressiveness that black can bring.

The flying owl, *Fly Free*, grabbed me as it was such a poignant picture – just days before I had experienced a huge barn owl fly in front of my car on a late autumn evening. I decided to incorporate the salt and spatter to demonstrate the movement of such silent wings.

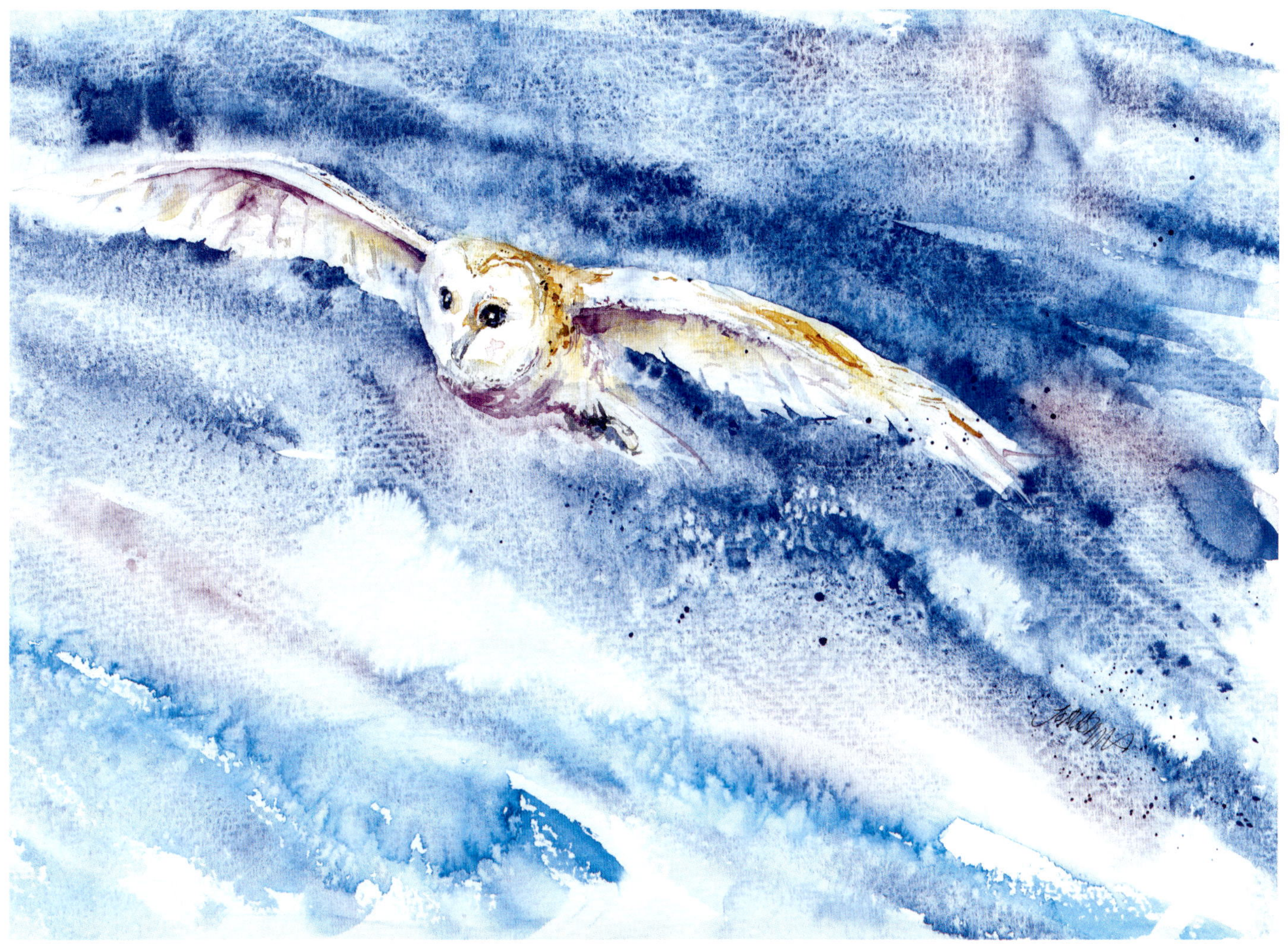

Fly Free
31 x 22cm (12¼ x 8¾in)

Making artistic choices

A good sketch is what will ensure that your finished painting of a cat will look like a cat – the proportions of the face must resemble that of a cat, the ear shape and nose size must be correct, and so forth.

However, we don't have to paint the cat brown just because in real life he is brown. The painting stage is where we can have fun and enjoy our colours. Perhaps we will brighten our cat up with reddish-brown fur, and add a little green shadow under the chin instead of the black or grey of the photograph. By using the complementary pair of red and green, the subject will bounce off that paper and will look much more vibrant and lively.

As part of the composition, the colour of my subject often determines the background colour I use. I like my animals to jump off the page and so will opt for a complementary colour to the subject. If I do not use complementary colours in the background, I often introduce complementary pairs another way. In a painting of a yellow bird, for example, I might introduce purple flowers nearby even if in reality the flowers are a completely different colour, or absent entirely.

Such artistic licence is what will make your paintings unique to you, and add to your enjoyment.

Planning

When drawn to a particular subject, I try to sketch it accurately and don't make many changes – but this is purely the way that works for me. If you enjoy adapting your photograph or sketch, you should feel free to do so.

Colour is where I allow myself much more freedom and expression. I paint whatever colour takes my fancy that particular day and use different techniques as a painting progresses. Unless I am teaching something specific, I do not plan: when I am left alone to be creative, it is an organic, involving process that gives me so much joy.

You don't always have to have a plan, you don't have to have restrictions. Sometimes it is good to just let go and go with the flow. Feel that freedom. Paint from the heart.

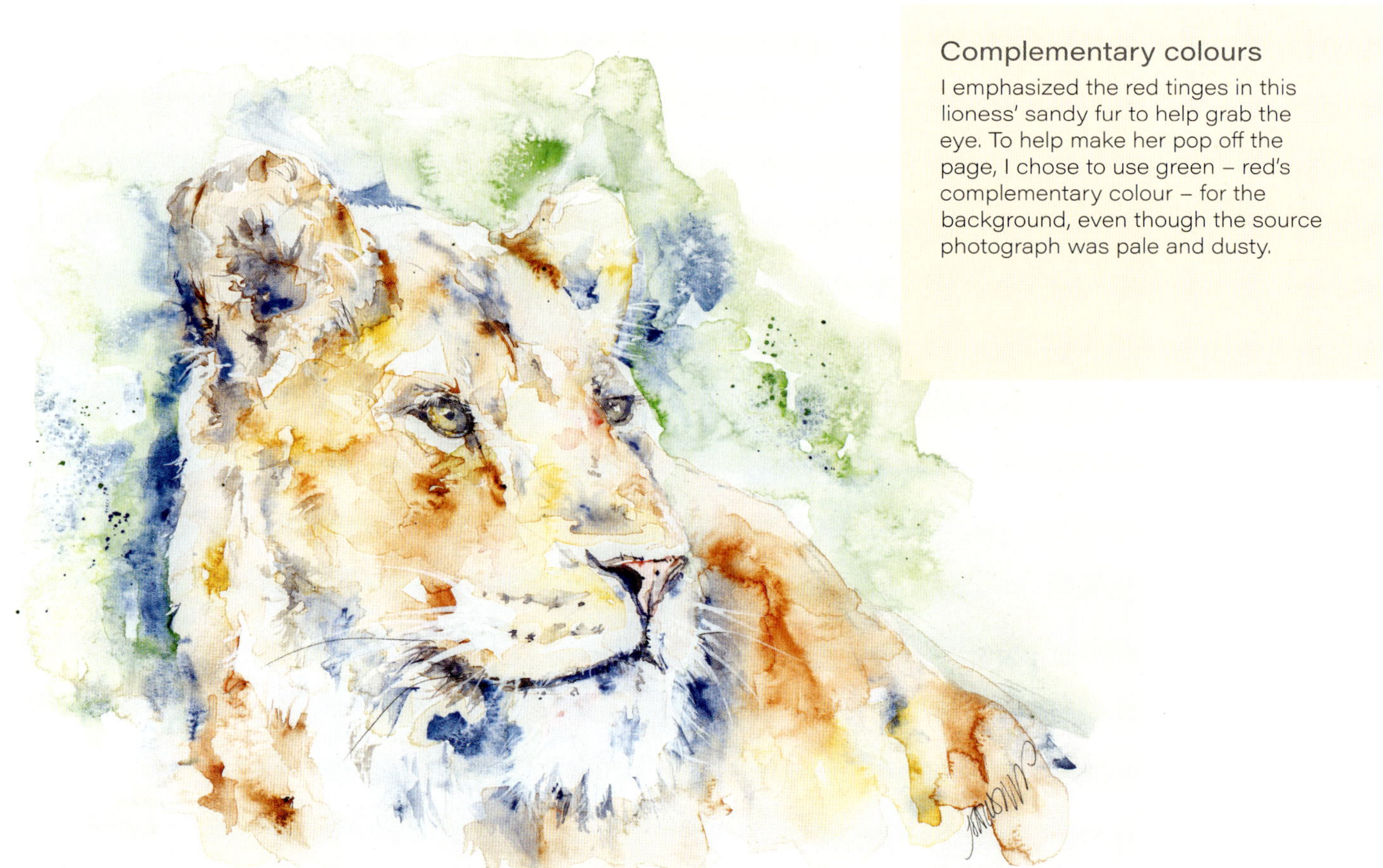

Complementary colours

I emphasized the red tinges in this lioness' sandy fur to help grab the eye. To help make her pop off the page, I chose to use green – red's complementary colour – for the background, even though the source photograph was pale and dusty.

Focal points and hot spots

The focal point is where you want the viewer to pay particular attention: give them something to look at. Leaving other areas looser is important, or the painting will be over-detailed and tight, and the viewer won't know where to look.

You can use colour to help direct, too. As red is an advancing colour and draws the eye, I will often use this colour on the face somewhere to gain the attention of the viewer. Even if there is no red on the animal at all, mine will often have a little eye-catching 'hot spot'. Likewise try using cool blue colours, which appear to recede, for less important areas.

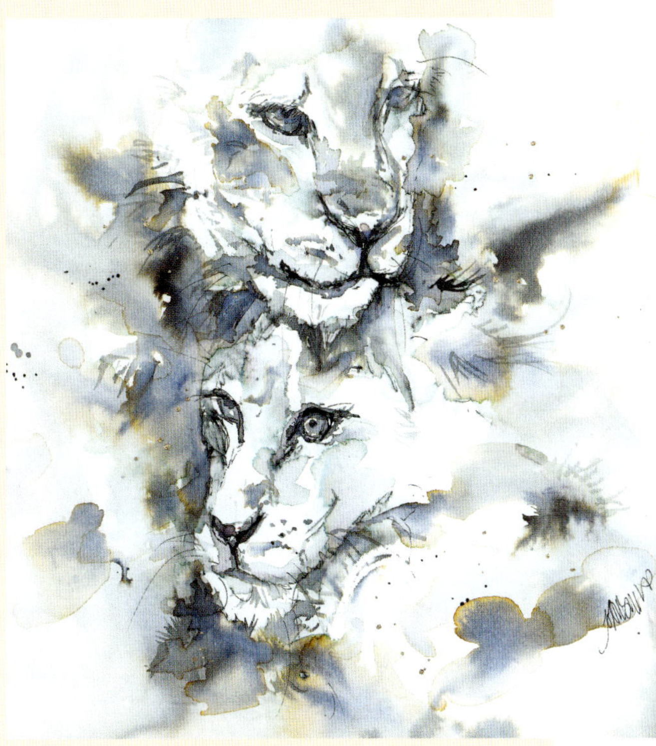

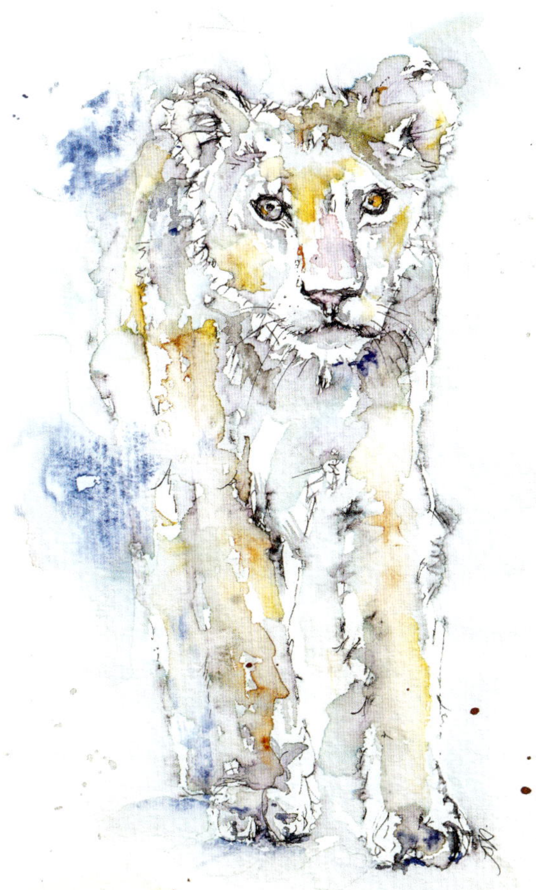

Leading the eye

The main focal point here is the face of the lioness. Note how much more detailed the eyes, nose and mouth are than the legs and body, and that I've used a splash of pink-red on the nose as a hot spot.

Once you've grabbed the viewer's attention, you can hold it with a second focal point: in this case, the paws. These have more detail than the legs and body, but less than the face – the viewer's gaze will therefore move back and forth between the face and paws. Note that the legs and background include blue, a cool, receding colour, so the eye drifts over them.

Approach and style

Making choices – whether in terms of the drawing, the colours you use or the techniques you employ – will affect the final result. Over time you'll find that you are developing your own personal style.

I like to keeps things fresh – and so swapping and changing mood and medium helps me to constantly develop my style. Just compare the three pictures of lionesses on these pages to see how the same subject can be approached in lots of different ways. There are no hard and fast rules in art, so be brave and have fun.

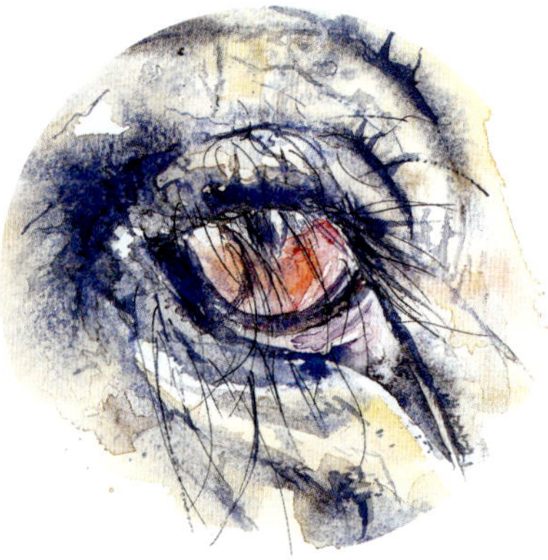

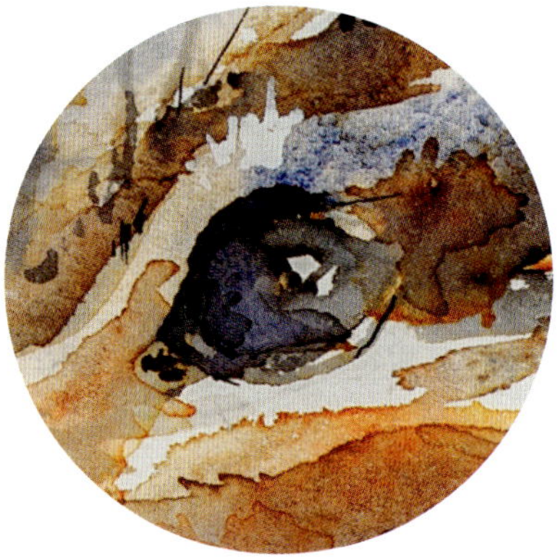

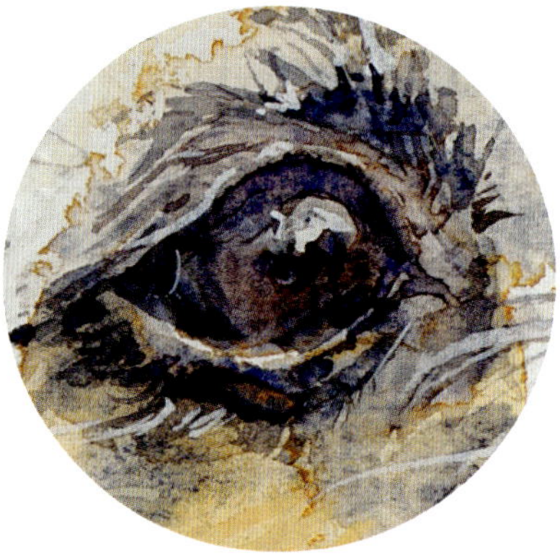

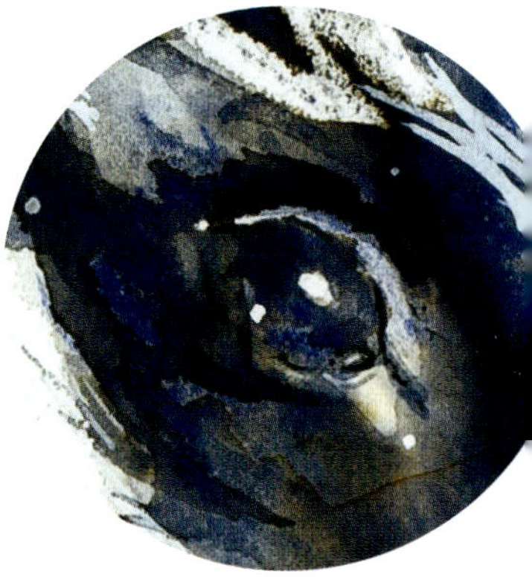

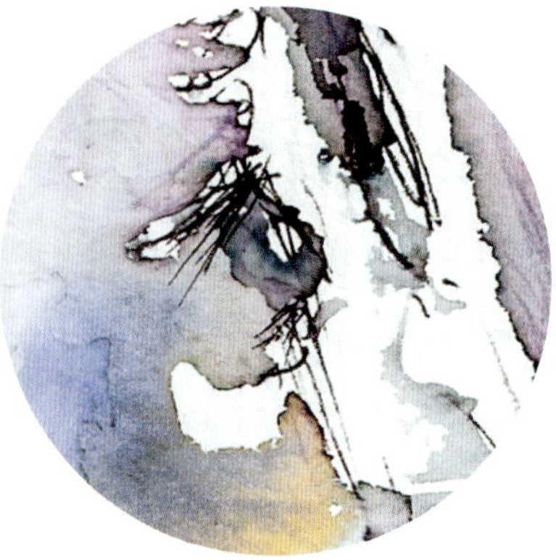

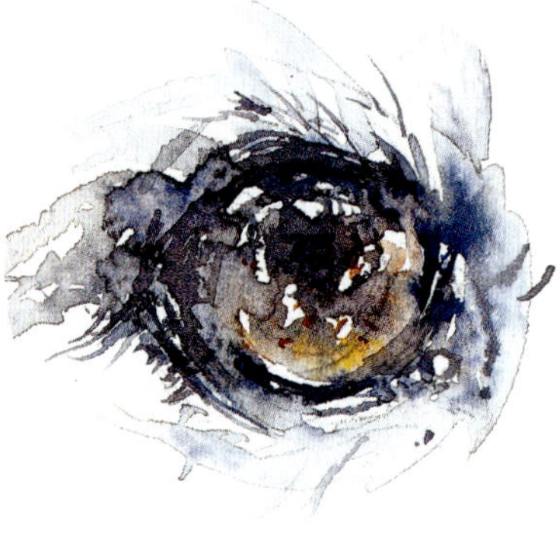

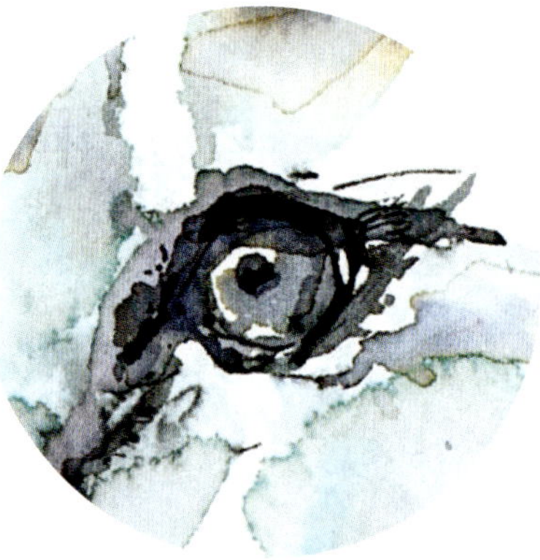

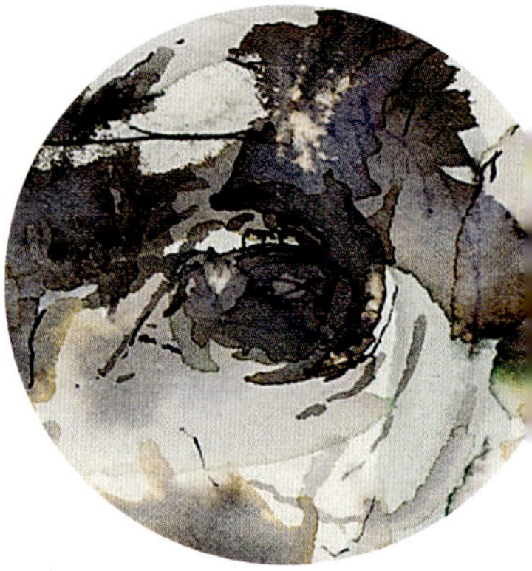

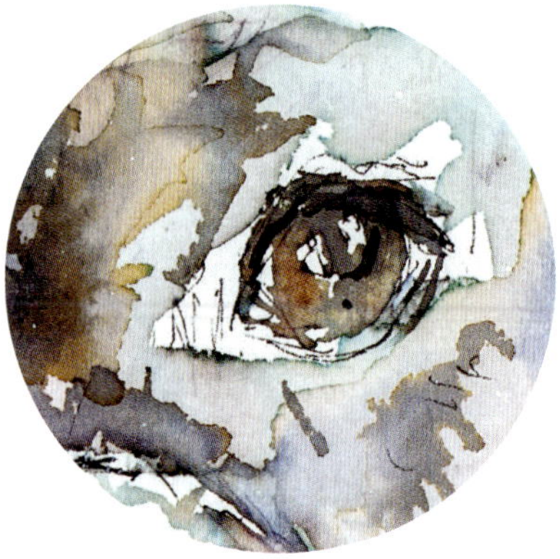

The eye is in the detail

I paint freely and loosely, but as a common focal point, the eyes often need an extra bit of attention, with the detail being built up until it is just right. Some artists prefer to get the eye detail in very early on in a painting, but I prefer to build up eyes slowly in the later stages of a painting, applying the detail using my baby brush.

This approach works better for me for a couple of reasons. On occasion I have changed my mind as to exactly where the eye should go, midway through a painting. It's much easier to lift out if there's not a lot of detail already in place. Secondly, and more importantly, I find adding the eye later on brings my painting to life near the end, reigniting my enthusiasm. I just adore the feeling of seeing my animals come to life before my very eyes – the satisfaction is just immense to have them finally looking at me.

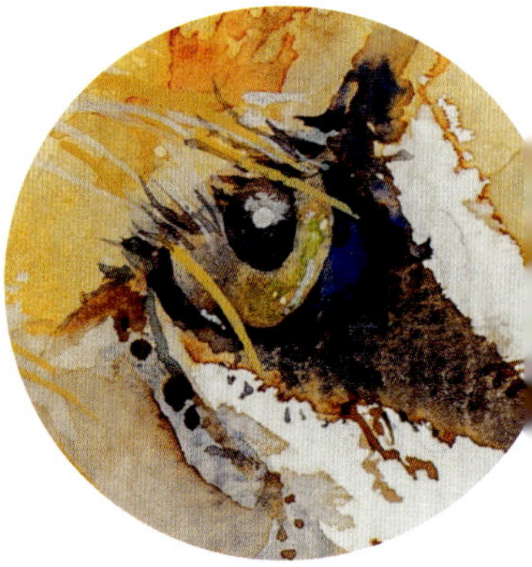

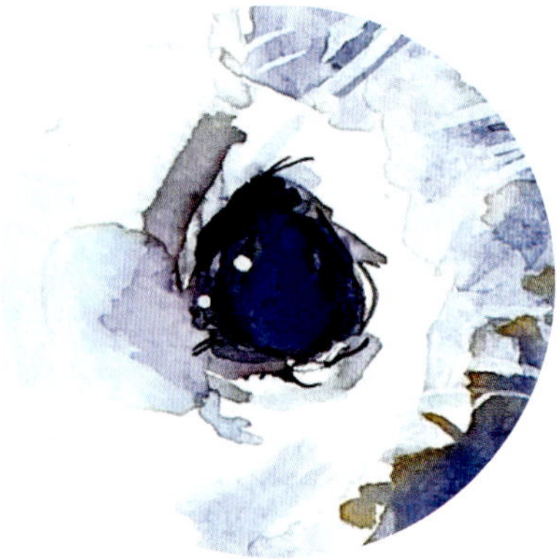

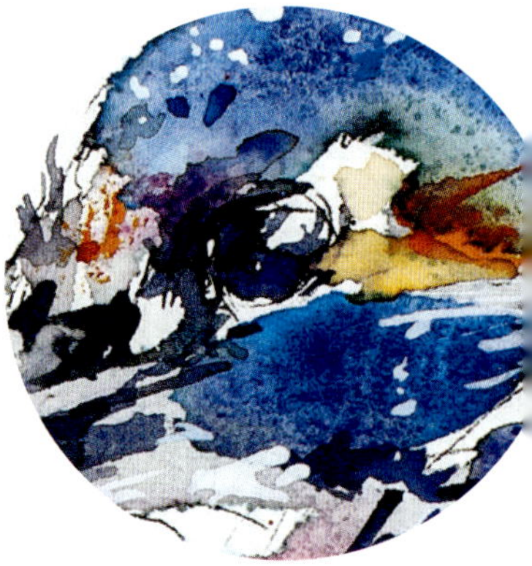

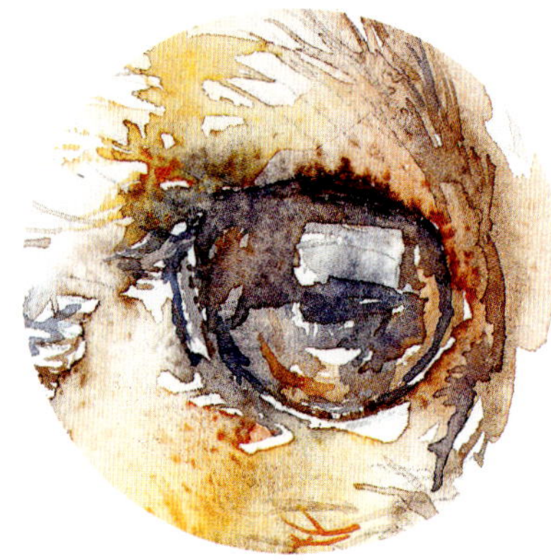
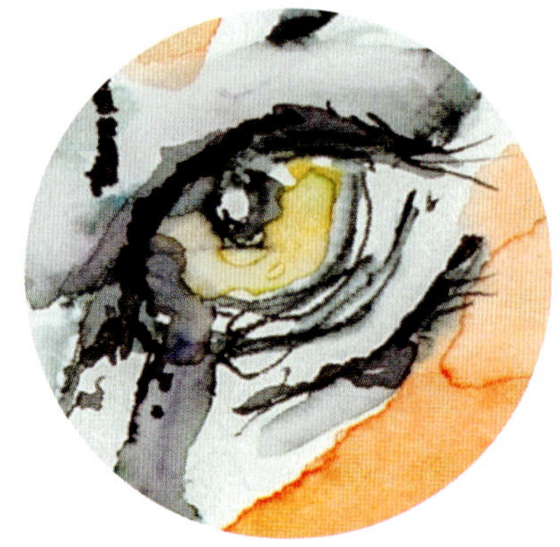
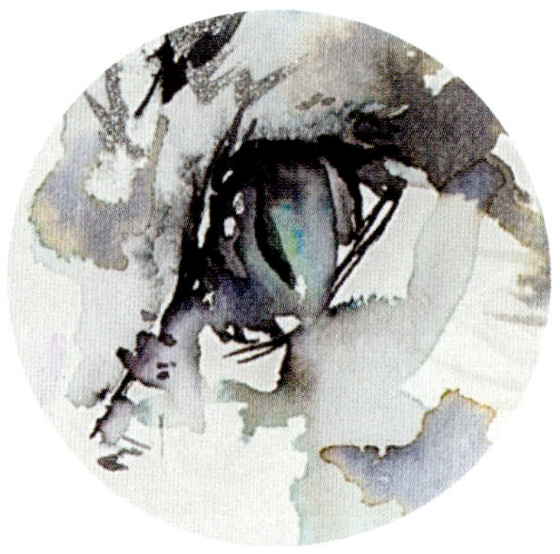
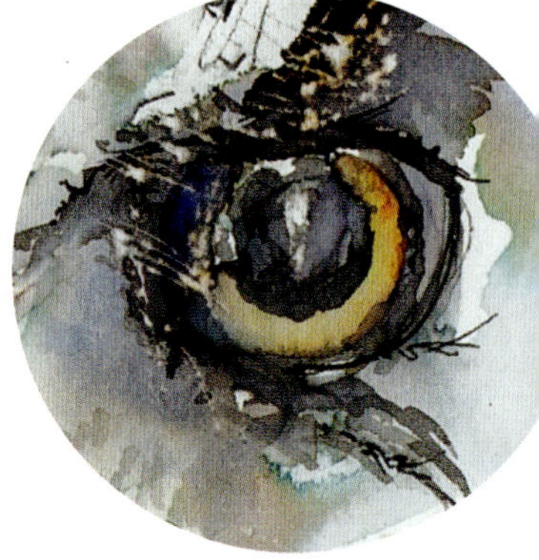

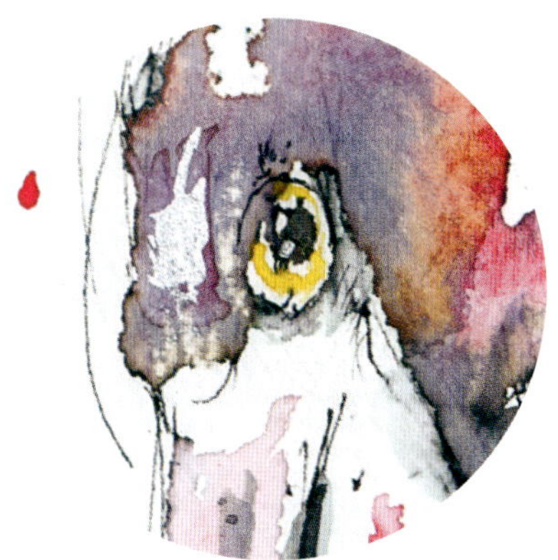

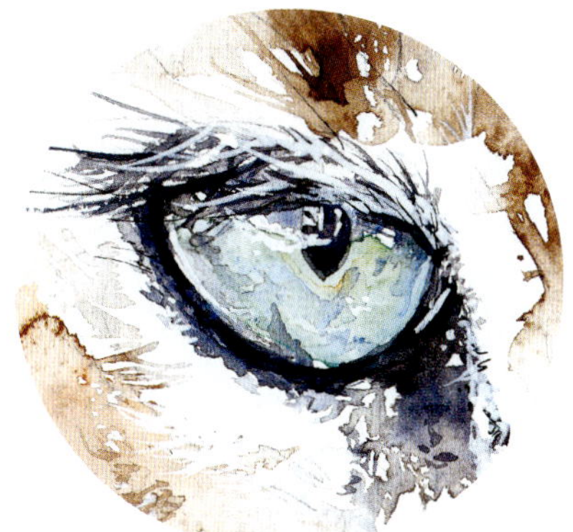

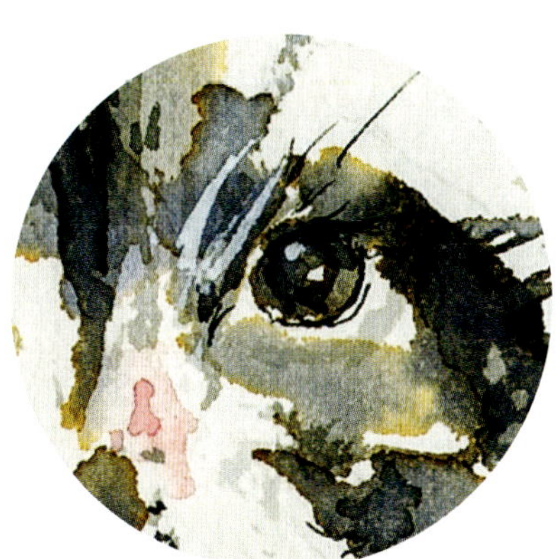

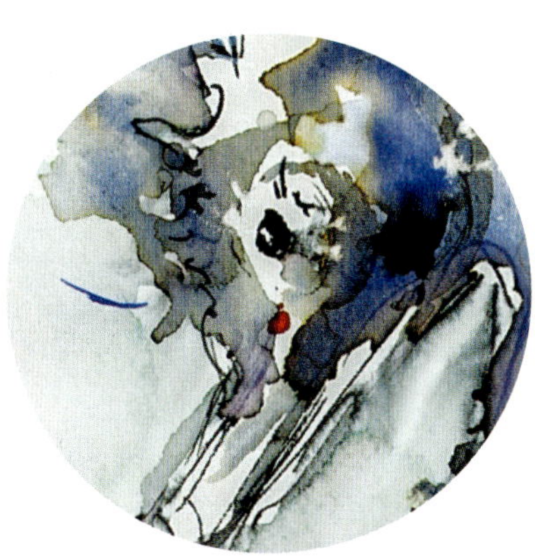

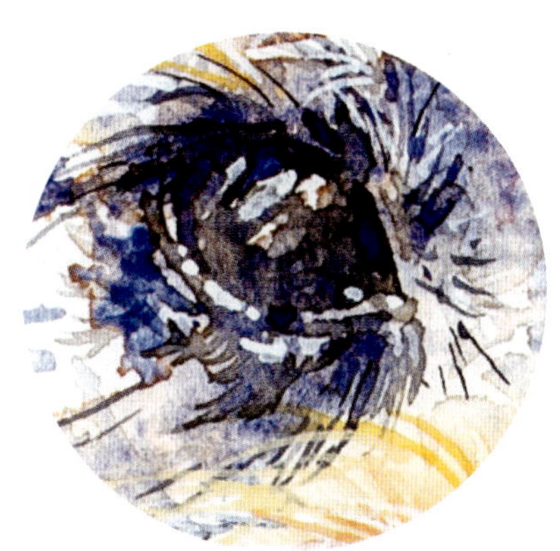

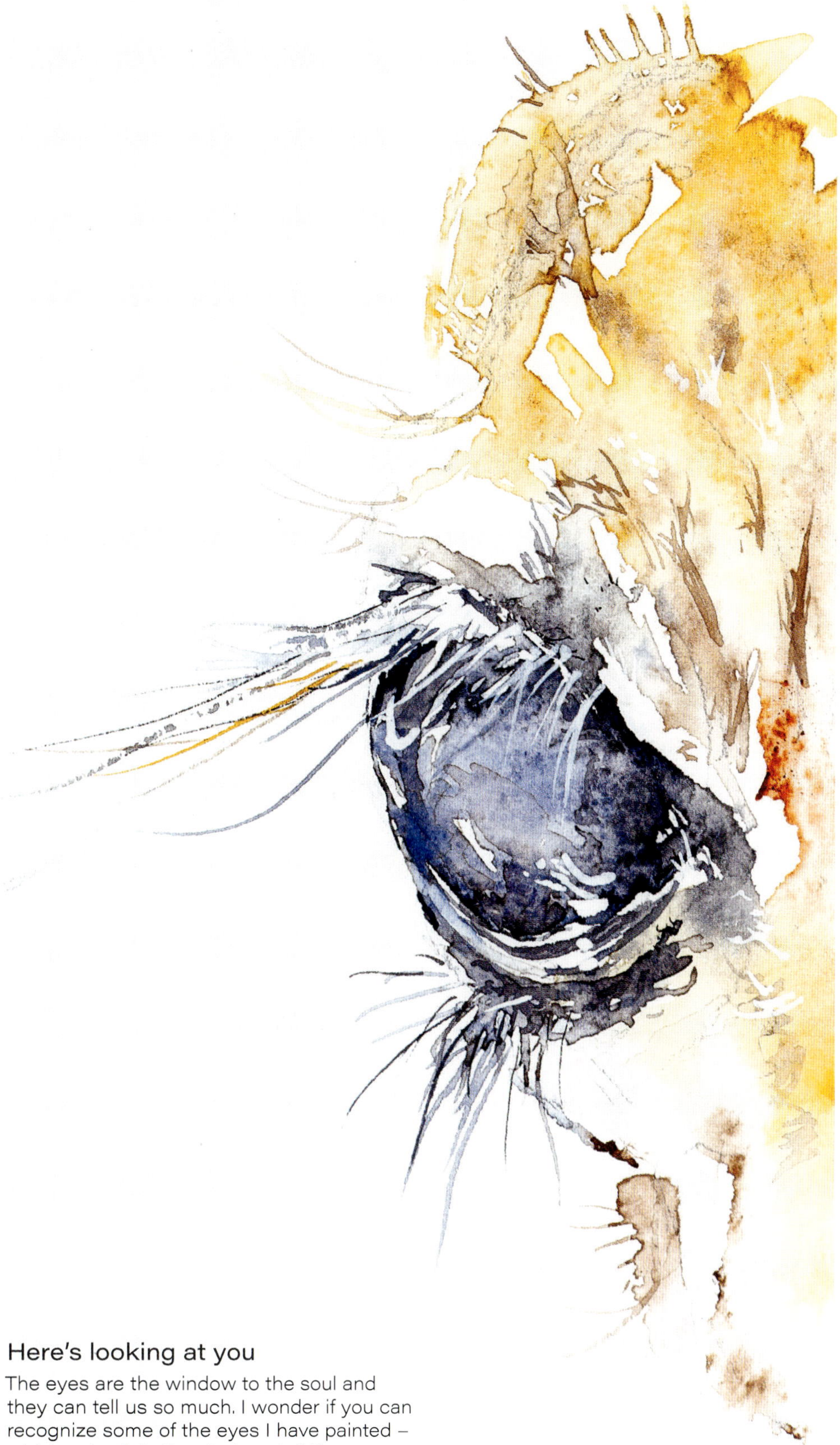

Here's looking at you

The eyes are the window to the soul and
they can tell us so much. I wonder if you can
recognize some of the eyes I have painted –
which animal do they belong to? If you can
see from where they come, this means I have
done a good job.

Patterns

Sometimes we get lost in a painting or drawing. We struggle
to work things out – proportions, shapes, patterns… These
important elements get lost as we over-focus on the details.
When this happens, we need to take a step back.
The simple tips here will help you get back on track when
you are concentrating too hard on the subject – in this
example, a lion.

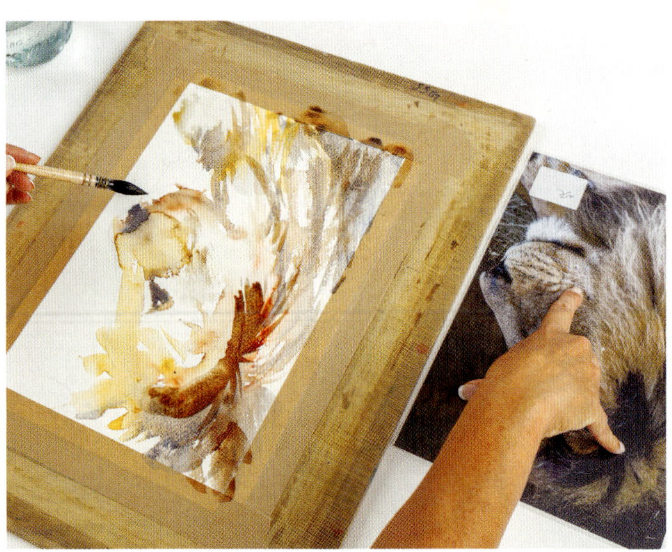

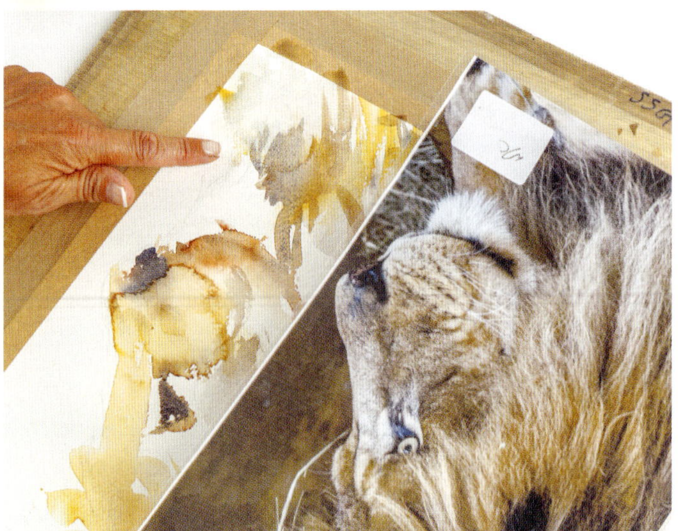

Turn the picture – make it unfamiliar

Turn both your painting and your reference upside down. This
change in perspective will reduce what we recognize as a lion
to simple shapes and patterns. By concentrating on drawing
and painting just these simple shapes, you'll find it really helps
to identify – and accurately paint – subtle parts that are easy to
miss the other way around.

Look for shapes and marks

Take a little time to compare your painting with the reference,
trying to find simple shapes rather than identifying parts of the
animal such as nose, cheeks and so forth.

Concentrating on abstract areas of tone, rather than thinking
in terms of particular parts of the animal, will make it easier
to identify subtle shapes and marks – and to apply the
paint accurately.

Look at it from another angle

There's no reason that you have to turn your painting completely upside down. You might find that turning the image sideways or at another angle works better for your particular painting.

It's worth trying different angles to ensure you keep your brain from getting familiar with what's in front of you. In turn, this helps to ensure a direct, natural response to what is actually in front of you, rather than painting what you think is there.

Finer detail

Once you've got the basic shapes in place, try turning it the right way up again to carry on with the finer detail. Note, however, that there's no need to do this – you might choose to paint the whole thing upside down if you find it helps.

You will likely find that having had the image upside down helps you understand the picture as a whole. Here, for example, I spotted that the eye that I had put in initially was actually much lighter, so I used a wet brush to lift out the colour a little.

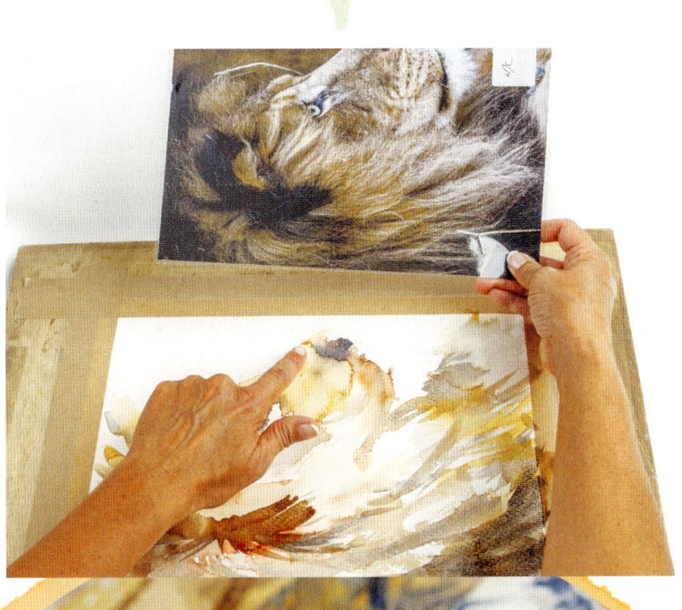

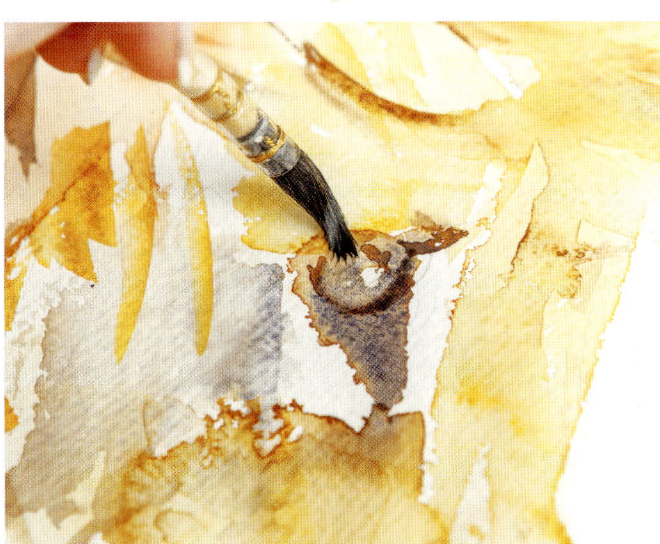

Don't stick too closely to your reference

Sometimes it's useful to deliberately break shapes and patterns, to avoid things looking too solid and fixed. Spattering is a great technique for this, as it will always have a slightly uncontrolled result.

To spatter, load your brush with fluid paint and gently flick the paint onto the surface. The spattered marks will instantly add a sense of movement, texture and interest.

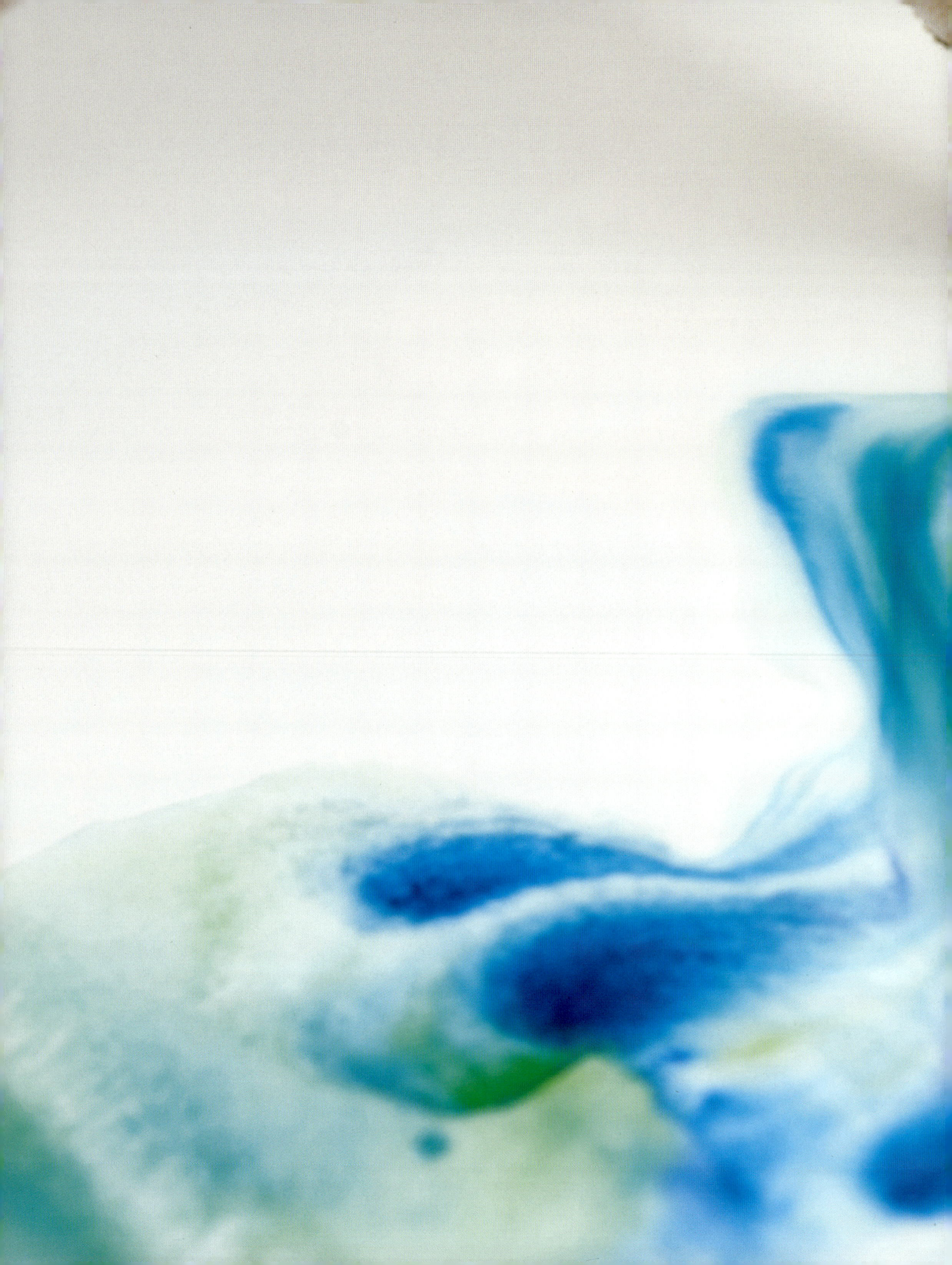

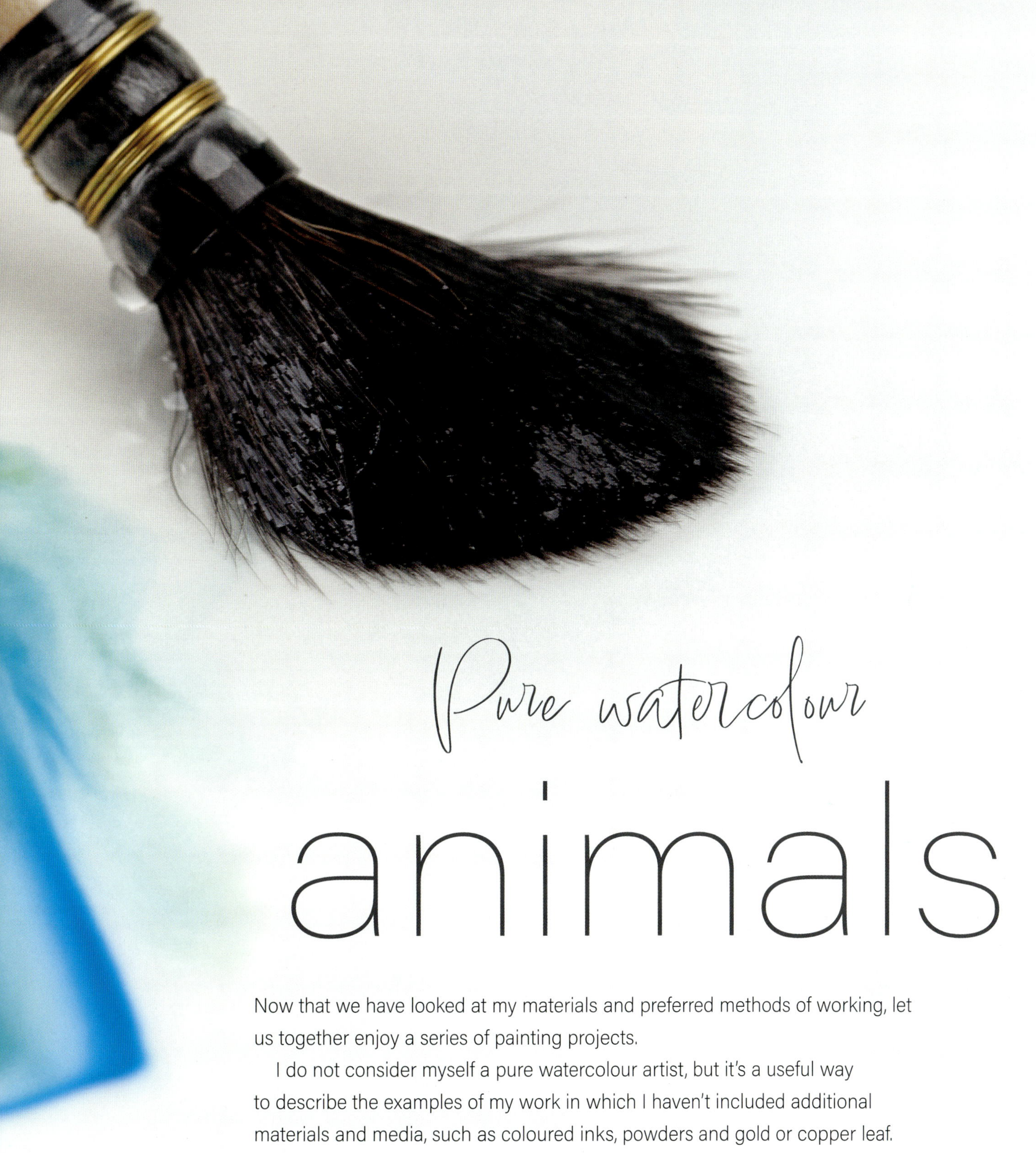

animals

Now that we have looked at my materials and preferred methods of working, let us together enjoy a series of painting projects.

I do not consider myself a pure watercolour artist, but it's a useful way to describe the examples of my work in which I haven't included additional materials and media, such as coloured inks, powders and gold or copper leaf.

We'll start working with pure watercolours so you can find your feet with the loose style, and then we'll move on to introducing some exciting mixed media elements later on.

On your marks, get set... go!

How to approach the projects

I have tried to include as broad a selection of animals as possible, so I hope there are lots that you find appealing. There is no particular order in which to approach the projects, so whether you want to dive into an inky peacock straight away or stick with a pure watercolour fox, that's fine.

Always draw and paint things that please you. When you are enthusiastic, you are much more likely to produce a better piece than forcing yourself to do something you are less passionate about. I suggest that you look through the book to see which subject, material or technique appeals to you the most.

Each project is followed by further ideas to explore – by the end of the book, you'll have all you need to come back to tackle any of the paintings I've showcased.

Avoid becoming mechanical

If you're just starting out, the steps will give you a plan to follow. Don't panic, however, if things don't look exactly like my paintings at every stage. Watercolour is an unpredictable medium – but this is a good thing. Allowing the paint to do its own thing in places will help you to achieve this loose, free style.

Start on a positive and not a negative. Every mark you make will be another step forward. Think of all that practice you are getting!

Play with colour

As explained on page 38, it's important to have a fairly accurate initial sketch – but you can use whatever colours of paint you like. I've included the information on what paints that I have used, but these are just suggestions. Have fun, substitute my colours for your own, and really enjoy this process.

Likewise, don't be slavish to the picture: if there's a fussy background you are not confident with, you do not have to paint it. You have the choice to opt in or out of anything: it's your painting, and no one else's.

Opposite:
Thorn
20 x 20cm (8 x 8in)

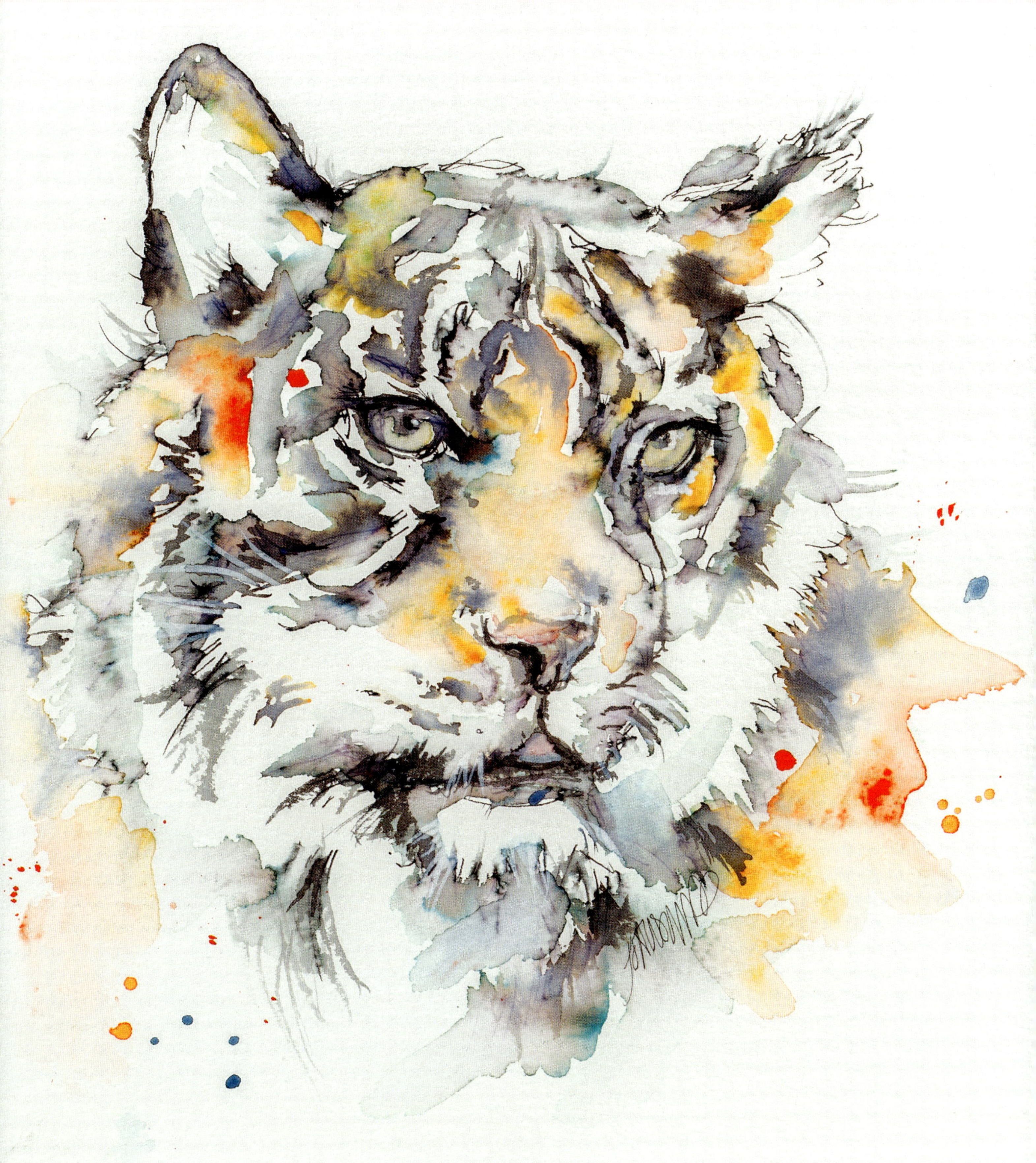

Border Terrier

I wanted to paint this picture of my dog Alfie, as I know exactly when and where we were when this was taken. Do not be fooled by Alfie's innocent face; he is a little red devil! Alfie is not at all receptive to any of his four-legged 'friends'. The only one he would tolerate was my other terrier, Oscar, who was top dog.

Red is an aggressive colour and I felt it apt here to reflect this part of Alfie's character, so wanted to include it where I could. Despite being red, I made the decision to omit the bulky harness from my painting – it risked drawing too much attention – and instead included just his hot red collar. You'll spot that I even gave him a little suggestion of red on his face too.

Rather than using greens for the background I decided to use red here too, for a unifying effect. I kept it simple to make him the star.

I have fond memories of my late Oscar being mischievous with Alfred this particular day – they got wet and smelly in the pond. I often visit this local beauty spot, with just Alfie now.

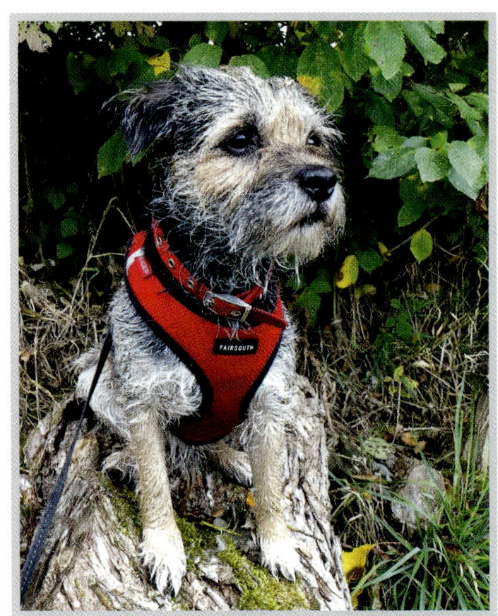

Source photograph
Alfred the Great! With the plan in mind, I decided that Rough surface paper would be great to demonstrate Alfie's rough coat.

You will need

Bockingford Rough surface watercolour paper
25.5 x 35.5cm (10 x 14in)

WATERCOLOUR PAINTS:
Yellow ochre, burnt umber, French ultramarine, rose madder, vermilion

Large, medium and small brushes

HB pencil and putty eraser

Beeswax candle

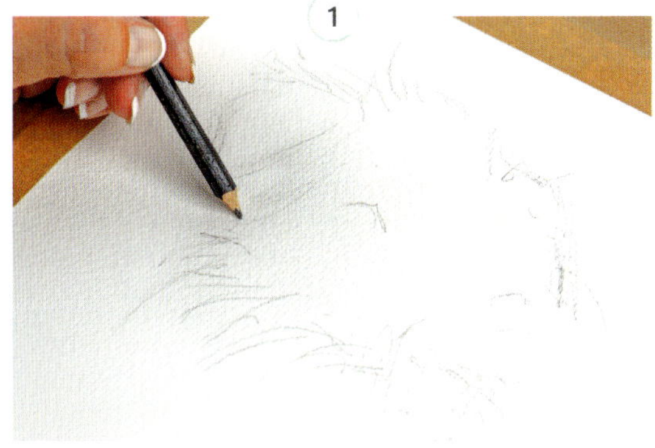

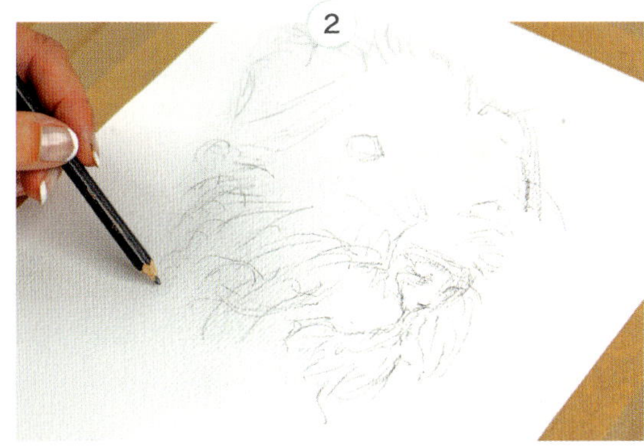

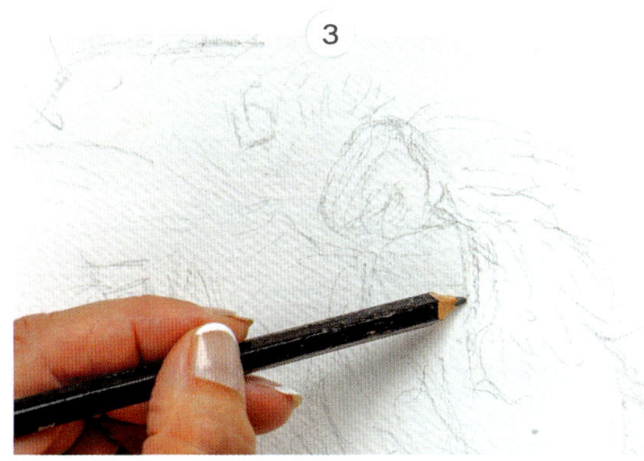

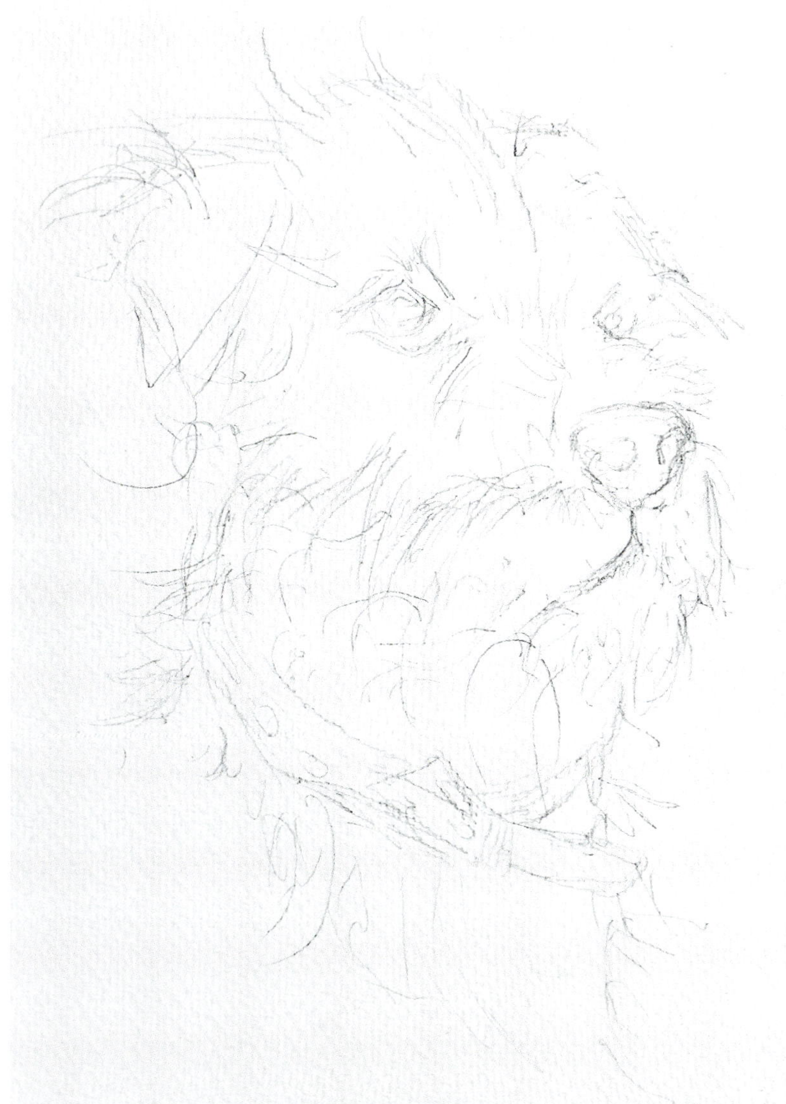

The sketch

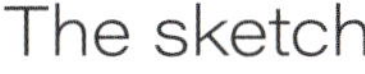

In cases like this, where obvious face shapes are hidden somewhat by thick fur, look for a feature that'll give you a way in. Here, Alfie's ear is ideal; a simple triangle that I can pop in at the top left.

While I want the collar in the finished piece to provide a pop of colour, I don't want to include the harness, so I've left it out of the sketch, using the shapes that are present to help me work out what's underneath.

1 Begin sketching using the HB pencil, building up the sketch with reference to your source photograph.

2 Use the early marks to assess the shape, width and height of the head and features. Pay attention to your source photograph.

3 Turn the piece on its side to help assess what you've done. Here, I realized that I had placed the nose too low on the face – the pose means it appears higher than you might expect. This is a good example of how drawing what you think is there, rather than what's in front of you, can lead you astray. Rely on turning the picture (see pages 42–43) to help you adjust accurately, and without any expectations.

Painting Alfie

For this piece, I'm adding more wax than I might usually. This is because his fur is scruffy and textural, and will benefit from the marks of wax on the Rough paper surface.

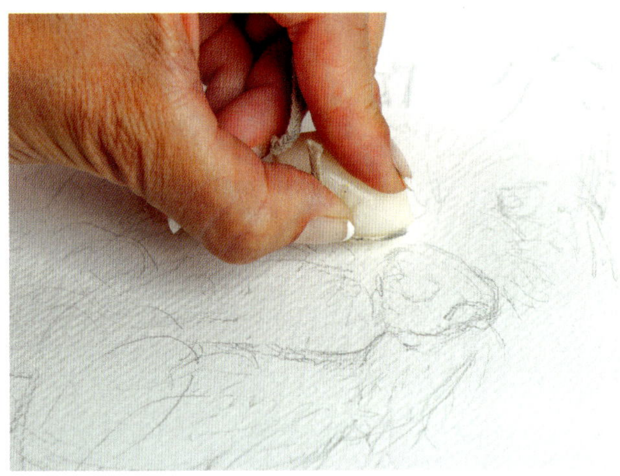

4 Use the wax like a pencil to add directional strokes that follow the lines of the fur. Place these marks very loosely, almost randomly. You can read more about wax resist on page 115.

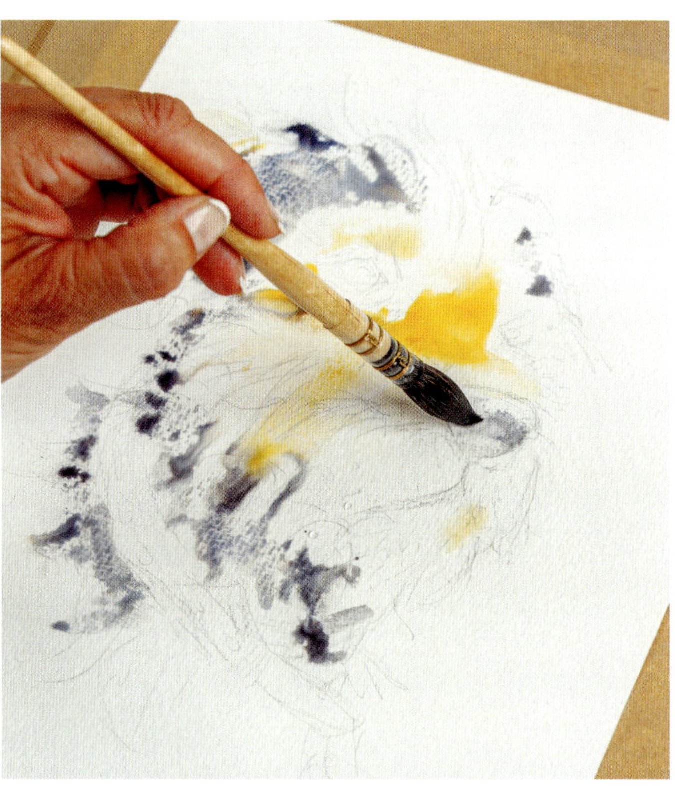

5 Using the large brush, apply yellow ochre around the nose and eyes before mixing burnt umber and French ultramarine to make a neutral grey. Use this to build up the fur with a mix of brushstrokes.

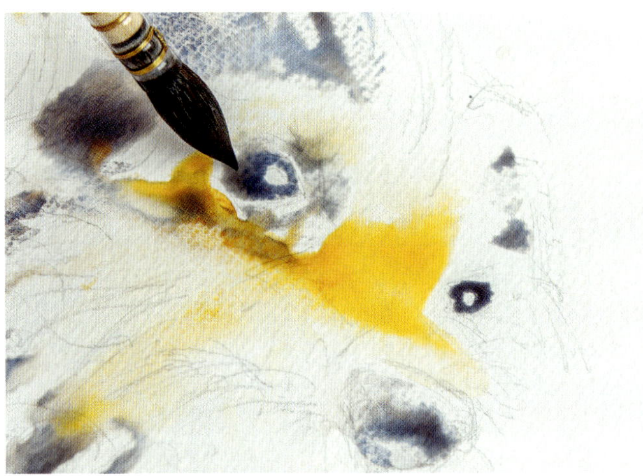

6 Establish the eyes using the same mix and brush, leaving a glossy highlight in the centre of each.

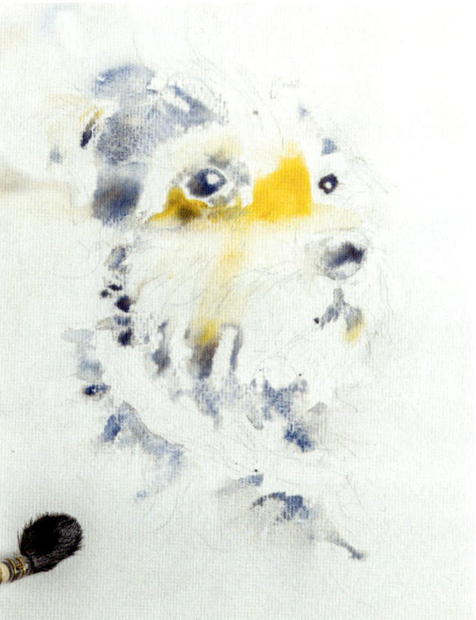

7 Rinse the brush and bring clean water in from the edges in towards the wet paint. Allow it to 'tickle' the wet paint so the pigment bleeds outwards slightly.

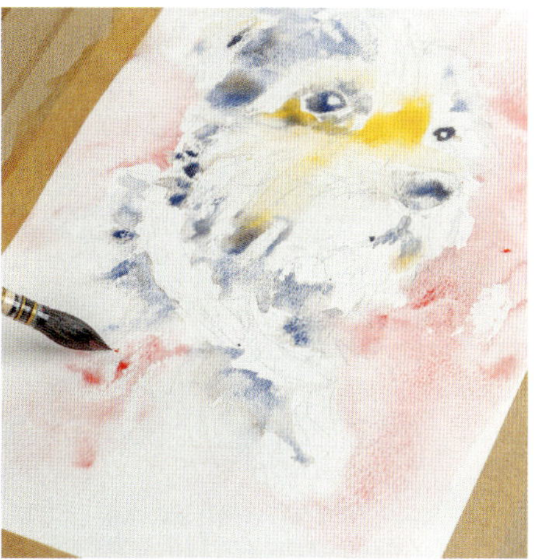

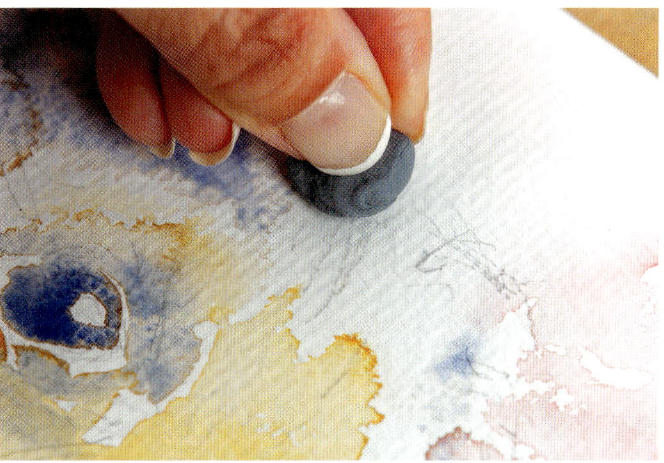

8 Add rose madder into the wet background, aiming for an interesting but not distractingly detailed result.

9 Allow to dry completely. With the shapes in place, you can now remove the pencil lines with the eraser.

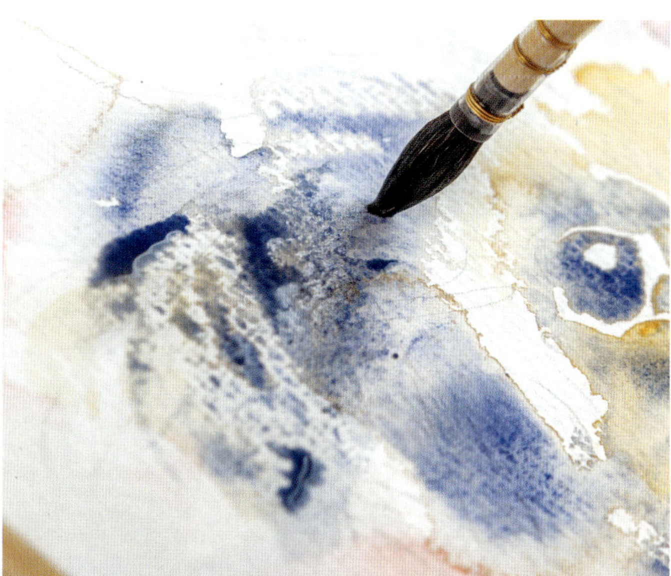

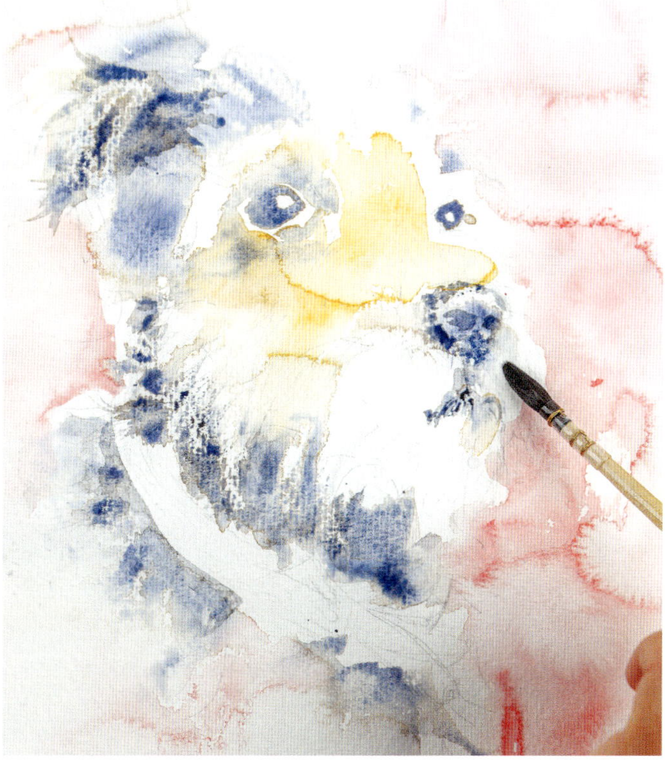

10 Swap to the medium brush and use a dark mix of French ultramarine and burnt umber to paint the ear. Use the belly of the brush to work outwards from the head. Note how the heavy use of wax on the paper surface helps to create additional texture. With the paint remaining on the brush, use the tip to draw a few marks in towards the head.

11 Continue over the rest of the dark areas including the nose, using the small brush to draw out a few finer marks, particularly on the left-hand side of the painting. Add more water for the darks on the right-hand side, to help them recede. Use the small brush to draw out a little more of the wet paint towards the right and to develop the muzzle area.

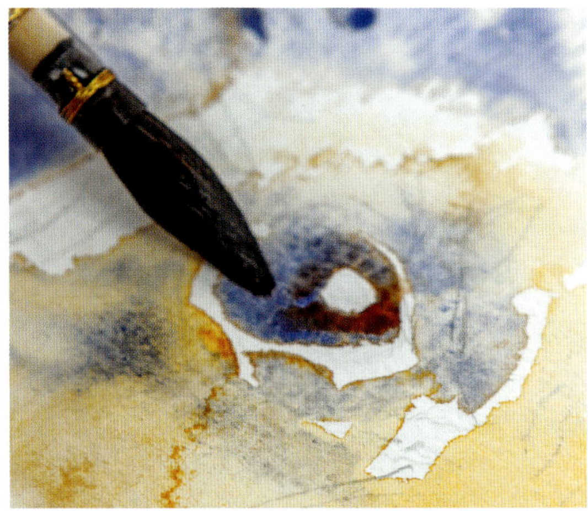

12 Use the tip of the medium brush to touch in a few dots of burnt umber to the eyes, then add a little water to draw it out and give a lively, glossy result.

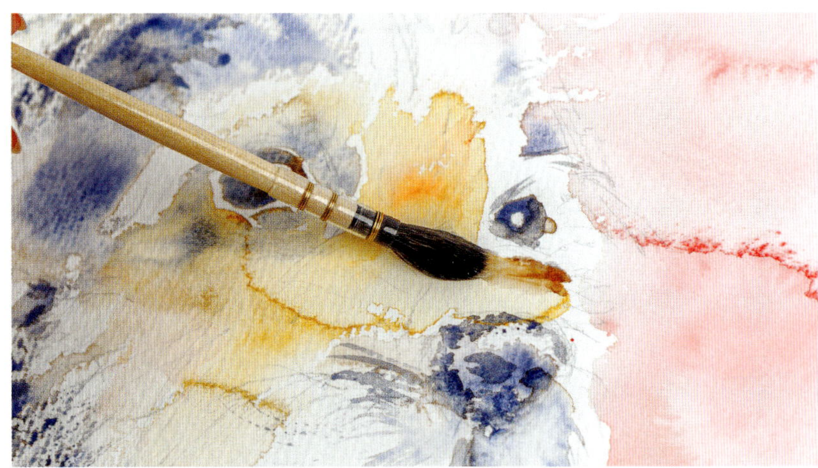

13 Use very diluted vermilion to paint over the peach-coloured fur. This is a glaze – a wash that's thin enough to allow the paint underneath to show through. The result is an optical mix of both colours, and part of what makes watercolours so jewel-like and vibrant.

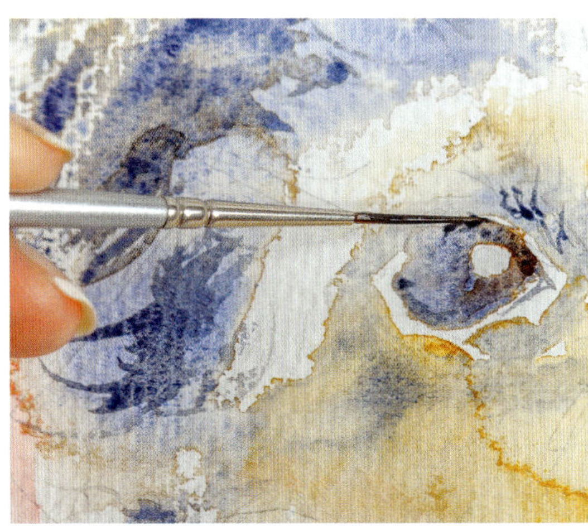

14 Switch to the small brush and use the dark mix of French ultramarine and burnt umber to pick out fine marks around the ear and eye on the left-hand side with the tip of the brush. Rinse the brush and soften them into the surrounding fur with the side.

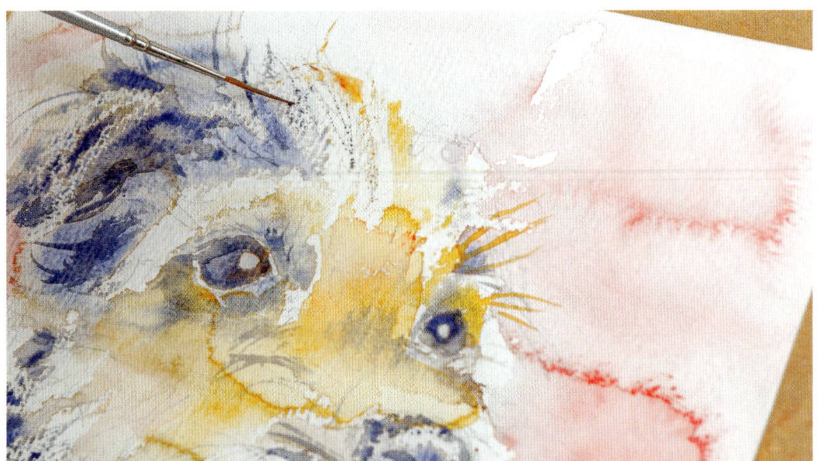

15 Switch to yellow ochre for the longer hairs on the right-hand side and the top of the head. Add some hair using the dark mix, too. These subtle marks help to define the top of the head. Add some finer details with a stronger mix of the French ultramarine and burnt umber.

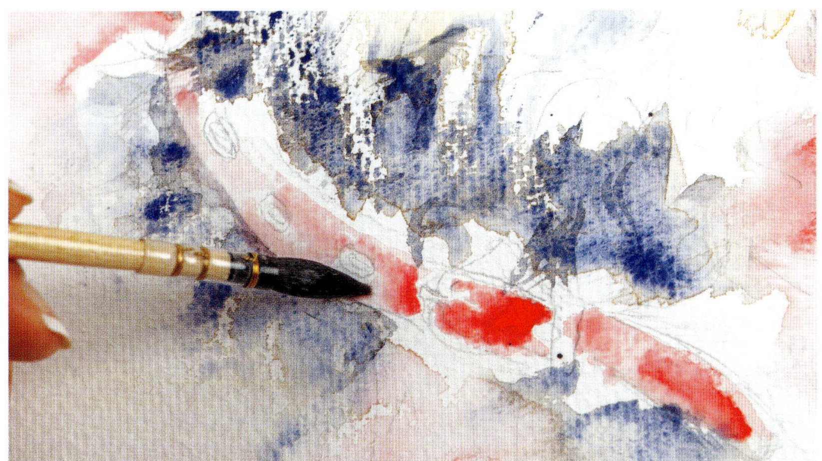

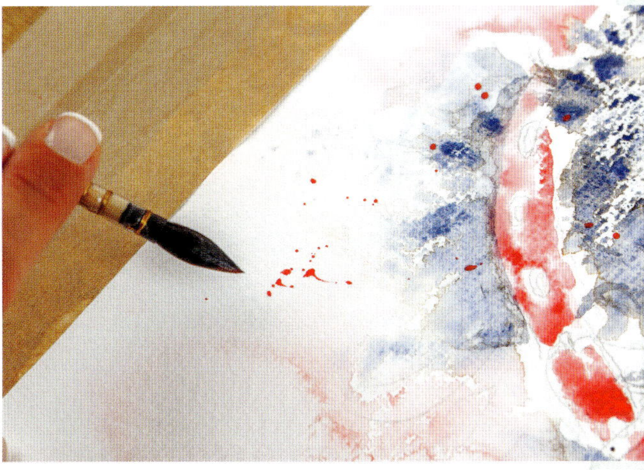

16 Use dilute rose madder to paint the collar with the medium brush, working around the metal eyelets carefully. While the paint is wet, drop in stronger colour to strengthen the result. The paint will only flow where you have wetted, so the eyelets will remain clean.

17 Add a little spattering (see page 43) with the paint remaining on the brush. This breaks up the shapes and enlivens things.

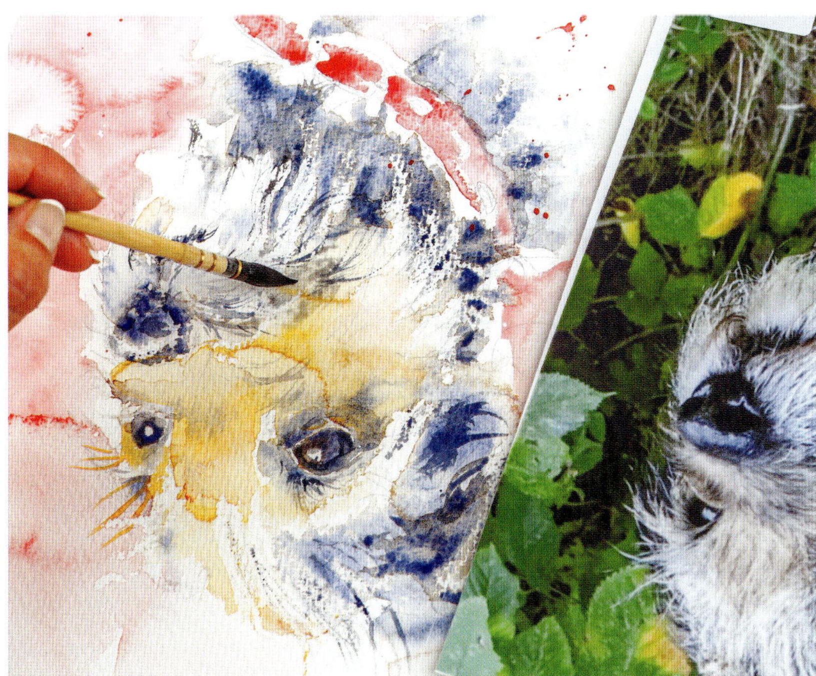

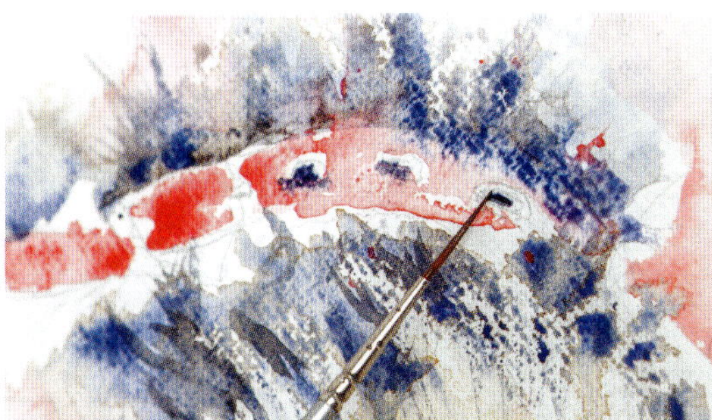

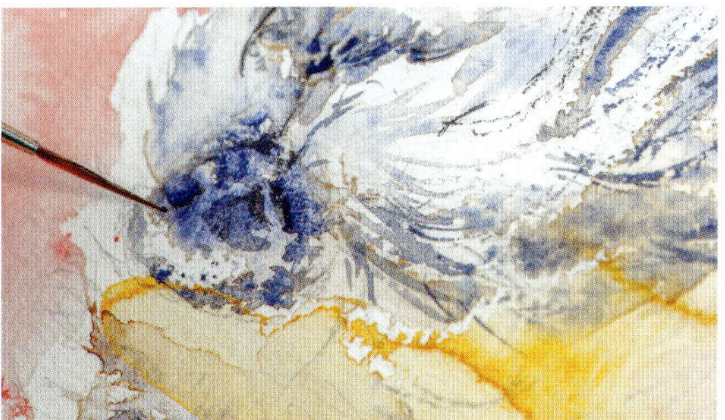

18 Add some longer fine dark marks with the small brush around the mouth to suggest the longer scruffy hairs. You can use negative painting to suggest white hairs. If you're struggling to make sense of the complex fur, try turning the painting on its side or upside down to make areas of tone easier to spot.

19 Still working upside down, and with close reference to the photograph, use the small brush and dark mix to touch in the eyelets (see top), leaving a little white space around the dark marks. Detail the nose with the same brush and mix (see above). Getting the details right is key to making this look not just like any dog's nose, but Alfie's (or your subject's) nose in particular.

Finishing touches

Don't work upside down for too long. Turn the piece back over and step away for a few minutes before coming back to assess. Walk away, have a coffee and clear your mind, so you're not over-focussed on the painting.

It's a good idea, if you can, to take a photograph when you think the painting is nearly there, but needs a little more work. Not only will seeing it in a different context help you to spot areas that you want to work on, but if you do it every so often as you reach the end of the work, you'll be able to go back and compare. This will allow you to assess whether (and when) you have taken it too far, and made it too detailed. Over time, you'll work out how refined you like your artwork, and be able to better judge things as you work.

Finishing the painting

There's no-one stopping you making adjustments even late in the process. Here, after stepping away, I decided that the ear on the left-hand side needed to be bigger, so I adjusted the sketch with the HB pencil, then used the same mixes and techniques as previously to paint in the ear.

When you're confident that you're happy with the overall painting, use the small brush to add a glaze of rose madder near the nose to draw the eye and provide a focal hot spot.

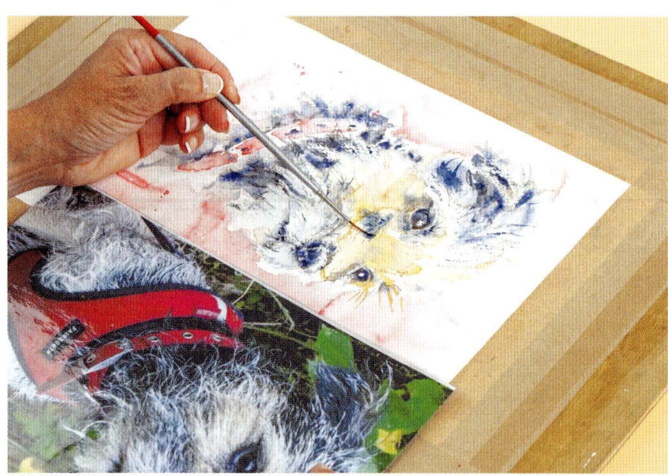

20 When you return, try turning the painting to another angle again. You'll likely find that any parts you want to work on will now jump out immediately. (If nothing does, then you've probably finished!) Here, I decided that the shadow on Alfie's muzzle needed strengthening, so I used the shadow grey mix (French ultramarine and burnt umber) to glaze the area.

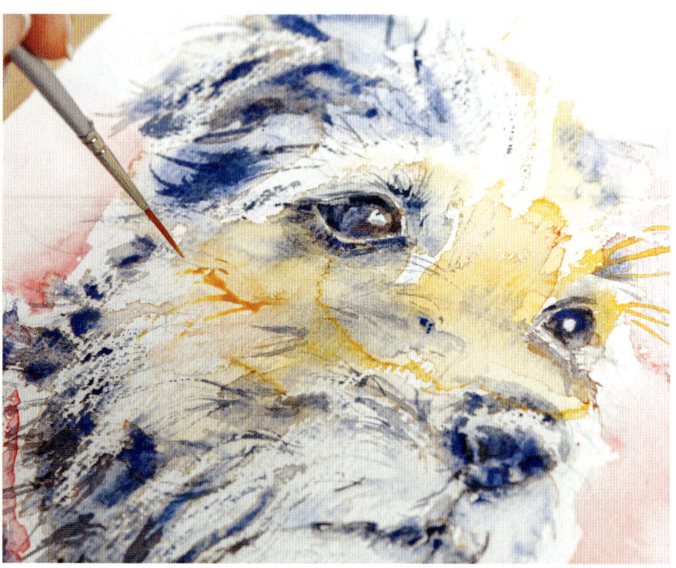

21 Continue refining until you're happy with how the painting looks, but be careful that you don't overwork it, or you'll lose the freshness. To make areas of white fur stand out, work negatively around them with a very watered-down version of the dark grey mix.

Opposite:
Alfred the Great
25.5 x 35.5cm (10 x 14in)

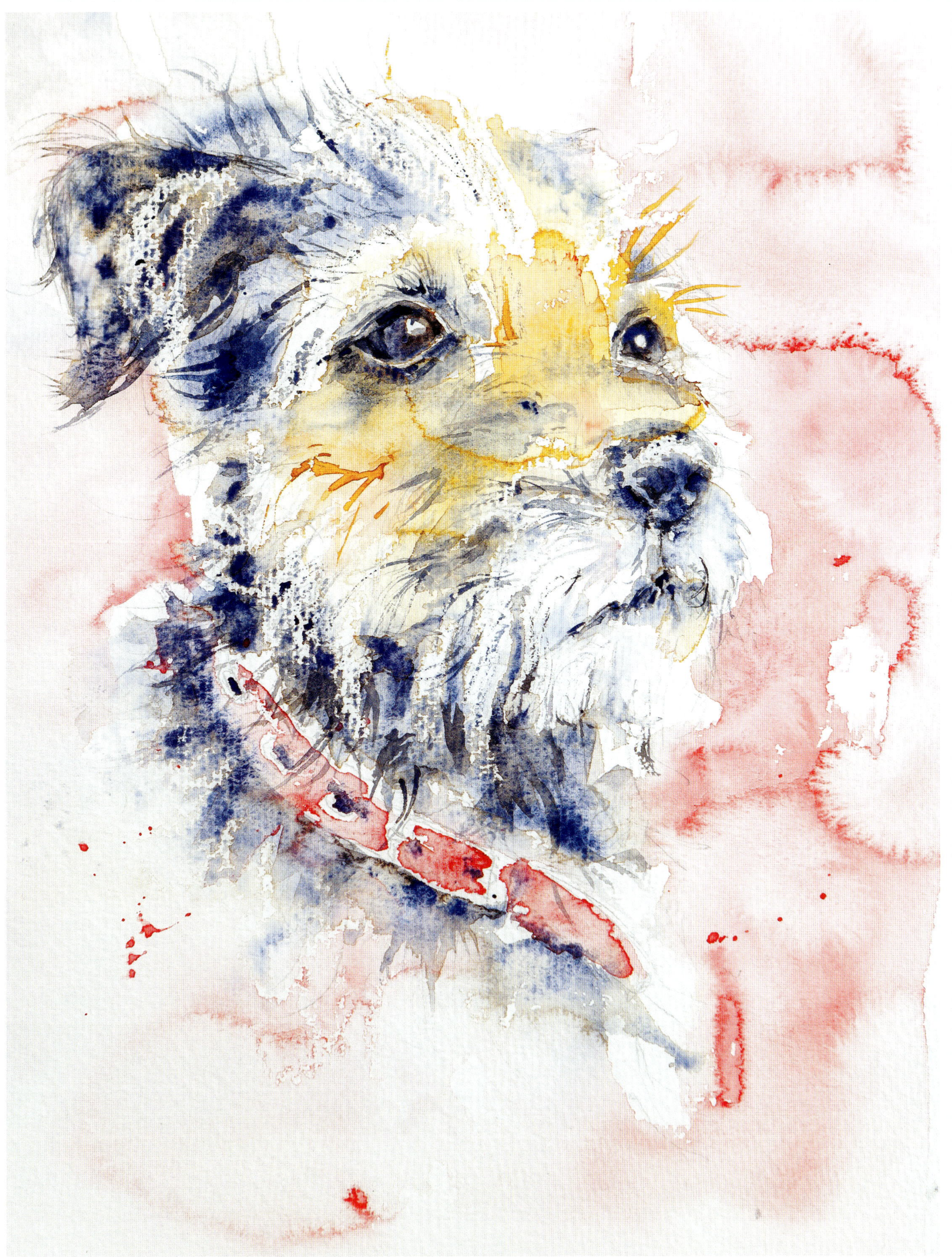

Exploring
sketching with pen

Instead of sketching using a pencil, try going straight in with a pen. Working this way from time to time can be a great confidence builder.

Working with a pen usually means that you get a sketch that is very hard and fixed, and cannot rub it out, but the pen I used here, a Staedtler Triplus fineliner, is very forgiving as the watersoluble ink 'melts away' somewhat when wet, meaning small mistakes in the sketch are not too noticeable. This will encourage you to free up a little and avoid the tendency towards stiffness when working with a pen. You won't be able to completely rub out small errors, but adapting to them will add life to a picture rather than appearing too contrived or perfect – a constant risk when sketching.

As with the *Border Terrier* project, here I concentrated on just a head-and-shoulders composition, and used a similar background colour and style. Whereas on Alfie the black was a mix of French ultramarine and burnt umber watercolour, here I used Quink ink for the black. I also decided not to use wax resist to reserve white on the bulldog as the wax texture would not be a good representation of his smoother coat. Instead, I simply avoided painting the white areas; they're left as the clean paper.

One of the other benefits of sketching with a pen is that switching back to pencil will feel even easier!

Using watersoluble ink means that the hard lines will soften as soon as you work over them with water. This ensures the lines aren't too hard in the finished painting: they'll blend right in.

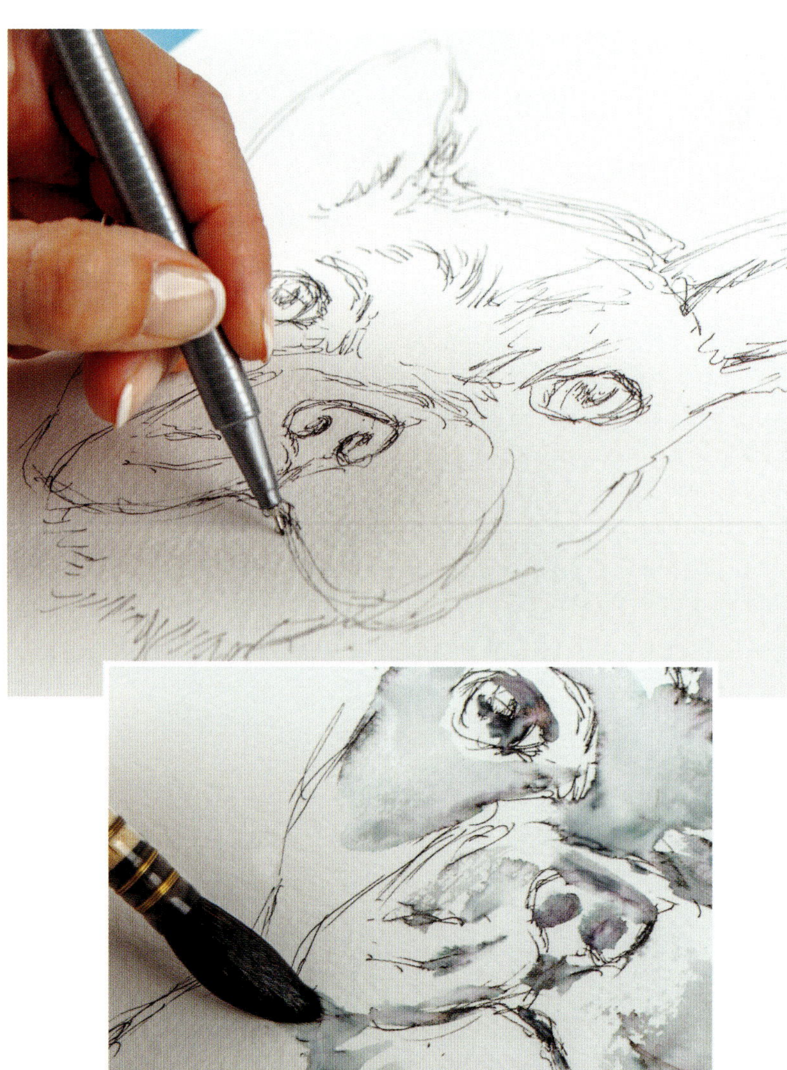

When you come to paint, use a light touch with the brush; don't scrub or apply too much water. The ink will flow very readily, so small, gentle movements are best.

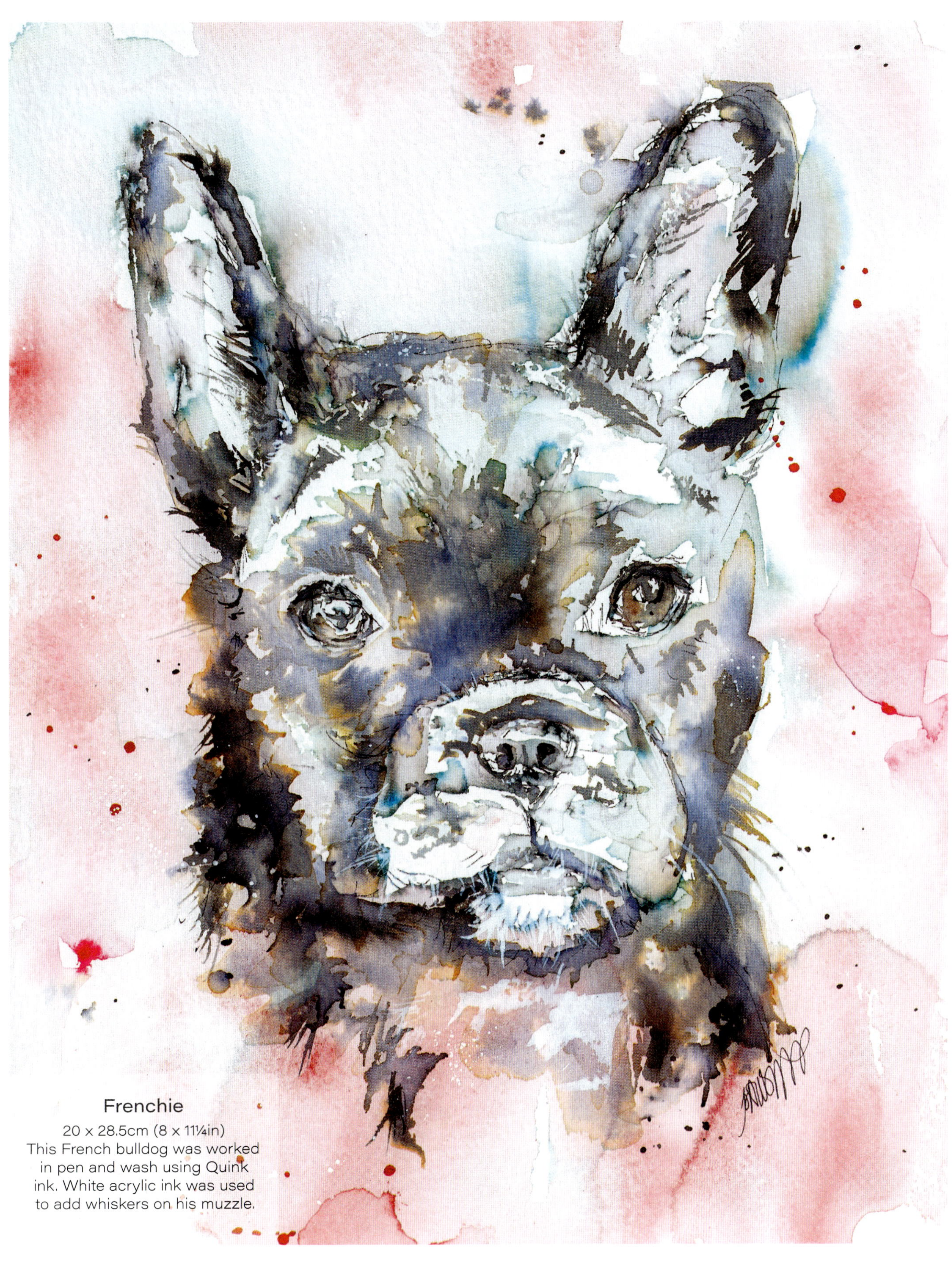

Frenchie
20 x 28.5cm (8 x 11¼in)
This French bulldog was worked
in pen and wash using Quink
ink. White acrylic ink was used
to add whiskers on his muzzle.

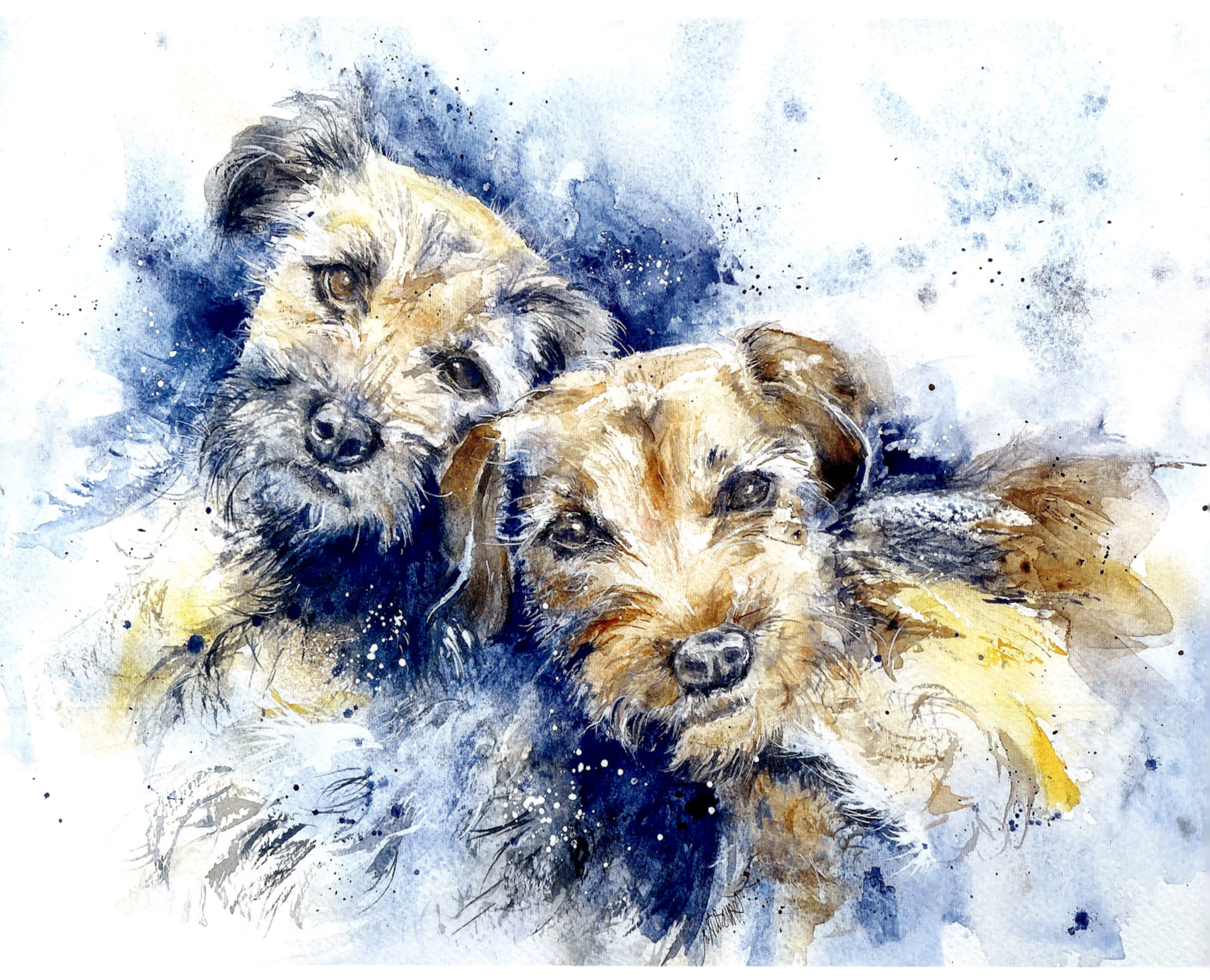

Alfie and Oscar – My Boys

38 x 27.5cm (15 x 10¾in)

In contrast to the bright red background I used for Alfie's portrait (see page 55), here I opted to use a cool, relaxed blue for the background as my boys were exactly that. There was no fire in their bellies that day, just love and relaxation; happy in each other's company.

The cool background blue complements the warm orangey-browns in my boys' fur, and as it recedes, the colour also ensures the subjects came forward. If you look closely, both have a little pink near their eyes too, forming hot spots as described on page 39.

Curled up in contentment together, this is one of my favourite pictures of my two border terriers.

Exploring colour

The colours you choose for your painting, whether in the background or the subject, are fun to explore. You can create different responses or feelings by choosing different colours – just compare the relaxed, calm feeling of the painting opposite with the bright, engaging background of the lioness to the right.

My main advice when it comes to colour is not to feel you have to copy the photograph or the colours I've used in these projects. Boldness and strength of colour will help your paintings to feel exciting and full of life, and there's no reason at all that colours need to be realistic.

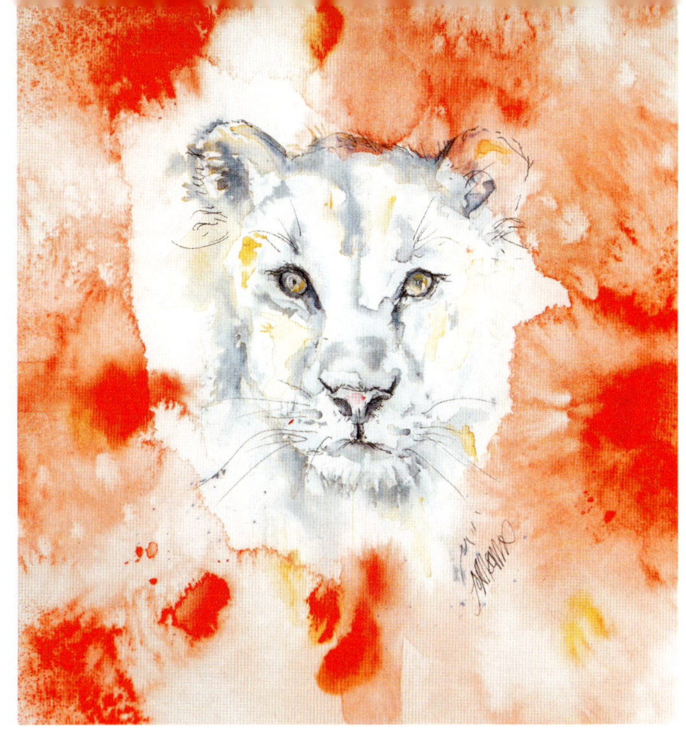

Lioness
20 x 27cm (8 x 10½in)

Dare to go dark

Watercolour dries lighter, so if you like how it looks when wet, you'll need to add more colour than you think to keep that effect. You can do this by using stronger washes (see right) – that is, those made up with with more paint and less water.

Alternatively, you can add colour to a partially dry or damp surface to strengthen the colour. This can result in blooms, or backruns. I embrace these as they add a sense of texture and unexpected movement that I think adds to the appeal of the painting.

If you don't like backruns, then the best approach to add more colour and impact is to let it dry completely, then rewet areas and introduce more colour wet on dry. In effect, you're glazing (see step 13 on page 52), and that builds up the depth of colour.

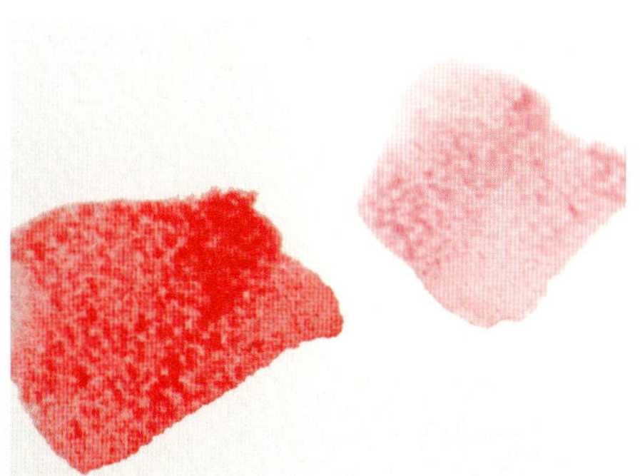

Wet watercolour

Here, the colour I'm after in the finished painting is shown on the right. I know it's not going to look like that when it's finished, so I've painted another swatch of much stronger colour, too.

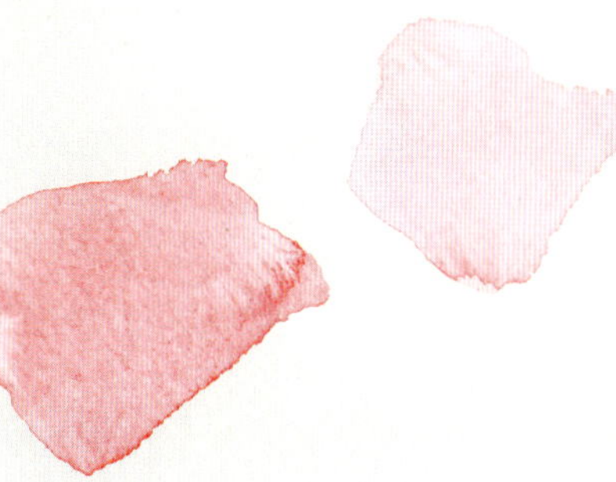

Dry watercolour

Now the colours have dried, you can see the top swatch, which looked right when wet, is now too pale; while the seemingly too-strong version looks closer to what I wanted.

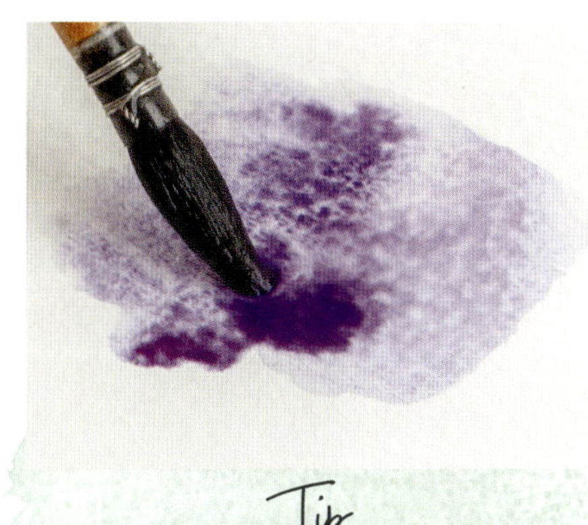

Tip

To strengthen a too-pale wash, try adding more colour wet in wet.

Reuse and repaint

We all have a tendency to be critical of the things we make and do – and this absolutely includes our art creations. It does not matter whether we produce something exceptional or below par, we will always find fault. Well, it's time we did not. Ultimately, a painting starts as just a plain piece of paper. By making our marks, we're either improving on what's there – that is, nothing – or we are practising and we are learning. What does it matter if that's sometimes by trial and error?

The evil of the bin

I stopped putting any of my paintings in the bin a long time ago, and I encourage you to keep all of your paintings too. By keeping them to one side, you will be able to check back after six months or so and, by comparing them to newer pieces, assess your progress. You'll be surprised with how far you've come.

Another reason is to experiment. Try playing around with other ideas on the reject to see how you might improve things. This will give you invaluable practice and learning, and working on something that you already think is a failure takes away any pressure. Here are some starting points:

- Does it require a few highlights? Try adding white ink or scratching out highlights.

- Is the scale out, or the proportions wrong? Re-draw the animal directly on top of the old one, and see which set of marks work better.

- Would it benefit from some brighter washes over some areas? Add some straight on top.

- Are the colours too dark and muddy? Try washing the painting under the tap – your watercolour paper will take it! While wet, secure it onto a board with brown gummed tape and it will just stretch itself as it dries; flat as a pancake to rework. The image will be lighter in colour but still there to work from. You can read more on washing on pages 95–96 and 100.

- Can other media help lift it? Pastel, charcoal, inks... Pretty much anything goes in mixed media.

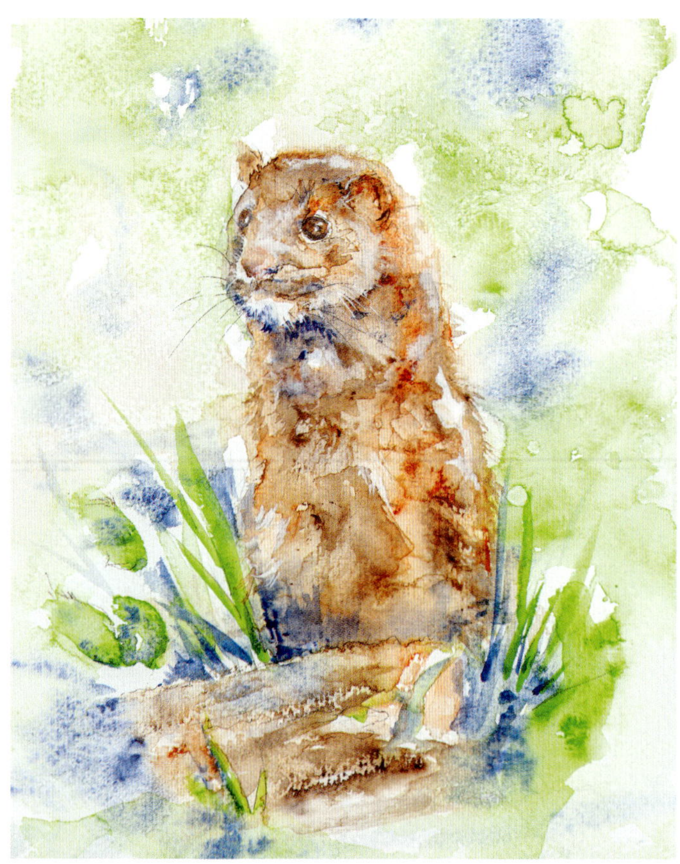

Unsuccessful first try

The face looked off, and the result wasn't as colourful as I wanted. In addition, the piece of wood in the foreground, which was intended to help unify the colours of his surroundings with the subject, ended up as a barrier – your eyes are drawn to it, rather than the subject.

However, you don't need to analyse your paintings to work out that something is wrong. Trust your gut. If you're not happy, then something is wrong with it for you. Use this as a lesson, and decide whether to press on to improve it, or start again with what you've learned in mind.

Sometimes I will leave a piece for a few days and then look with a fresh eye (when I am feeling less ratty!). I usually find this allows me to spot more easily what is wrong with it, so I can try to put it right. Even if the reworking doesn't become a success, you will definitely have learned something. The more practice you have, the more lessons you will learn.

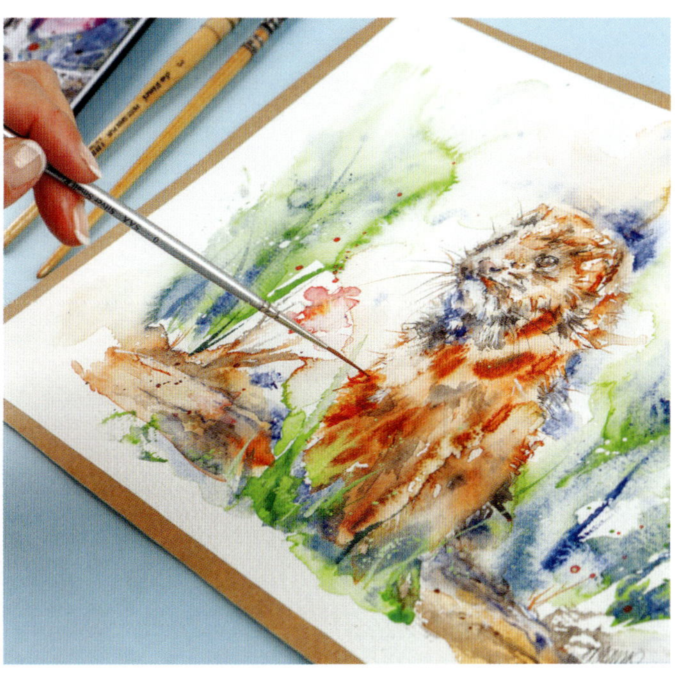

Making the change

Learning from the first painting, I decided on a compositional change from portrait to landscape format. This allowed me to still include the foreground wood, but here I had the space to break it in two and remove the sense of it being a barrier.

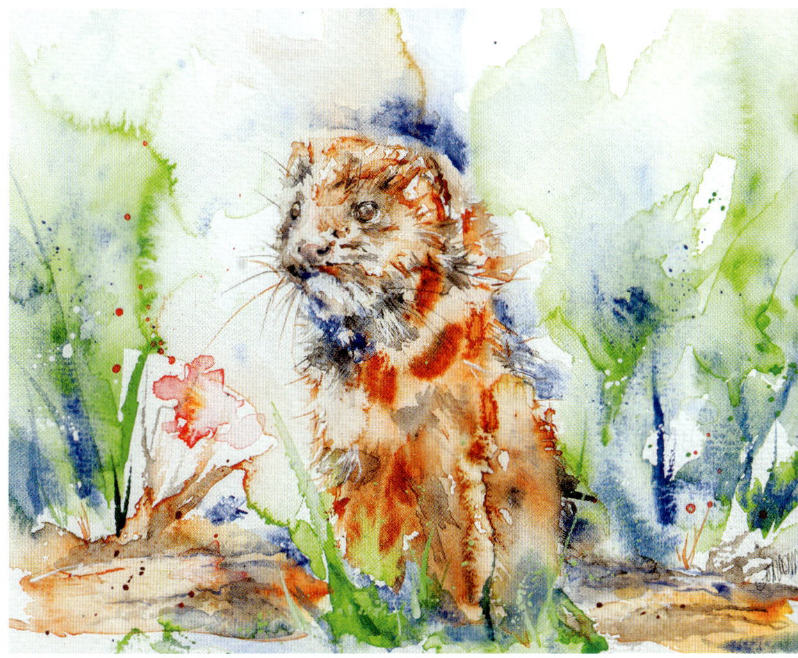

Refined and improved

In the new version, you'll see that I've brightened the painting with the inclusion of red spattering and a red flower. Most of all, however, the depth of tone and detail in the face is warmer, stronger and more engaging.

Tip

A painting that you don't particularly like is a great place to try out a new technique, both because you can see whether it enhances it, or simply to practise before you use it on your masterpiece.

Fox

I decided to paint this beautiful fox as they are a favourite animal of mine and my husband Geoff's. I was particularly drawn to the eyes. Although the photograph has a dark grey background, I wanted a contrast to the glorious orange fur, so opted for the complementary colour, blue, to make him pop. The same blue was used for shadow areas under the chin and ears to tie in for a harmonious result. This project is a great example of how you can make simple colour choices to set off your work.

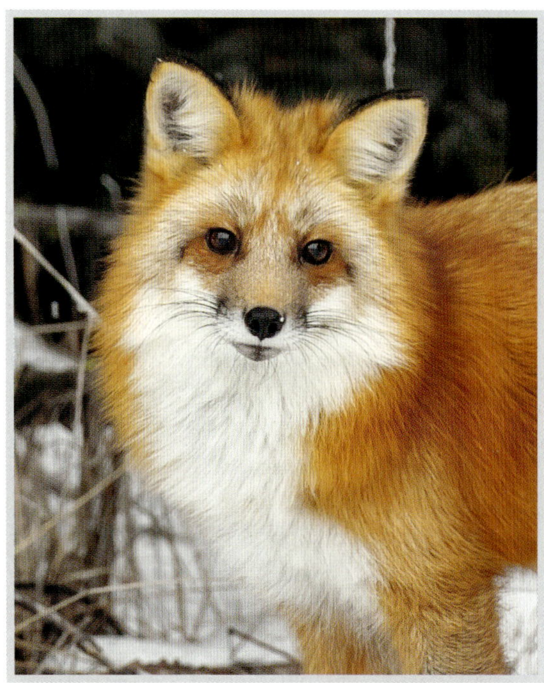

Source photograph
Foxes do have gorgeous faces, there is no doubt about it. The eyes in this photograph are so beautiful and that stunning red fur certainly got him noticed.

You will need

Bockingford CP Not surface watercolour paper
25.5 x 35.5cm (10 x 14in)

Large, medium and small brushes

HB pencil and putty eraser

WATERCOLOUR PAINTS:
Yellow ochre, vermilion, vanadium yellow, burnt sienna, French ultramarine, burnt umber

Beeswax candle

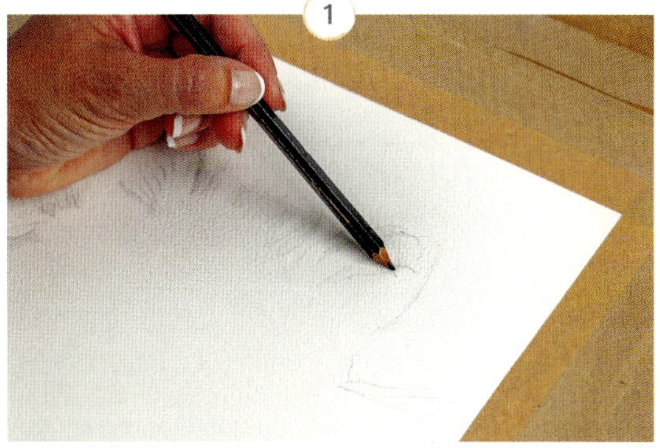

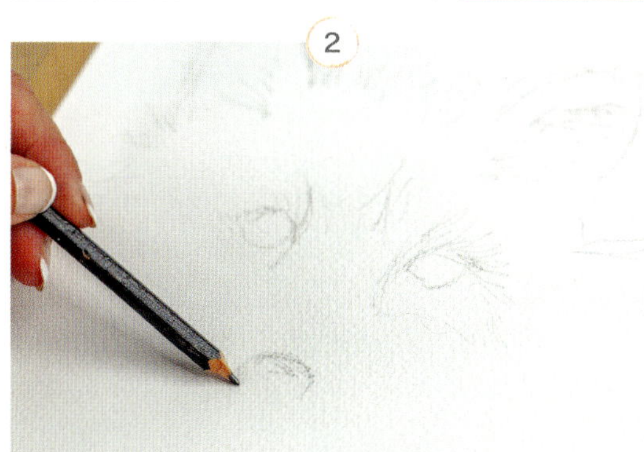

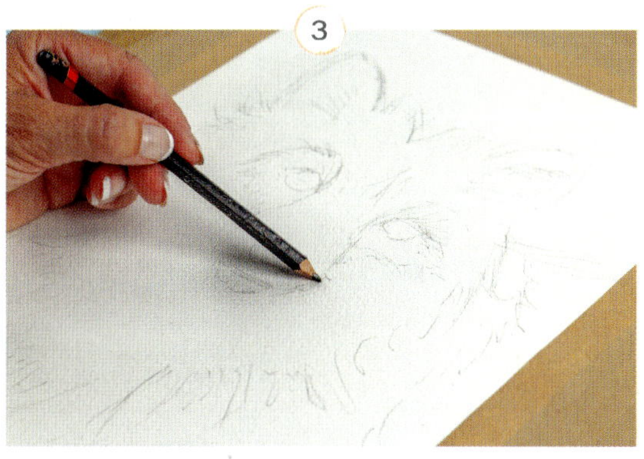

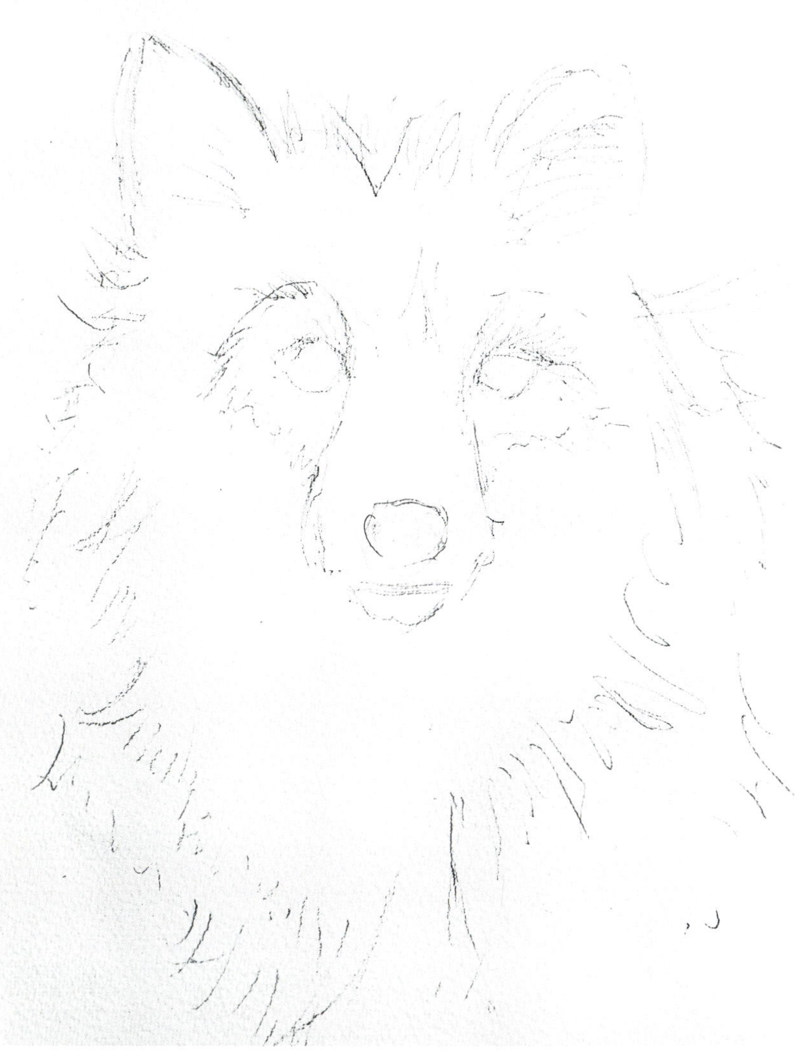

The sketch

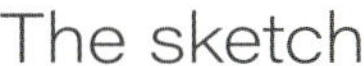

Don't overwork the sketch – if you draw
a stiff, detailed and complicated initial
drawing, this will inhibit your painting. If we
start with a contrived drawing, it tends to
result in a contrived painting: you're guided
by too much detail, and lose the chance
to improvise. Just aim for the image to be
recognizably this fox.

1 Using the HB pencil, begin to make a loose sketch. With constant
reference to the photograph, transfer the shapes to the surface.
Constantly flick your eyes to the picture. Here, I start with the ears,
as they're big, obvious shapes and help me place the fox on the
paper. You'll note that I don't start with the eyes; I just roughly place
them to begin with.

2 Get the overall shape onto the paper – the bigger picture: the head
and neck of the fox – then begin to add the features. Avoid the
tendency to over-focus on an area; just get it down, then move on.
You can always come back and refine later.

3 To help make sense of the fur, look for changes in tone and colour
as well as shape. Mark these lightly with loose flicking marks.

Painting the fox

We want to ensure a rich start to the painting, so be bold with your application. It's key to have a sopping wet surface to start: make sure you get plenty of water on your paper before you start to add the paint.

Adding wax before you begin will ensure we have some added sparkle, interest and movement in the finished picture – and because it will protect the surface from the paint, we can work quickly, boldly and loosely, and really enjoy the process of painting without worrying about being too neat and tidy!

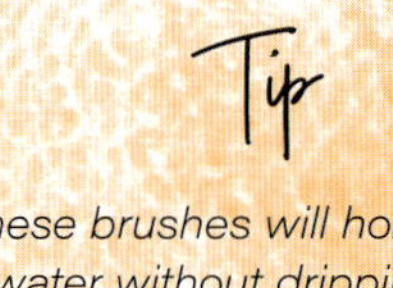

These brushes will hold plenty of water without dripping; this is the great advantage of natural hair brushes.

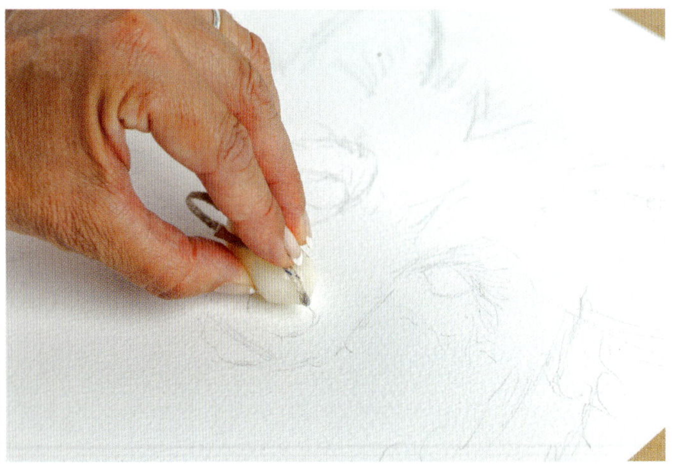

4 Use the candle like a brush to apply the wax, keeping your movements loose and using the whole of your arm. Add wax to the top of the ears, around the nose and on the chest. It's worth noting that, although the fox is largely white, we're not using the wax to try to reserve all that area – just to add interest to it.

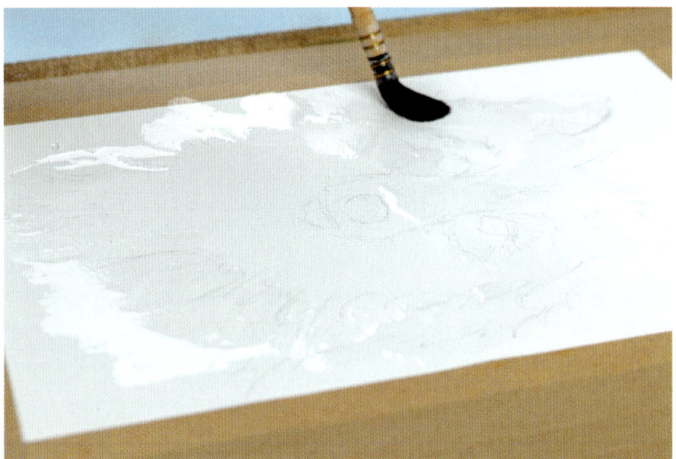

5 Dip the large brush into your water pot and really load it up – you want plenty of clean water. It needs to be absolutely sodden. Apply water to everywhere you want the paler orange areas – all over the mask and back; and don't worry if a little goes onto an area that'll eventually be light, as it'll add some dynamism and excitement.

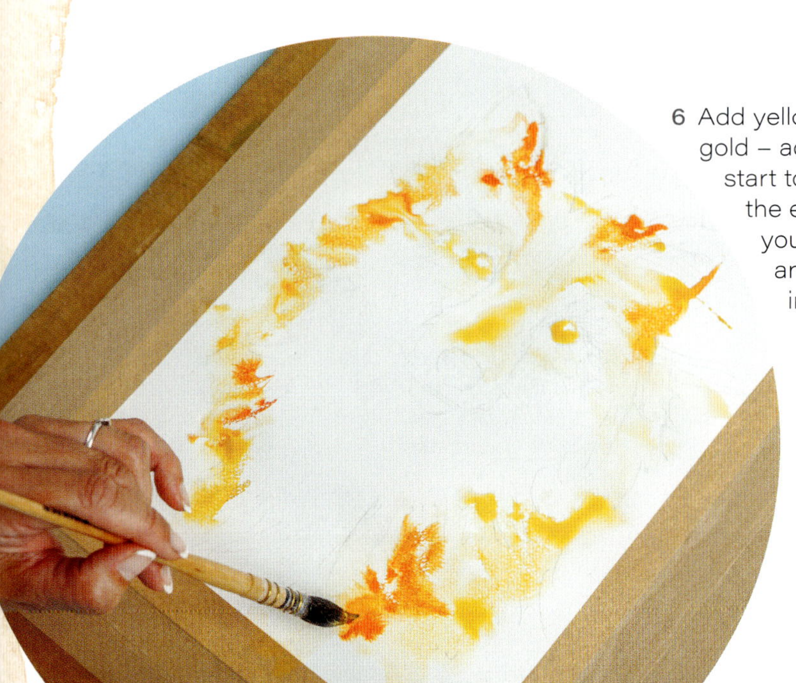

6 Add yellow ochre – one of my favourite colours; I call it my gold – across the redder areas of fur. This gives a nice rich start to the painting. Note I've also added this colour in the eyes. Add vermilion to the darker areas: anywhere you see the rich orange. Allow the colours to mix and merge on the surface, and vary the colour by introducing vanadium yellow wet in wet.

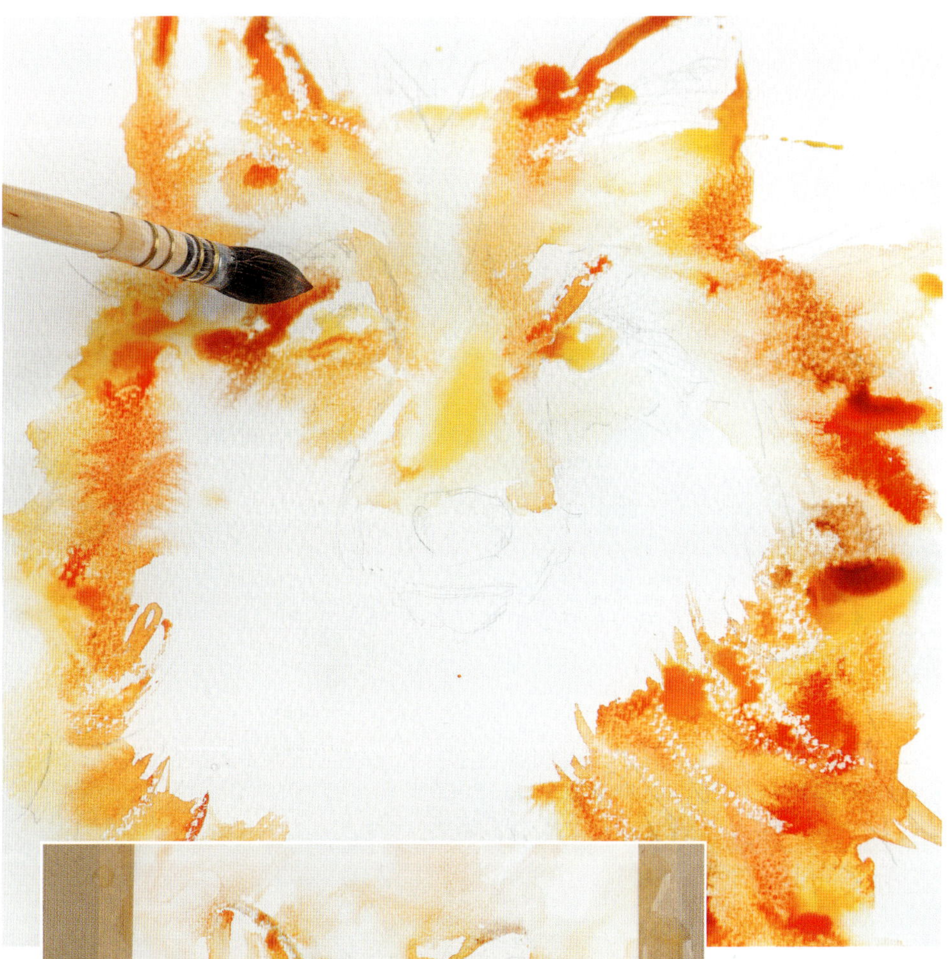

7 Use light, flicking touches with the tip of the large brush to pull the wet colour into the white areas of the fur. Think of pulling the dark into the light. Rinse your brush, then add burnt sienna. Use your marks to unify areas; work almost randomly.

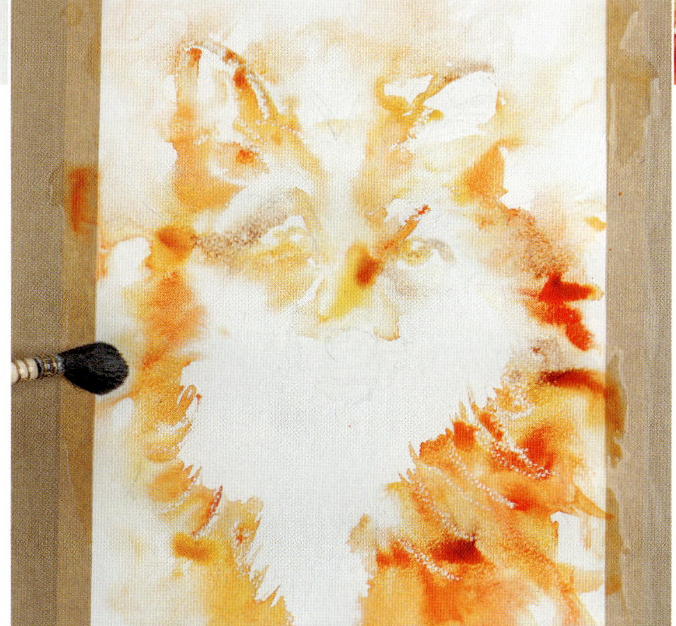

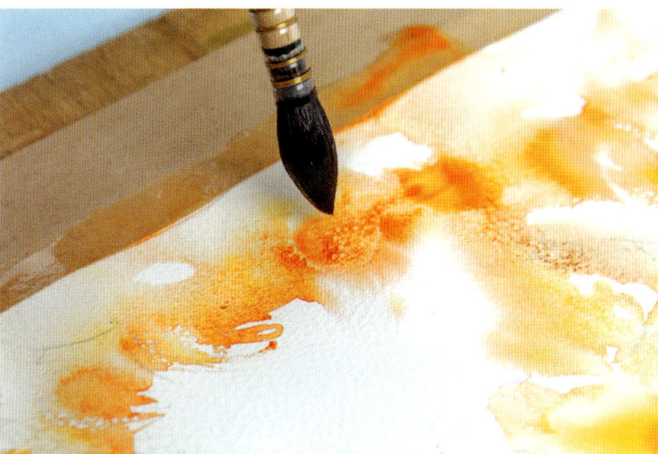

8 Wash the brush thoroughly, then load it with pure, clean water. Working from the outside of the painting inwards, bring the brush up to just touch the edges of the wet paint. A little of the pigment will flow into the clean water, and help to unify the painting.

9 Create backruns by dripping clean water into areas of the drying paint. This adds liveliness and randomness, so look for where the washes on your own painting are already starting to dry. Touching your brush here will create the backruns.

Painting the background

With the rich reds in place, we'll use a bold blue to contrast in the background. I've used French ultramarine for my background, but you could use any blue (or other colour!) that you choose.

To ensure the finish stays fresh, it's important to apply the background paint a little distance away from the fox – or the colours might bleed into one another, risking losing the outline of the fox.

10 Add French ultramarine into the background (apply the paint a little distance away from the fox, as noted above), then use any remaining on the brush to tickle in shadow below his muzzle. Flick the tip of the brush upwards into the muzzle area to suggest the fur texture, then soften the colour away into the white with a clean damp brush.

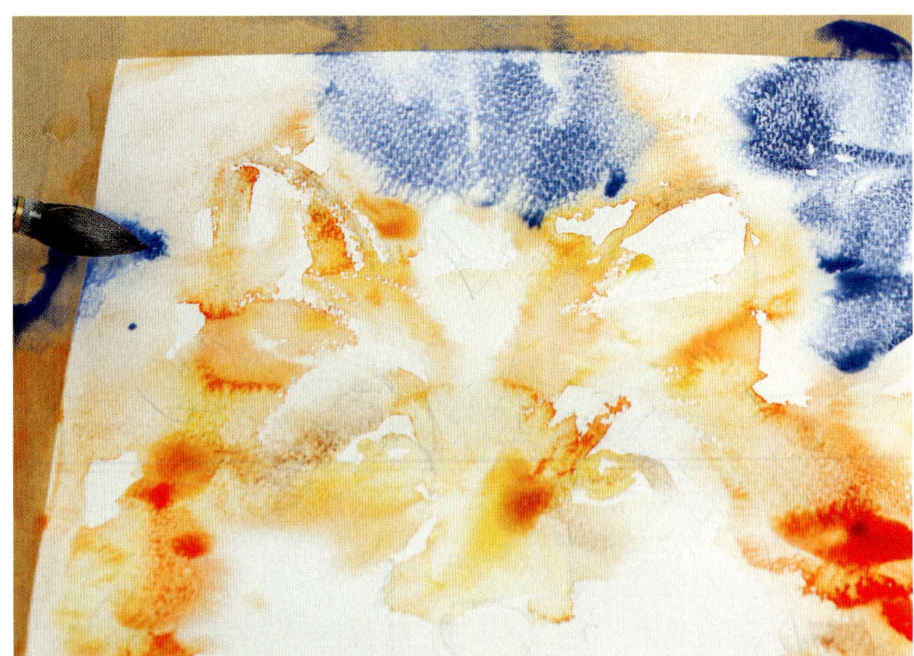

11 Dot in the pupils at this point, too – though keep the tone light; you're just finding the placement at this stage.

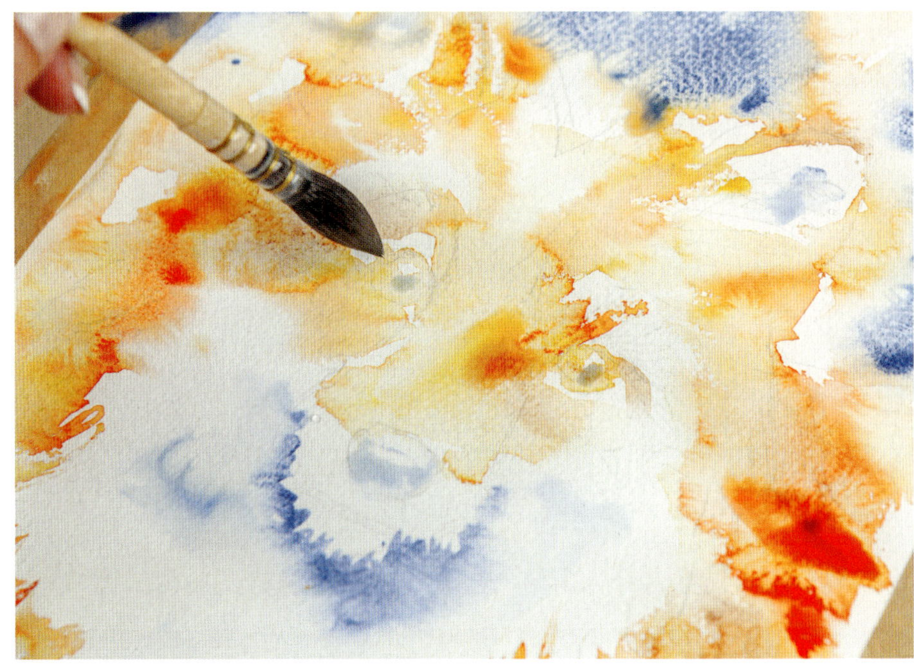

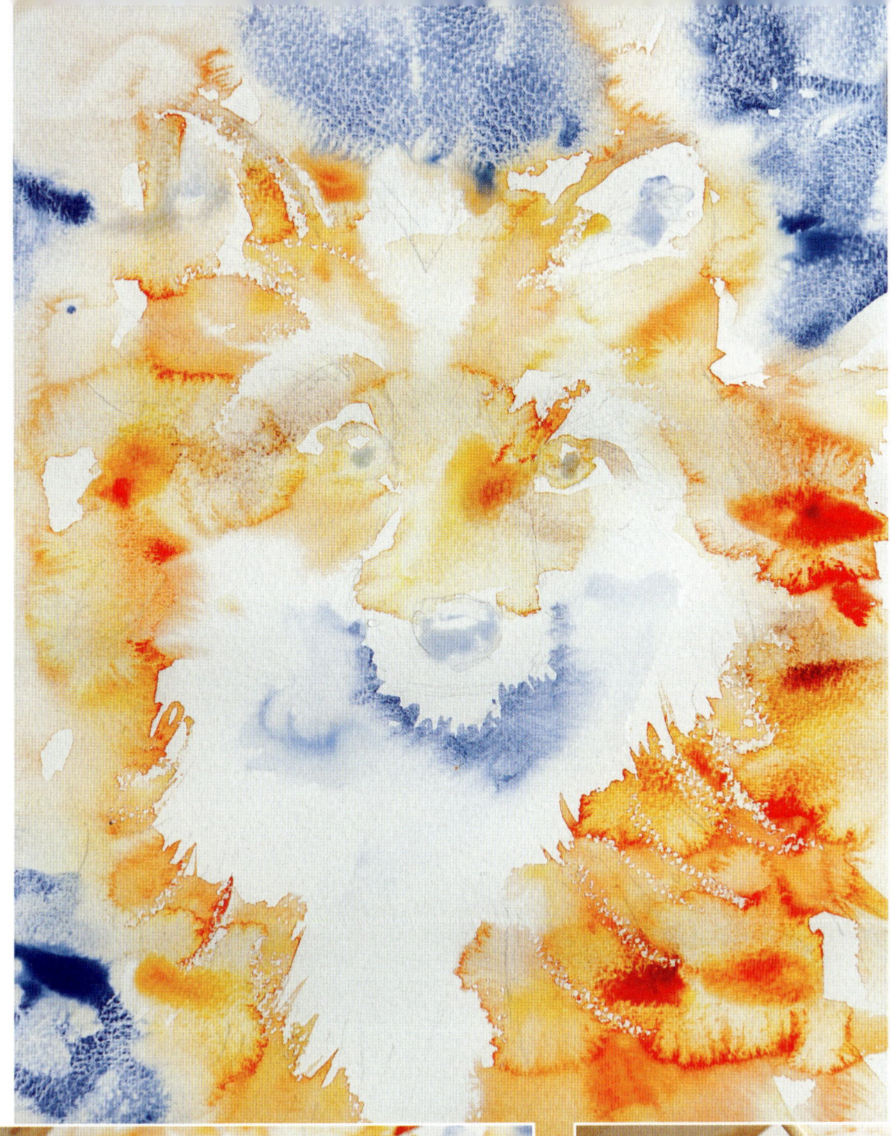

This is a good stage to pause if you need to, but if you're enjoying the flow, you can carry straight on!

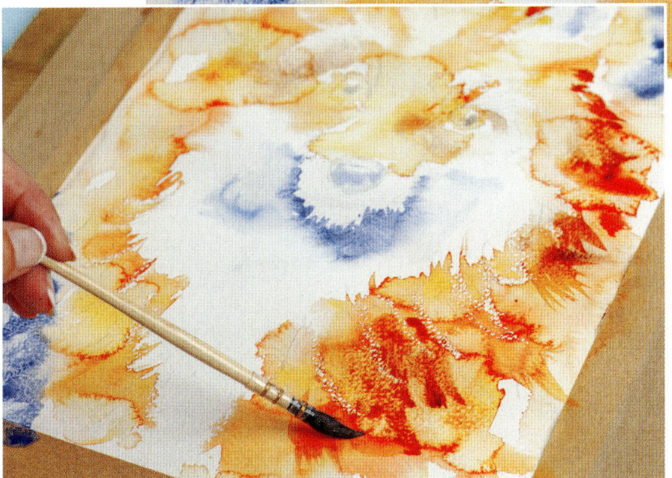

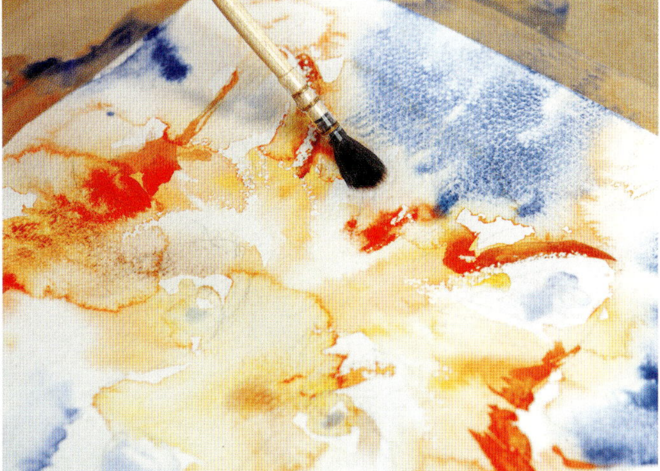

12 Identify the darker areas on your reference image. Swap to the medium brush and apply burnt sienna to these areas. You can work both wet in wet and wet on dry here; the more variety the better.

13 Using the same colours as before (vermilion, vanadium yellow and burnt sienna), re-establish any shapes that have become obscured. I have re-established the ear, for example. However, don't be slavish to your reference photograph. If there's a random shape or an area that you particularly like, save it.

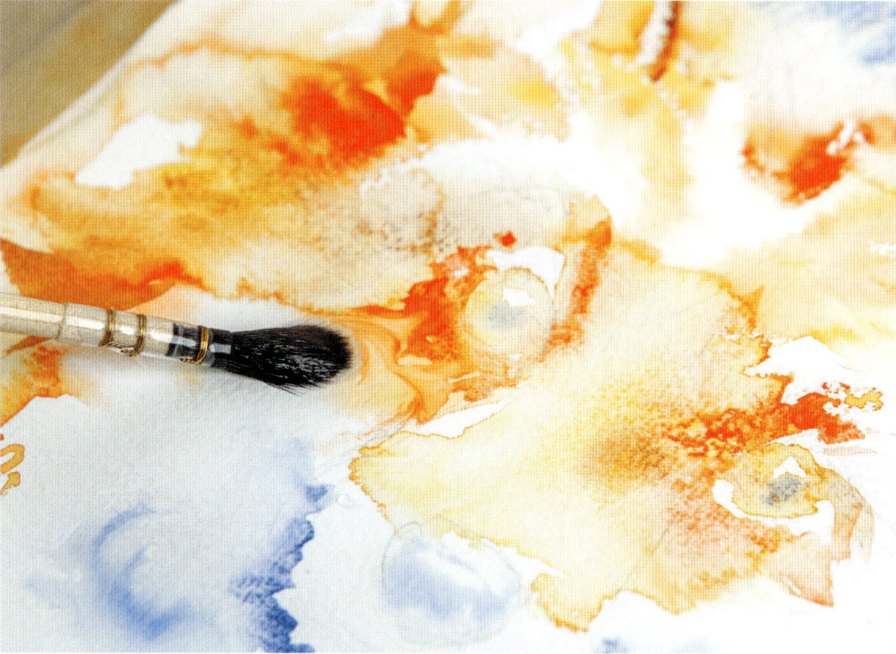

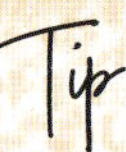

14 Use the red to frame the eyes a little, with flicking marks of the brush tip to suggest texture. Don't worry if this looks a bit stark: as I often say, 'Dare to go brighter, as it'll dry lighter.' Avoid this looking stiff by drawing a little clean water up to the edge of the area. The paint will bleed in and away, leaving the texture.

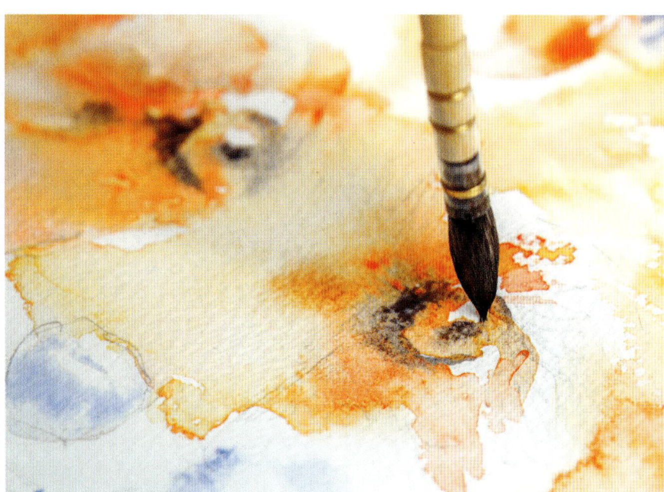

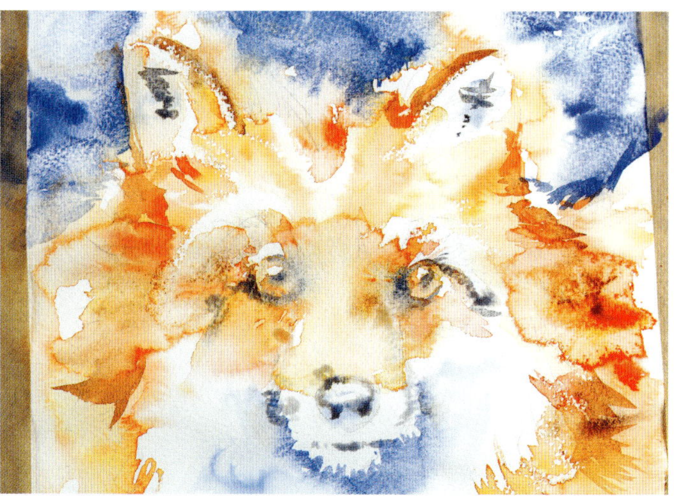

15 Add some French ultramarine and burnt umber to a well in your palette to make a natural grey mix. Use this to add some punchy tone around the eyes. You're not applying eyeliner here, so it's good to let a little bleed away. You don't want hard lines at this point: don't go too heavy, too soon.

16 Use the same mix on the nose, ears and around the whiskers as well. These should be soft. If the underlying paint is still wet, great – let the dark mix soften away. If not, then apply the paint, then rinse the brush and draw a little clean water towards the wet dark area to encourage it to bleed.

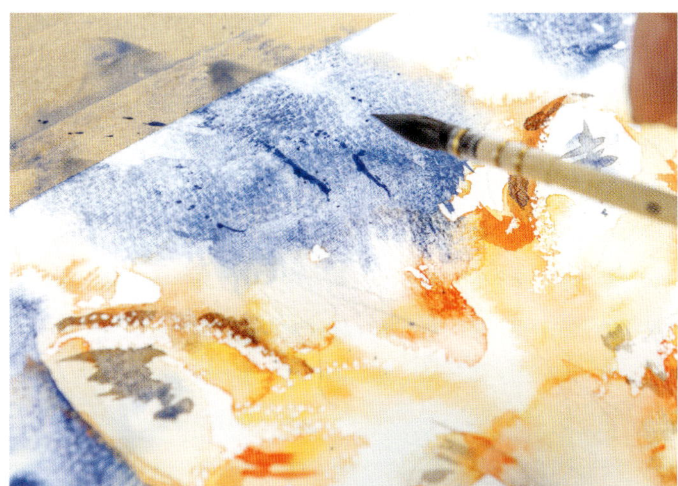

17 Carry on with the same colours, using your instinct to add some additional texture or marks. I've added a little spattering to the background by holding a brush loaded with French ultramarine a little way above the painting, then tapping the brush handle with my fingernails.

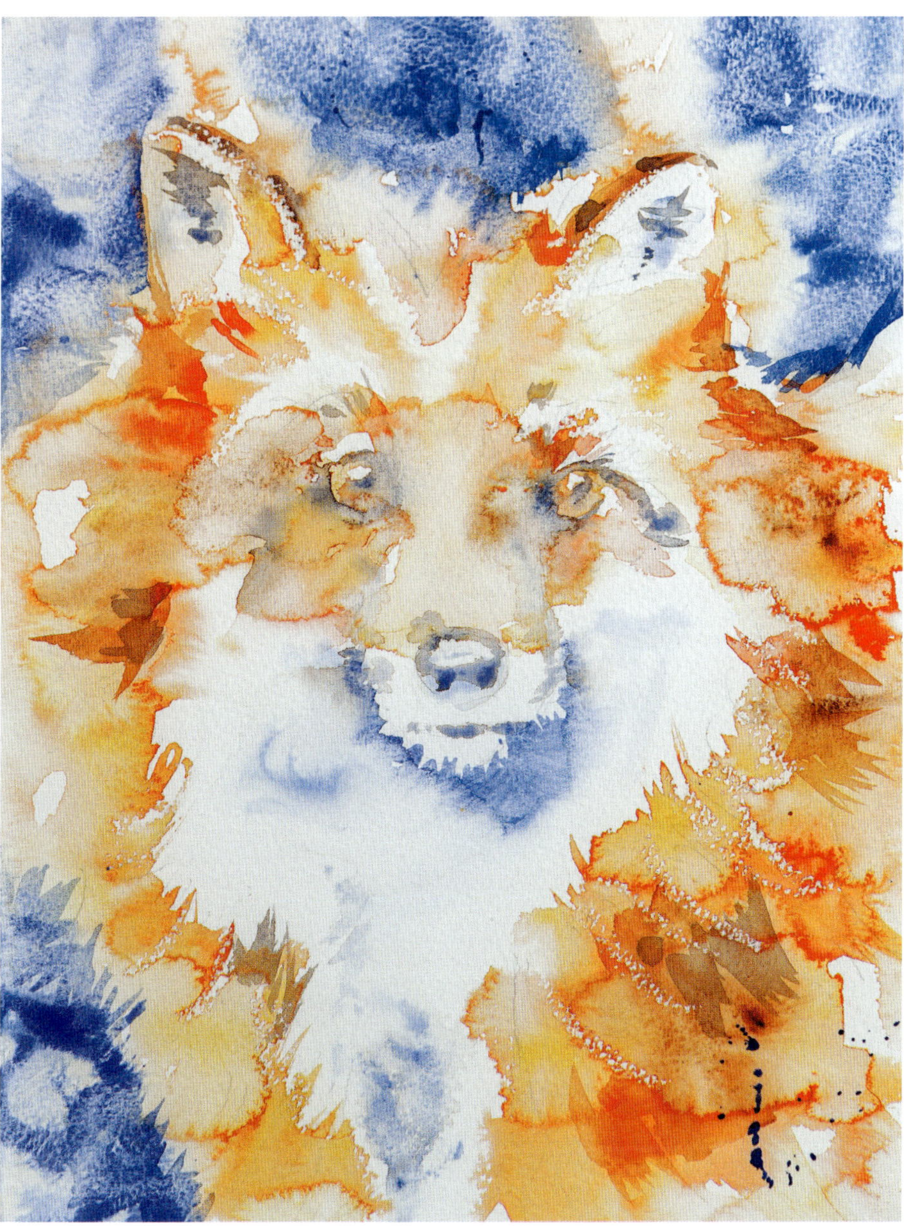

Allow the painting to dry before moving on. Take a break and come back with fresh eyes to your work.

Making the painting yours

With all the main shapes, colours and tones in place, it's now time to do your own interpretation. Pay less attention to the reference photograph now, and instead make your own judgements on how you want your painting to look. Here are some suggestions for how I decided to finish my fox. You can follow them as closely, or as loosely, as you wish.

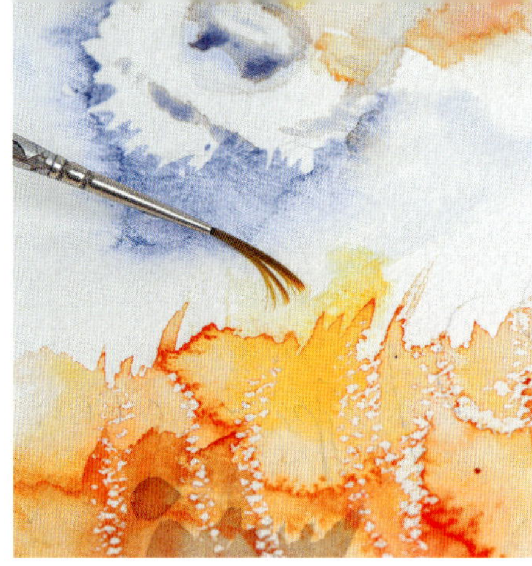

Use the side of the brush

Swap to the small brush and load it with a mix of vanadium yellow and vermilion. Using it almost on its side, drag the hairs across the surface. This isn't great for your brush, but it gives a brilliantly natural and loose mark.

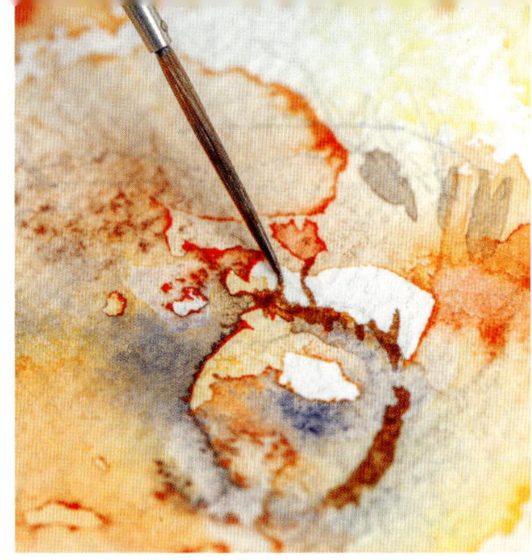

Take control for contrast

If you need more control for delicate, important areas like the eyes, hold your brush closer to the tip. Having some areas that are tighter will create contrast and draw the viewer's eye to them – not everything has to be loose. In fact, if you want an overall loose feel, you need some clean, focused detail to help it sing out from.

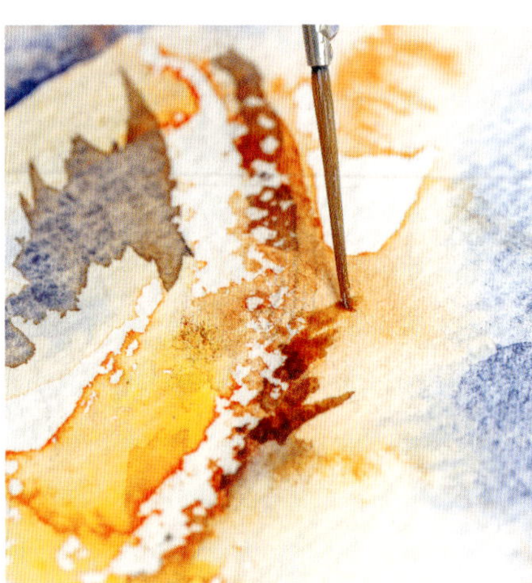

Small brush, varied marks

Use both the side and tip of the small brush to pick out and emphasize areas that are already on the painting. Here I'm adding some burnt umber touches around the ears, to suggest the texture of the long hairs of the fox's fur here.

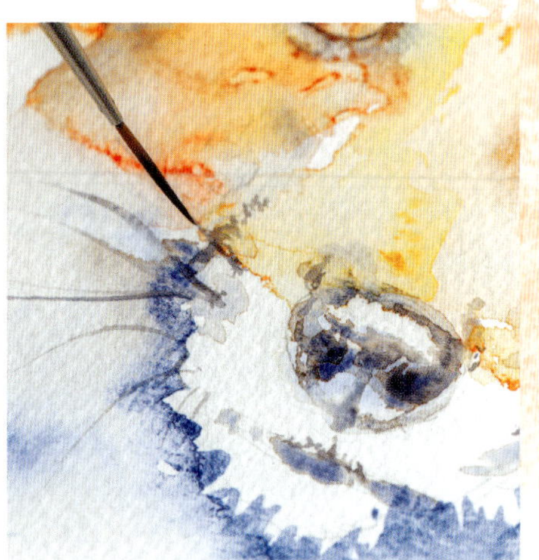

Subtle colours

Try French ultramarine and burnt umber, both alone and in a mix together, to soften and detail the nose. For the whiskers, use the same grey mix, fairly dilute. Place the tip of the brush on the muzzle, then draw it lightly away to the side, lifting it away from the surface at the same time to create a fine, tapered mark.

Finishing the painting

Continue to develop and detail your painting. I swapped back to the medium brush to create a harder mark near the mouth and re-establish a lost shape.

As you start to feel the painting is nearing completion, add a hint of rose madder above the nose. This flash of hot pink will draw the viewer's eye to the focal area.

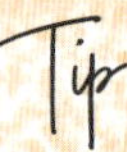

Tip

You'll likely find it easier to draw whiskers in one direction than the other. Turn the painting over so you can draw them in the direction you find easier.

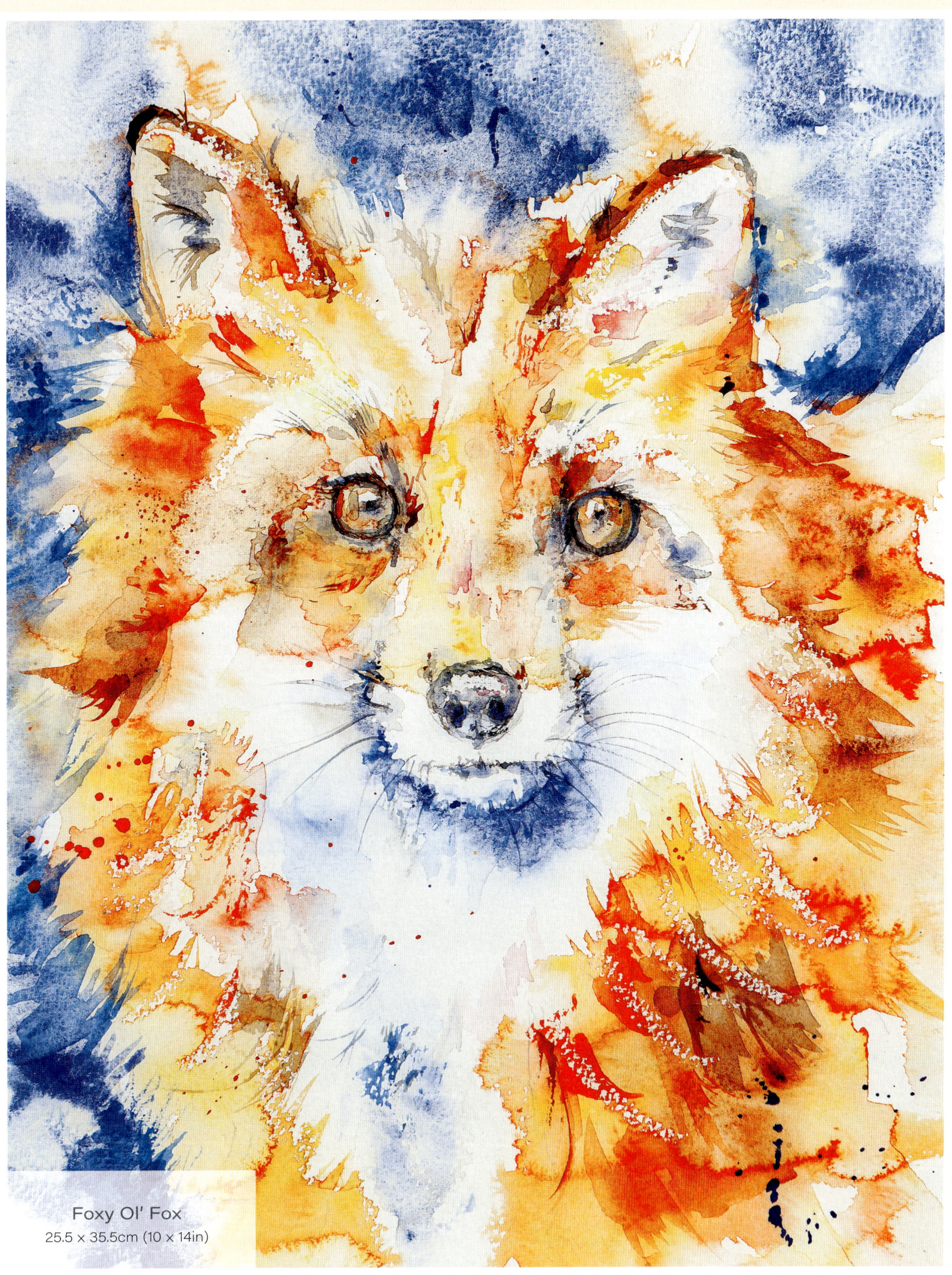

Foxy Ol' Fox
25.5 x 35.5cm (10 x 14in)

Setting off black and white animals

Whereas *Foxy Ol' Fox* was painted using just watercolour, this badger was painted using mixed media: watercolour, Quink ink, acrylic ink and a tiny touch here and there of water-resistant pen. What is similar to the project is the use of the wax – you can make this out on the right side of his face. It was also used to create some light grasses.

As with *Foxy Ol' Fox*, I used blue to help knock back areas – for example in the undergrowth and under his chin, and the back of his head. As a badger is mainly black and white, I decided to add some bright red flowers against the green grasses to brighten up the painting and put the same red on his nose too.

The purple – another receding colour – was added to suggest more distant flowers, as well as to lend more colour to my monochromatic badger. As with the fox painting, spatters were added with some of the colours I had already used which I felt created movement to suggest him scurrying through the wild undergrowth. You'll spot some interesting texture to the right of him, which was created using salt.

Badgie
32 x 23cm (12½ x9⁷in)

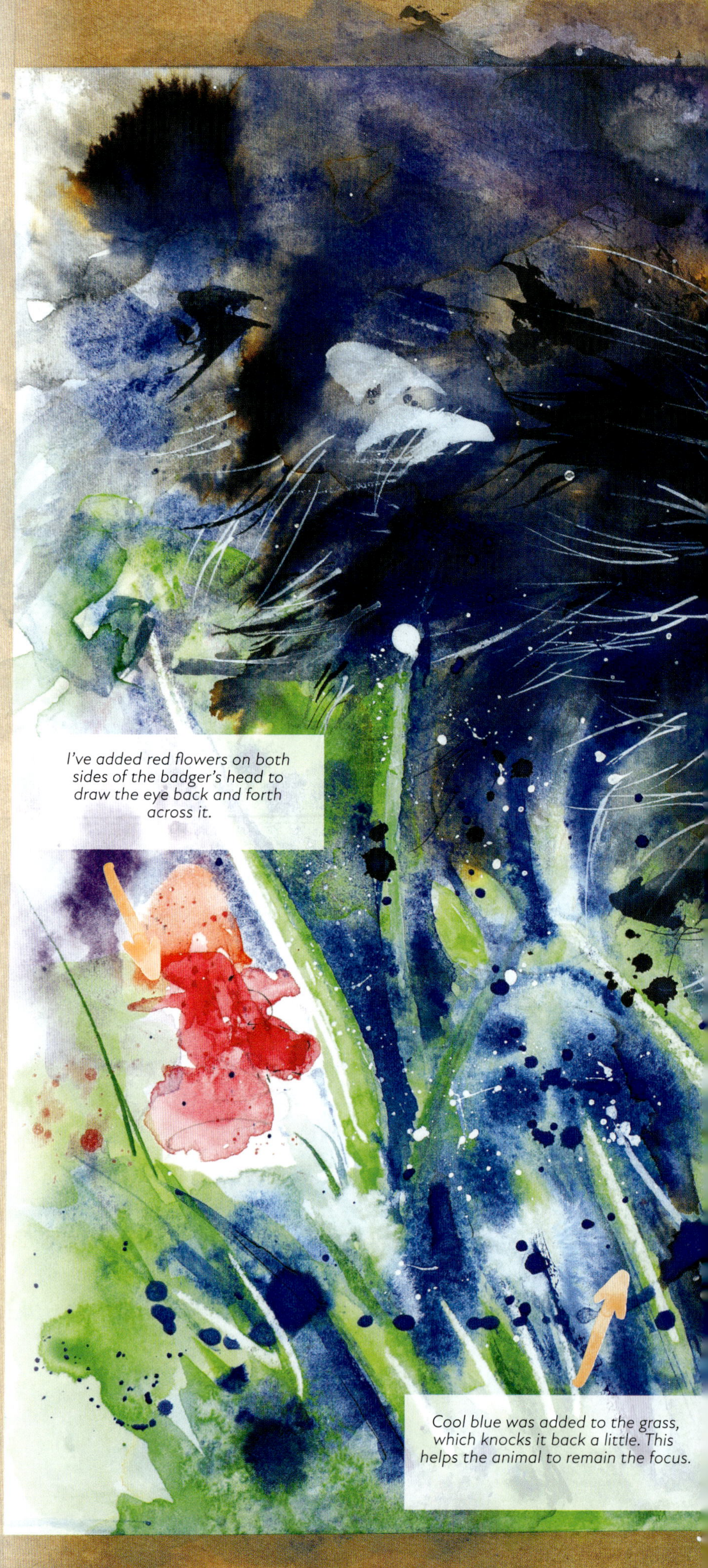

I've added red flowers on both sides of the badger's head to draw the eye back and forth across it.

Cool blue was added to the grass, which knocks it back a little. This helps the animal to remain the focus.

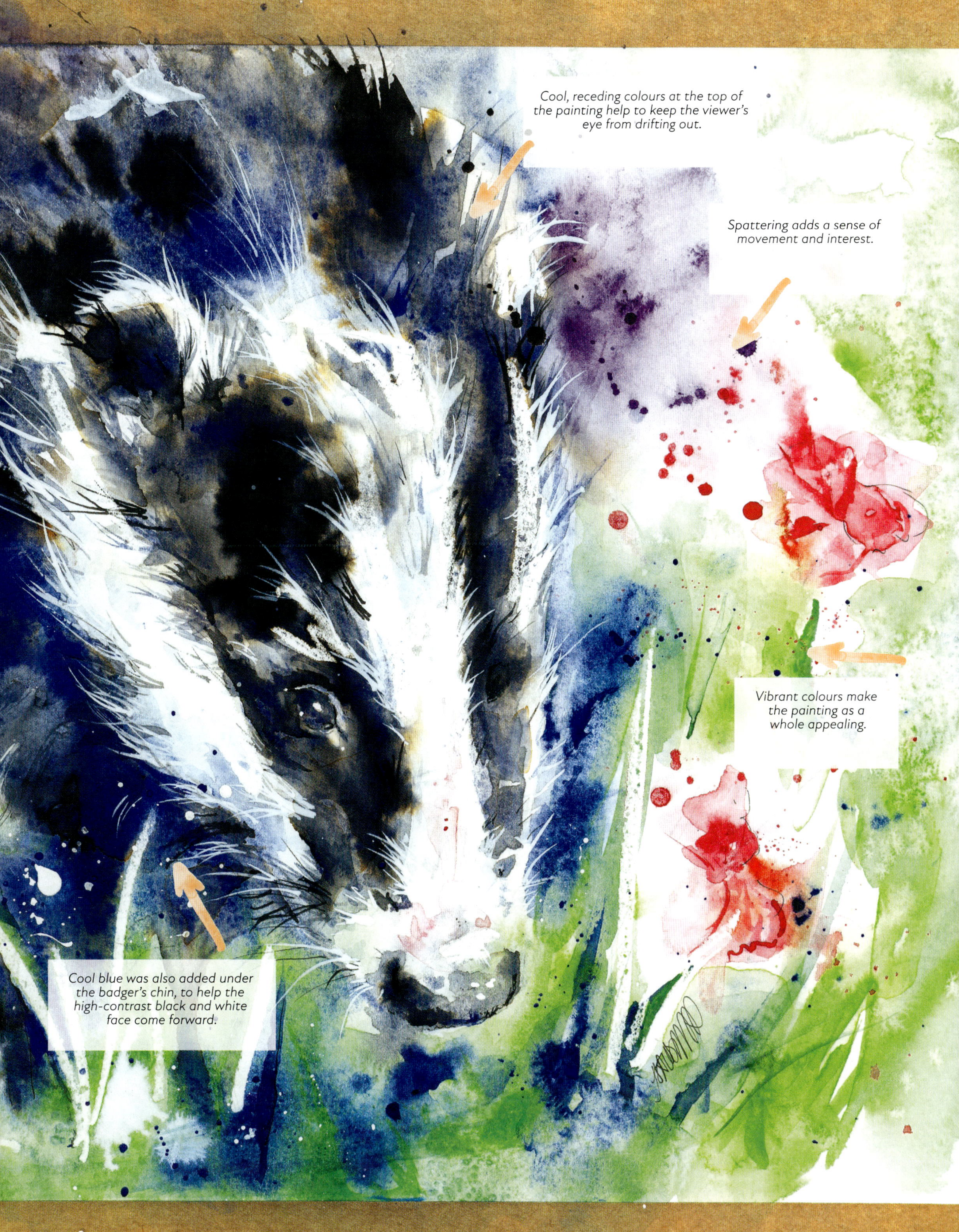

Cool, receding colours at the top of the painting help to keep the viewer's eye from drifting out.
Spattering adds a sense of movement and interest.
Vibrant colours make the painting as a whole appealing.
Cool blue was also added under the badger's chin, to help the high-contrast black and white face come forward.

Exploring backgrounds

You can decide whether or not to include a background in your painting. Backgrounds offer you lots of options. My paintings tend to fall into three categories:

- Those that have a complex background as an important part of the composition from the start.

- Those where I decide to add a soft or simple background while painting.

- Those added to a finished paintings to improve the result.

The important lesson here is that I leave my paintings open and free to adaptation, depending on how I feel. How a painting starts to unfold will influence the decisions I make – or even the surface I am using can sometimes determine whether or not I fill the page. Stay flexible, adapt as you go, and do what you prefer.

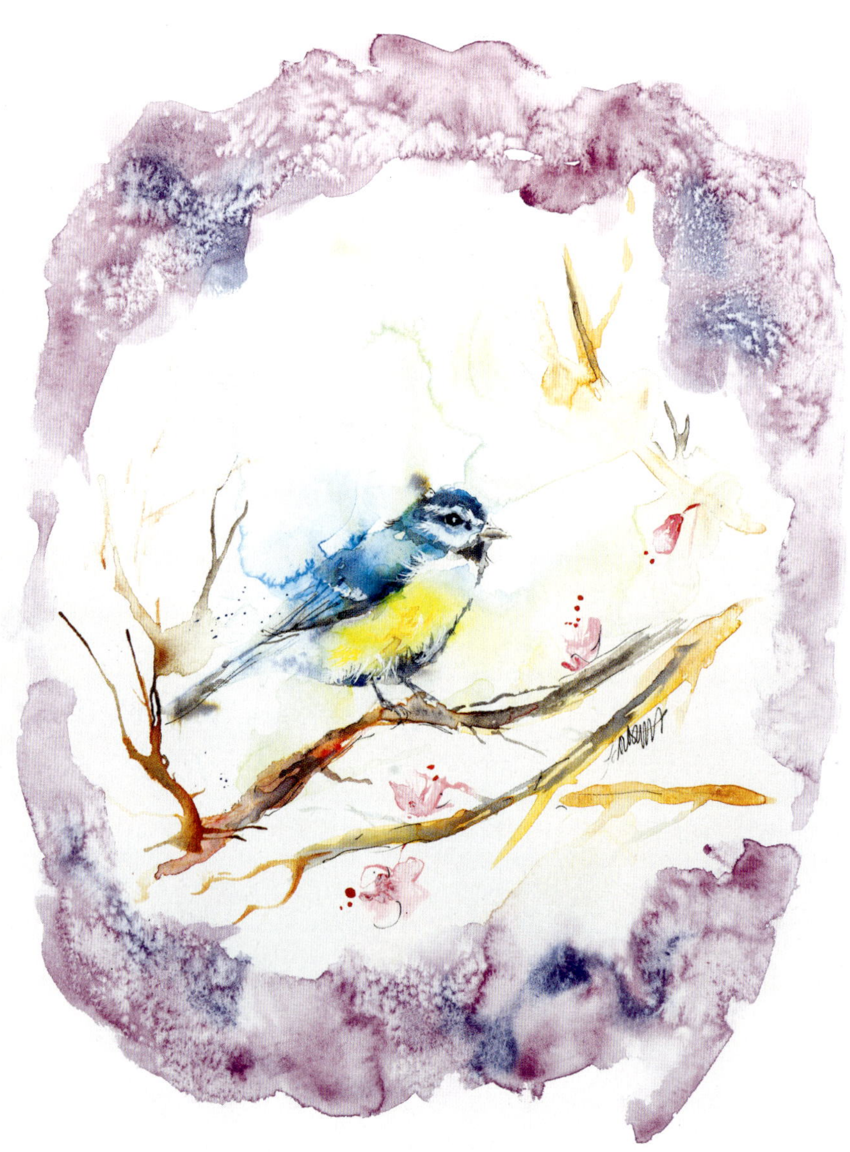

Bird's Eye View

23 x 31cm (9 x 12¼in)

The inspiration for this blue tit comes from a bird box we have in the garden. I videoed the male coming and going with food for the nesting female, and I wanted to hint at the idea of the circular entrance to the bird box.

The purple halo is how I chose to interpret that – there's a sense that you're looking through the eyes of the female blue tit, waiting.

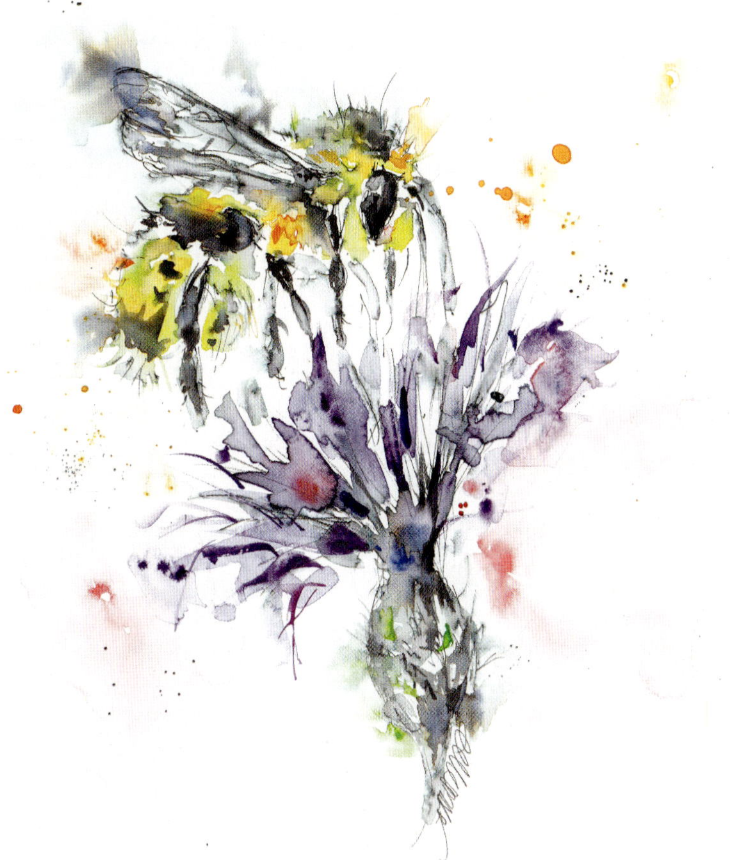

Queenie
23 x 31cm (9 x 12¼in)

There is virtually no background at all in this painting, and that's because there's another element just as important as the animal – the flower. Having two subjects makes the composition more complex, and having a background can fight with it. Here, I've deliberately left things very simple, just letting a hint of colour bleed out from the bee and flower.

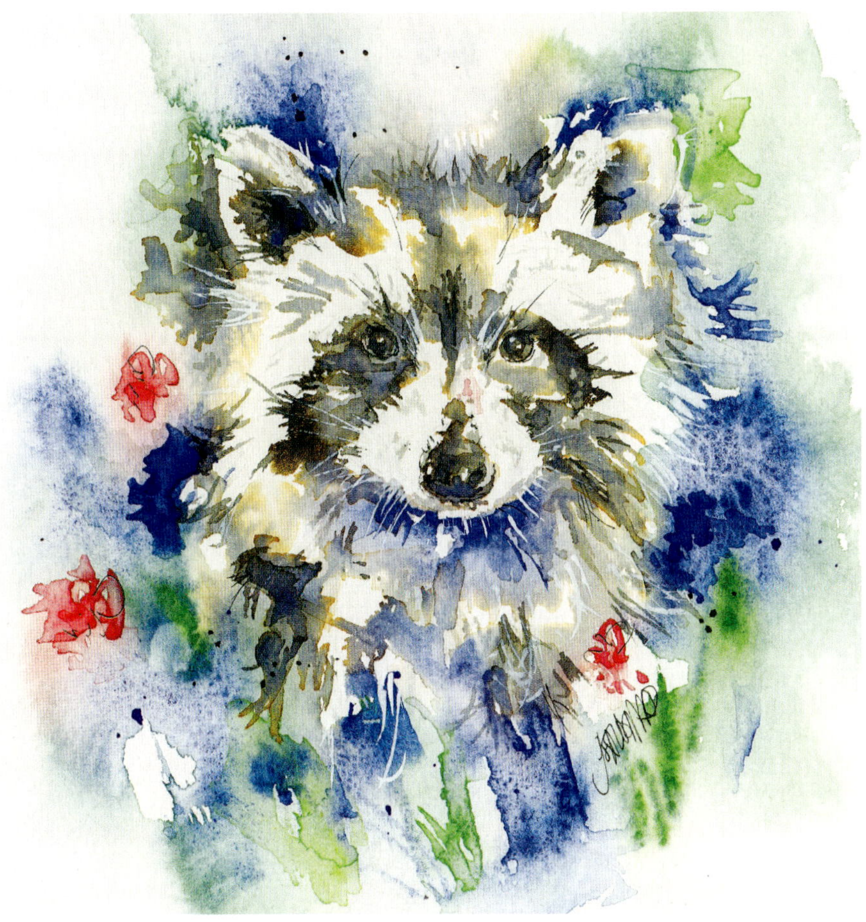

Rockie Raccoon
20 x 20cm (8 x 8in)

Like *Badgie* on pages 72–73, here I decided to bring bright watercolour around the raccoon's monochromatic head and shoulders. He looks like he has just lifted his head up from the undergrowth, having been disturbed.

The background is a combination of cool blues and greens with a burst of red here and there with the trio of flowers. While they are aggressive, the reds do not dominate but rather enhance this painting as the more detailed raccoon takes you to him. Did you notice the hint of red on his nose too?

Squirrel

I adore the striking colour of the red squirrel, and that's what we're going to explore in this project. The main challenge here is to ensure that texture, colour and detail are clear around the front of his body, without that striking tail drawing the eye too much.

The tail in the source photograph below is very bushy and textured, and we need to make it lighter and less detailed so that it will recede. This could be tricky, as the red-brown colour is naturally warm and advancing. Using a little artistic licence, we'll therefore use a little bit of blue in his tail to help push it back – even though this is not evident in the source photograph.

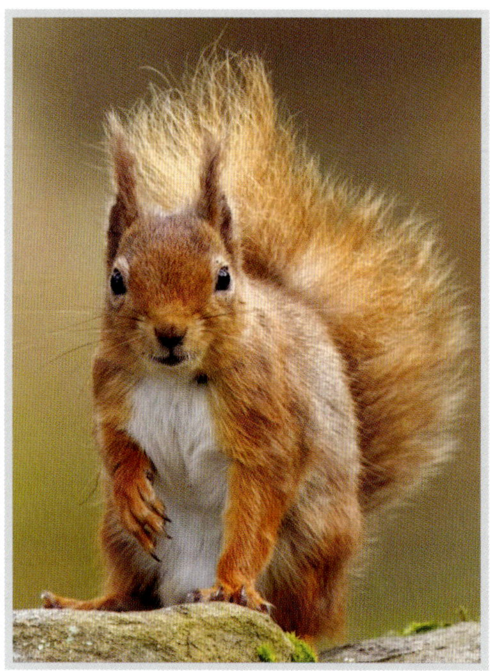

Source photograph
Since my Nan, herself a redhead, used to liken me to this creature, I'm very fond of them. The striking red fur, his fixed eyes and that tail – wow!

You will need

Bockingford CP Not surface watercolour paper
25.5 x 35.5cm (10 x 14in)

Large, medium and small brushes

HB pencil and putty eraser

WATERCOLOUR PAINTS:
May green, French ultramarine, yellow ochre, burnt sienna, burnt umber, vermilion, rose madder

Beeswax candle

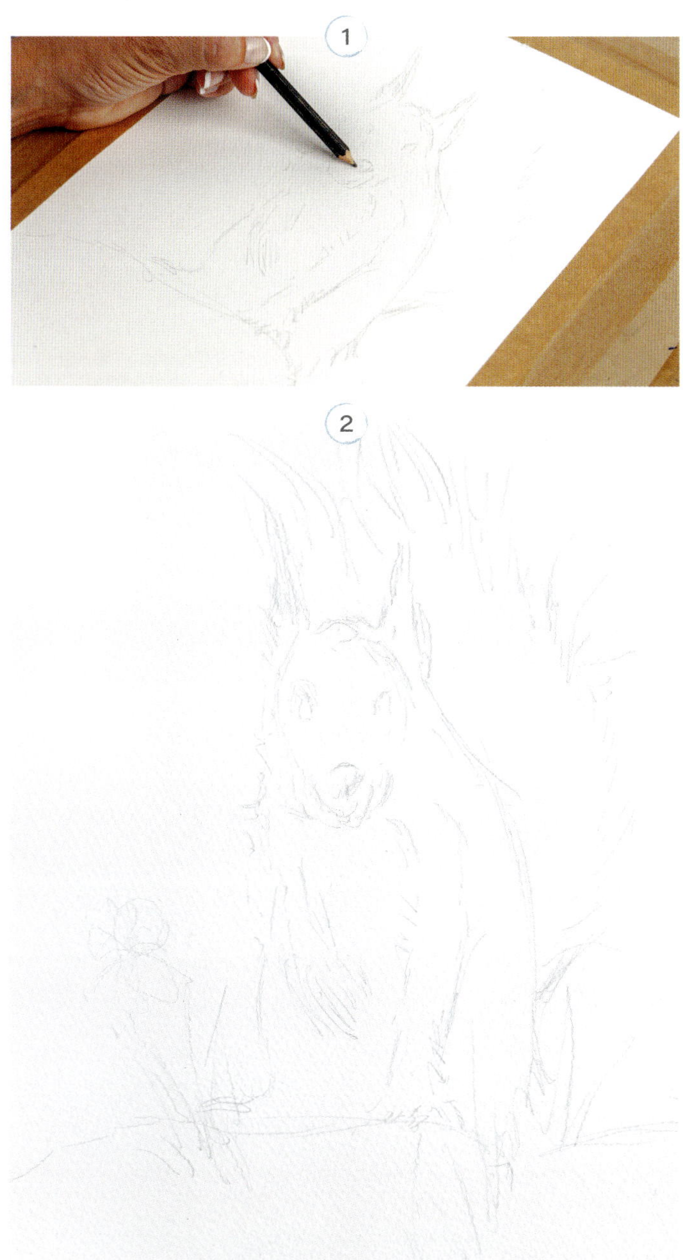

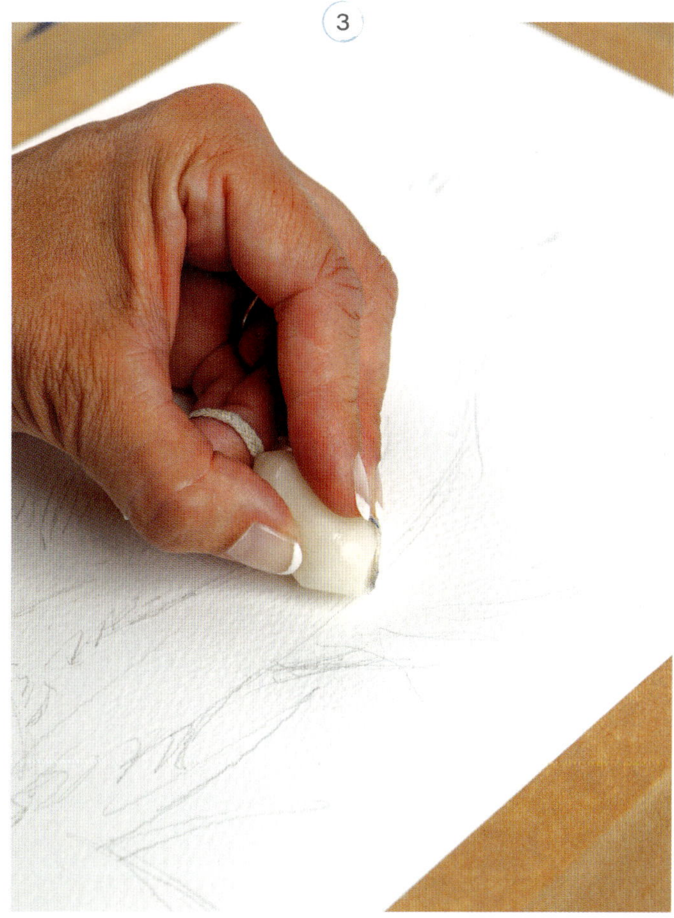

The sketch

I'm not keen on fussy backgrounds in paintings – these could detract from my animals, and I want them to be the stars of the show – so I've added just the line for the squirrel to sit upon. I'll develop that with a little foliage, perhaps some flowers, later on.

1 Draw your sketch, transferring the main shapes to the paper. You need only a little hint of the rock beneath him.

2 Don't overwork your sketch; instead concentrate on the main elements of the squirrel and the position of the facial features.

3 Add some marks using the wax, following the contours of the squirrel's body and picking out highlights here and there. Although there is some light-toned fur on the tail, avoid putting wax here. The reason for this is that you'll make the painting look flat if everything is treated the same. In general, reserve the wax for foreground areas.

Main shapes

This stage involves lots of wet in wet painting with a large brush. The key is not to panic if the paint bleeds in a way you don't want. Don't try to lift it out at this stage; all you'll do is end up with a white patch. Although it looks very obvious here, it'll dry much lighter and become very subtle. Together with the more striking paint added elsewhere as we develop the painting later, you'll barely notice such marks at the end.

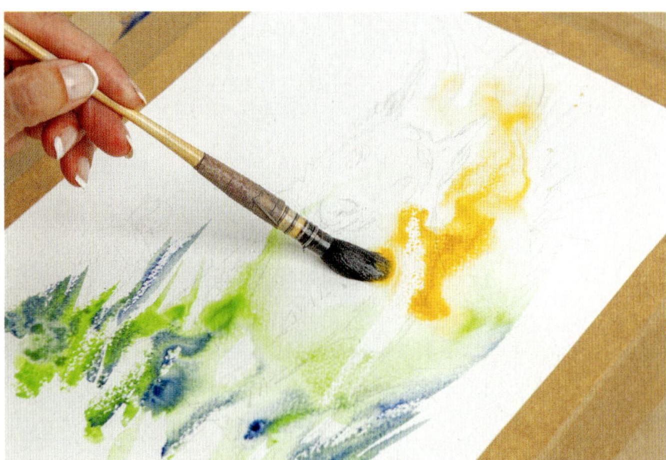

4 Using the large brush, add some foreground grasses with May green and French ultramarine. Working wet in wet, use yellow ochre to start to paint the squirrel.

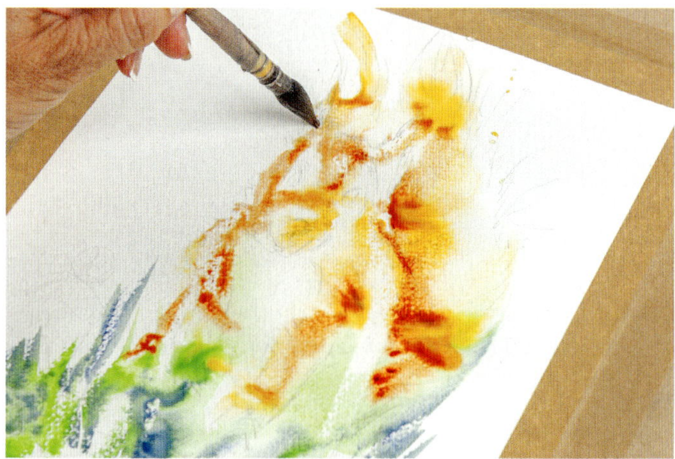

5 Work from light to dark, adding burnt sienna to paint the warm, gingery areas. Introduce burnt umber to enrich and deepen the darks, applying the paint with the point of the brush.

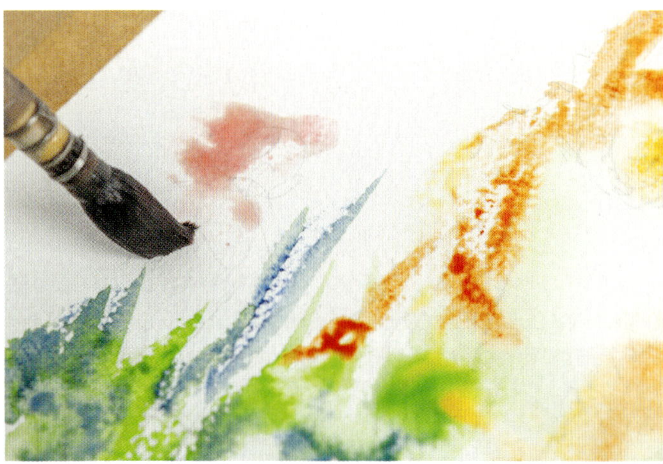

6 Throw on some bold marks in the background to the left of the squirrel using rose madder.

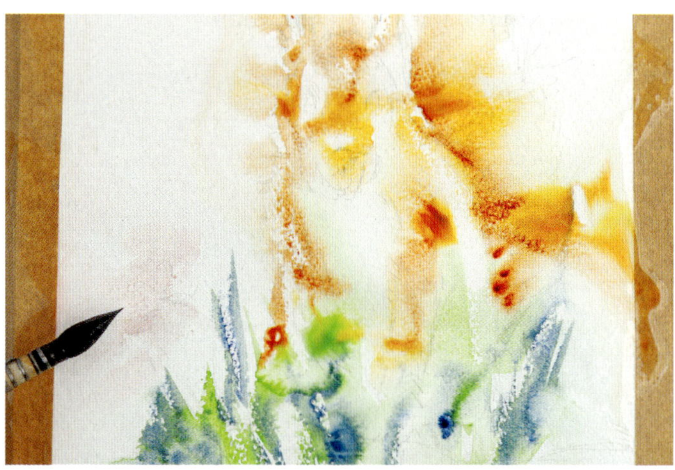

7 Push clean water up to the subject and wet colours to encourage the colours of the squirrel to bleed into the background.

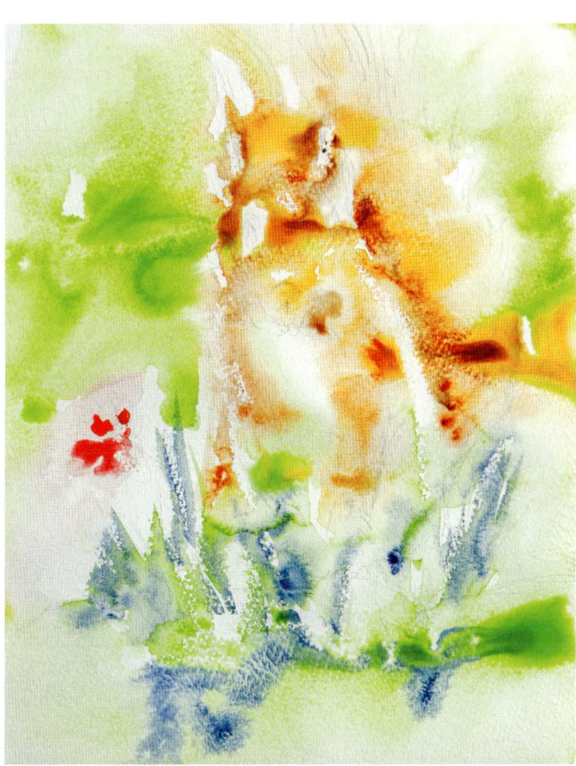

8 While the paint remains wet, drop in May green to the cleaner areas of the background, applying the paint into the gaps around the squirrel. Extend the green over the ground beneath the squirrel, and add some French ultramarine wet in wet to create some variety and interest.

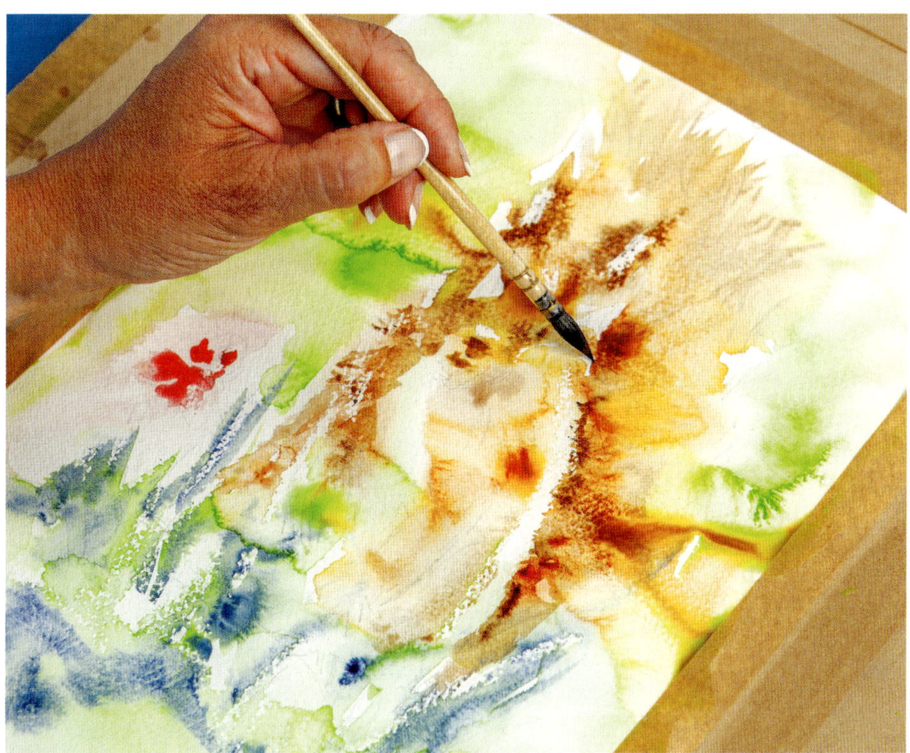

9 Swap to the medium brush, and assess the painting. While the background is still wet, apply burnt umber strokes with the tip of the brush. This will hint at the texture of the fur whilst drying to a much softer texture to help push the tail back. Lost edges help to emulate an out-of-focus result.

Refining and defining

The squirrel's body eventually needs to be more defined than the tail, so that it sits forward of it in the painting. This can be achieved through found edges, to contrast with the lost edges on the tail. However, we don't need to make hard, obvious marks just yet. They can be built up gradually as the painting develops. For the moment, we'll make the most of the wetness on the squirrel's body to create an overall sense of softness to the fur.

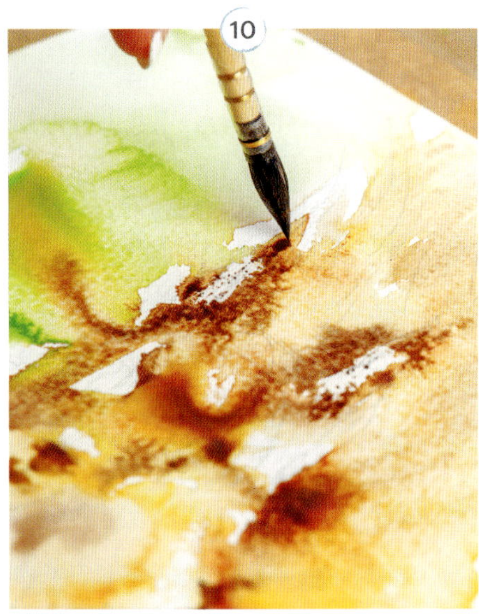

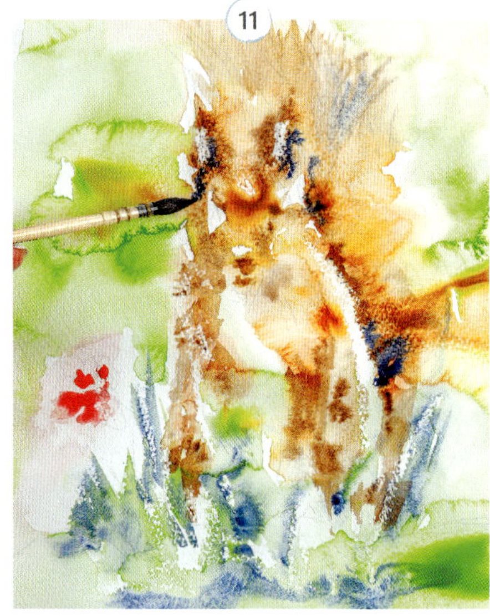

10 Using burnt umber and the tip of the medium brush, start to add depth to the squirrel's body, avoiding the tail.

11 Draw a few marks of burnt umber down from his legs into the stone, to integrate the different parts of the painting and prevent him looking stuck-on, then swap to French ultramarine to add some darks wet in wet around the painting, particularly around the ears to help push back some parts and add some definition.

12 Use French ultramarine to add some shadow to define the squirrel's chin. Use the wet medium brush to soften the colour away towards the chest, then quickly swap to the small brush and use the tip to tease the paint into the muzzle area to suggest the furry texture. Use burnt sienna to pick out the nose.

13 Add the claws with the small brush and French ultramarine, then allow the painting to dry. You can use a hairdryer to help speed this up – and this also allows you to add some dynamic marks. Move the hairdryer close to the surface to drive pools of paint in particular directions.

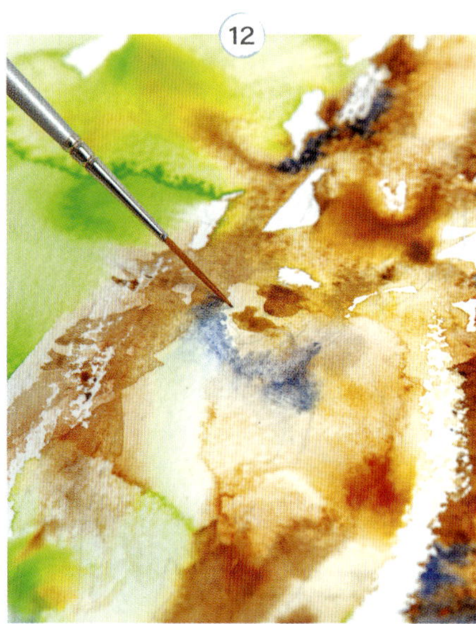

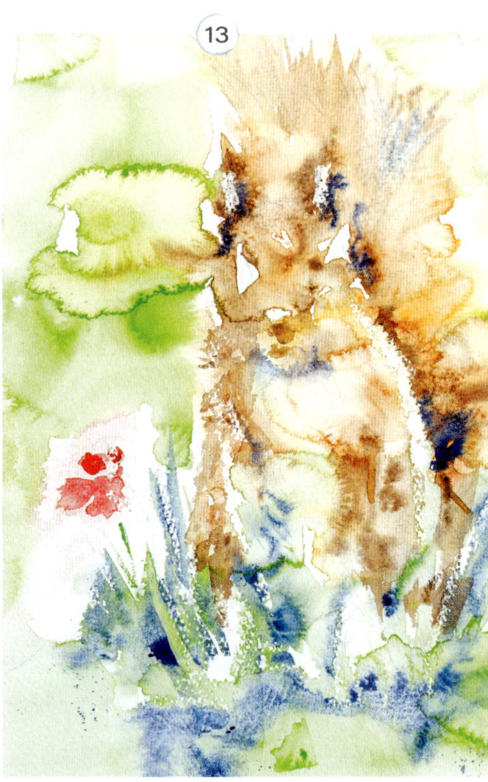

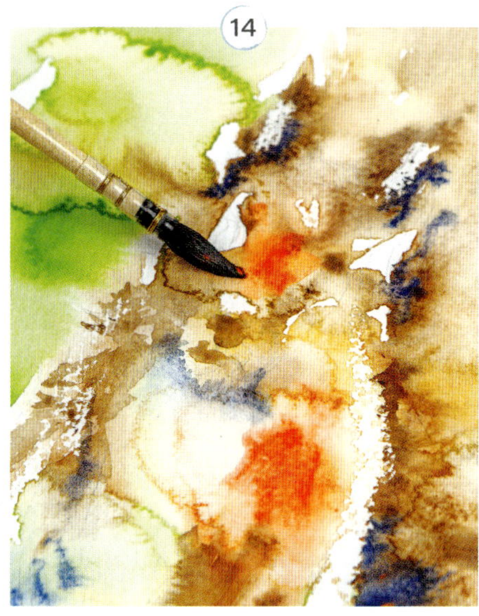

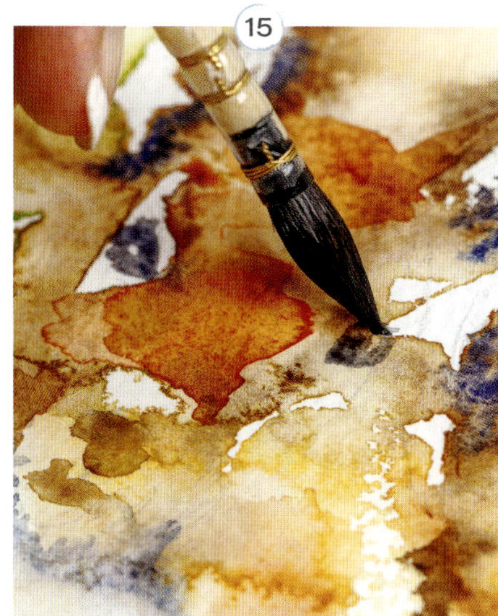

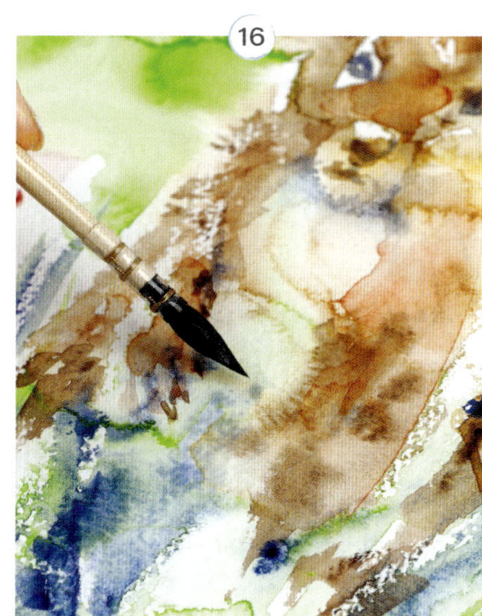

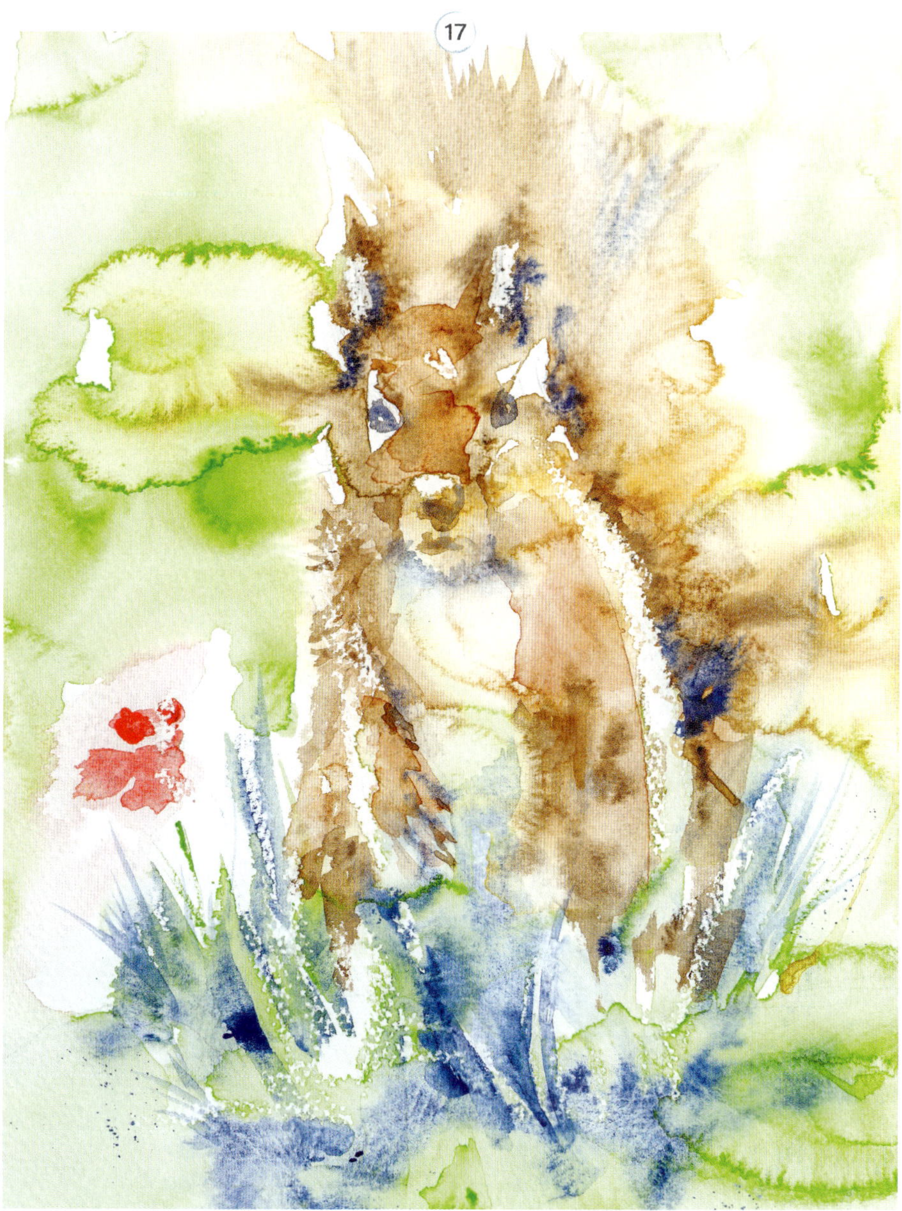

14 Vermilion, applied to the forearms, hands and face, will help these parts of the painting to come forward. There's no need to mix a reddy-brown, as this diluted colour will let some of the underlying paint come through. Apply the paint with the medium brush, and avoid the more distant areas of fur to avoid bringing them forward.

15 Use a grey mix of ultramarine and burnt umber to paint in the eye, leaving a small highlight in each as a glossy highlight. I've used the point on the medium brush, but if you feel you want a little more control, you can swap to the rigger.

16 Add some more French ultramarine to knock back the belly area, blending it away into the blue on the ground.

17 Add some flicking marks up from the ground to suggest grasses in shadow, then allow the painting to dry.

Making the painting yours

It's now over to you to finish off your animal as you wish. You can use these ideas to achieve something like my finished painting opposite.

When making marks to bring definition to the key areas like the features, it's important that nearby marks don't distract. Bleed the colour away from softer edges so the marks aren't making too bold a statement.

You might find turning the painting upside down not only makes painting details like the whiskers much easier, but also lets you assess the painting as a whole at this stage.

Finishing the painting

Use the small brush and the appropriate colours to make any additional tweaks to the painting to finish. Here I've added a little warmth on the right-hand side, some more definition to the face, and whiskers using the grey mix of burnt umber and French ultramarine.

There's no perfect time to stop, but aim to draw a line under the painting before you overwork the piece. You can always come back to add more, but you can't take it away as easily.

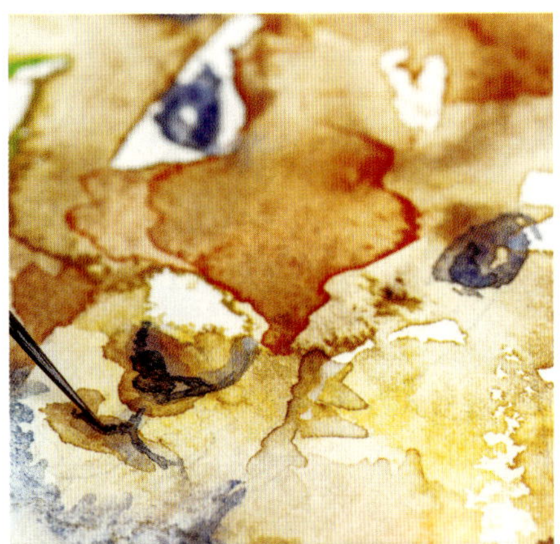

Focal features

Using the small brush, develop and detail the eyes, nose, claws and similar features with a grey mix of French ultramarine and burnt umber. Tiny marks that hint at eyelids can subtly change the character of the eyes or mouth.

When adding these marks, don't feel you have to pay attention to the previous layers. As you can see, the tone of these dark marks makes the underlying colour almost irrelevant.

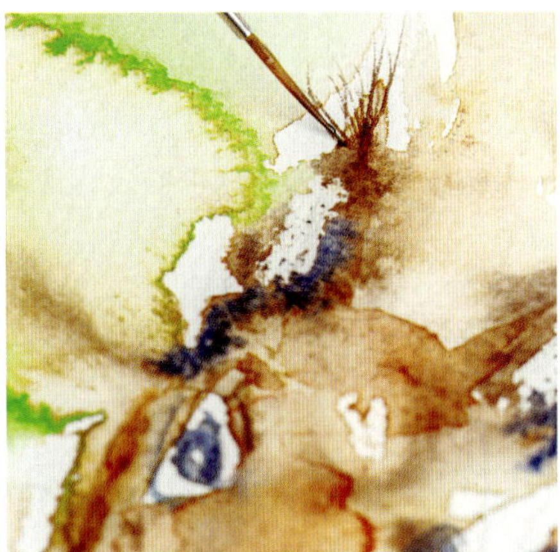

Warming areas

Use the side of the brush to apply dilute burnt sienna to warm areas of the fur; these will help them to come forward. Burnt umber is great to use for the distinctive ear tufts – apply the paint with light, flicking marks of the brush's tip.

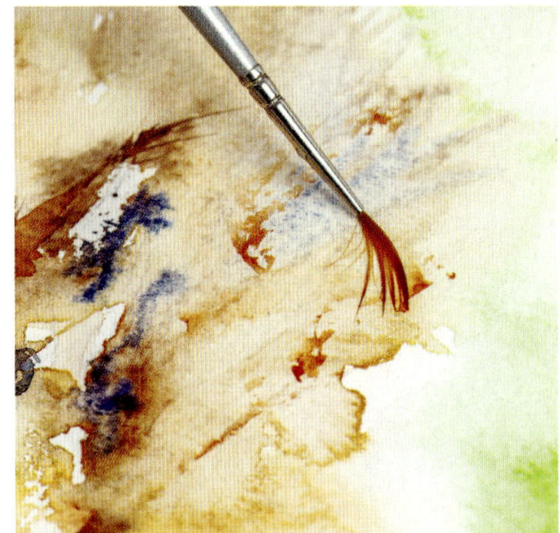

Keep the distance subtle

Develop the tail with the side of the brush and stronger burnt sienna. Use a flicking, dry brush technique to hint at the fur's texture without overdetailing it and throwing it forward.

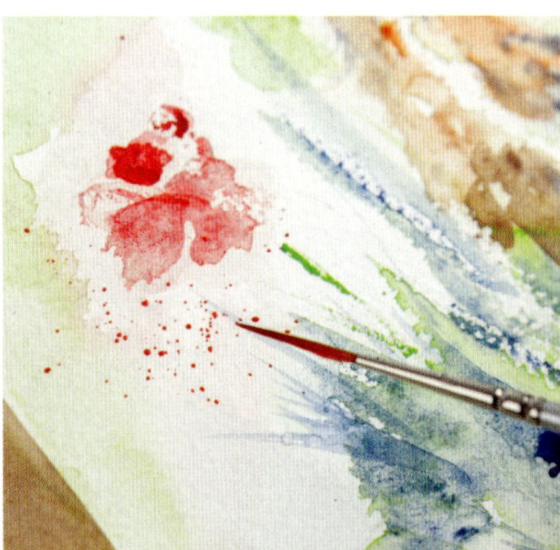

Flowers and interest

Add a little scribble with rose madder to the centre of the flower. This is a bit of a signature of mine. To avoid the flower drawing all the attention, add a little spattering of rose madder elsewhere amongst the foreground flowers.

Opposite:
Rusty
25.5 x 35.5cm (10 x 14in)

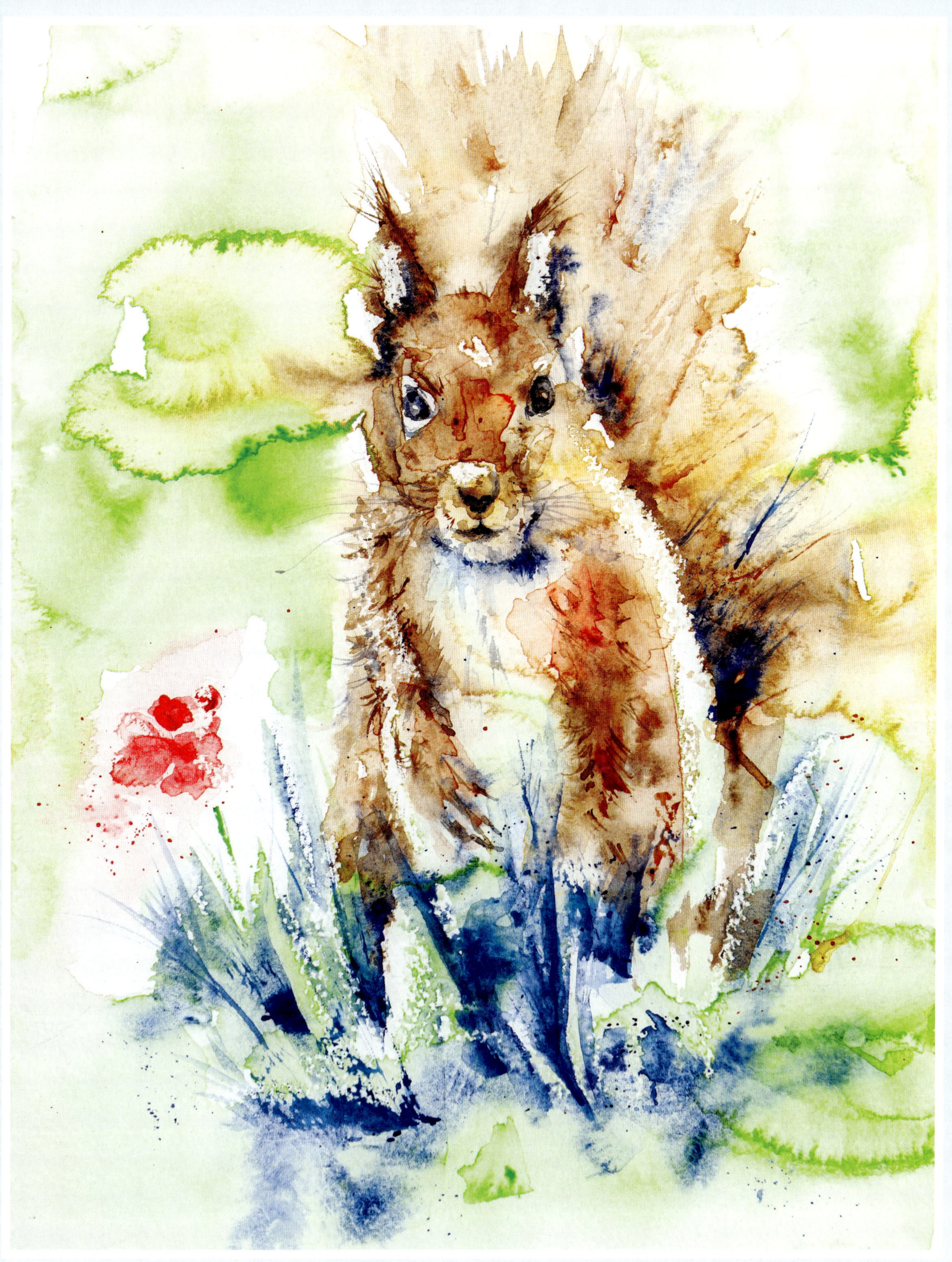

Putting the animal in context

In comparison with the red squirrel in the project, this grey squirrel uses a little more artistic licence to make for a more interesting painting. For example, the photograph I used here – shown below – was almost black and white, with hardly any indication of colour. The finished painting, by contrast, is bright and fresh; the grey tones replaced with bright blues and reds.

Colour was also used to bring out the acorn he's holding close to his chest. This detail is almost lost in the original photograph, but a bit of artistic license allows us to highlight it and add a sense of story to the painting. It's also worth noting that the red colour of the acorn acts as a hot spot, particularly against the blue of the fur shadow. There are other little flashes of these autumnal colours around him to help set off his blue fur.

There was also no evidence in the photograph of the autumn leaves that I chose to include, but these added elements help to surround the squirrel with warm browns and create an interesting background.

As with the squirrel project earlier, I used wax resist and spattering. Painting this squirrel also involved the use of both white acrylic for some of the light fur and spatter, and a water-resistant fine black pen for a few little suggestive marks here and there.

Opposite:
The Collector
23 x 31cm (9 x 12¼in)

Another beautiful squirrel, *The Collector*, was painted – as always – using lots of wet in wet to create blooms, just as in the red squirrel project on the previous pages.

He's pictured here with warm leaves, getting himself organized for winter – hence the inclusion of the cooler blues and greens – and collecting treats to squirrel away for tougher times.

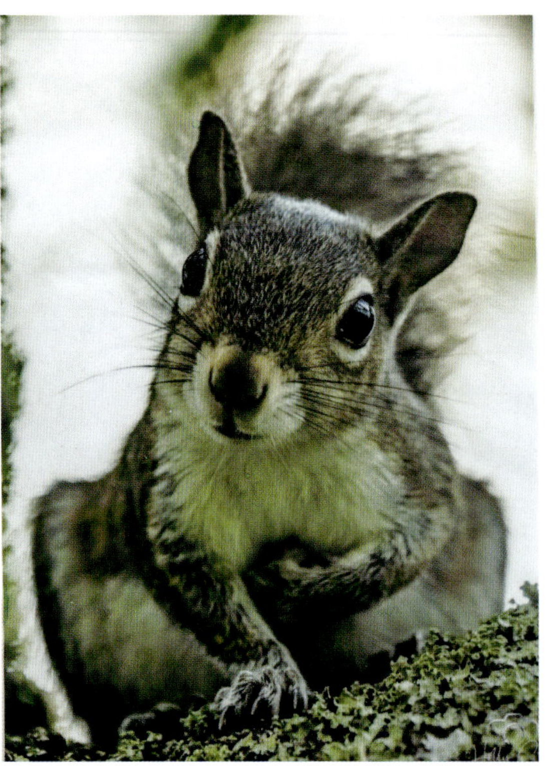

Source photograph
Those big eyes pulled me in, but I knew I wanted to include colour to lift this image.

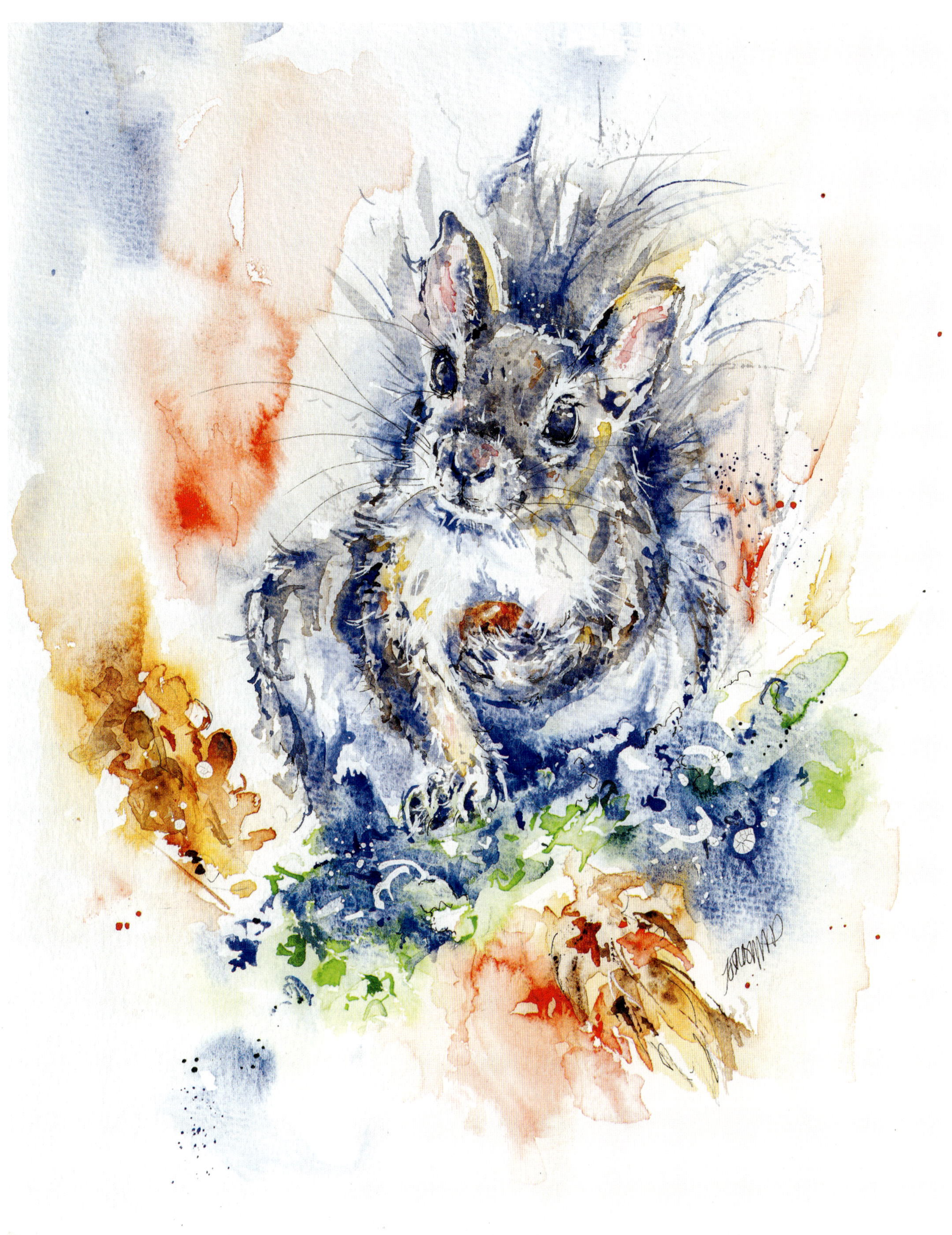

Adding more impact

If you want your paintings to reach out and grab the viewer's attention, you need to bring impact into your painting. The key to this is contrast: in colour, tone, texture or all three.

Contrasts of colour

Some subjects, like parrots, lend themselves well to contrasting colours as they're already very colourful. When your animal is more muted, you can add impact by adding unexpected contrasting colours, or simply making it up! There's no reason you have to stick to what's in front of you in your photograph.

Warm, vibrant colours can be introduced in the background or in the subject – and it's warm hues like reds, oranges and pinks that will draw the eye.

Contrasts of tone

Tone refers to how light or dark a colour is. This is obvious with black and white, but it applies to all colours. Placing your lightest lights to the darkest darks in your compositions is a great way to get viewers to look at a particular area.

Contrasts of texture

Detail draws the eye, and you can use this to help lead the eye around the painting. Consider lost and found edges. On a photograph, everything looks in focus and sharp. Sometimes you need to soften some areas so that they're not fighting for attention. In this tiger painting, for example, I've used sharper, harder lines for the fur texture on the face, as I want the eye to rest here. To help this, I've used soft marks and blending for the tiger's body, so that they don't draw the eye.

Colour contrast
The original photograph here was drab greens, greys and black – just look at what some flashes of super-vibrant colour do to bring this crab to life.

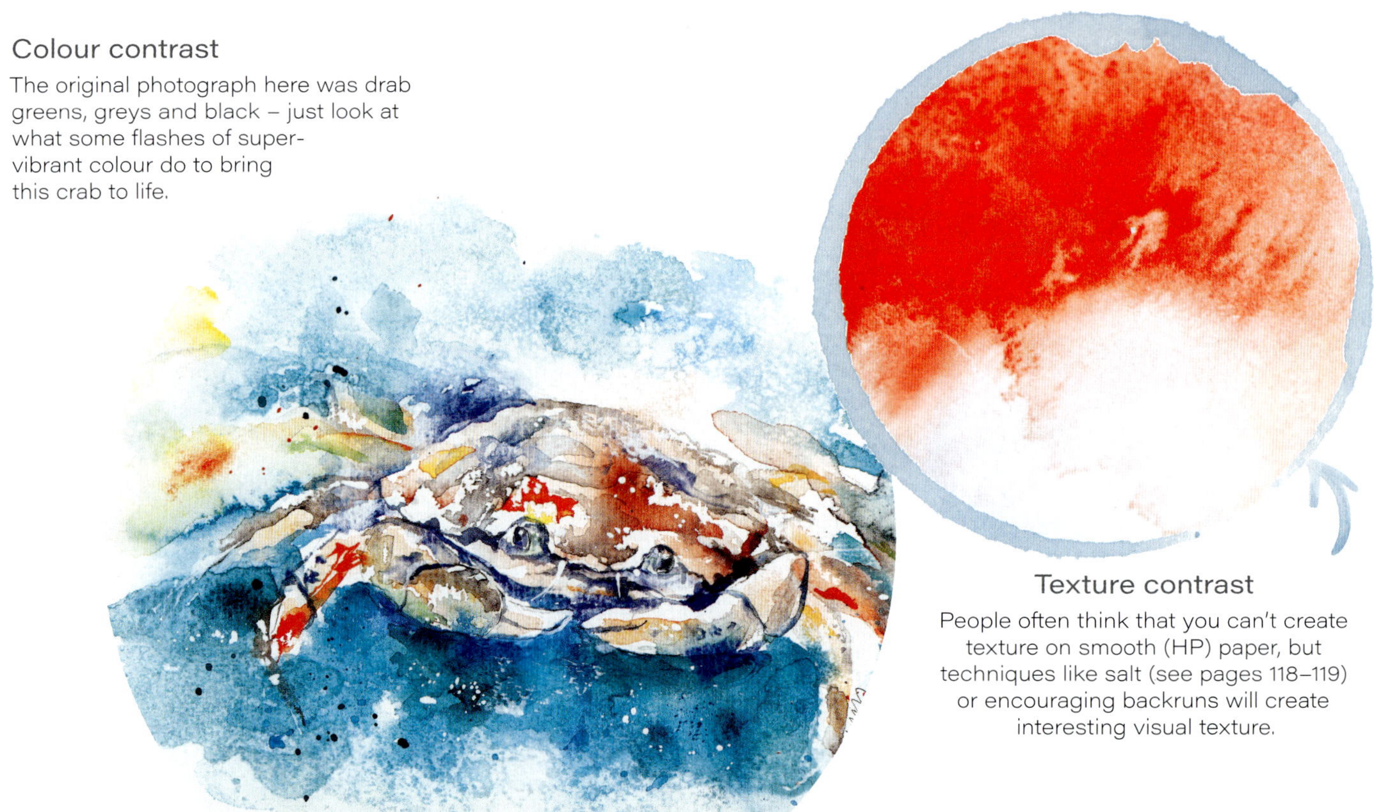

Texture contrast
People often think that you can't create texture on smooth (HP) paper, but techniques like salt (see pages 118–119) or encouraging backruns will create interesting visual texture.

Tiger
35.5 x 25.5cm (14 x 10in)

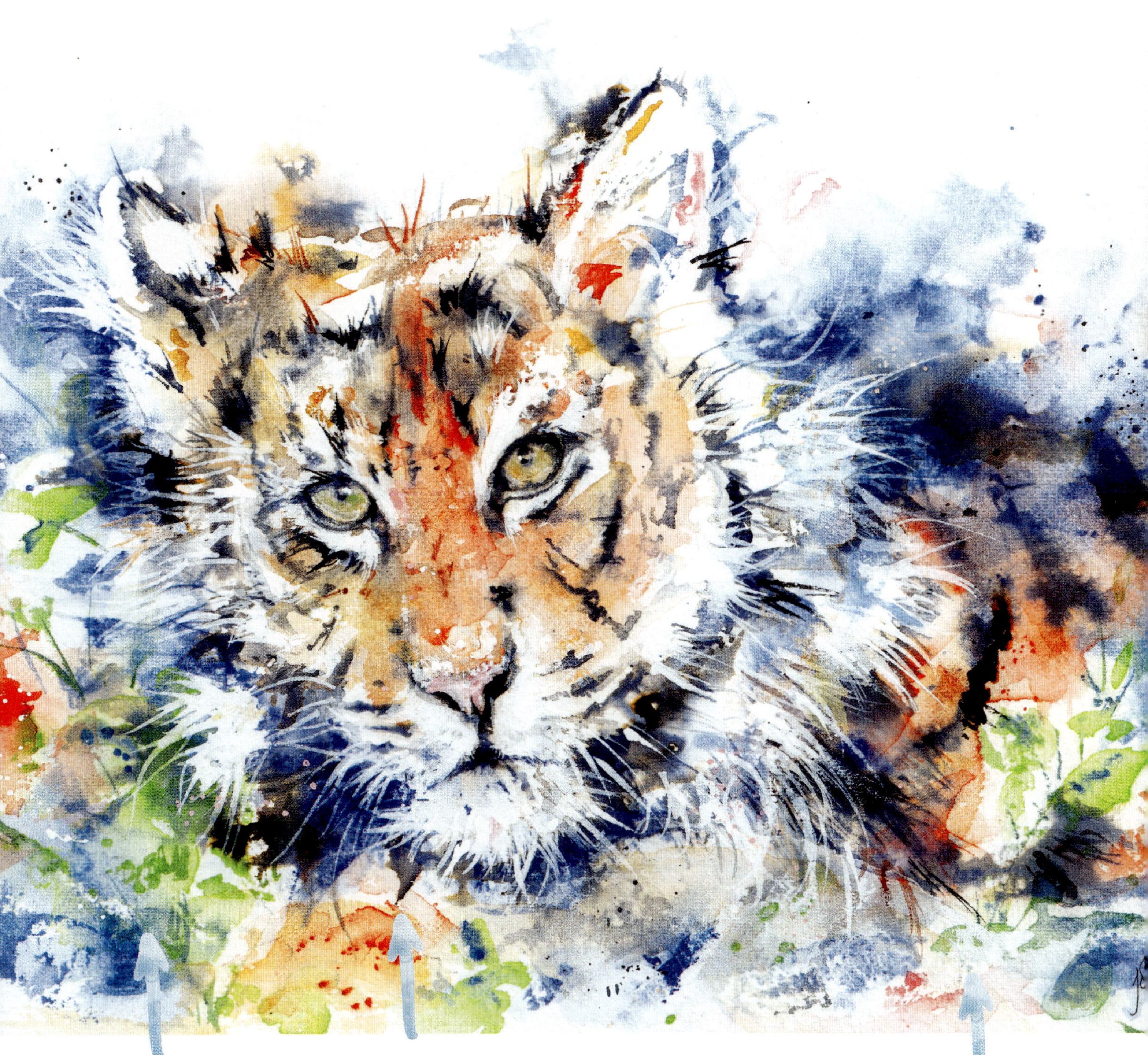

Textural contrasts of hard
lines against soft edges.

Tonal contrasts of dark
against light.

Colour contrasts of warm
reds and oranges against
cool blues and greens.

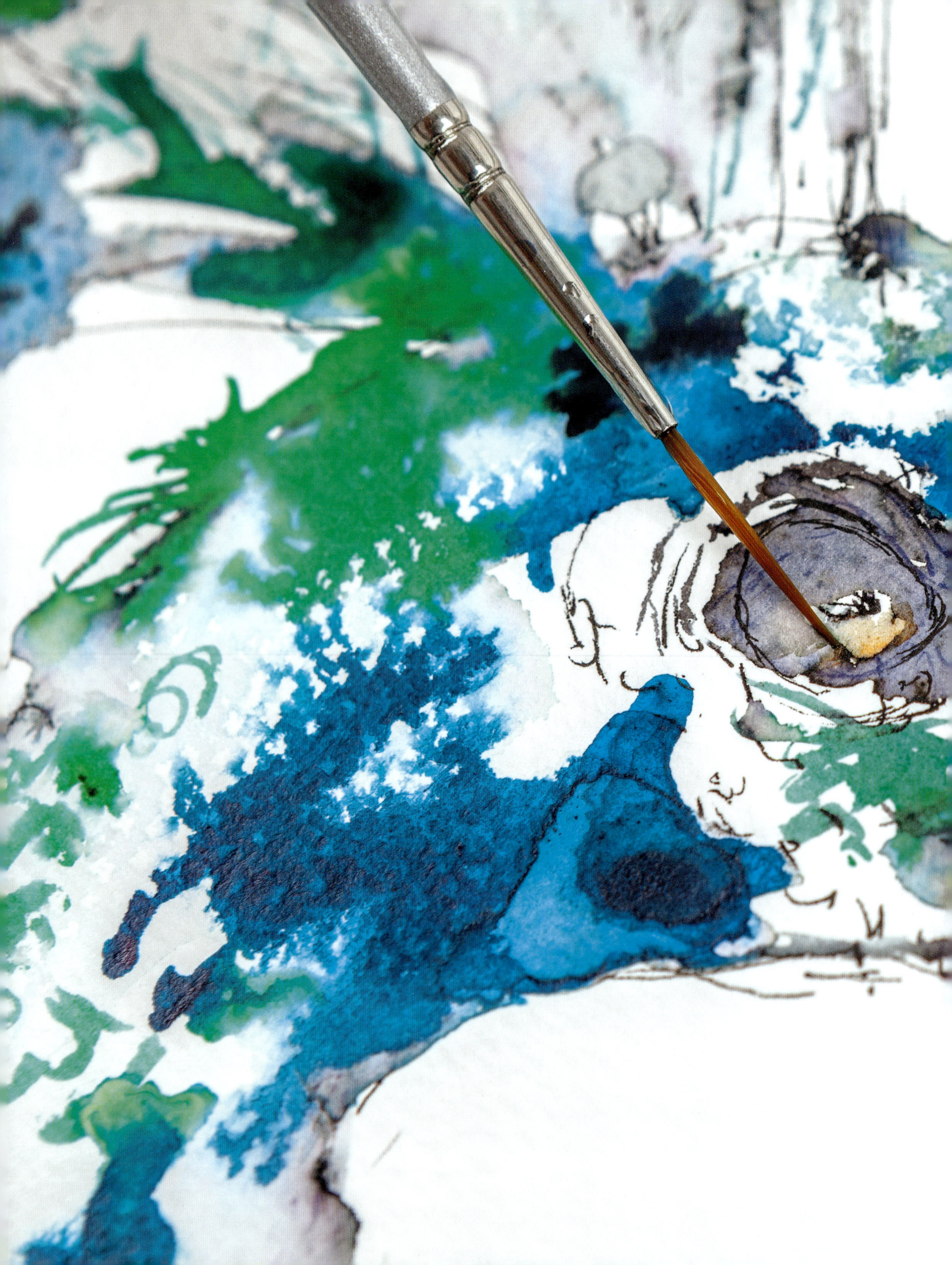

Animals in mixed media

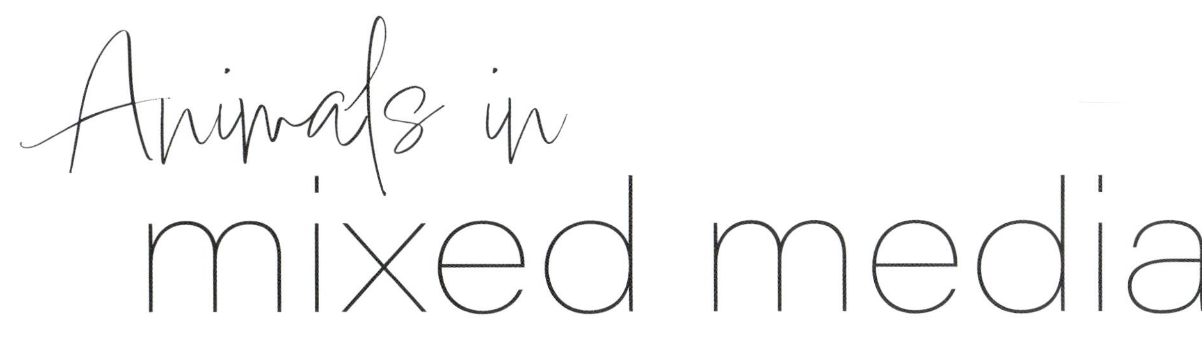

There are so many other things we can do with watercolour. Mixed media is a fabulous option, particularly if things are not going your way. If, by adding a little acrylic paint, we can hide an error, who is to know? Will they even care?

We can improve and enhance a painting with the addition of other media, whether pastels, watercolour pencils, acrylics, gouache or wax crayons. I personally love to use some bling here and there, by adding bronzing powders. All are beautiful, and I use bronze, silver and gold powders: they are a good reminder of the trophies I have received in my martial arts. Being able to reflect your achievements or pride from other areas of your life in your painting will go a long way to improving your enjoyment of your art.

Experiment to your heart's content with whatever takes your fancy. In these projects, I have used some of my most favoured diluents, additions and techniques – and I encourage you to experiment and find your own favourites. Remember, it doesn't matter how you get there, as long as you get there in the end.

Mixed media materials

FW acrylic inks

These acrylic-based inks are available in a variety of colours and, as they are opaque, can be painted over the top of watercolour. They dry hard and cannot be reconstituted – and so can ruin brushes. Always ensure that you wash out your brushes thoroughly after you finish and in between washes. These inks are wonderful for putting into a wet watercolour wash because of how they react and swirl into beautiful patterns. They are also the perfect consistency for painting whiskers using my rigger brush.

Bronzing powder

For additional bling here and there, bronzing powders are excellent. These can be added directly to wet watercolours, or mixed with water on a plate and used like a paint to add sparkle to paintings. I favour Schmincke's Aqua Bronze range of powders. Available in gold, silver and bronze, they create a lovely iridescence, especially when you view the painting at different angles, where they add a sparkle to your work.

Bleach

Pour a drop or two of bleach – any household bleach will do – into a china receptacle. Be careful not to get it on your skin or near your eyes, but otherwise you can use it like any other paint.

Parker Quink Ink

When added to water, this black ink breaks up to create beautiful blue and yellow-orange hues – people sometimes don't believe that some of my pieces have been painted using only black ink with water and assume I must have used other colours! When working with ink, I sometimes wash the whole painting to create effects and patterns. Quink also reacts well with bleach for another added dimension.

Salt

Everyone should have some salt in their kit box. Both table and rock salt create beautiful patterns in watercolour, which are hard to emulate. Do experiment on a spare piece of paper first, as the results will be different depending on how wet or dry your paint is. Different pigments and papers can also alter the effect. I find that good, strong dark pigments create fabulous contrasts that allow you to see the patterns more clearly. Let the wash dry naturally after adding the salt, so as not to disturb the process. Patience is a virtue.

Plastic food wrap

Laid over wet paint that's then left to dry, this creates an interesting effect. I often use this to emulate waves on water.

Isopropyl alcohol

Isopropyl is fantastic. It can be sprayed into a wet wash to create beautiful textural effects which are difficult to emulate any other way. If used before a wash, this gives a batik effect. You can add alcohol to your water pot prior to painting, too, which speeds up drying times.

Metallic foil

Gold leaf (also silver or bronze leaf) will add some different texture and vibrancy to a painting. I usually add it to strong inky paintings rather than the 'pure watercolour' paintings. It is secured by painting white glue (PVA) onto the surface, then placing the foil with tweezers.

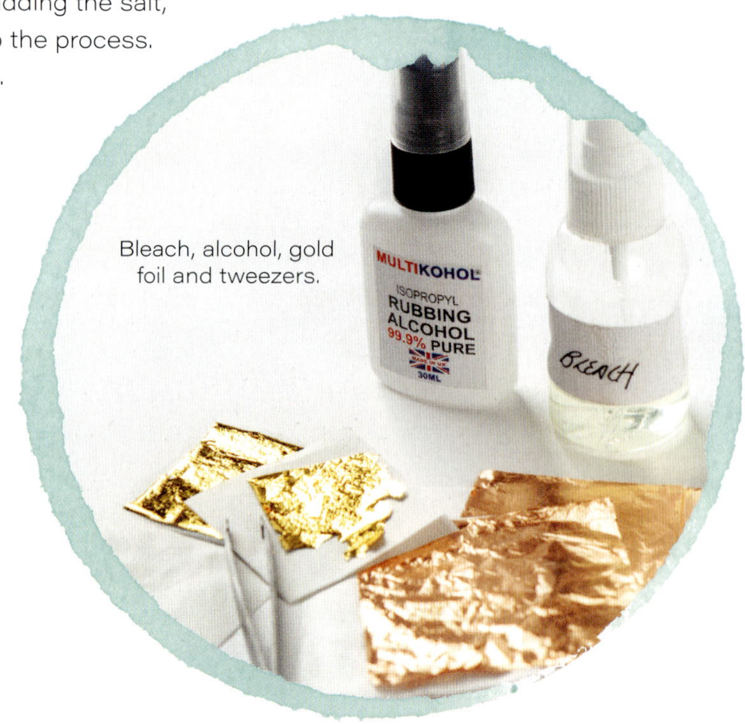

Bleach, alcohol, gold foil and tweezers.

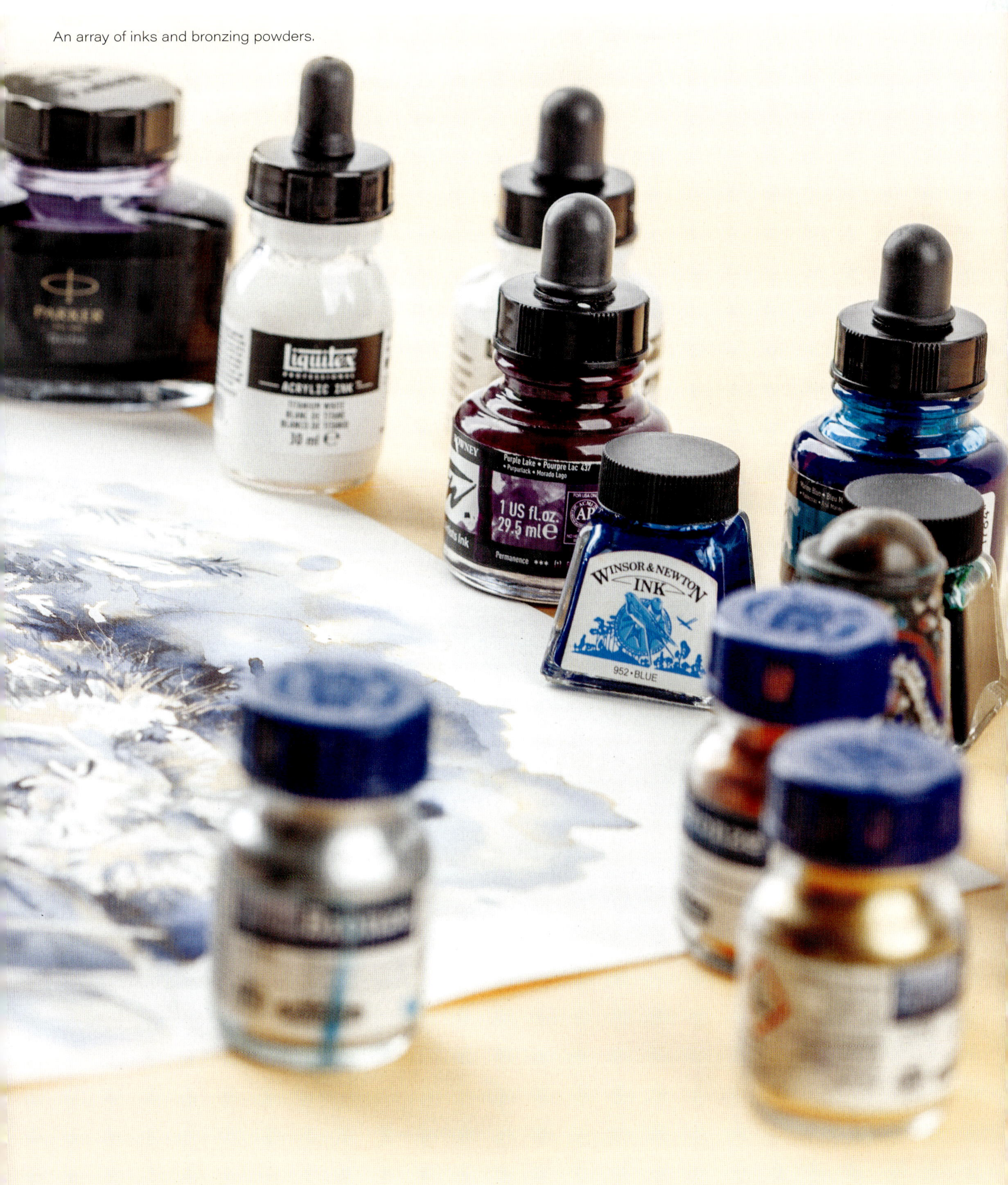

An array of inks and bronzing powders.

Sand Cat

I do love cats' faces; they look so very demure – but cats are both extremely independent and very assertive. I was attracted to this cat for a few reasons: one was that I had taken a similar pic of a cat curled up asleep in Rhodes and, two, because it reminds me of the big cats I adore.

This is perhaps why I decided on quite a subtle approach with the initial melt of the pen and the softer tones, but then added in some harder, darker inclusions.

We'll introduce pen and acrylic inks to watercolours in this project, putting a fresh spin on the classic pen and wash approach.

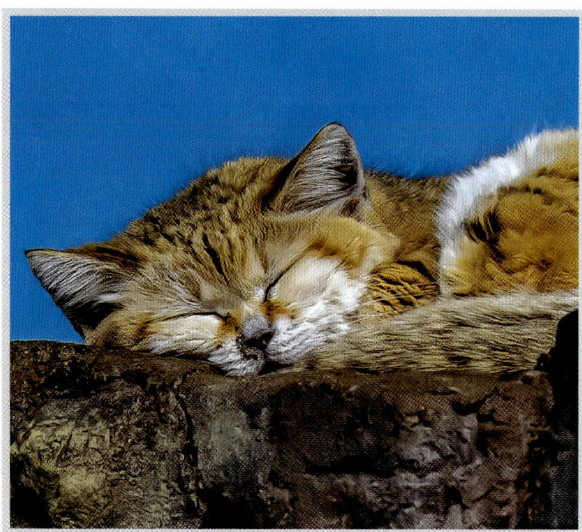

Source photograph

As soon as I saw this photograph, I felt compelled to paint it, as the cat is in a similar pose to one of my favourite paintings, *A Sleeping Lion*, which you can see on page 143.

You will need

Bockingford Rough surface watercolour paper 35.5 x 25.5cm (14 x 10in)

Large, medium and small brushes

HB pencil and putty eraser

WATERCOLOUR PAINTS:
Burnt sienna, yellow ochre, French ultramarine

INKS:
Daler-Rowney FW acrylic inks: white and purple lake; Parker Quink ink

Beeswax candle

Watersoluble black fineliner pen (Staedtler Triplus fineliner)

Permanent black Pigma Micron archival fineliner pen

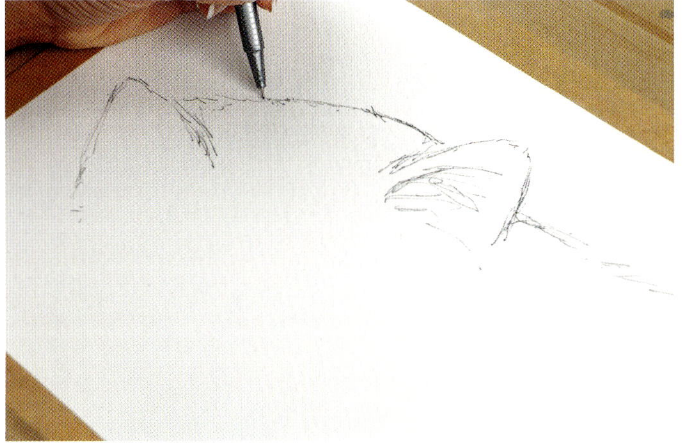

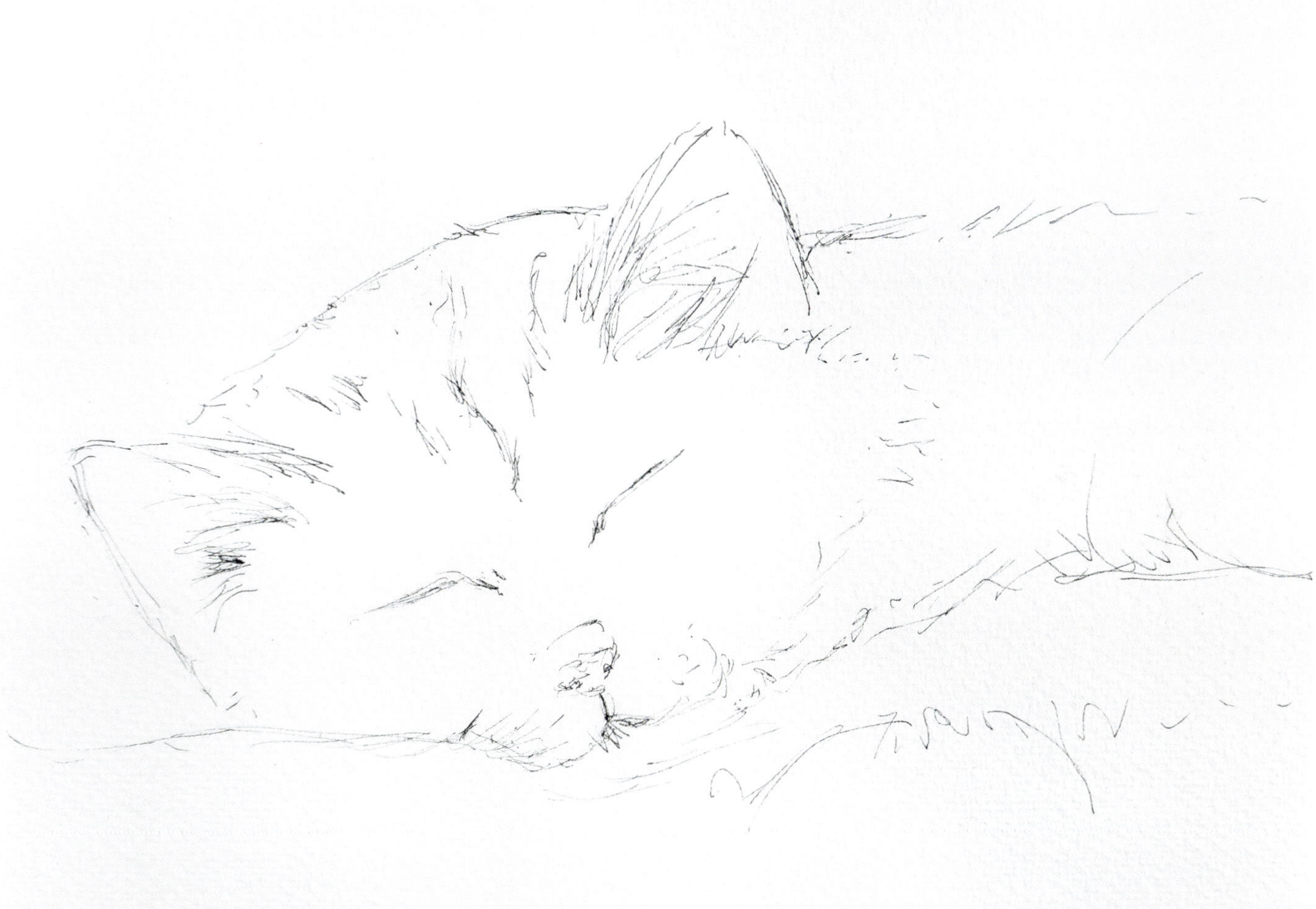

The sketch

Draw your sketch with the watersoluble fineliner. Work nice and loosely, just adding in the key marks. Concentrate on filling the space, and emphasize areas by working into the surface repeatedly where you want deeper tone, and lifting off for more subtle or lighter-toned areas.

Painting the cat

Even though the sketch is simple, we need to soften it down in order to evoke the soft, dreamy atmosphere we want. There's a new technique we'll learn here: washing-off. It's great for knocking back tone and line.

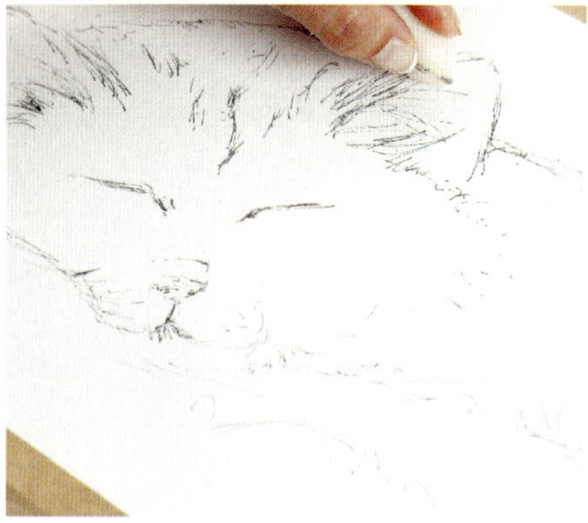

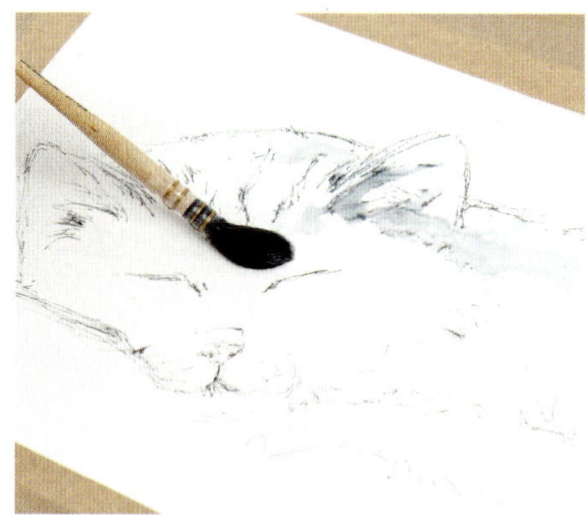

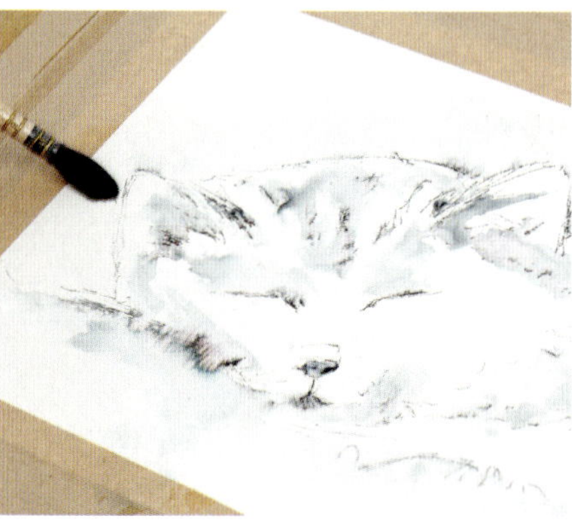

1 Add a little wax near the eye and at the top of the ears and head, plus a few little marks that follow the line of the fur – these will echo the stripes on the source photograph.

2 Load the large brush with clean water and lightly trail it across the lines of the cat here and there, to allow the lines to bleed out. Draw the brush to create areas of shadow, allowing the ink to bleed into it. Avoid obscuring the features.

3 Using a clean wet brush, pull the line of the fur on the cat's back up into the background. Work outwards from the fur to create a wet area all around the cat.

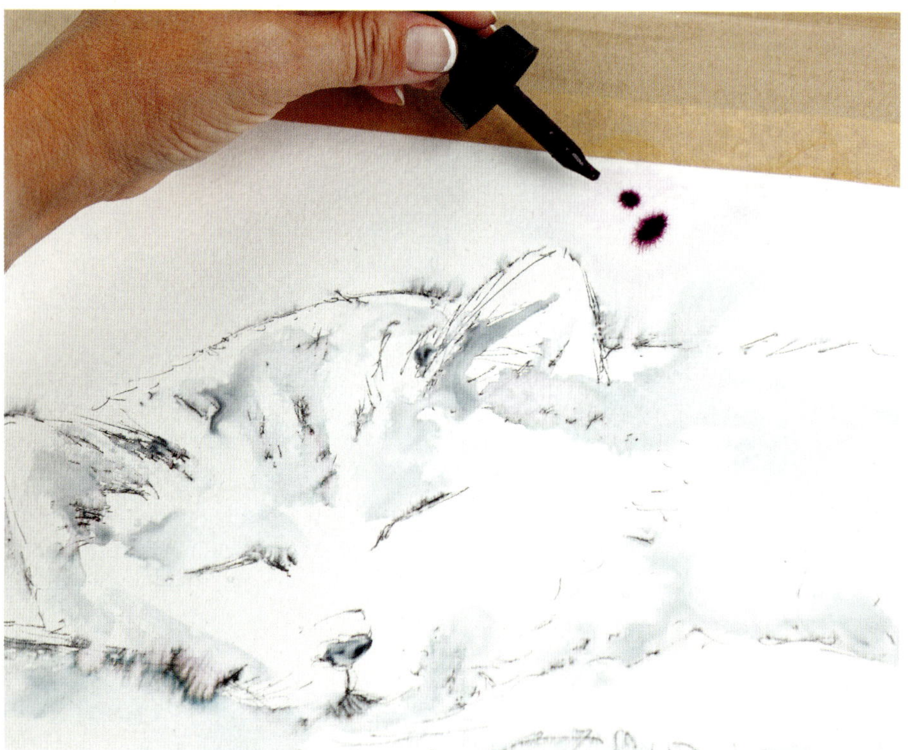

4 Using the dropper on the bottle, start to drop in touches of purple lake acrylic ink.

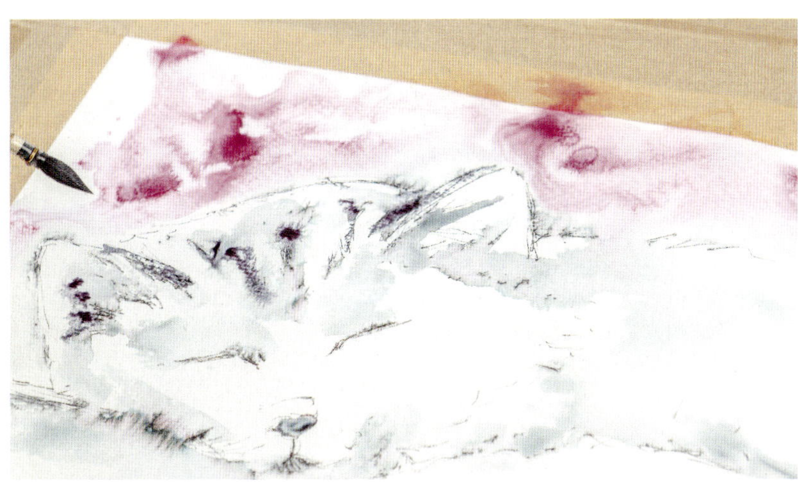

5 Move the purple ink around a little to create some shapes and curves in the background.

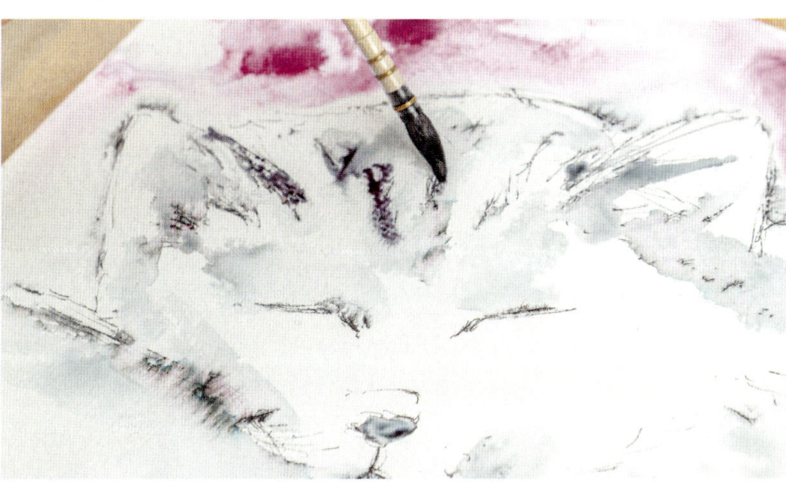

6 Change to the medium brush and add Quink ink wet in wet in the darker areas of the cat and blanket, touching it in lightly to encourage it to diffuse into the wet surroundings.

7 Tilt the board upright and pour a jug of clean water over to encourage the ink to flow. You can run the board under a tap, if you prefer. The important thing is to get plenty of clean, flowing water in a single direction, to carry the water down and off the surface. Hold the board upright until it stops dripping.

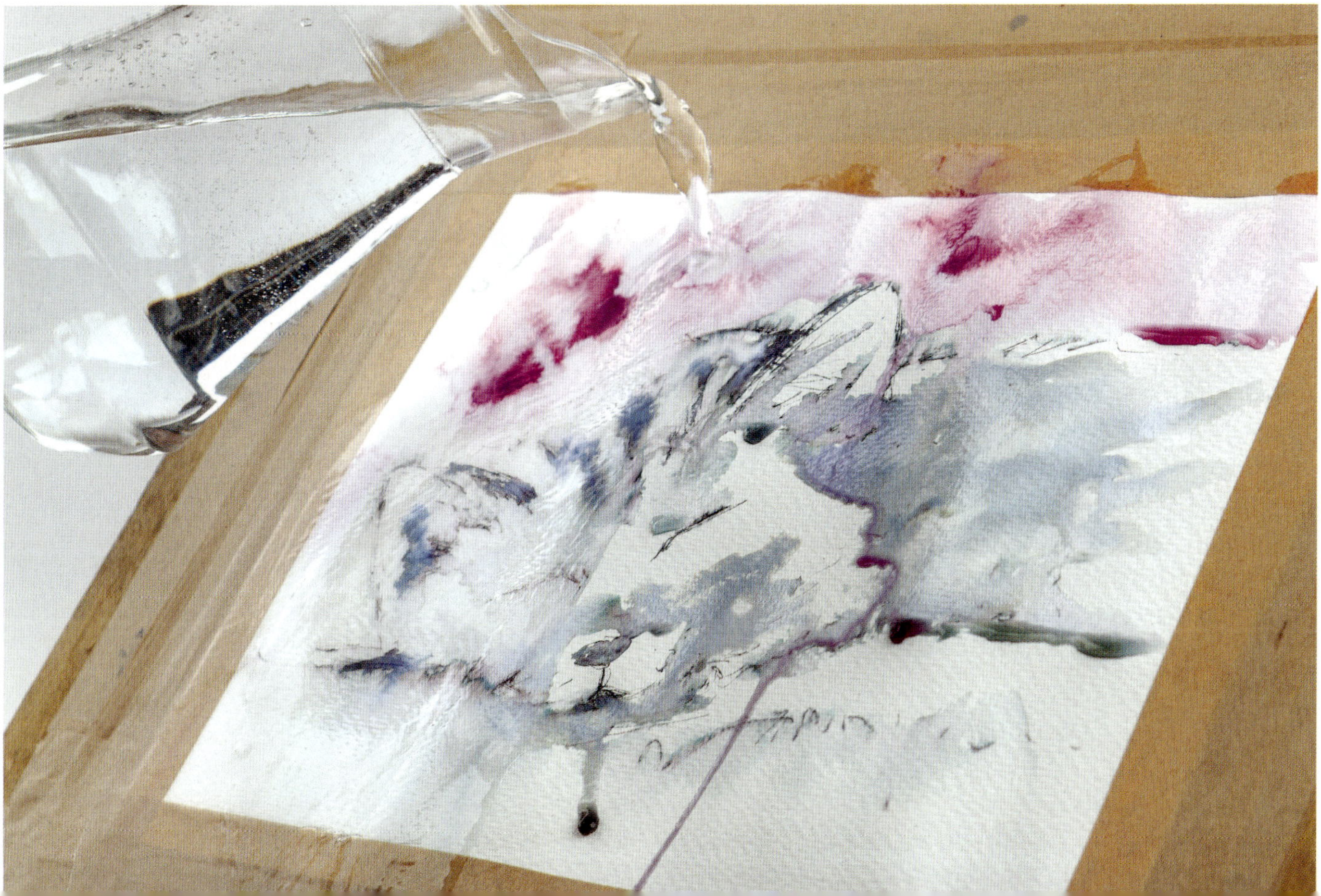

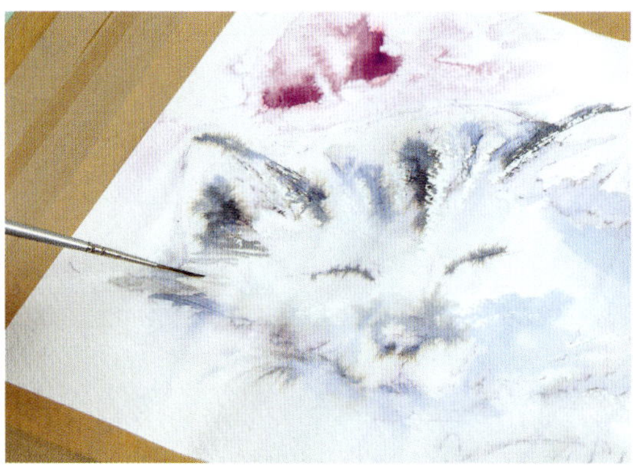 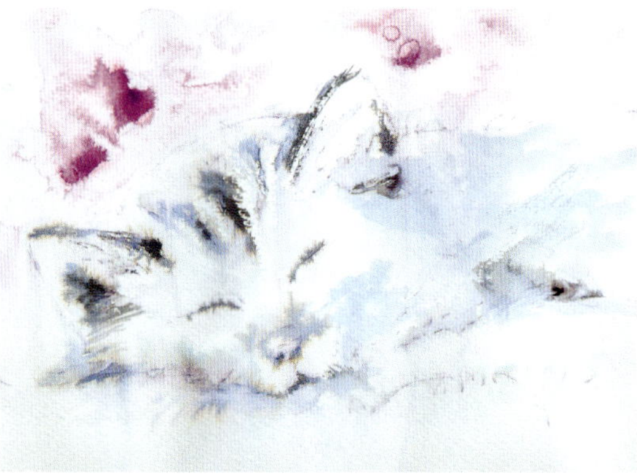

8 While the surface remains wet, use the small brush to begin re-establishing the darker lines and areas of shadow wet in wet, using Quink ink.

9 Continue developing the shadows and features. As the surface starts to dry a little, you can add some texture on the right-hand side with the side of the brush, picking up the texture of the paper.

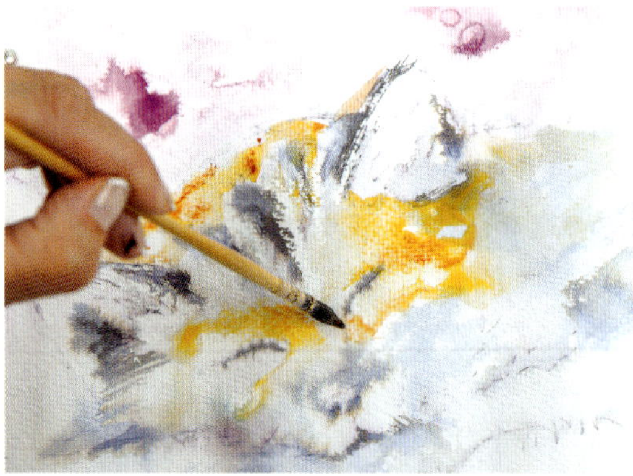 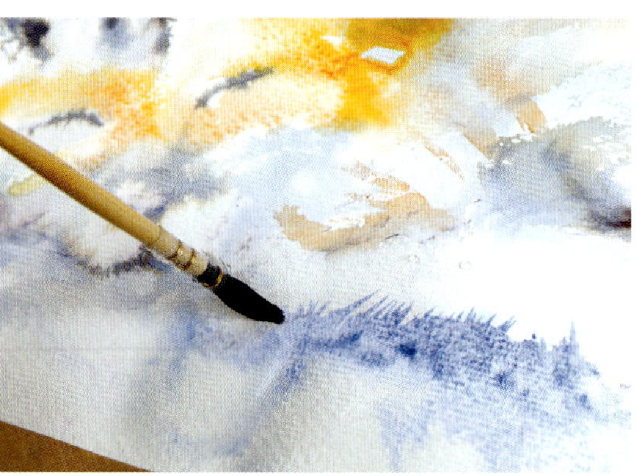

10 Start touching in some burnt sienna and yellow ochre wet in wet using the medium brush. Re-wet areas that you want to become ginger with clean water, then add the colours. Avoid areas that you want to be white – just avoid them when applying the clean water, and the paint won't flow into them.

11 Add French ultramarine below the tail in the same way. We're painting this area in shadowy blue to avoid drawing the eye too much from the cat's face. Pull the paint upwards to suggest longer white hairs.

12 Add some wet in wet spatters of French ultramarine around the foreground. Don't be too energetic with the spattering here – we want a soft, peaceful feel.

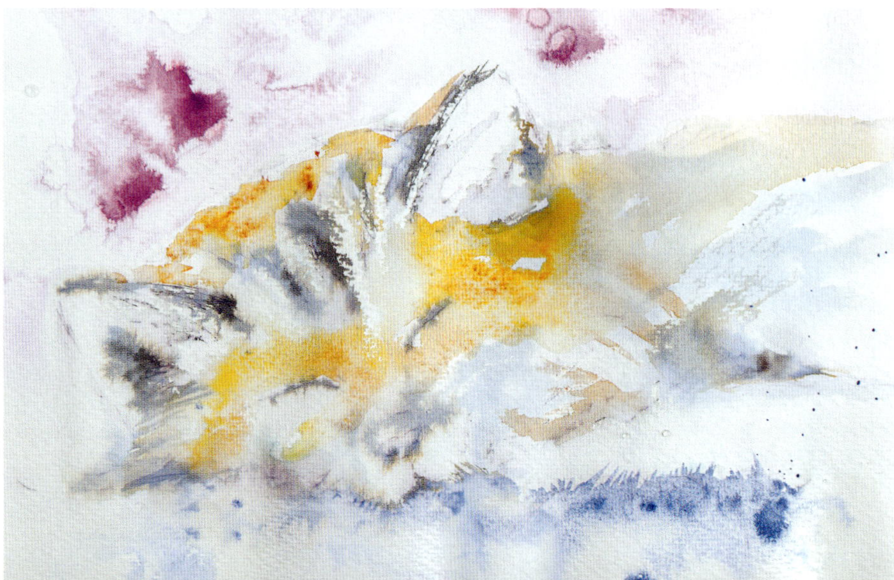

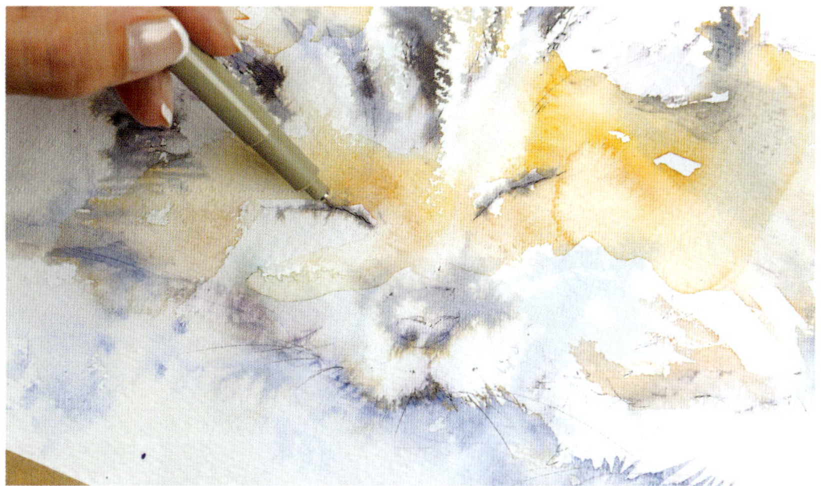

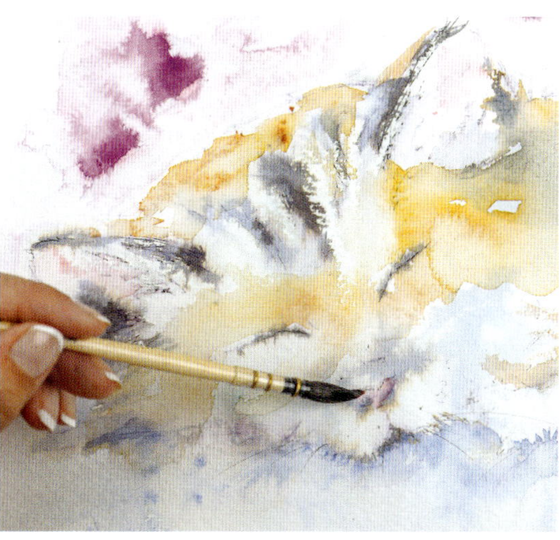

13 Make sure the painting is absolutely dry, then use the permanent fineliner to pick out and develop the features, adding longer fine lines on the ears, a few whiskers, and some subtle touches to the nose and eyes. Be careful to avoid any areas of wax.

14 Using the medium brush, add dilute rose madder to the nose and insides of the ears.

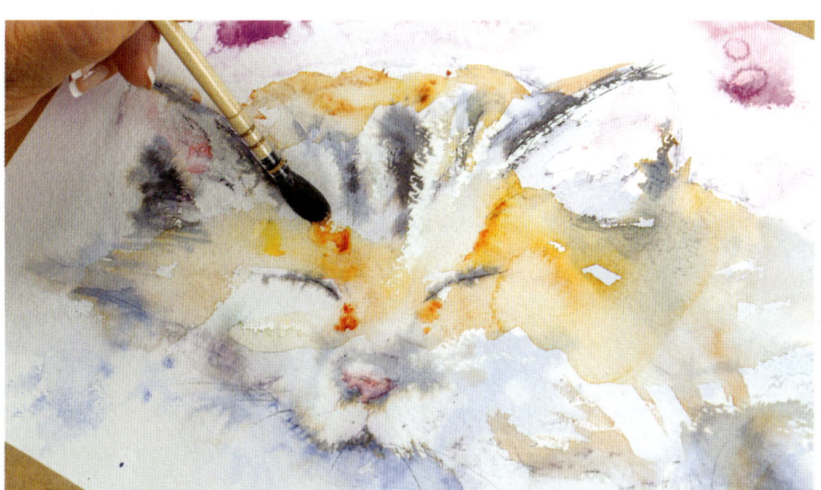

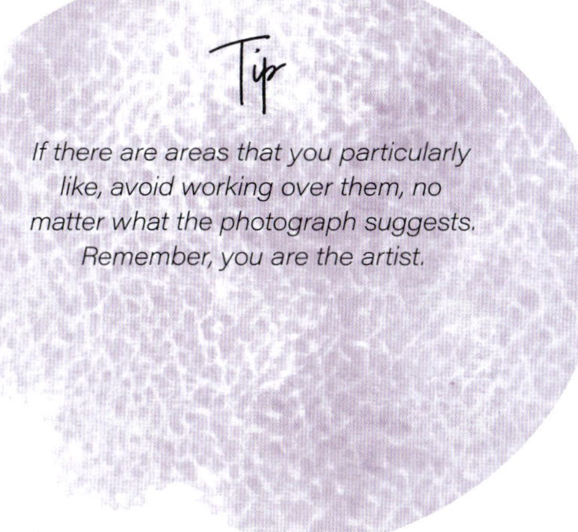

Tip

If there are areas that you particularly like, avoid working over them, no matter what the photograph suggests. Remember, you are the artist.

15 Using a combination of wet on dry glazes and wet in wet additions, develop the darker ginger areas on the cat's fur with stronger mixes of yellow ochre and burnt sienna.

16 Glaze the cat's body on the right with French ultramarine to help knock it back a little.

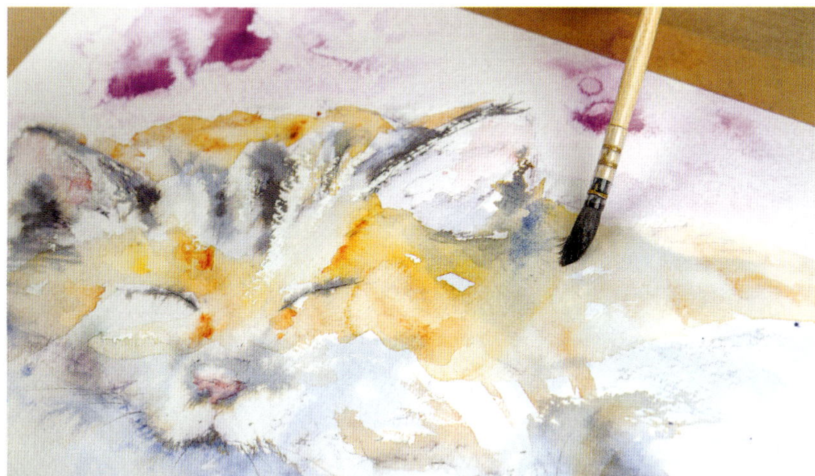

Personal touches

From here, you can develop the details as much, or as little, as you like. Adding more detail at this stage can tighten things up – so if you think you're happy with it, walk away and come back with a fresh eye before doing anything else. After all, it's easier to add later than it is to remove something added too early.

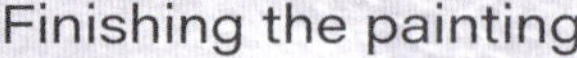

Finishing the painting

For final tweaks, I decided to develop the lower left-hand corner with additional darks and purple lake additions.

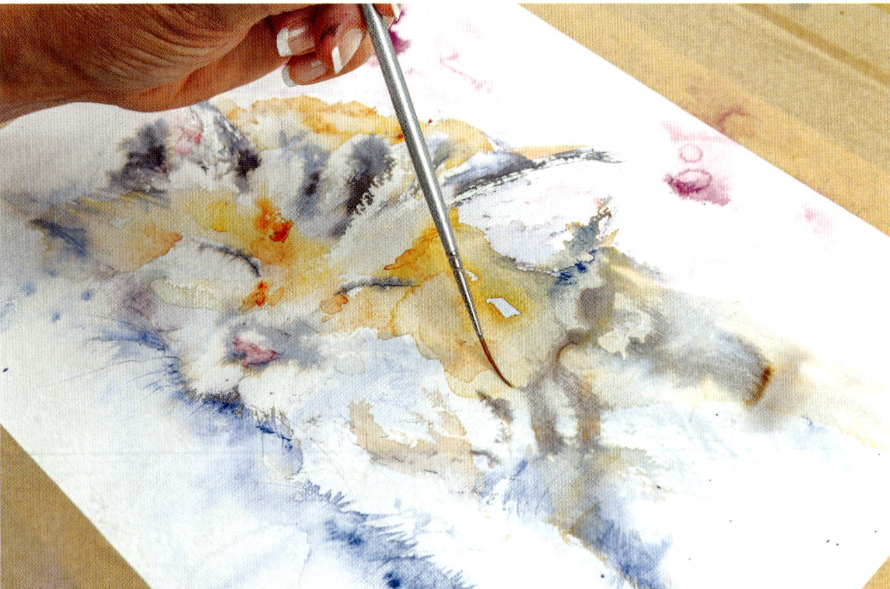

Increasing the contrast

Once dry, add clean water over the same area where you want the darker stripes. Add diluted Quink ink wet in wet with the medium brush, then swap to the small brush to draw it out and help to suggest the texture of the fur.

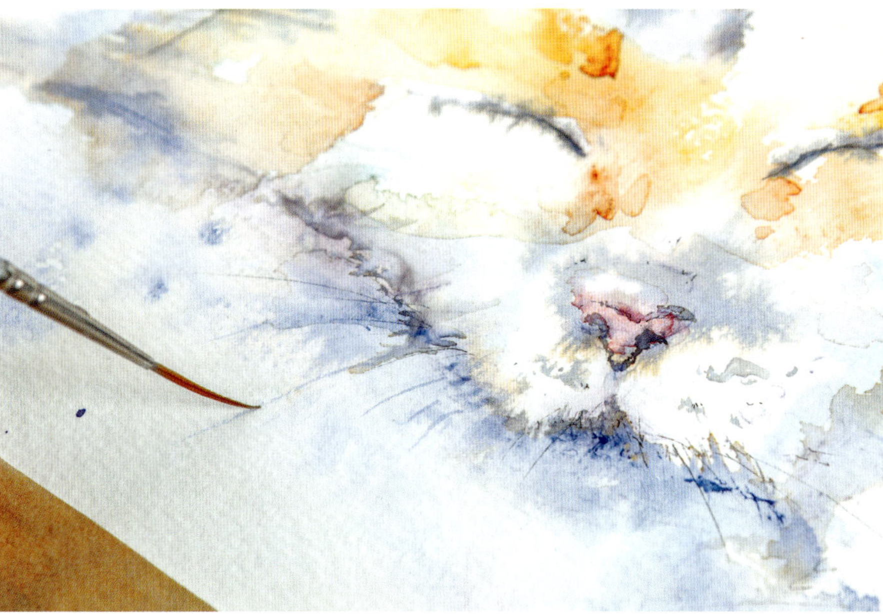

Subtle refinements

Build up the tone in the features and dark areas with more Quink ink, swapping between the medium and small brush for larger or finer marks.

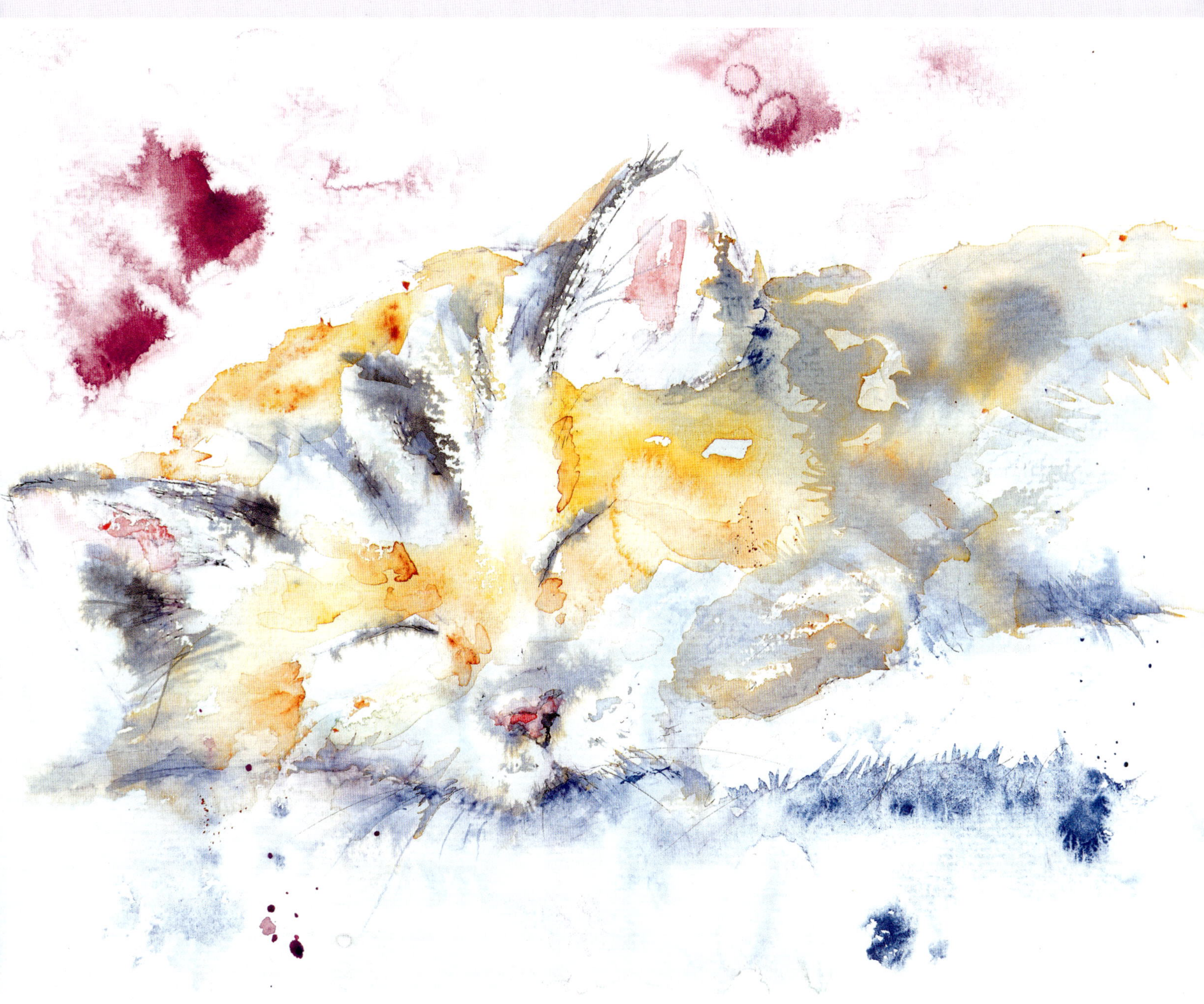

Sand Cat

35.5 x 25.5cm (14 x 10in)

Rescuing an overworked painting

Even with the best of intentions, it's easy sometimes to get caught up in things and layer too much colour on your painting. Perhaps the colours have become muddied and overworked, or you've simply gone into too much detail and ended up with a tight painting.

Don't worry. We can use the washing-out technique, explained on pages 95–96, from the sand cat project to soften lines and lift off some colour, leaving a lighter, fresher result that can either be left as-is, or worked back into.

This technique will work more obviously with some colours than others. Staining colours, like burnt sienna, will lift less than non-staining colours like French ultramarine. Likewise, permanent or dry acrylic inks will be almost unaffected, while water-soluble inks will be considerably lightened and softened.

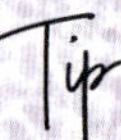

Tip

Note that light areas created by leaving white paper will be stained slightly by the washed-out colour. The only areas that will remain truly white are those that were reserved with wax at the start of the painting.

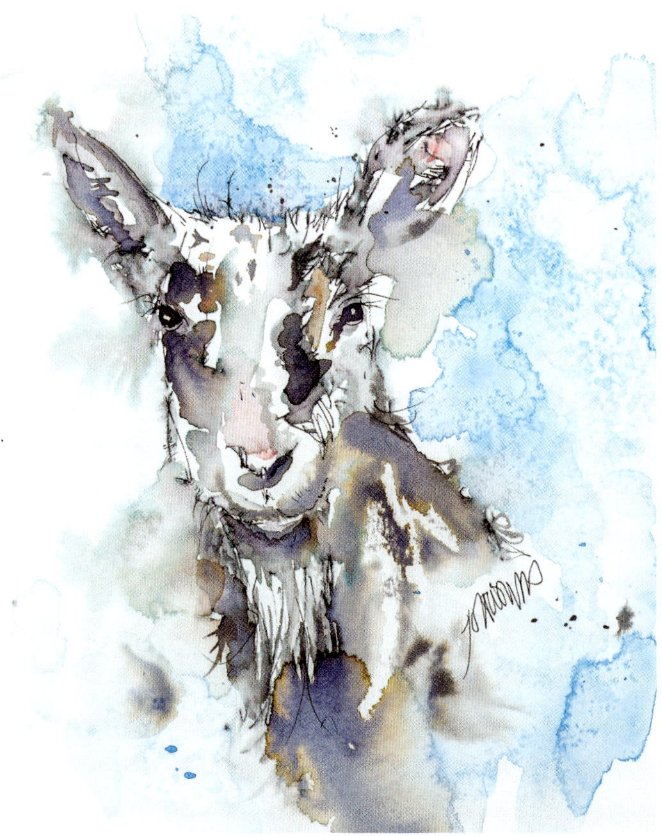

Before

I was quite pleased with this painting, *Billy*, but felt that I wanted to lighten the tone of the inks and give an overall softer appearance.

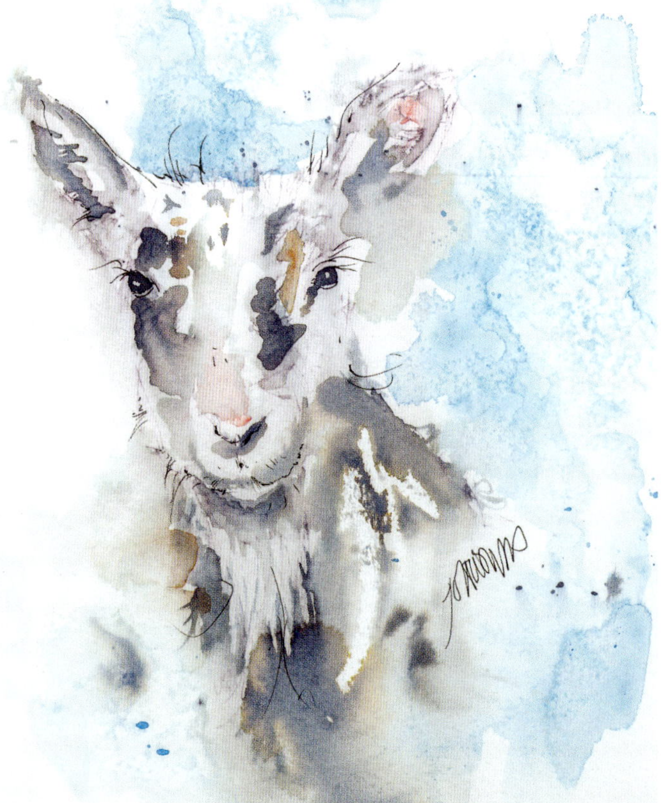

After

The painting was held under a cold running tap for a minute or two, then secured to a board with gummed tape before being left to dry.

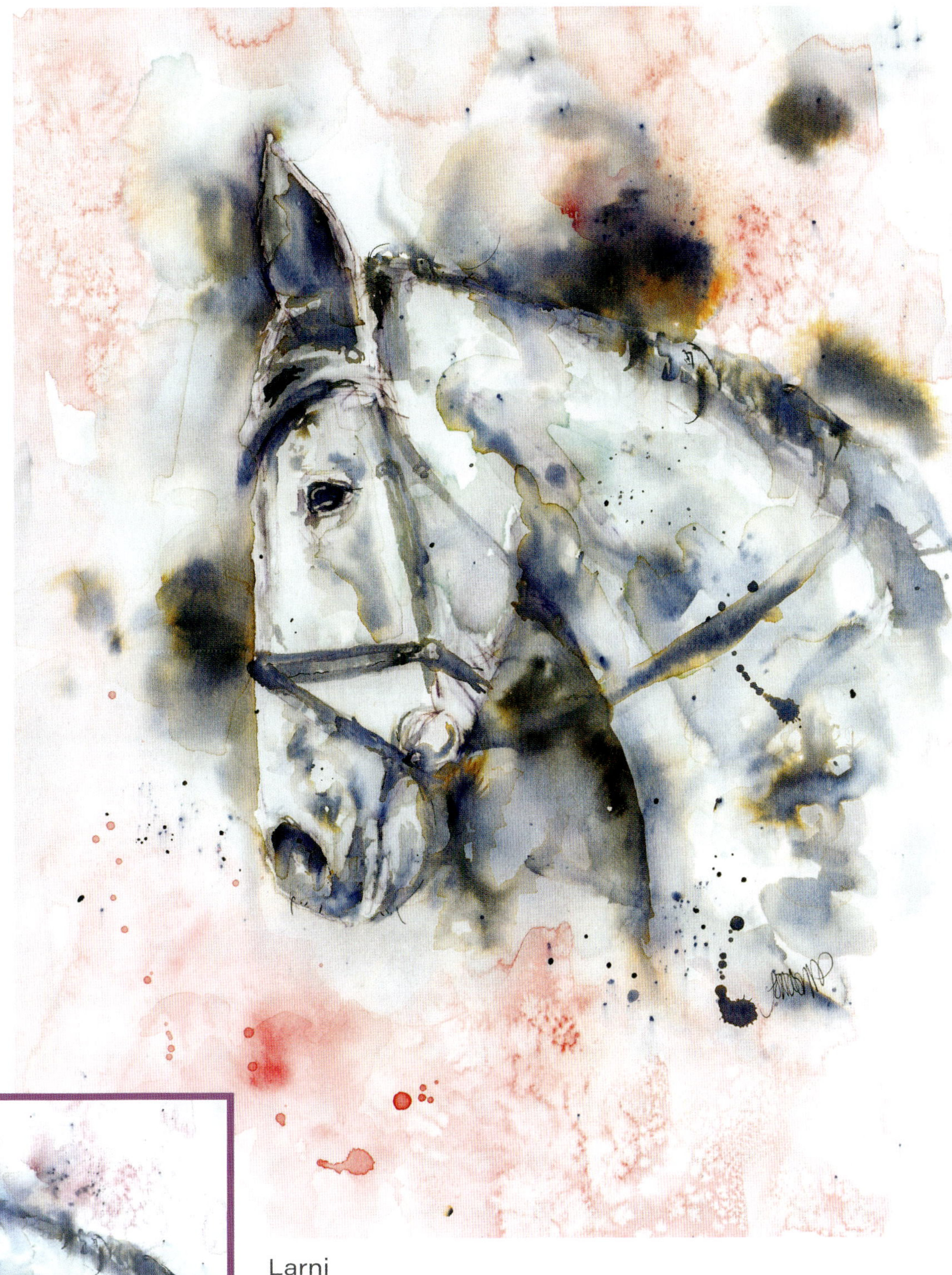

Larni

21 x 28.5cm (8¼ x 11¼in)

Sometimes, rescuing a painting means nothing more than continuing to work on it. Here, I finished this painting, but some days later decided he was too light in tone (left). I went back into the painting and applied more layers of glazing to build up the tone and impact.

Clouding

This is a technique I quite often use to lighten a darker/ muddy part of my painting. I call it 'clouding', both because the shapes formed remind me of clouds and because the paint also goes cloudy and less transparent. The technique involves wetting an area and dropping in neat white acrylic ink either from my brush or straight from the pipette. As it hits the colour, it pushes the wet pigment away and creates a light cloud-type shape.

This technique is useful to remedy an overworked piece, but I sometimes use it simply to create some interesting shapes and patterns to liven things up a little. The technique works best on dark areas.

You can also add watercolour to the white acrylic on a receptacle to tint the ink a particular colour – a technique we examine opposite.

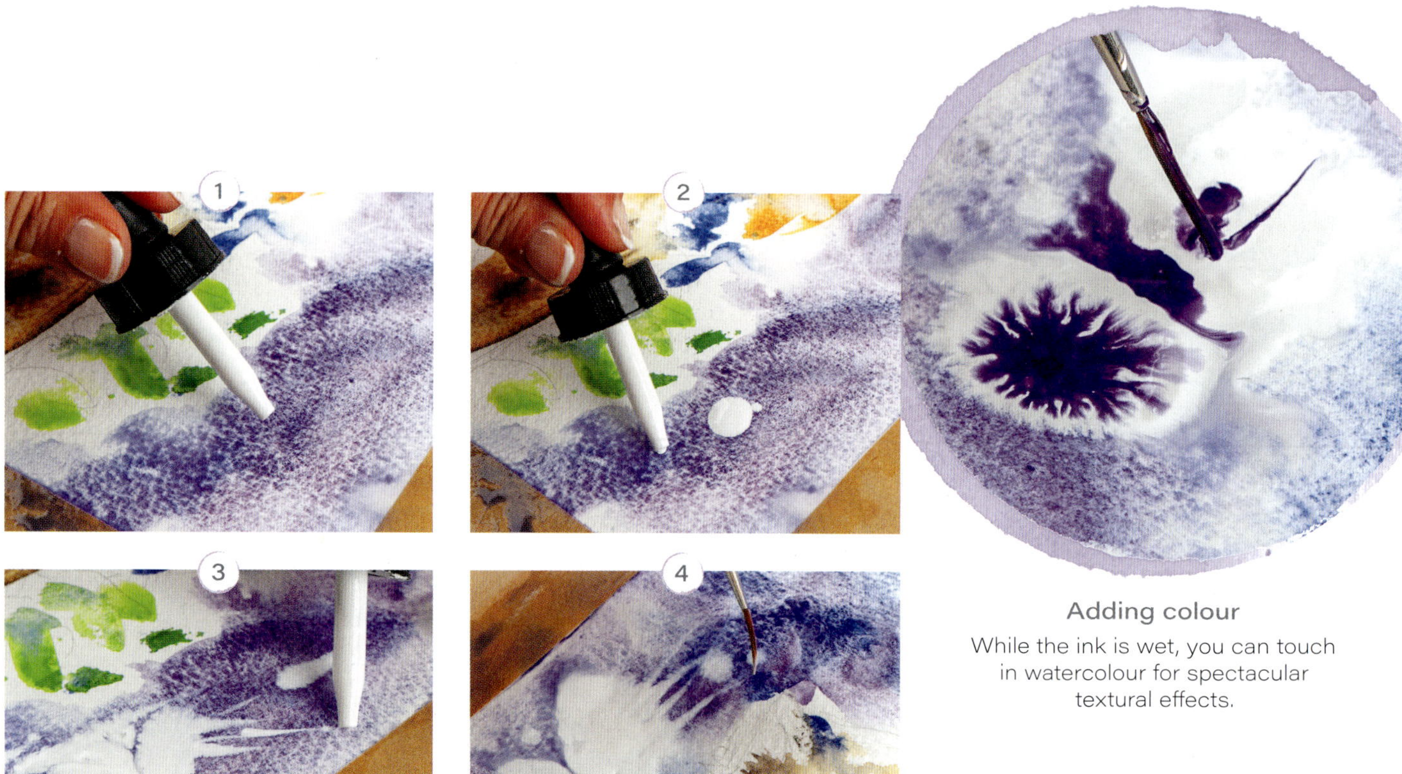

Adding colour
While the ink is wet, you can touch in watercolour for spectacular textural effects.

1 Working into wet paint, position your white ink dropper over the area to which you want to add the clouding.

2 Add the ink in small amounts. You can either squeeze the dropper to release individual drops, or simply touch the dropper to the wet surface.

3 You can create lines by drawing the dropper through the wet ink drops.

4 Alternatively you can draw a small brush through to create lines.

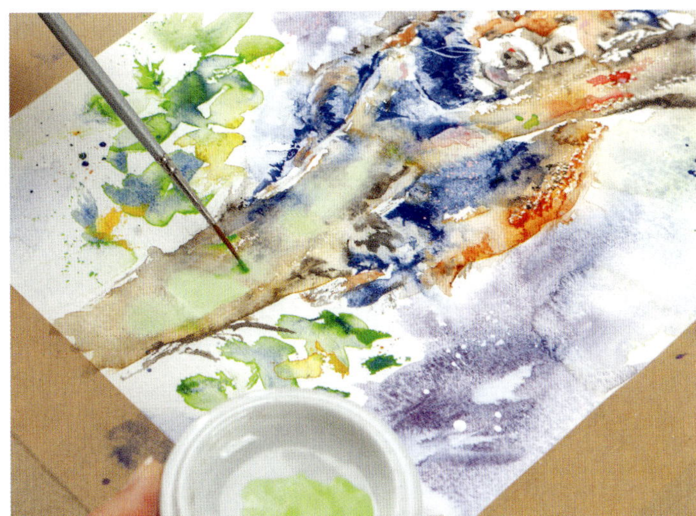

Clouding near the end

If you decide you want to knock an area back later, perhaps near the end of a painting, clouding is useful here, too. Allow the painting to dry completely, then re-wet an area (in this case the branch) with clean water. You can then add ink as before. Here, I've tinted the ink with a little green watercolour in a separate small palette well – give different colours a try!

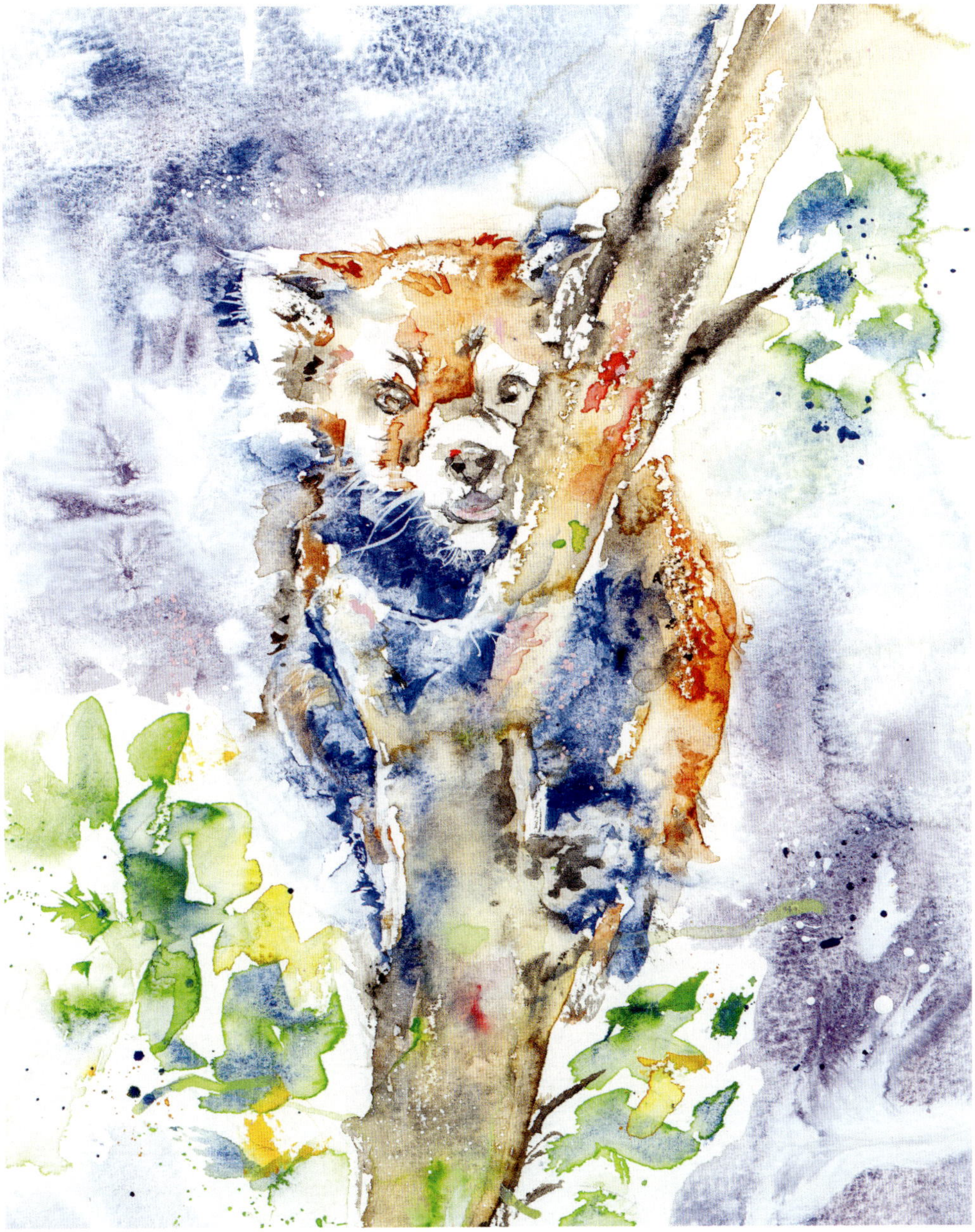

Red Panda
20.5 x 29.5cm (8 x 11½in)

Peacock

I was attracted to the confident look of this peacock: upright and proud – and why wouldn't you be, with a crest like that? To draw more attention to the crest, we'll include a hint of red to further show it off. We'll also use the spattering technique behind his head, to give the impression he is tossing his head back as he parades off.

Acrylic inks are my medium of choice here: they're perfectly suited to the vibrant colours of the peacock's plumage. I've also used calligraphy inks and Quink for further variety.

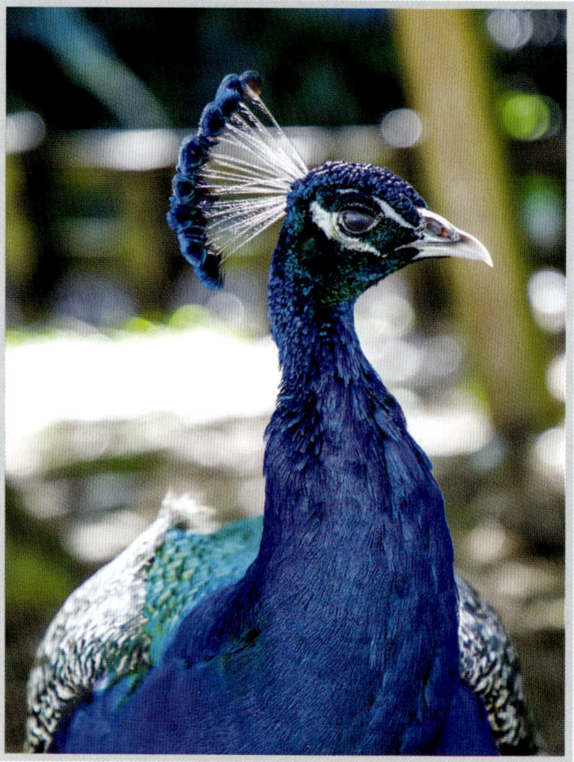

Source photograph
This bird looks as though he has attitude. I loved him for this, he looks a real character.

You will need

Bockingford CP Not surface watercolour paper 35.5 x 25.5cm (14 x 10in)

Large, medium and small brushes

Watersoluble black fineliner pen (Staedtler Triplus fineliner)

Permanent black Pigma Micron archival fineliner pen

INKS:
Winsor & Newton calligraphy ink: emerald; Parker Quink ink; Daler-Rowney FW acrylic inks: marine blue, white

WATERCOLOUR PAINTS:
Helio cerulean, rose madder, burnt sienna

Beeswax candle

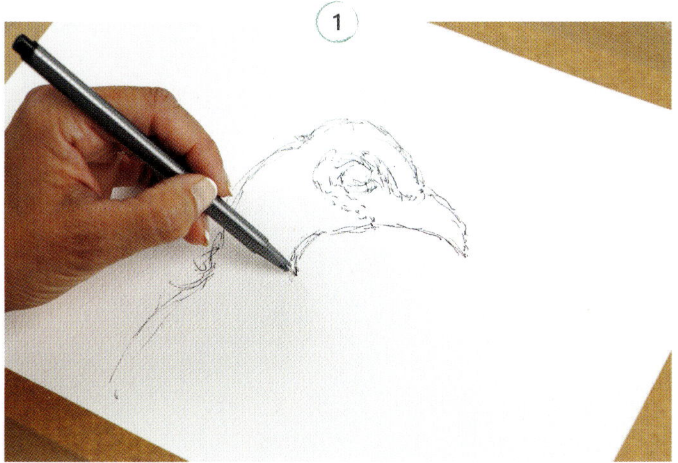

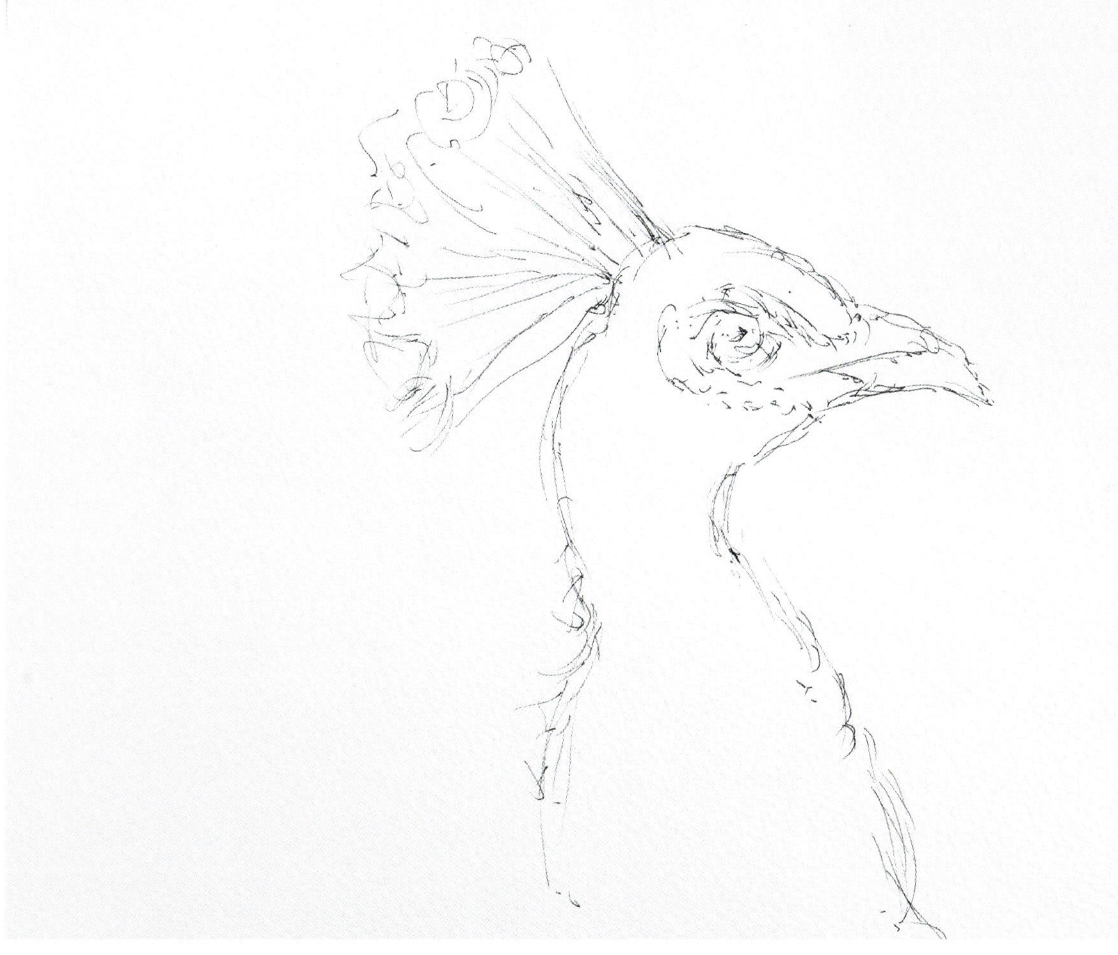

The sketch

Use the watersoluble fineliner pen to sketch out the basic shapes.

1 Sketch exactly as you would with a pencil, looking for shapes and comparing proportions against a particular feature. Here, the beak is slightly shorter than the width of the head, and the crest feathers are approximately the same width as the head. Because you can't erase the lines, it's important not to overwork things.

Inky investigations

Inks are fun to use, but a couple of things need to be borne in mind. Firstly, inks are very true to colour – unlike watercolours, they won't get lighter as they dry, so you need to apply the colour at the strength you want it.

Secondly, ink pigments are stronger than watercolour, so will push it out of the way or overwhelm it. That's why you need to avoid the watercolours interacting too much with the inks at this stage.

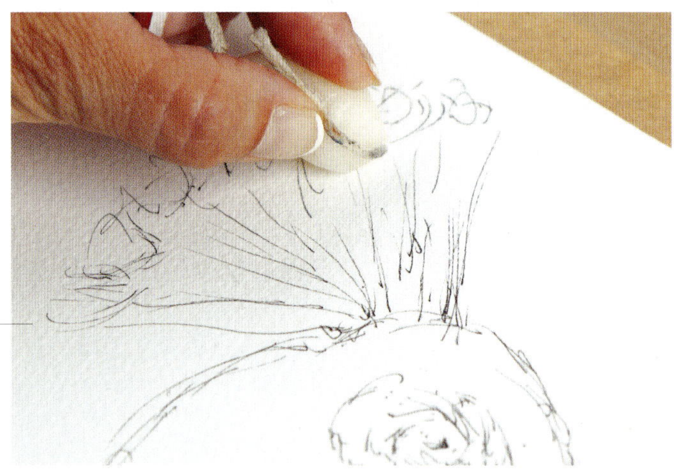

2 The top of the head naturally catches the light, as does the curve of the body, so add a little wax to these areas. Inks interact with wax in much the same way as watercolour – that is, it will resist the ink unless you apply the ink really thickly.

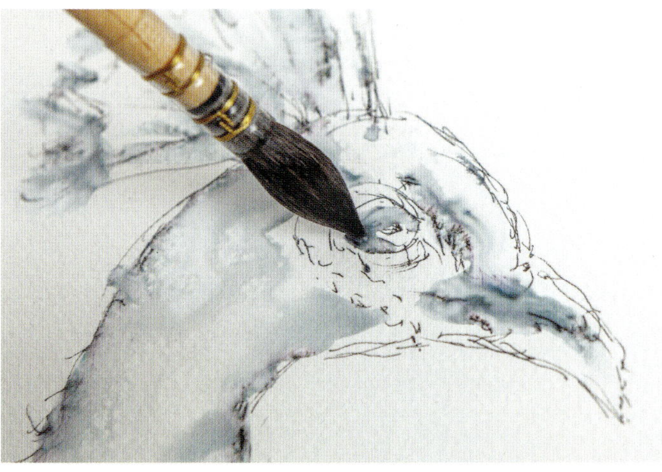

3 Wet the large brush and use it to gently disturb the ink sketch, drawing the brush around within the outline. The ink in this pen breaks up into beautiful greens and purples.

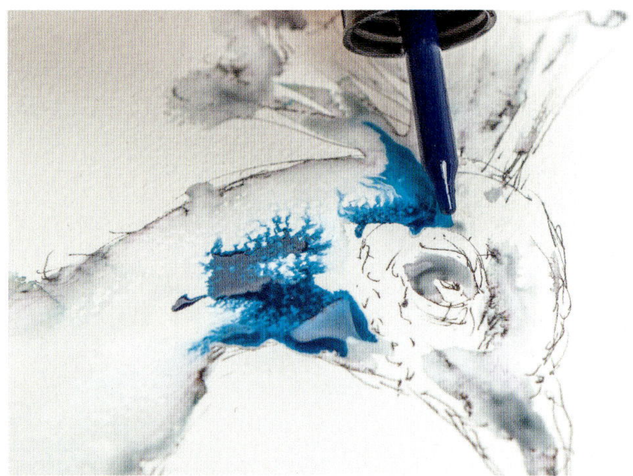

4 Use the dropper to apply marine blue acrylic ink to the peacock, aiming for the dark areas.

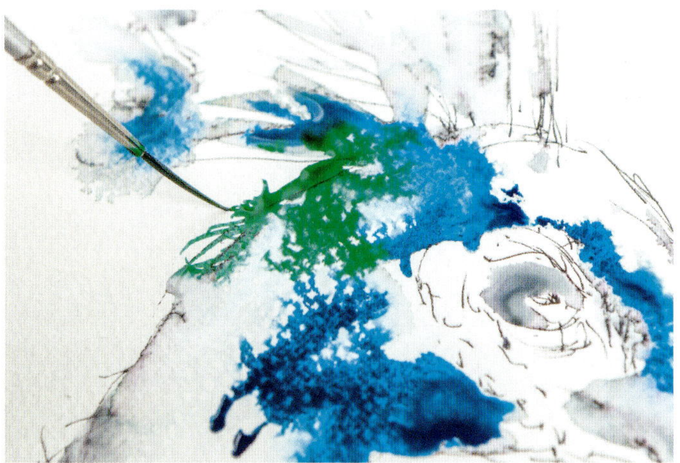

5 Swap to the small brush and use it to apply emerald calligraphy ink to the peacock. You don't need to follow the photograph exactly; apply it where you think looks best.

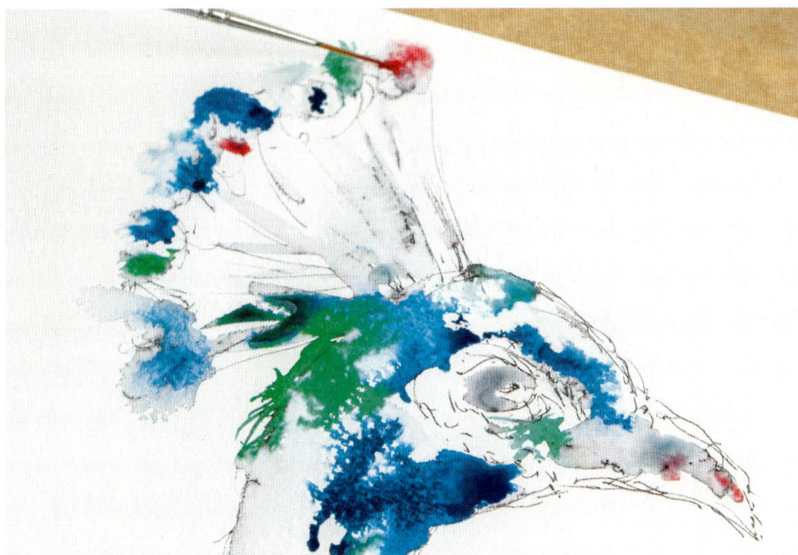

6 Avoiding the wet ink, use the small brush to apply helio cerulean and rose madder here and there across the painting. The small brush gives you control.

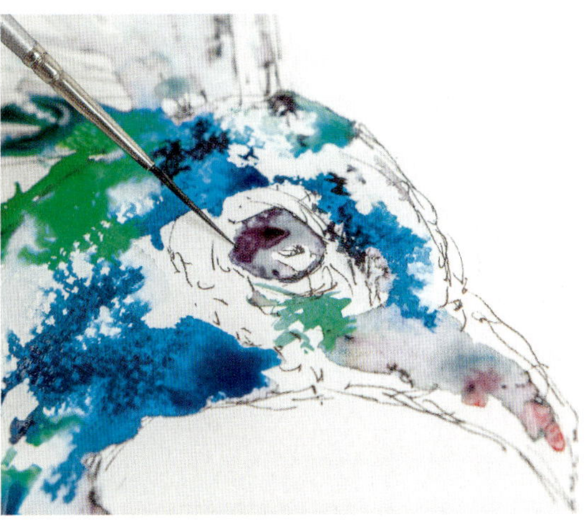

7 Apply the Quink ink wet in wet to areas you want darker, such as the eye. Use the small brush to allow you to put it only where you want it; and be sparing.

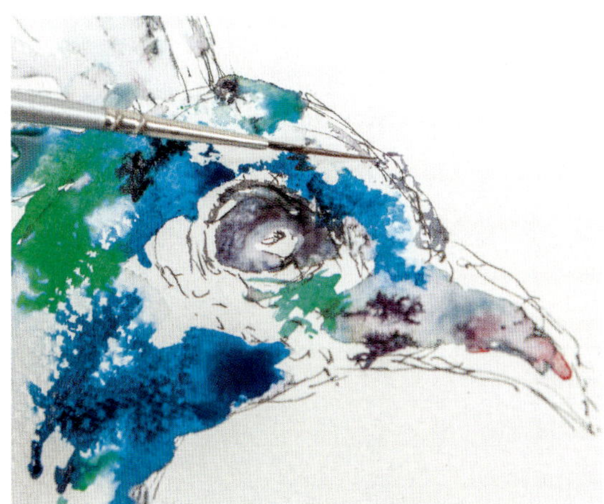

8 Dilute the Quink with water and use the fainter grey result to suggest a few outlined small feathers on the head.

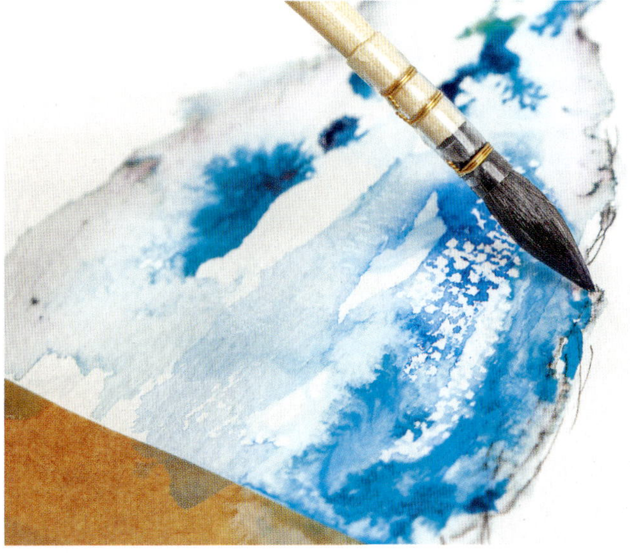

9 We've established the big bold marks and colours, so now we need to be a bit more subtle to refine them. Using the medium brush, add clean water to the body and add a little marine blue acrylic ink wet in wet.

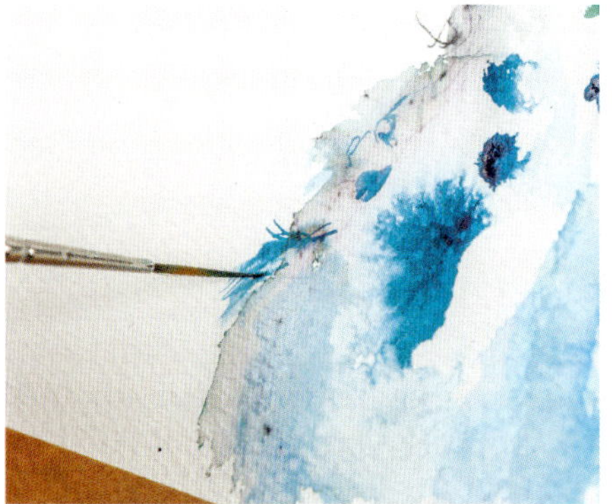

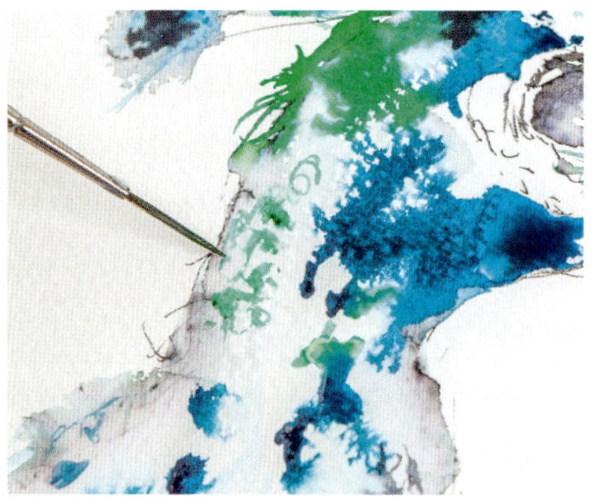

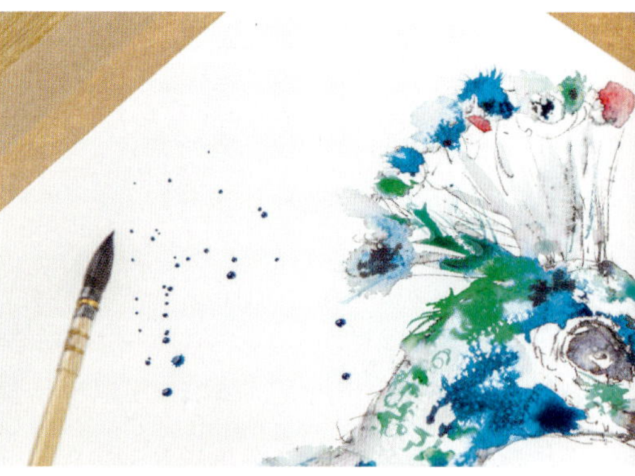

10 Swap to the small brush to feather out some fine lines of marine blue on the peacock's back.

11 Use curling, twisting marks with the tip of the small brush to add some emerald green calligraphy ink to the neck, suggesting the small feathers here.

12 Make some big spatters with the medium brush and marine blue acrylic ink. Pick it up with a damp medium brush, and use your wrist to flick the brush: you'll end up with larger, more uncontrolled spatters than tapping the brush.

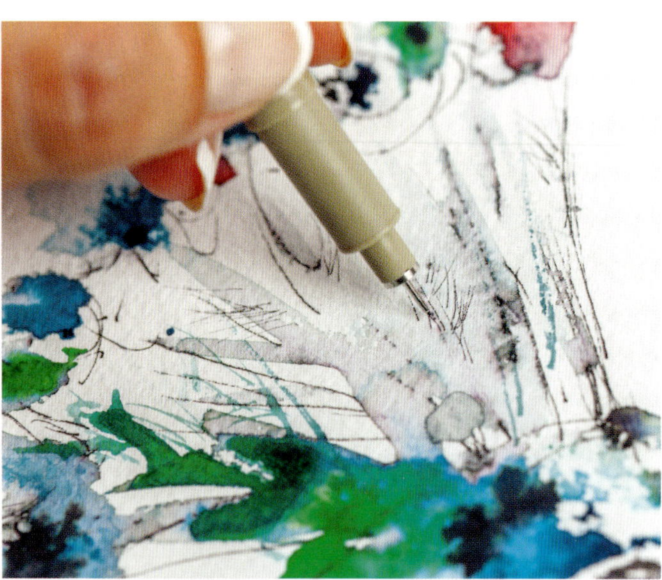

13 Allow the ink and paint to dry completely. Use the permanent fineliner pen to add detail to the crest. Use light, flicking strokes that lift off at the end to give a natural variety of thickness; and work with hatching and cross hatching to create the delicate lattice of the feathers.

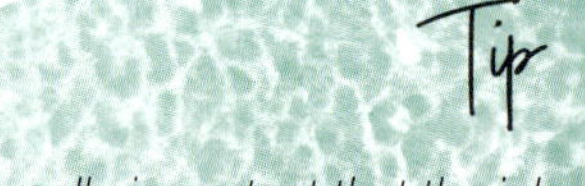

Tip

It's really important that the ink and paint are dry when using this very fine pen; likewise don't work over any wax or salt, or you'll damage the nib.

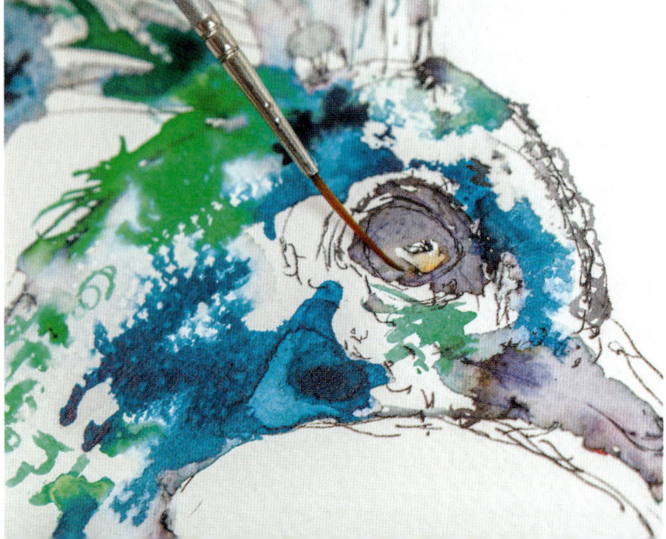

14 Develop the shapes in the eye with the same fineliner pen, then use the small brush to add burnt sienna to the eye. You don't need to worry about reserving highlights when working with mixed media, as we can work over the colour with white ink.

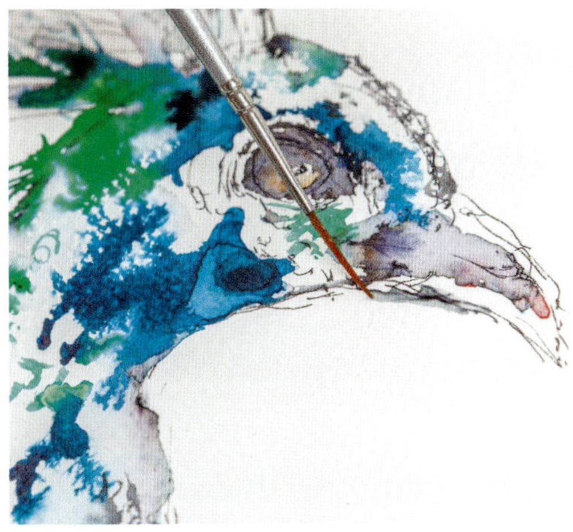

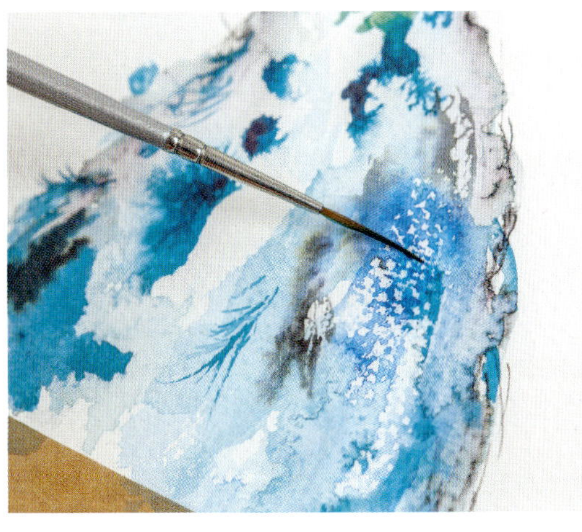

15 Rinse the brush and use the damp tip to gently agitate the ink lines on the lower beak. As these lines are made with watersoluble ink, you can reactivate them and create a soft grey shadow at the bottom of the beak.

16 Still using marine blue acrylic ink, add some additional textural marks wet on dry. Add overlapping fine lines to suggest feathers on the body.

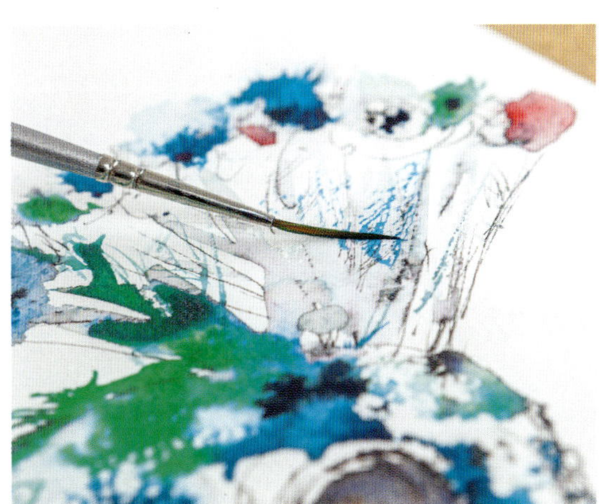

17 Gently drag the side of the small brush, loaded with dilute emerald green calligraphy ink, here and there across the feathers of the crest.

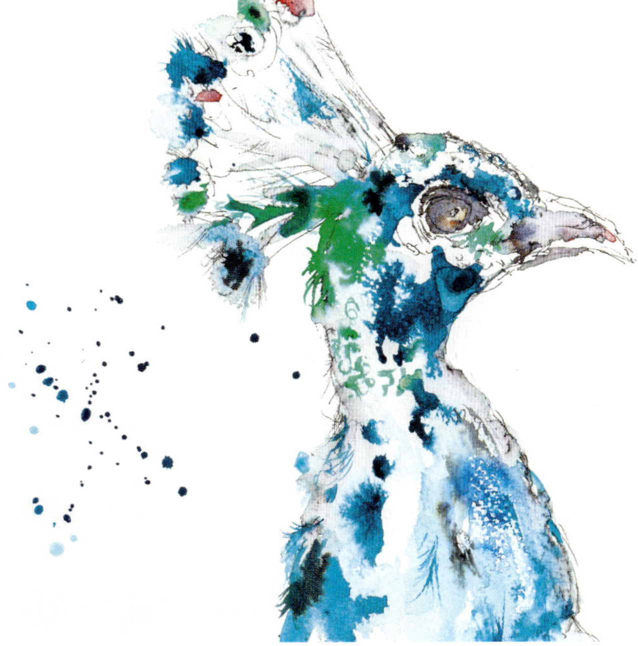

18 Dilute a little marine blue and add some finer, more controlled spattering over the dry area of spattered marks.

Making the painting yours

White ink is very fluid and allows you to apply clean, natural-looking lines – exactly those that are really hard to get with masking fluid or negative painting. The quality of white you get is also different from that created by the surface of the paper, so it gives you some additional variety. It's ideal for the finishing touches.

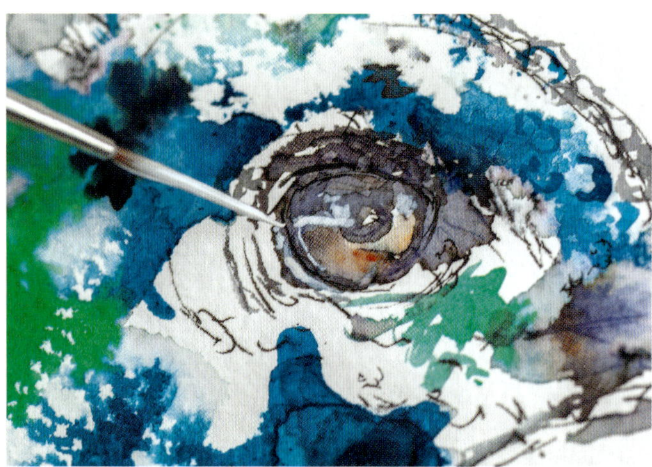

Glint in the eye

Use the tip of the small brush to apply very fine marks around the eye with Quink ink, then draw a small circle for the pupil itself, leaving a tiny white highlight in the centre. Using the tip of the brush and white acrylic ink, carefully draw the fine highlights in the eye.

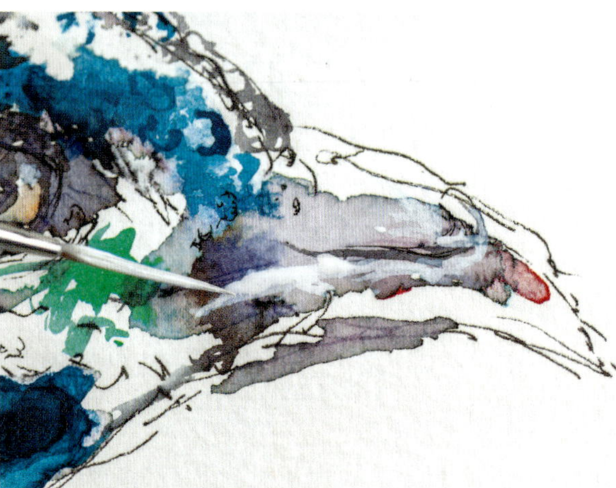

Beak

With very close reference to the photograph, develop the beak with Quink and the small brush.

Finishing the painting

Add the markings around the eye and add a few flicks in the crest as shown.

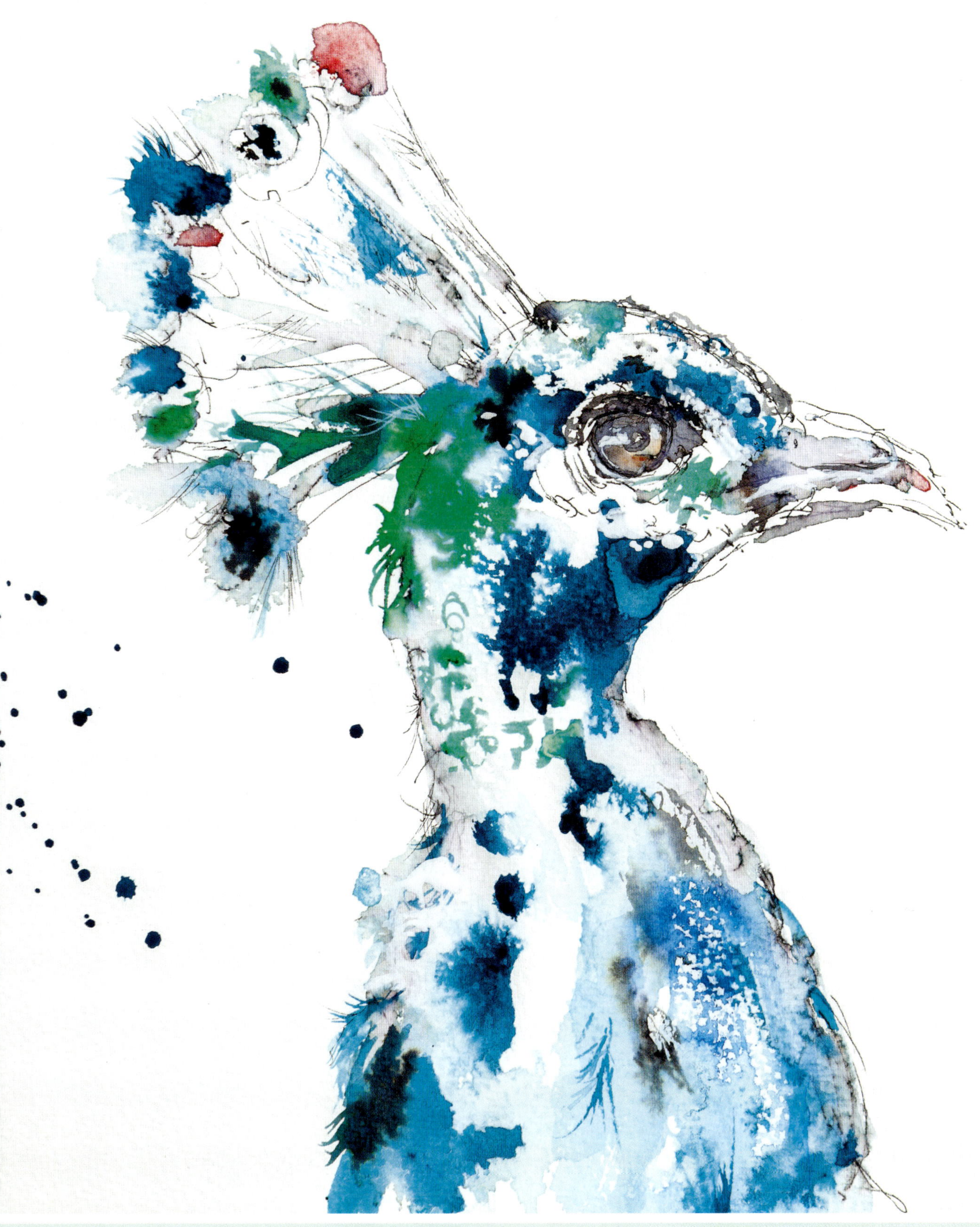

Cocky
35.5 x 25.5cm (14 x 10in)

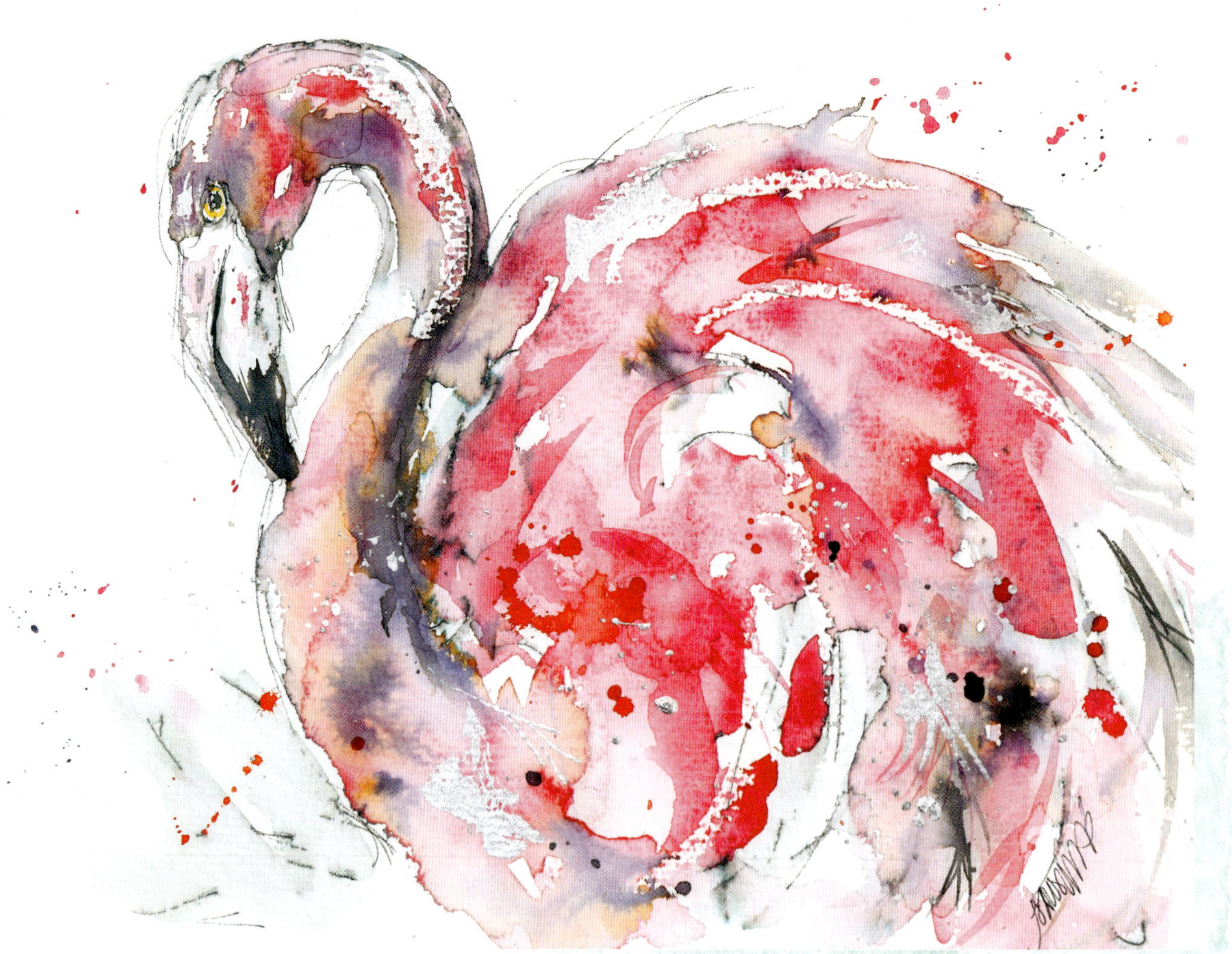

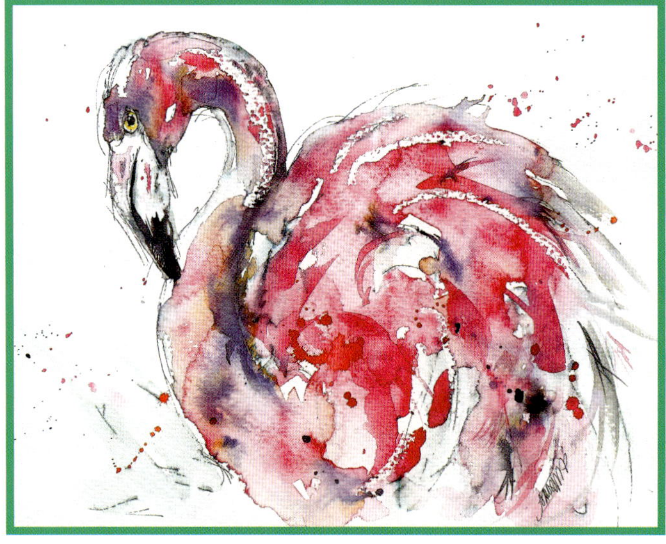

Pretty Flamingo

33 x 23cm (13 x 9in)

I had completed this flamingo and decided he was finished (see left). I didn't feel he needed a background as he stands alone extremely well, but later I decided he needed even more bling, so I applied some silver bronzing powder here and there over his body.

I used a lot of the same techniques as I did in the peacock project – spatter for movement, pen and ink, and wax resist. The medium, however, is different: instead of coloured inks, I used strong, highly pigmented watercolour, starting wet in wet with further enhancements wet on dry.

Exploring metallics

Metallics are a great way to add a finishing touch to your paintings. One of the nice things about them is that you can add them at the end gradually. Metallics are very eye-catching, so I suggest resisting the temptation to use them everywhere – less is more.

I tend to add metallics sparingly, and stick to just one metallic colour within a painting. They can add an extra little lift to your work.

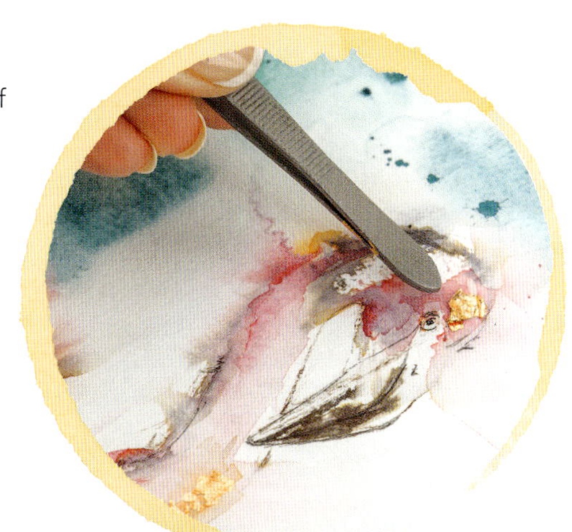

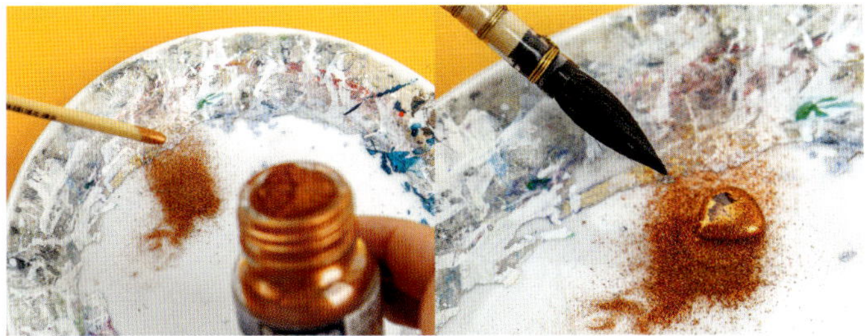

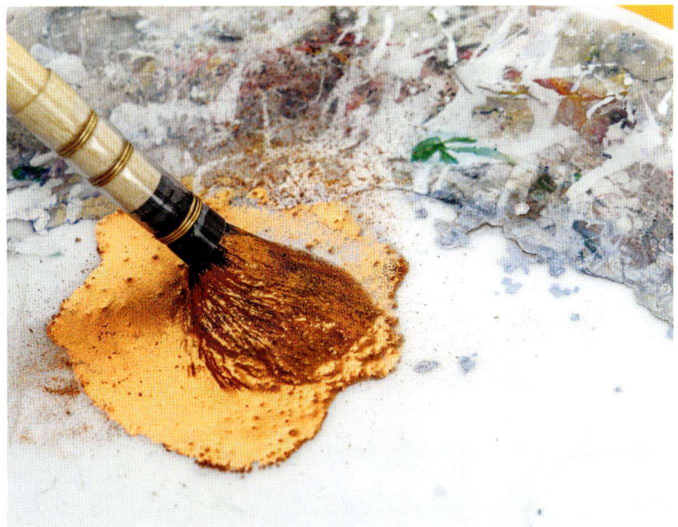

Preparing bronzing powder

Bronzing powder is available in a number of different colours, but they're all prepared in the same way. Use the back of your brush to scoop a small amount of powder onto a clean (well, 'cleanish' in this case!), dry saucer. Add a drop or two of water, then mix to a paint-like consistency. You can now apply it just like watercolour.

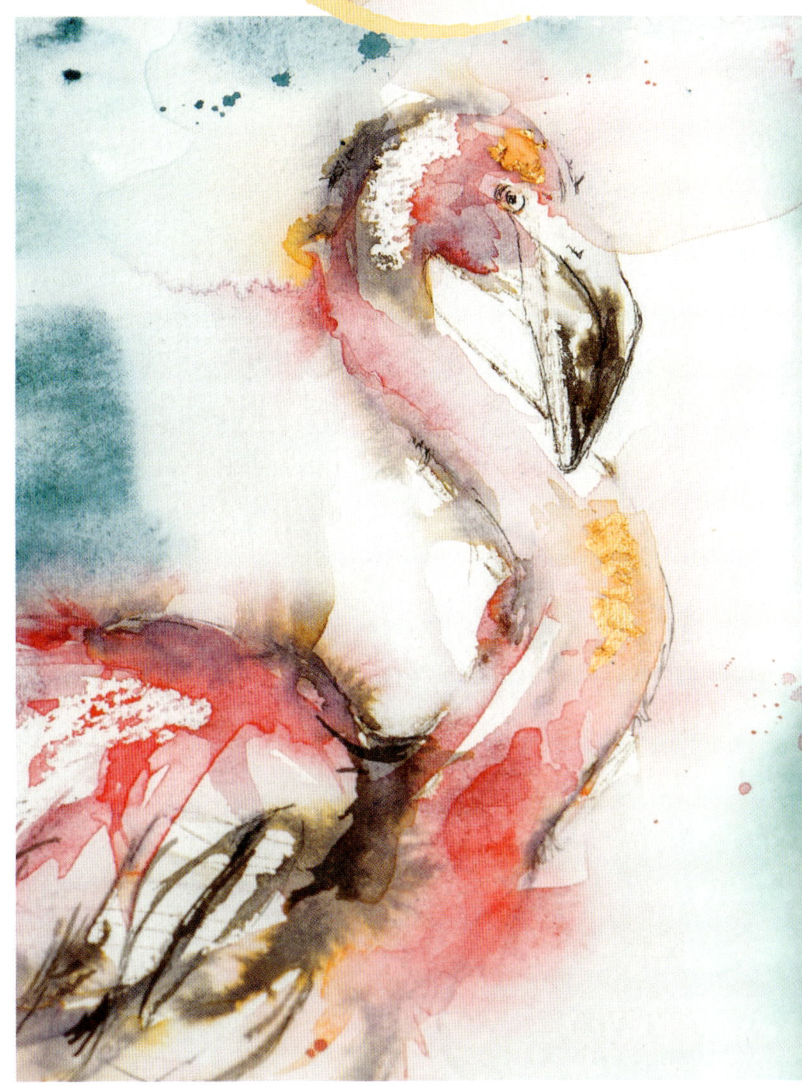

Metallic foil

Use a brush to apply a little watered-down white glue (PVA) to your dry painting, then use tweezers to place metallic foil onto the wet glue. Allow to dry, then brush away the excess.

Chimpy
21 x 28.5cm (8¼ x 11¼in)

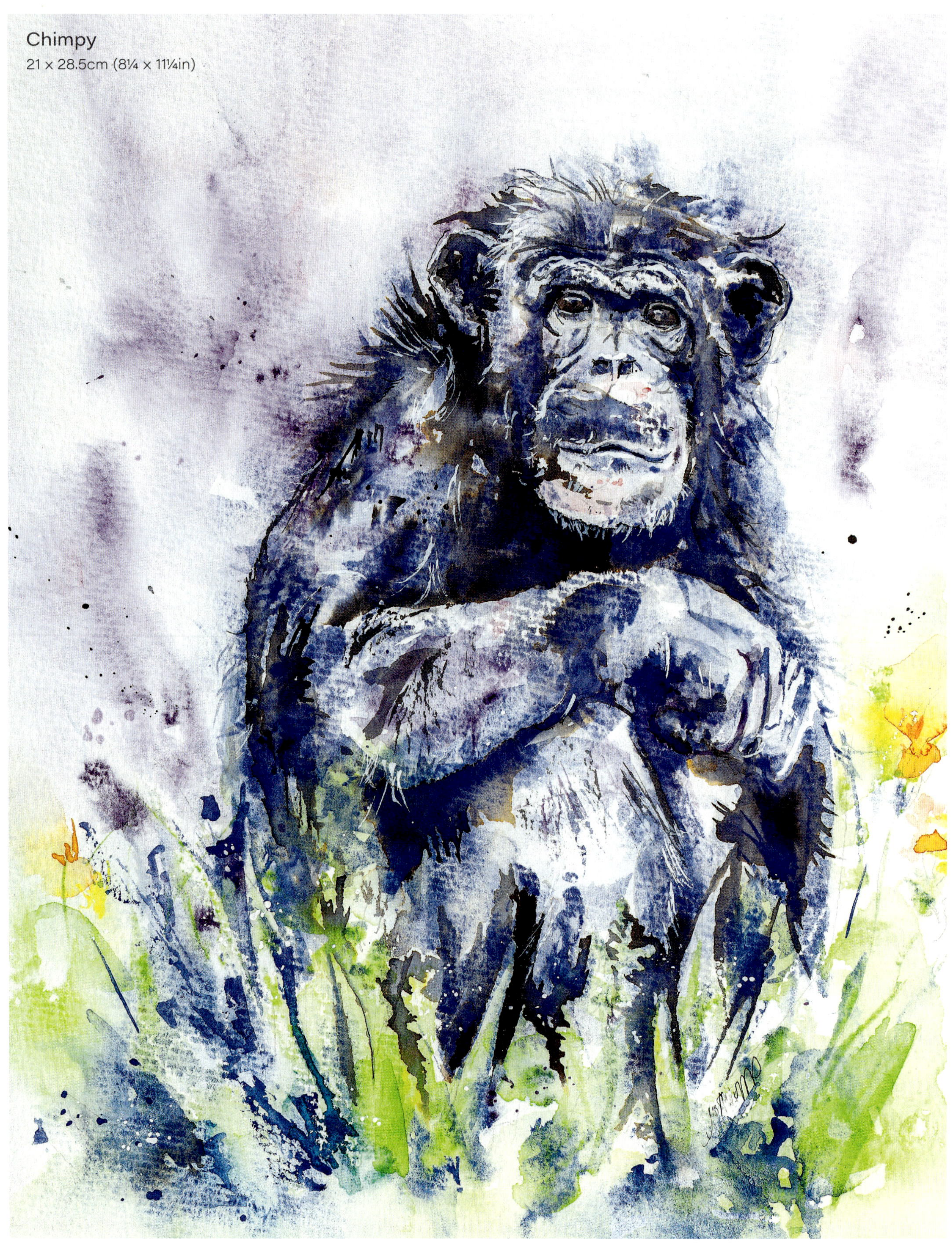

Exploring resists

A common step for me is to use my trusty wax candle to add some highlights and interest. Wax marks will prevent the watercolour from soaking into the paper, and so results in beautiful texture and highlights of clean white paper. I love that element of surprise – sometimes it's more of a shock! – when the effect suddenly appears.

As you work on your sketch, think about where you want the highlights and texture to be, and leave these areas blank. Wax will protect the surface, so you won't be able to remove or hide any pencil marks underneath them.

Reserving white highlights

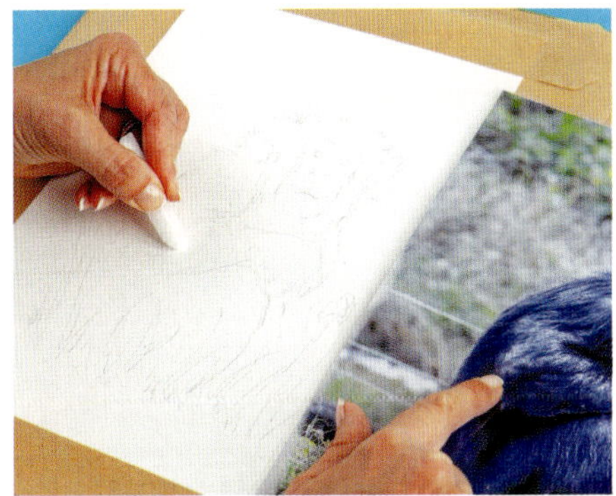

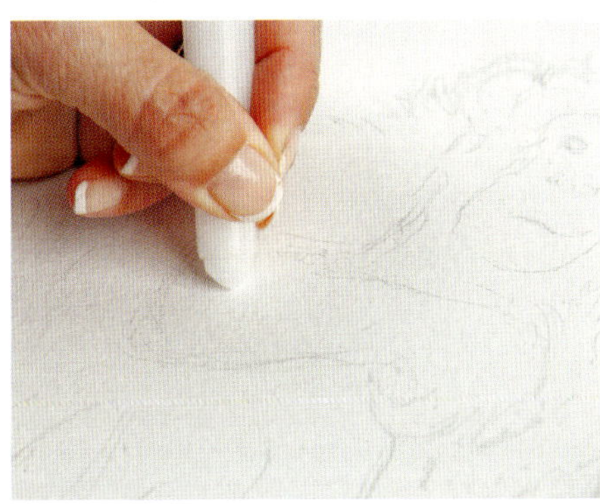

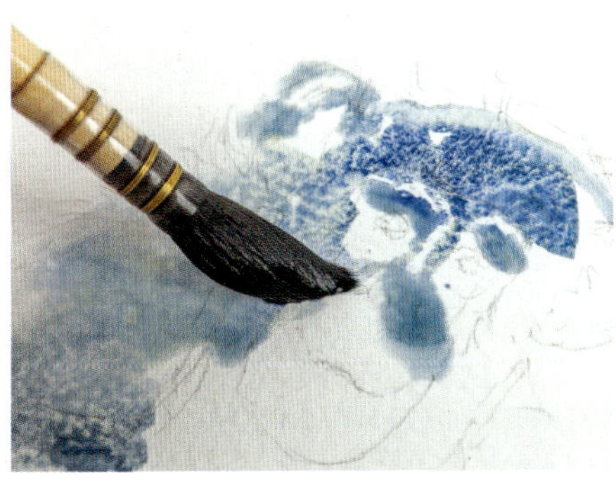

1 With reference to the source photograph and avoiding the pencil marks, gently rub the candle over parts of the image – not just the light bits, but some random bits here and there, too.

2 Follow the contours of the animal you are working on, and curve in directional strokes according to the image.

3 You can now paint over the wax, and the colours will be resisted.

Layering and depth

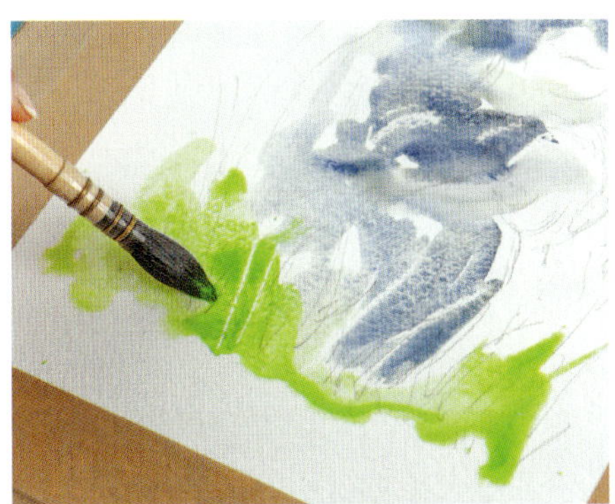

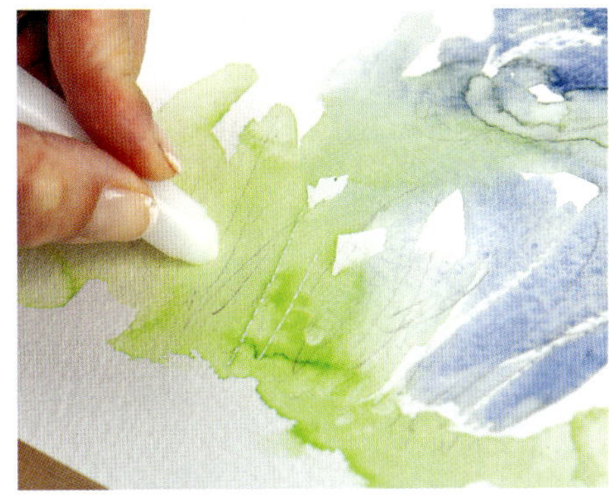

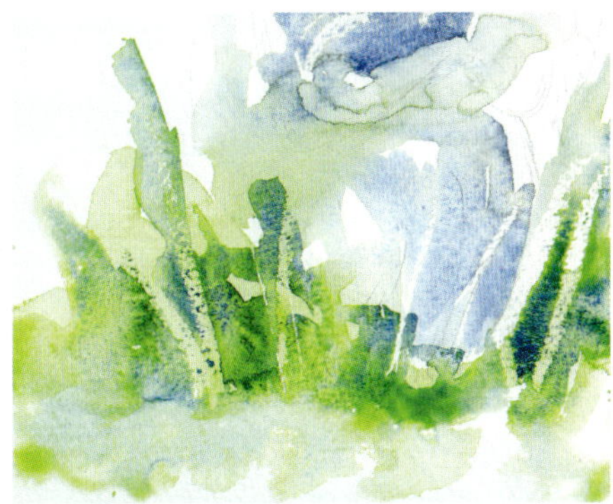

1 Wax can be used for more than reserving whites – you can reserve other colours, too. You can see here that the wax is resisting the green in the grass.

2 Allow the paint to dry, then apply some more linear marks with the wax over the light green.

3 Apply darker paints over the top, and you'll see both the original white and new lighter areas reserved.

Hyena

I have never before painted a hyena and so was very excited at this prospect. He looks rather cute and cuddly, but looks can be deceptive, of course…

In terms of composition, I liked the colours and his spots but decided to contrast the background against the warm orangey browns I used on him.

The salt effect works particularly well on hot-pressed paper, so that's a technique that we'll use here. It's perfectly-suited to the bristly, textural fur of the hyena.

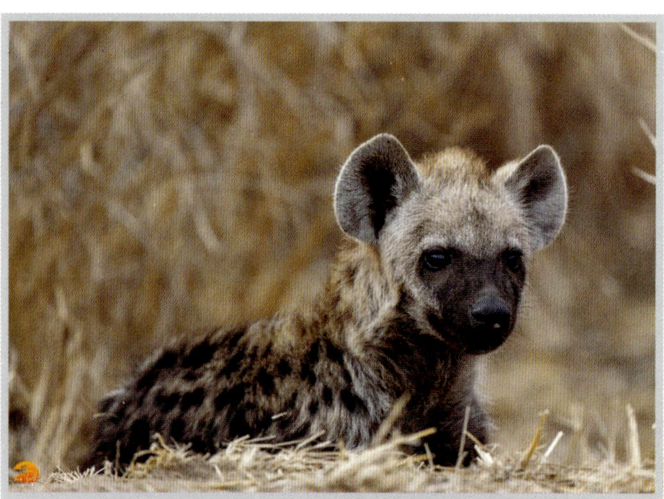

Source photograph

I fell in love with this photograph as soon as I saw it, and knew I just had to paint the subject. He seems fixated on something… I wondered whether it was dinner?

You will need

Bockingford HP (hot-pressed) surface watercolour paper 30.5 x 23cm (12 x 9in)

Large, medium and small brushes

HB pencil and putty eraser

WATERCOLOUR PAINTS:
Yellow ochre, burnt sienna, helio cerulean, French ultramarine, vermilion, burnt umber and rose madder

INKS:
Daler-Rowney FW acrylic ink: white

Table salt and rock salt

Permanent black Pigma Micron archival fineliner pen

Beeswax candle

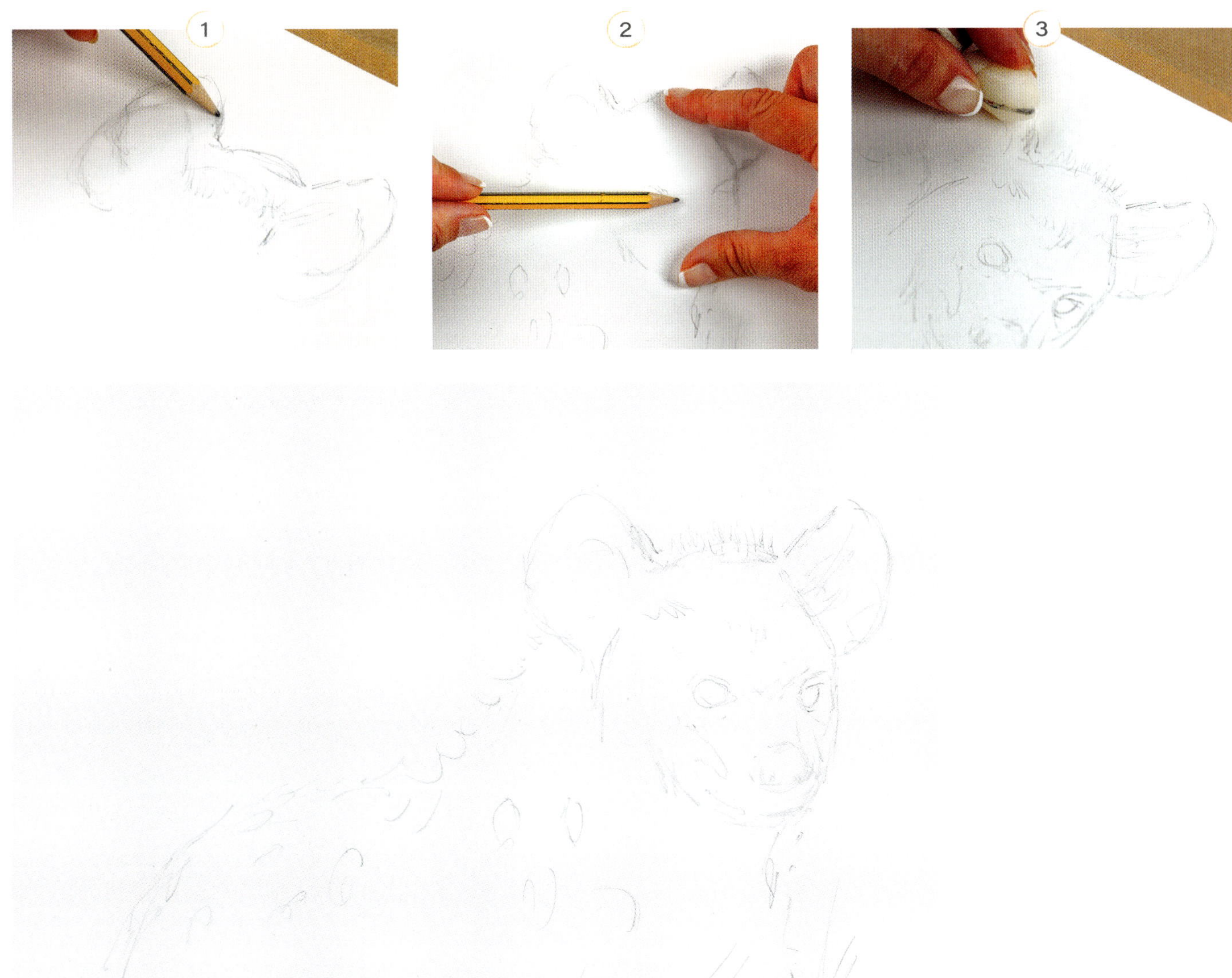

The sketch

You'll notice in the first step here that there are two lines for the top of the head – this was a mistake that I wanted to keep in, because it teaches a valuable lesson about thinking about the overall placement when you start sketching.

Here I started a little low – I want the hyena to have some grass to sit in – so I adjusted before I went too far with the sketch.

1 Using an HB pencil, start your sketch, adjusting if necessary, as described above. Here, note that I haven't erased the line before redrawing, as I'll unconsciously want to repeat the earlier mistake. By leaving it in place when sketching the new line, I can use the old line as reference when placing it.

2 Use the eraser to remove the old lines once the sketch is established, then continue. When placing the eyes, it's often helpful to use your fingers to take a measure of the overall head height on the reference photograph, note where the eyes sit, then take that measurement over to your sketch.

3 Once the sketch is complete, add a few light touches of wax to the hyena's head.

Basic shapes – and salt

When using salt, we need to make sure everything's good and wet as we drop it in. To do this, we need to apply plenty of paint and work fairly quickly. With that said, there's no need to rush – be considered with your application of paint and use the sketch to guide you.

It's worth reading through the steps below so that you know what you'll be doing at each step ahead of time. You might like to prepare all the paints in palette wells so they're ready to go.

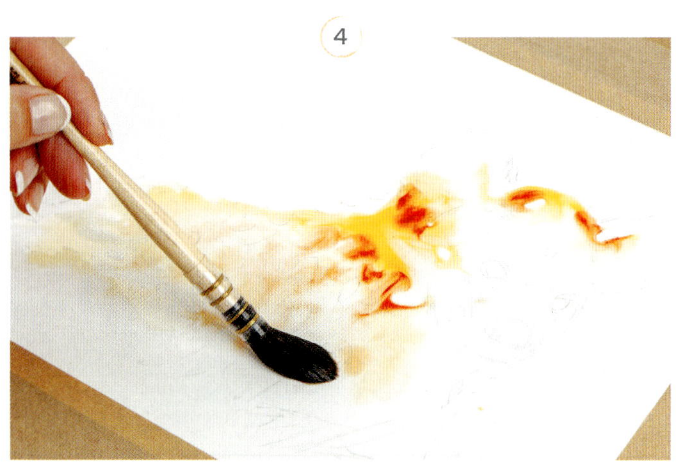

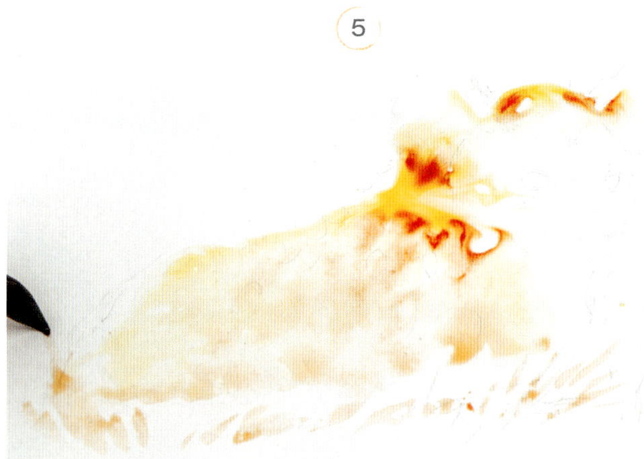

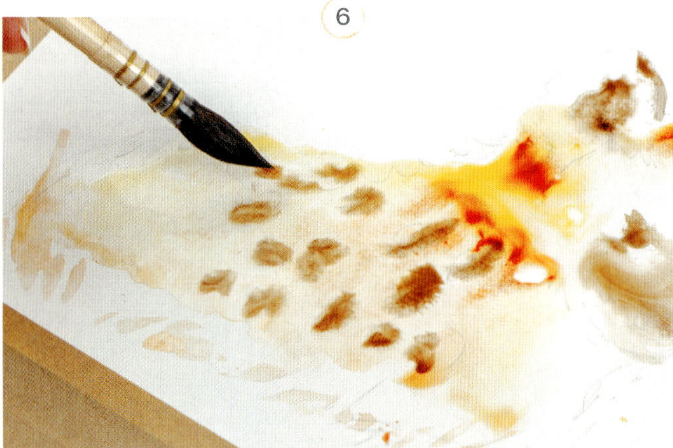

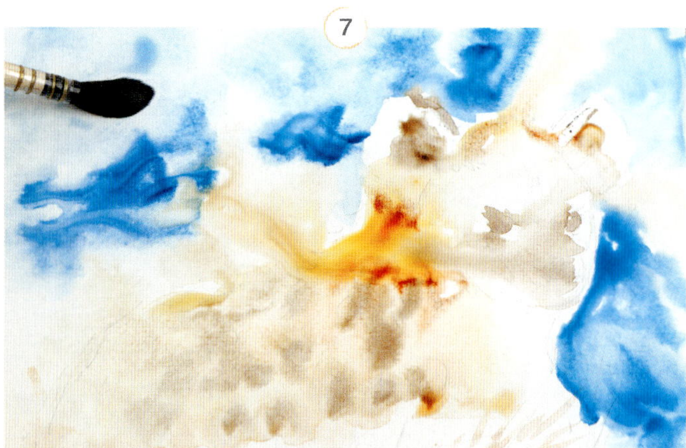

4 With the large brush, wet the whole of the hyena except for the eyes, then drop in yellow ochre. Add burnt sienna wet in wet.

5 With the paint remaining on the brush, use light flicking marks to add the dry grass around the bottom of the hyena.

6 Still working wet in wet, dot in the features and spots using burnt umber.

7 Bring in clean water from the edge with the large brush, but leave a small gap around the hyena, only touching here and there. Working quickly, drop in helio cerulean to the background. Make sure you're using plenty of pigment here: you want a nice strong colour as the salt will knock it back a bit.

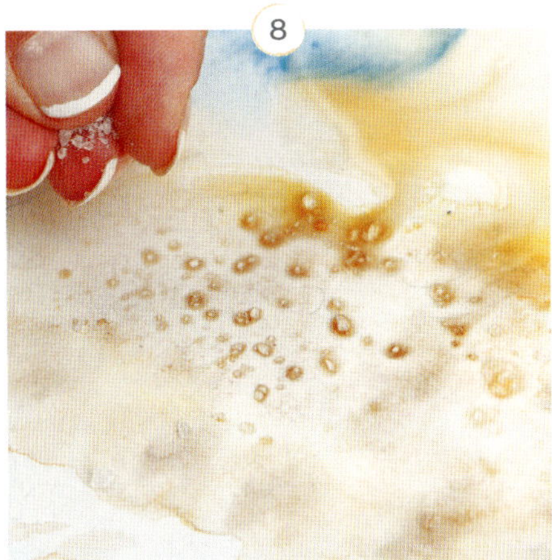

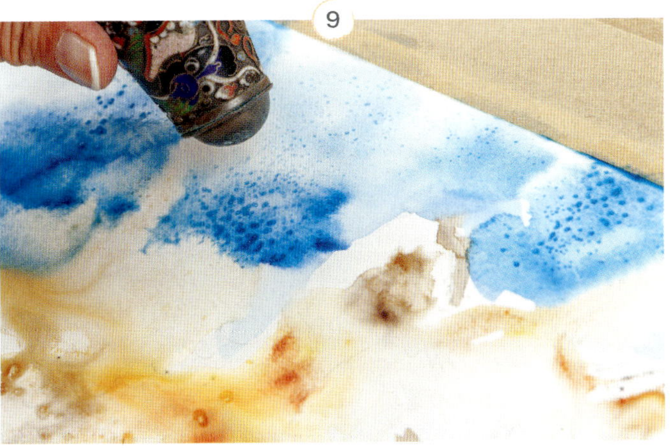

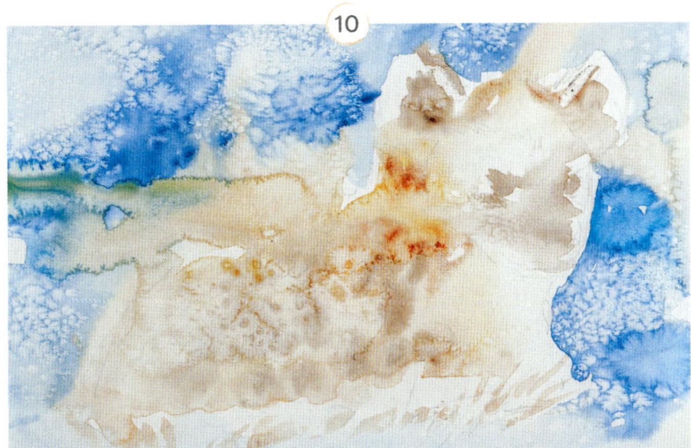

8 Drop in some rock salt on the hyena's back.

9 Sprinkle table salt generously over the background.

10 Allow the paint to dry naturally. The effect takes time to develop.

11 Before continuing with the painting, do make sure that the paint is completely dry. You can brush away the salt once everything is dry, then use the large brush to rewet areas and begin building up the colours on the hyena with glazes of yellow ochre and burnt sienna. Avoid any salt patterns or other points of interest that you particularly like, simply by not rewetting them. Reserve the burnt sienna for the focal area – the hyena's face and forequarters – and avoid the back parts.

12 Working wet on dry, add a glaze of French ultramarine to the hindquarters to help knock them back. Finally for this stage, add some dry grasses. Use short marks of the tip of the large brush to apply yellow ochre.

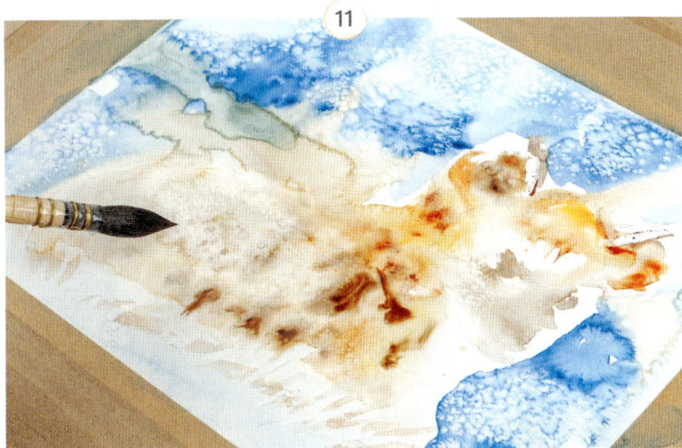

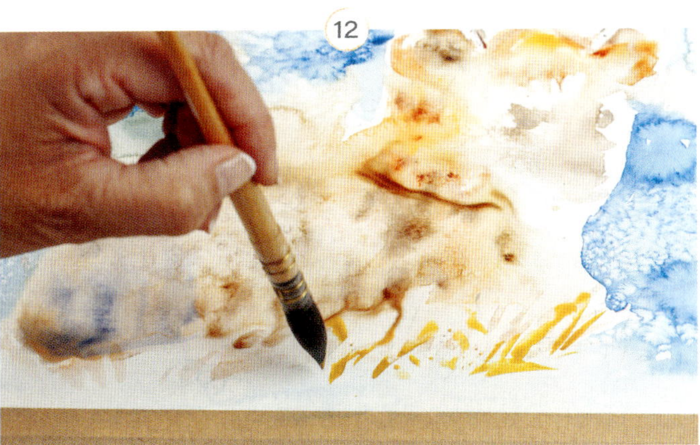

Refining

To help refine the front body and face, make sure you have the features in place. You might find it helpful to resketch in the nose, or other features, to help guide you.

Trying to paint the features all in one go, with one dark wash, will tend to look flat and stuck-on, while building them up gradually helps them to look natural.

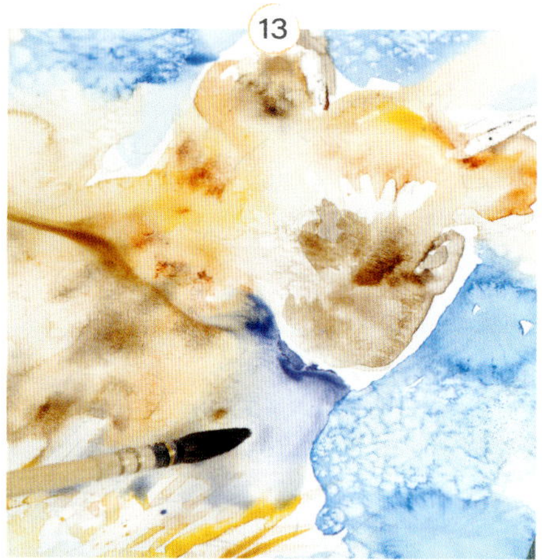

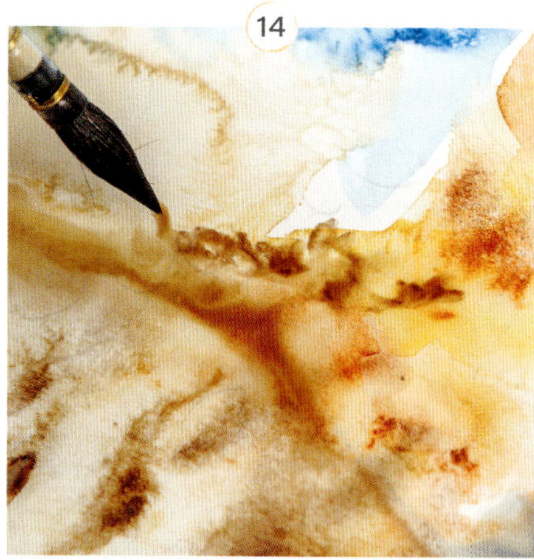

13 Change to the medium brush and begin creating the mask on the hyena's face using burnt umber. Add some shading beneath his jaw with a wash of French ultramarine.

14 Add some burnt umber spots to the hyena's flank, then tickle in some of the darker hairs on his spine, holding the brush at the end.

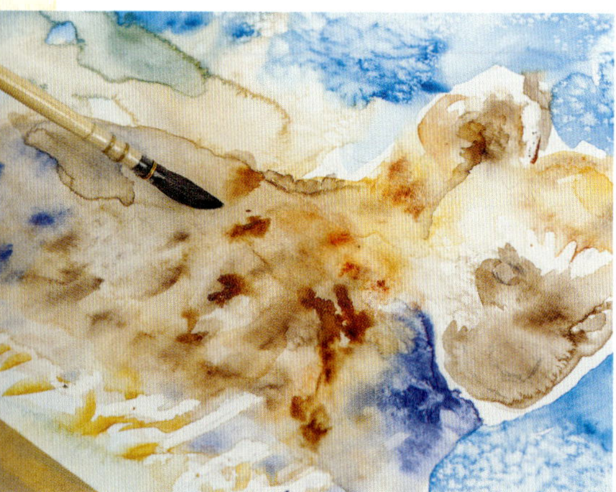

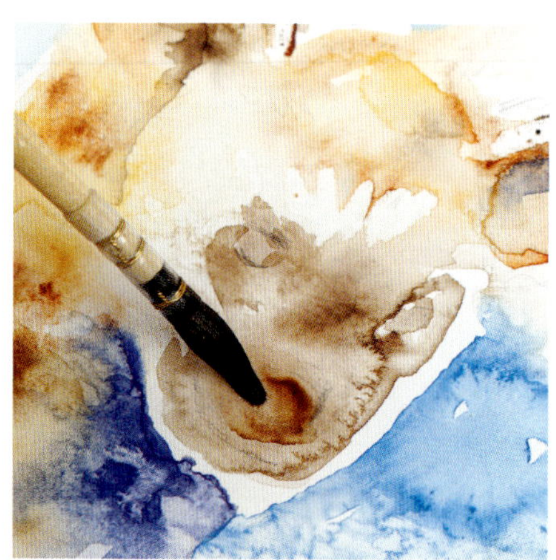

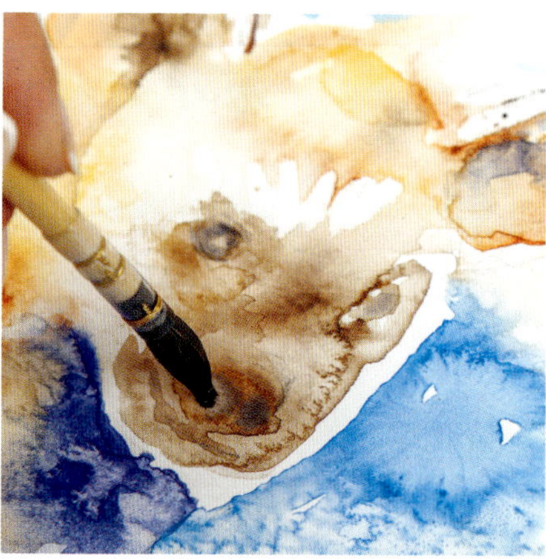

15 Allow the painting to dry, then begin building up the texture wet on dry. Use the medium brush to add more French ultramarine beneath the jaw, and add more burnt umber to the left-hand ear and spots along the back. Emphasize those nearer the forequarters, using more water in the mixes further away.

16 Push back the ears a little with glazes of French ultramarine. Wet the nose and put in a little dab of burnt umber, letting the colour flow in.

17 Use a mix of burnt umber and French ultramarine to begin to bring out the eyes. Add the water first, using the tip of the medium brush, then touch in the mix. While the eyes dry, add burnt umber to the nose.

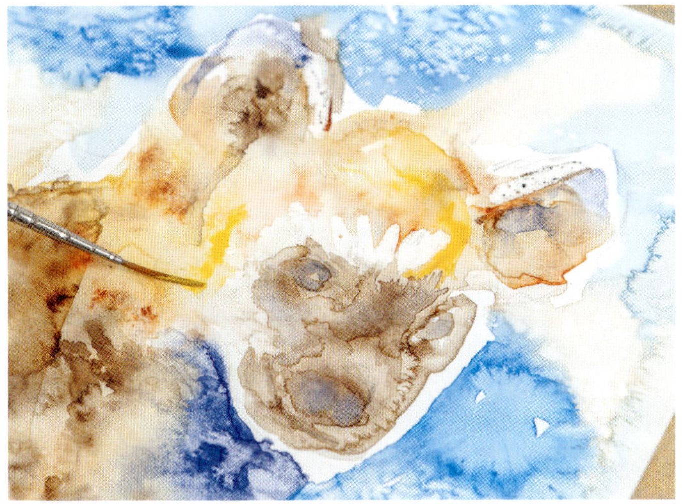

18 Swapping between the medium and small brushes, continue to build up the tone on the mask and features with burnt umber and the mix of burnt umber and French ultramarine. Strengthen the colours on his face with vermilion and yellow ochre glazes.

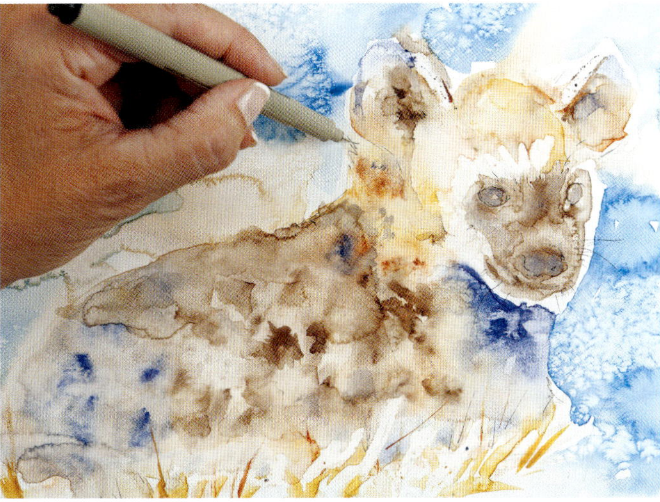

19 Use the tip of the small brush to flick in some light grasses with burnt sienna. Allow the painting to dry, then swap to the permanent fineliner to tick in some fine additional details around the face, and add some black whiskers.

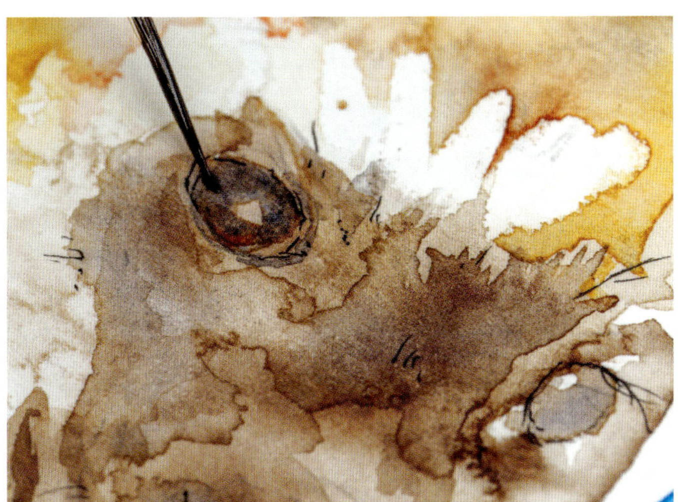

20 Build up the details on the eyes and nose using the small brush and a mix of burnt umber and French ultramarine. As before, wet the eye first and drop the colour into the wet area.

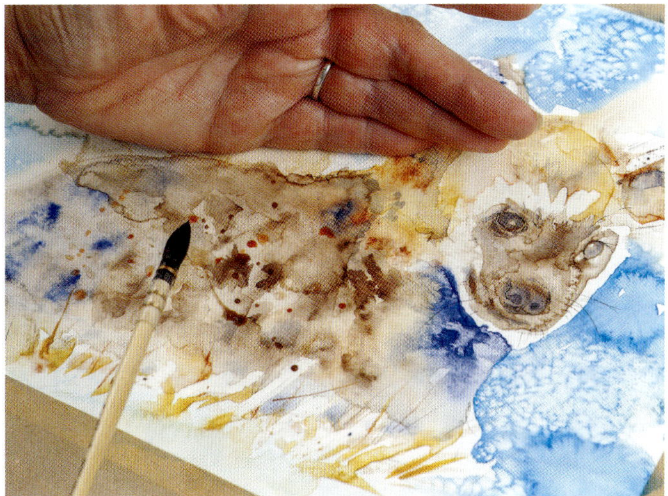

21 Use the medium brush to spatter some burnt sienna over the body, followed by some additional burnt umber. Use your hand (or a piece of paper) to protect the background.

Making the painting yours

Loose, wet washes and the effects of salt make for unpredictable results.
When adding your final details, be careful not to lose any happy accidents
by over-working your painting. If it looks good – leave it alone!

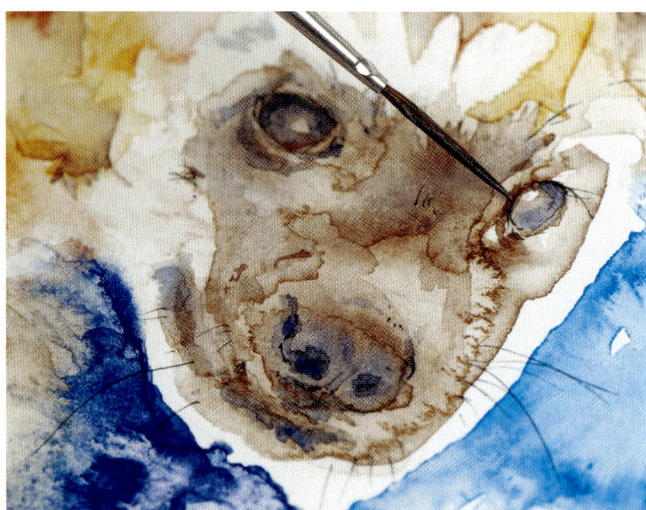

Bringing the face into focus

Once dry, enrich the detail in the nose
and eyes with glazes of the dark mix
of burnt umber and French ultramarine,
applying the paint carefully with the
small brush.

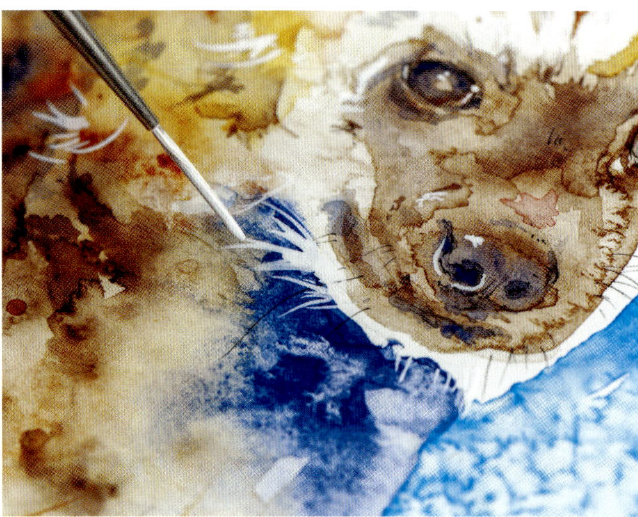
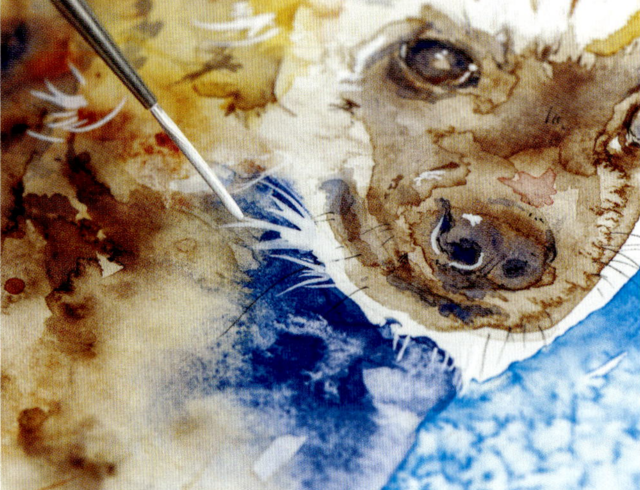

Warmth and light

Still using the small brush, add a hint of
rose madder on the top of the muzzle as
a subtle hot spot. Once completely dry,
add further details to the face with white
acrylic ink and the small brush.

Finishing the painting

Break up the foreground a little with
grasses painted with white acrylic ink,
and then add some spattering.

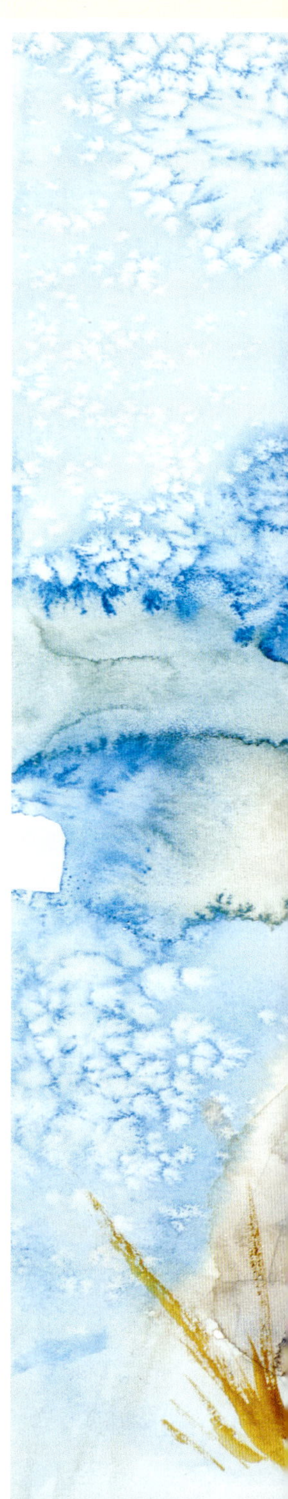

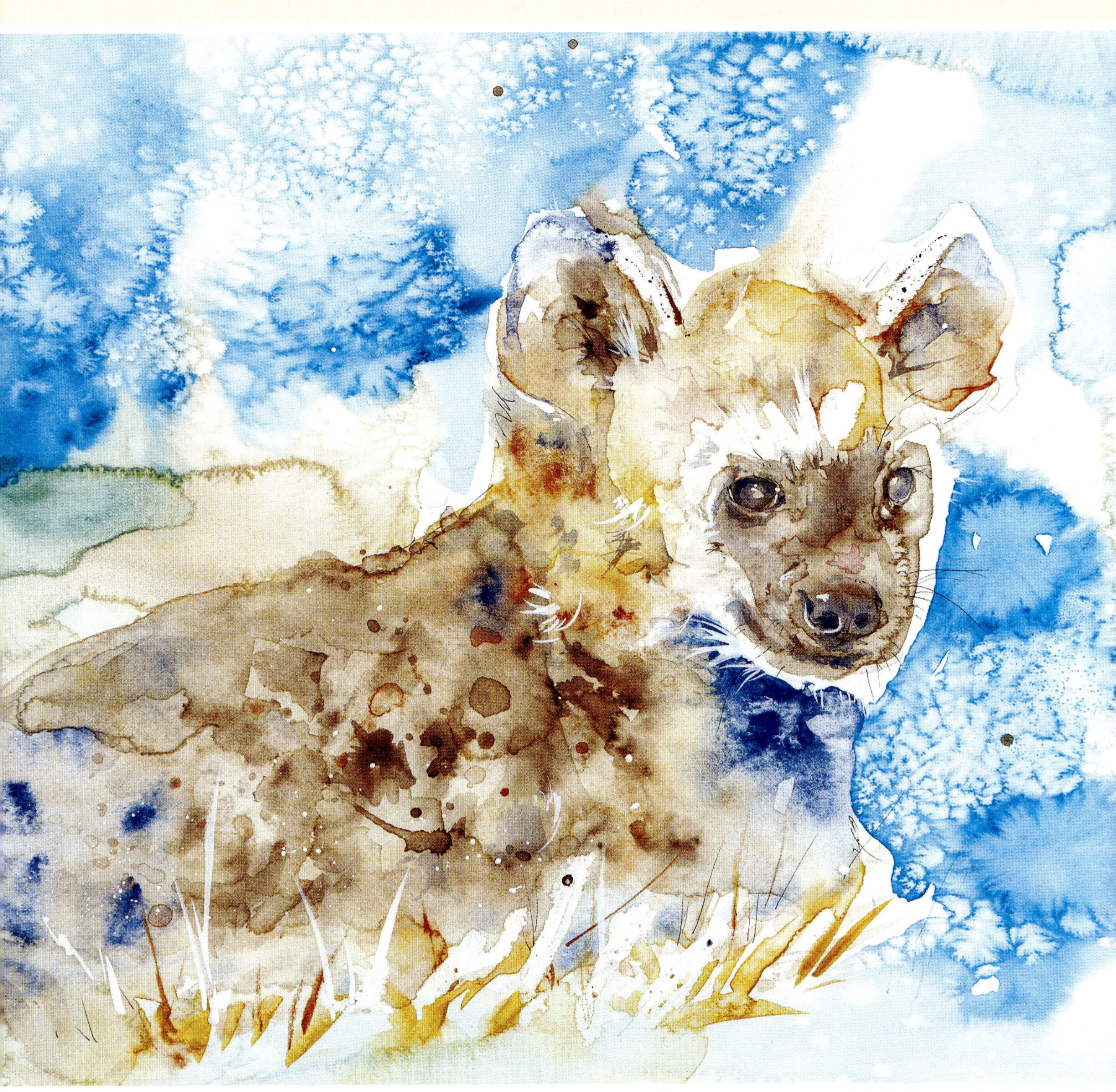

Hyena
30.5 x 23cm (12 x 9in)

Exploring isopropyl alcohol

Whenever you would like to form interesting textural effects in your paintings, there are different options to explore. The *Hyena* project demonstrates some beautiful shapes created with using salt, for example, but there are many other extras or diluents – I just call these 'stuff'! – that you can add. Isopropyl alcohol, for example, can create varying patterns in your paintings, depending on when and how it is applied.

Let's look at how alcohol works on the seahorse, in a completely different way to the salt on the hyena. Rather than textural and spiky, the alcohol creates bright, bubbly effects. Which effect do you prefer? Where would you use these? Experiment with them all and see which you favour.

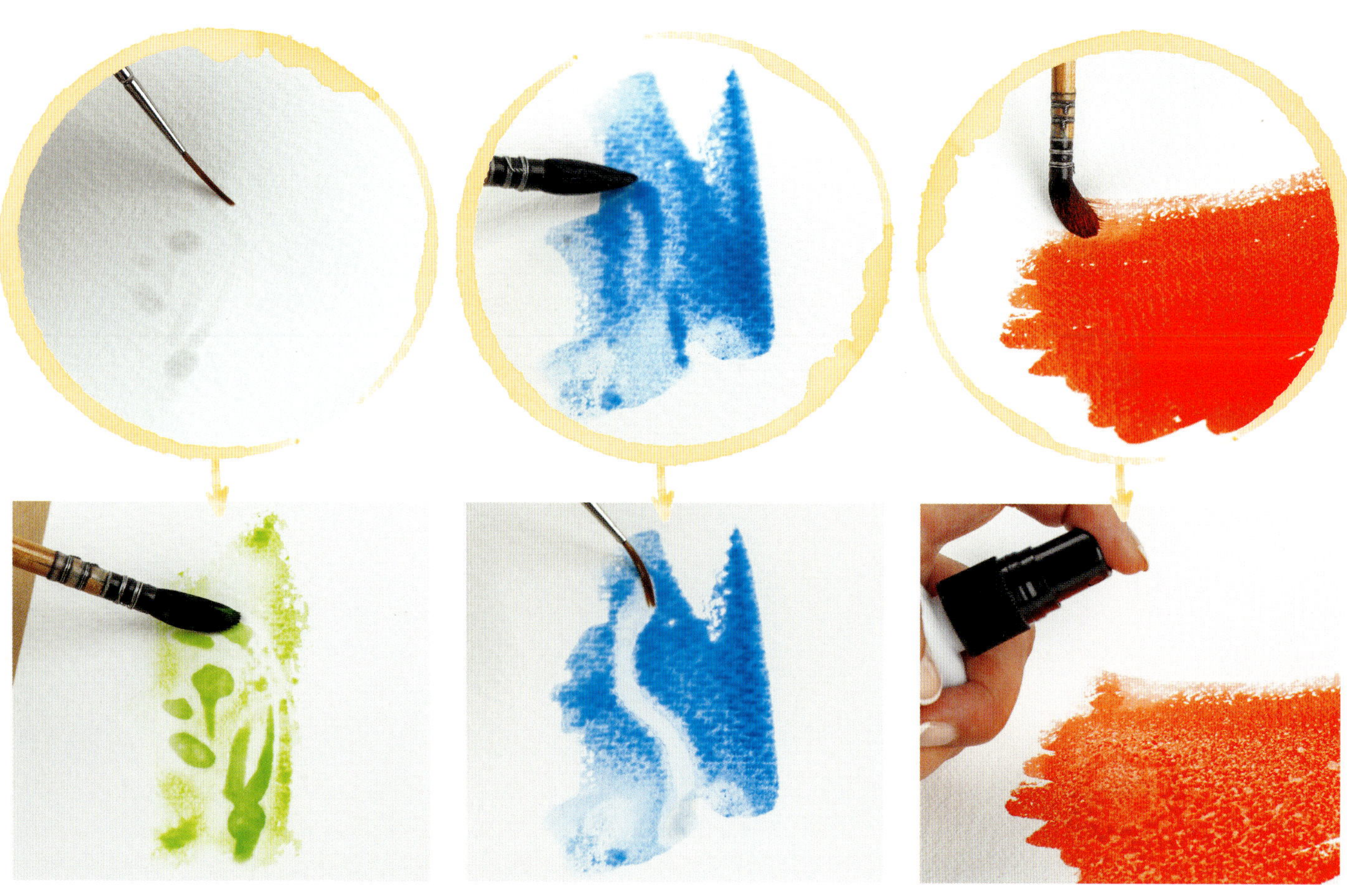

Added before painting

Tip a little alcohol into a small dish or palette well, and use a brush to make your marks on the surface (top). When you paint over this, you'll see the patterns emerge as dark marks.

Drawing through wet paint

A brush loaded with alcohol will cut straight through a wet wash on the surface. The alcohol displaces the wet paint and pushes it to the side.

Spraying into wet paint

Isopropyl looks great when sprayed into a wet wash. The alcohol adds instant texture than can emulate effects as diverse as foliage, surf on the water or lichen on trees.

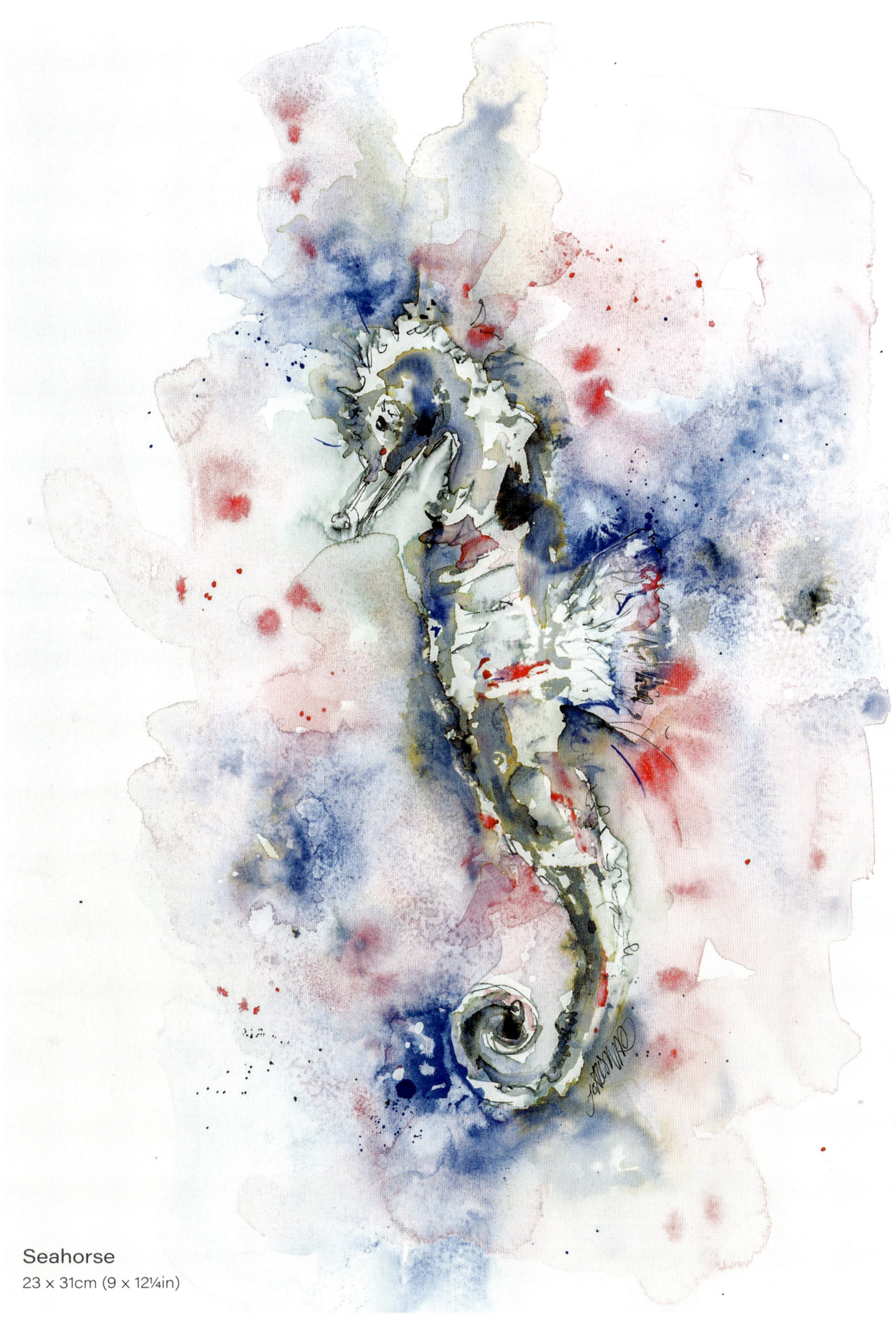

Seahorse
23 x 31cm (9 x 12¼in)

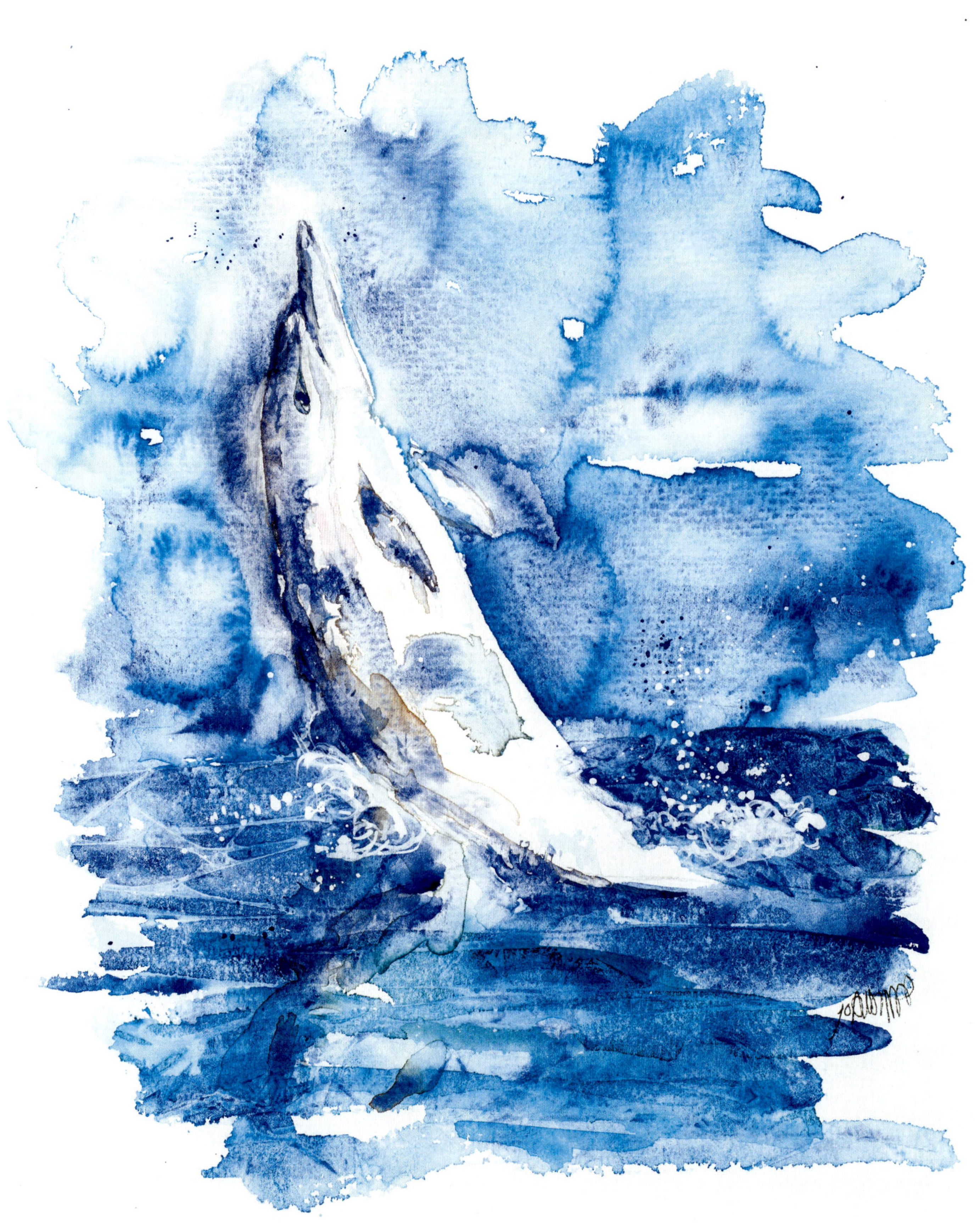

Exploring plastic food wrap

This technique is a marvellous method of creating not only texture, but dynamism to a piece. I will often use this technique to emulate water in my paintings, but you could use it whenever you like for adding texture – petals, flowers, tree bark, brick or stone are all good places to try this on.

I find this technique works particularly well for the ripples on water, as demonstrated on the dolphin opposite. The patterns achieved with food wrap are difficult to emulate in paint with a brush and are so very interesting – and also different every time. Allow this to dry for longer than normal as the plastic film over the watercolour paint slows down the drying time.

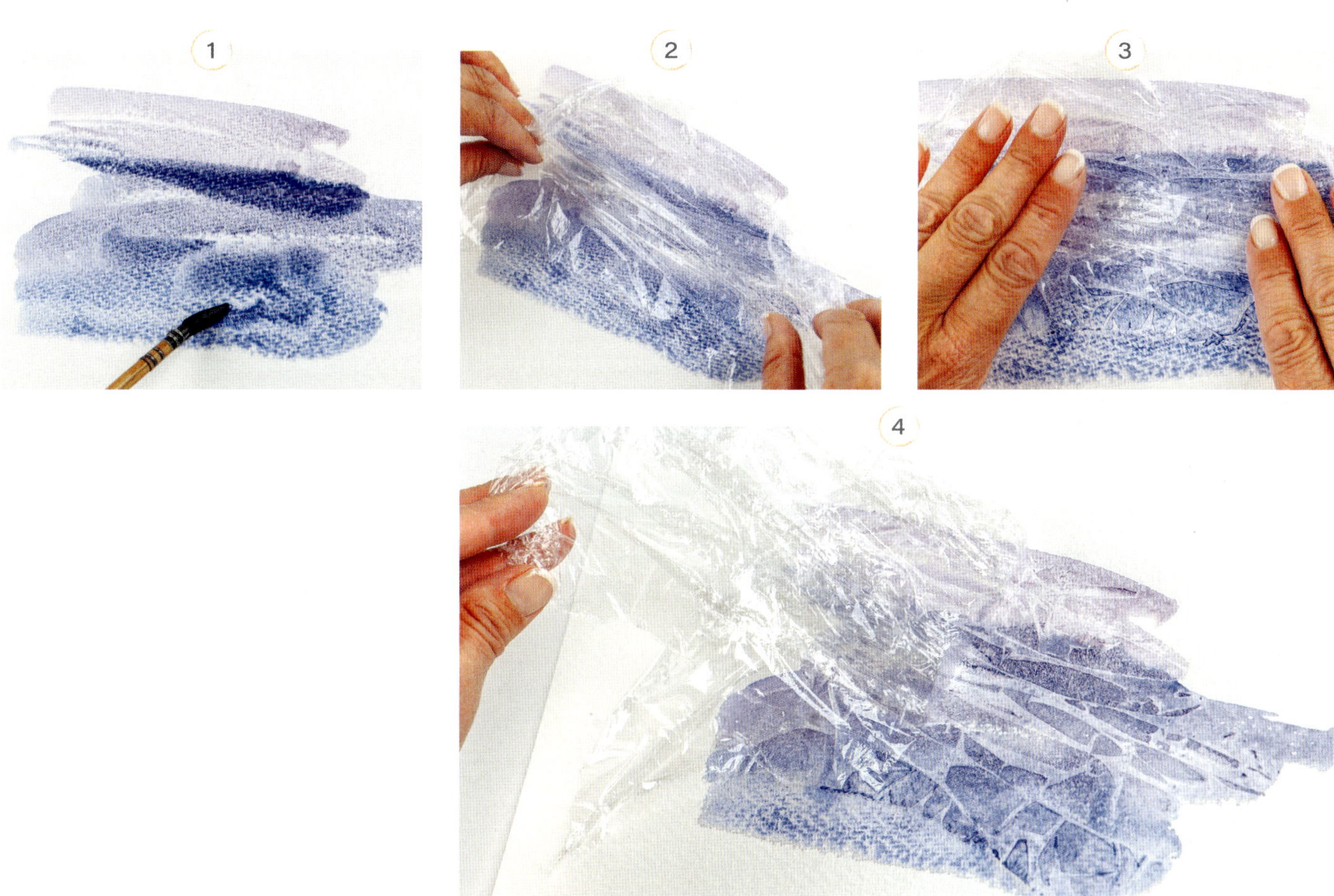

1 Paint a wash of colour onto the surface.

2 While the paint is wet, place a sheet of plastic food wrap over the top.

3 Use your fingers to manipulate it into place, then leave to dry thoroughly – give it an hour or two.

4 Once dry, carefully remove the food wrap to reveal the result.

Opposite:
Dolphin
23 x 31cm (9 x 12¼in)

Lennie
23 × 31cm (9 × 12¼in)

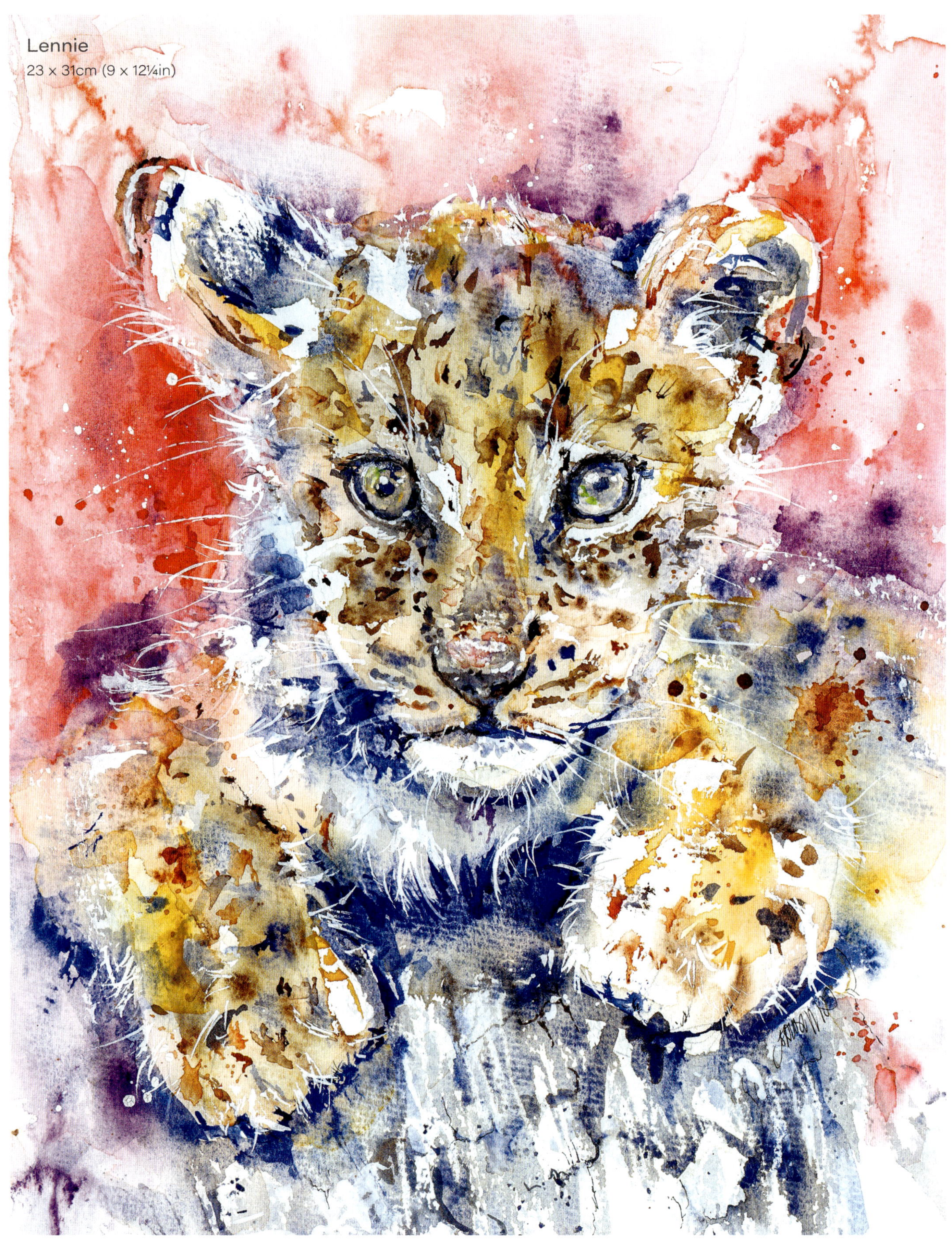

Six values

Including at least six values of light and dark in your painting will ensure a variety of tones and that all-important contrast. Irrespective of your chosen colours, the painting should include values that range from near-black (6) to the white of the paper (1) – which is the lightest tone you can get with pure watercolour.

Values are easier to assess in monochrome. Take a black and white photograph of your painting and the tones of the colours will become more obvious and easier to understand. In the picture below, for example, I've picked out examples of six different values, 1 being the lightest and 6 the darkest. This range is what ensures that the painting doesn't look flat.

If you now look at the version in full colour, you'll spot that some of the different colours are of the same value/depth. It is interesting how we can't always demonstrate these correctly as we sometimes assume one colour appears darker than the other – but as these pictures show, this is not always the case.

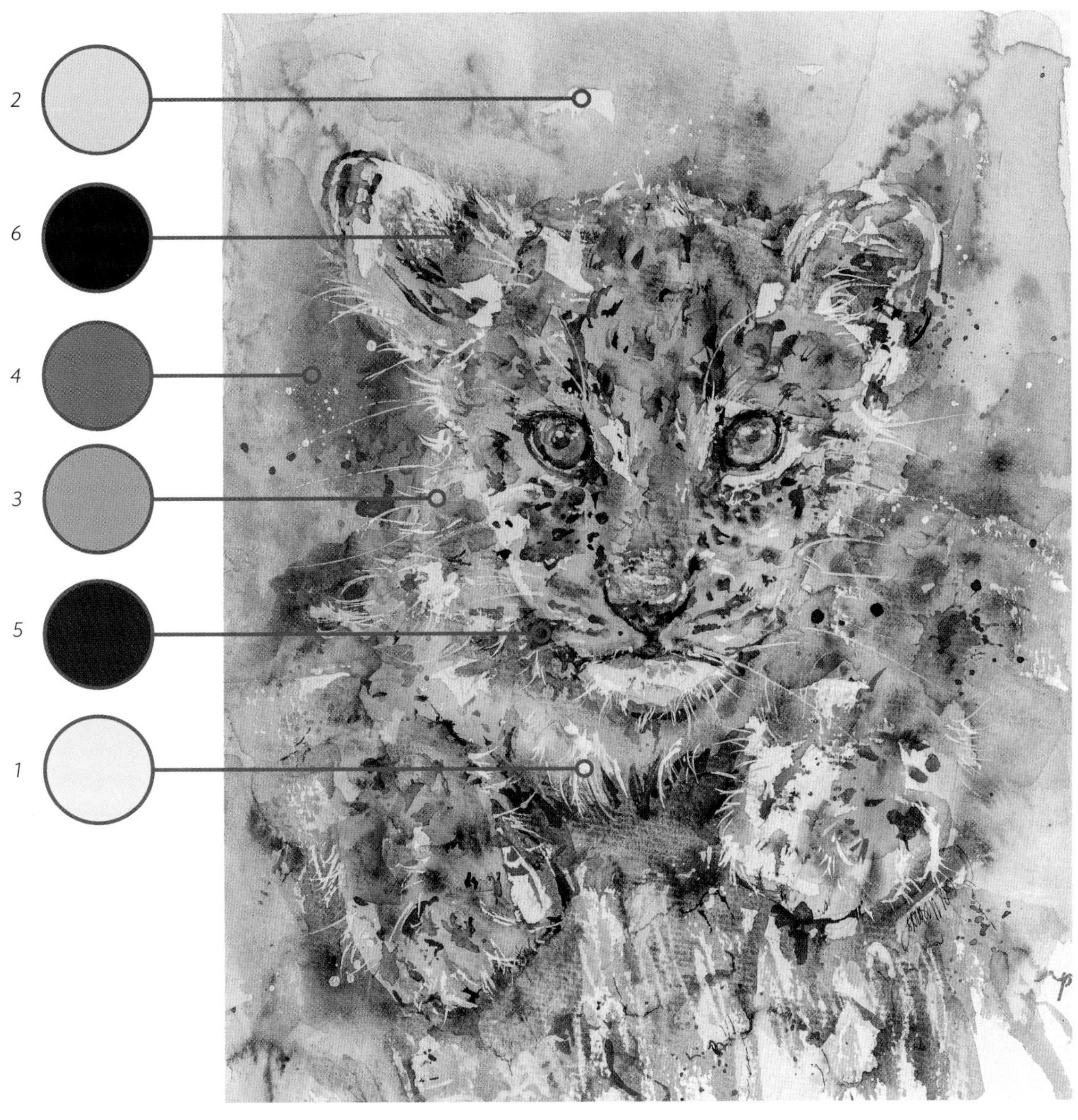

Zebra Foal

Black and white can be exciting when you involve Quink ink. A pen and ink approach suits the subject due to the zebra's strong dark stripes, and other subtle colours will appear from the ink as we work, creating liveliness and further interest.

In terms of composition, I wanted the pose to include the zebra's body, but also wanted to bring his gorgeous face more into focus, by losing his back slightly.

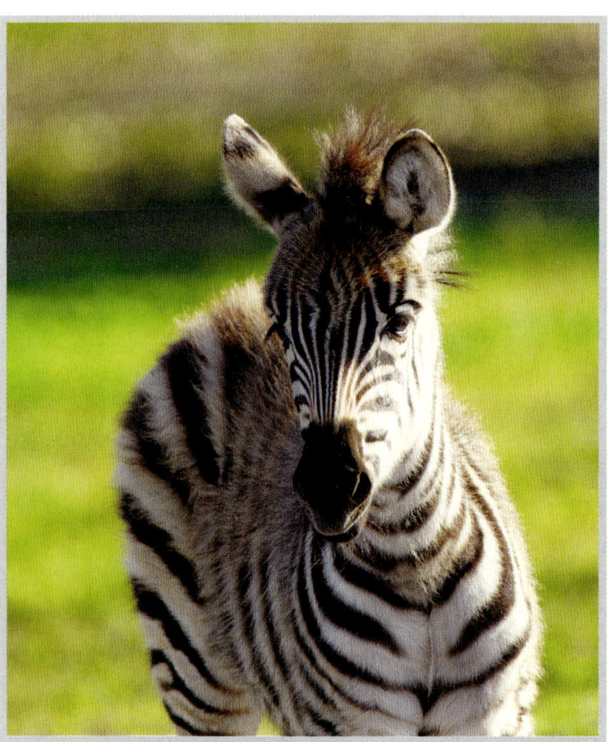

Source photograph
Zebras are such beautiful animals. This foal looks so fluffy that I just feel I would love to hug it – just look at those lashes, I'm so envious!

You will need

Bockingford Rough surface watercolour paper 25.5 x 35.5cm (10 x 14in)

Large, medium and small brushes

Watersoluble black fineliner pen (Staedtler Triplus fineliner)

Permanent black Pigma Micron archival fineliner pen

WATERCOLOUR PAINTS:
Rose madder

INKS:

Parker Quink ink

Beeswax candle

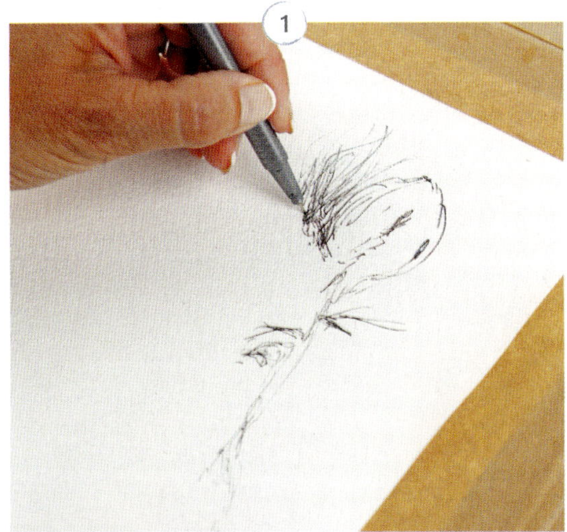

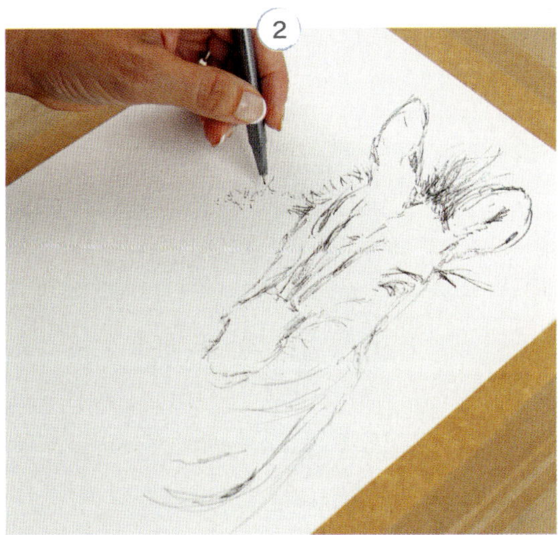

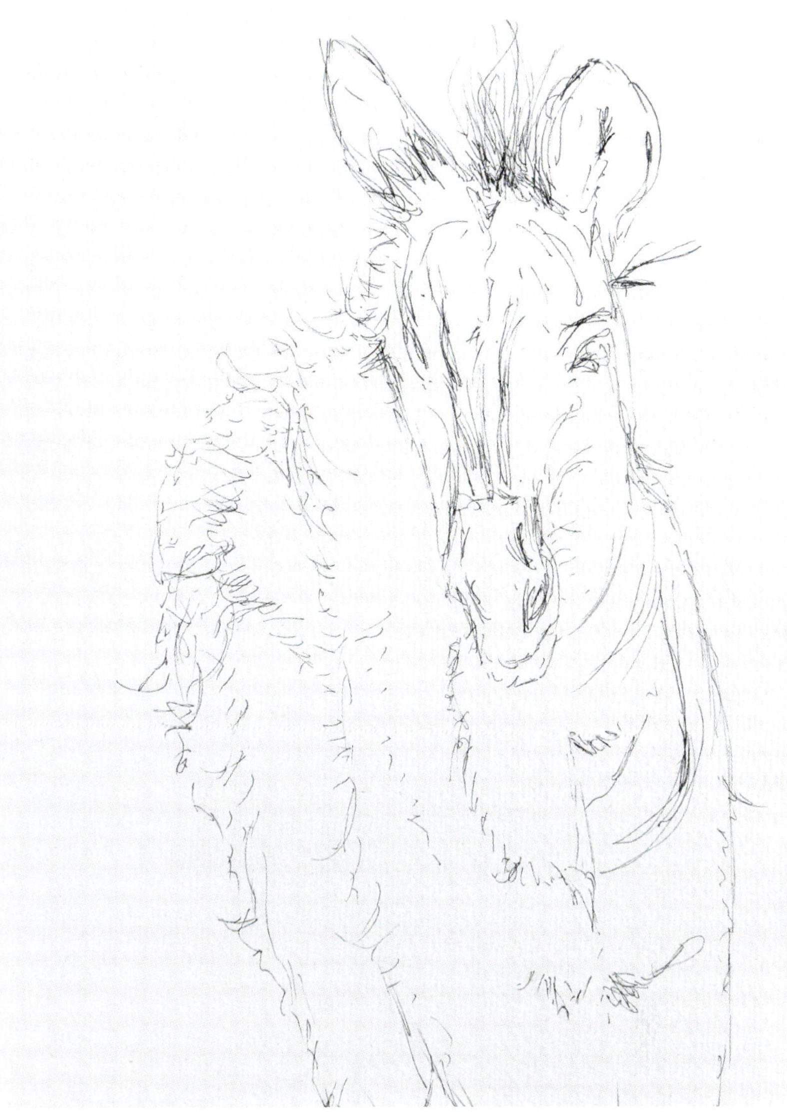

The sketch

Consider where you want the darker areas to be in the finished painting, and scribble a few more strokes in these areas to get more depth. Likewise, use lighter pressure and finer marks for areas you want to be lighter in tone and less eyecatching in the composition.

While the real strength of tone will come in later on, having these reference areas established from the start is really handy.

Don't worry about sketching in the stripes yet. If you find it helps, add a few marks to hint at them, but don't over-develop the sketch.

1 Working freehand, use the watersoluble fineliner to sketch in the zebra. I've started at the right-hand ear to give me a feature to use as reference for scale.

2 For darker areas, like the mane of the zebra, make quite a lot of marks and more pressure, rather than just hinting at the outline. The hindquarters and right-hand side in the sun need to fade away a little, so they're sketched in lightly.

Agitating ink

We're now going to wet the ink on the page to create the basic shapes. Prepare the ink on a separate palette or ceramic plate, putting the pure pigment on first, before dipping the still-inky brush into the water – not to wash it clean, but just to help to transfer the diuted ink left on the brush to the plate.

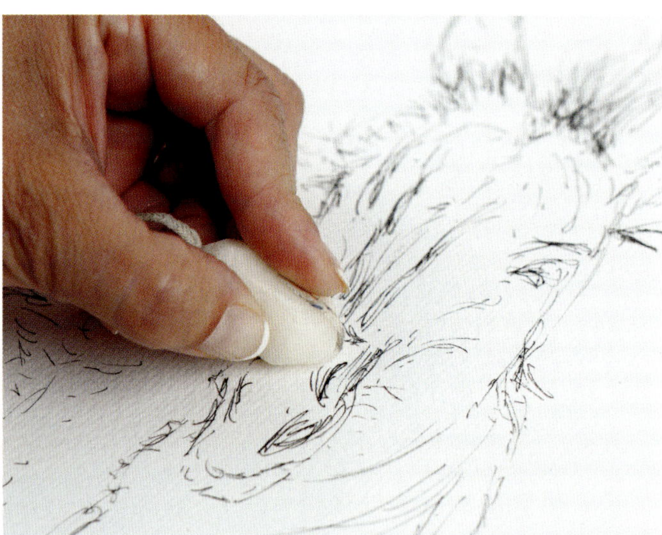

3 Add some wax marks on the head and forequarters.

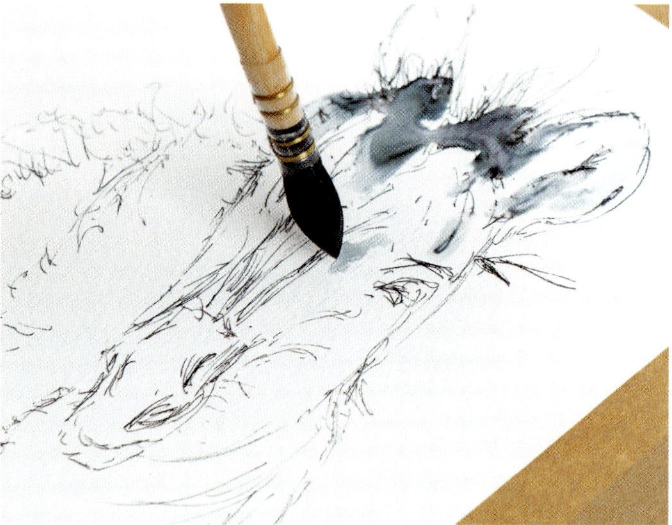

4 Load the large brush with clean water, tap off the excess on the side of your water pot, then begin to disturb the ink on the sketch. Don't just work over the lines and heavy marks of the sketch but use light dabbing marks to pick up some of the heavy ink and make some new marks.

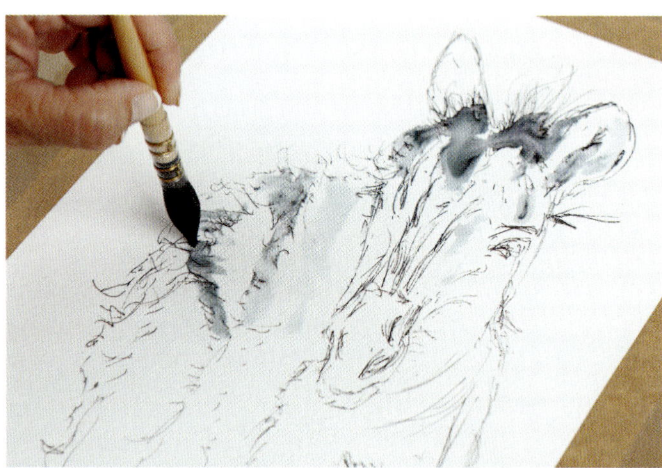

5 Start to develop the foal's body with clean water, using smooth sweeping strokes with a light pressure.

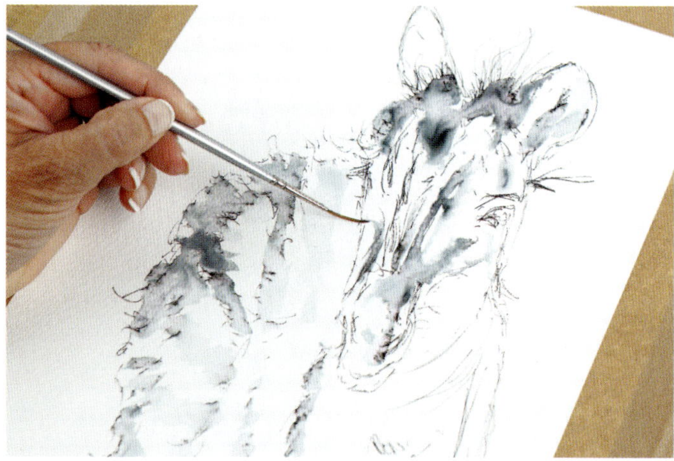

6 Put the large brush to one side without rinsing it. Swap to the small brush for finer details, like those on the muzzle.

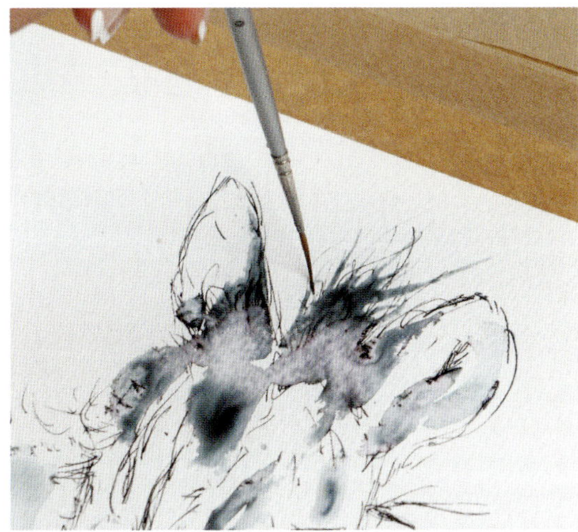

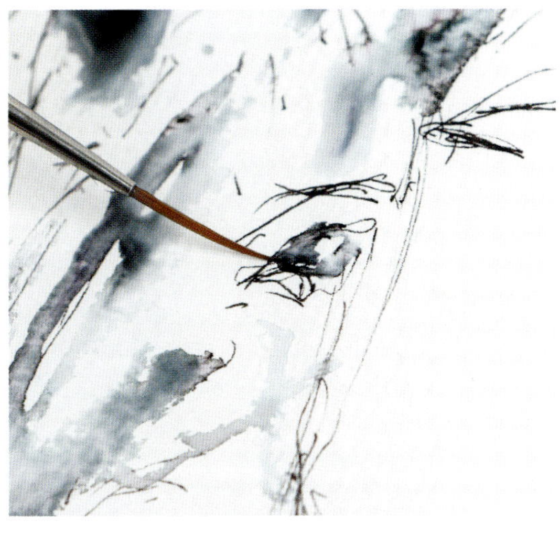

7 Where ink has pooled, draw the tip of the small brush through the pool to form the finer hairs.

8 Use the ink remaining on your small brush to touch in the details like the eye.

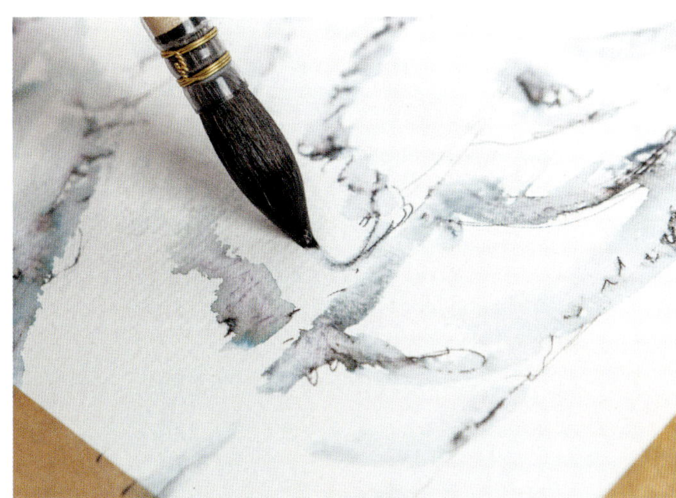

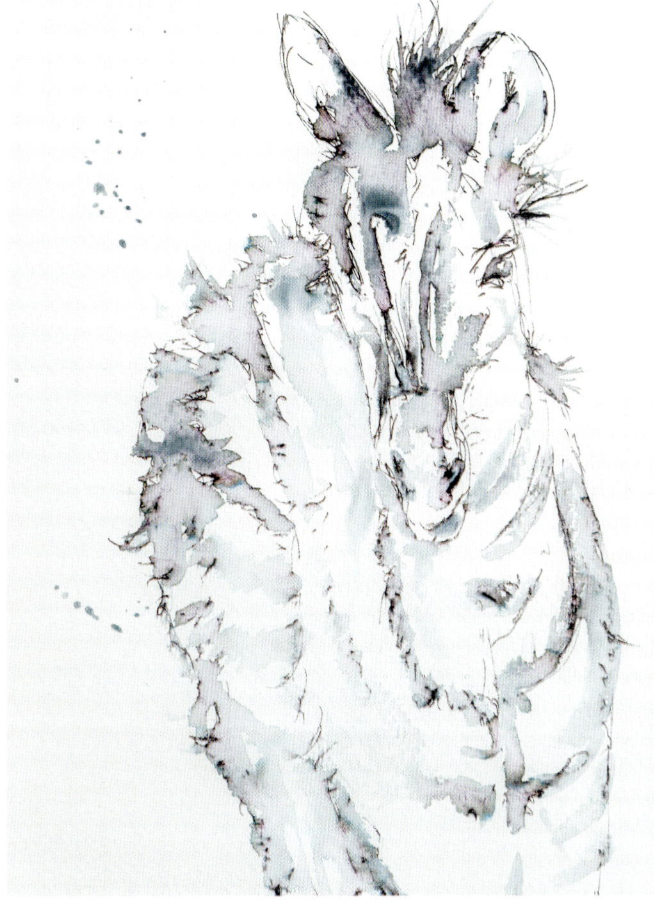

9 For the more subtle stripes, rinse the large brush and use the tip to gently draw outwards from the lines of the sketch.

10 Continue until you're happy with the basic shapes, then pick up the large brush again (see step 6, opposite), and use the diluted ink remaining on it to spatter some marks on the left-hand side.

The wonders of Quink

We're now going to add Quink ink, which will split into beautiful colours.

To avoid the Quink being too strong, transfer some to a plate with the brush. Quickly dip the brush with the remnants of the ink into the water pot, then take it back to the plate. This will give you a pool of more dilute Quink ink, as shown to the right, which can be used for light-toned areas.

Look at the colours that come from the inks at this stage – just amazing!

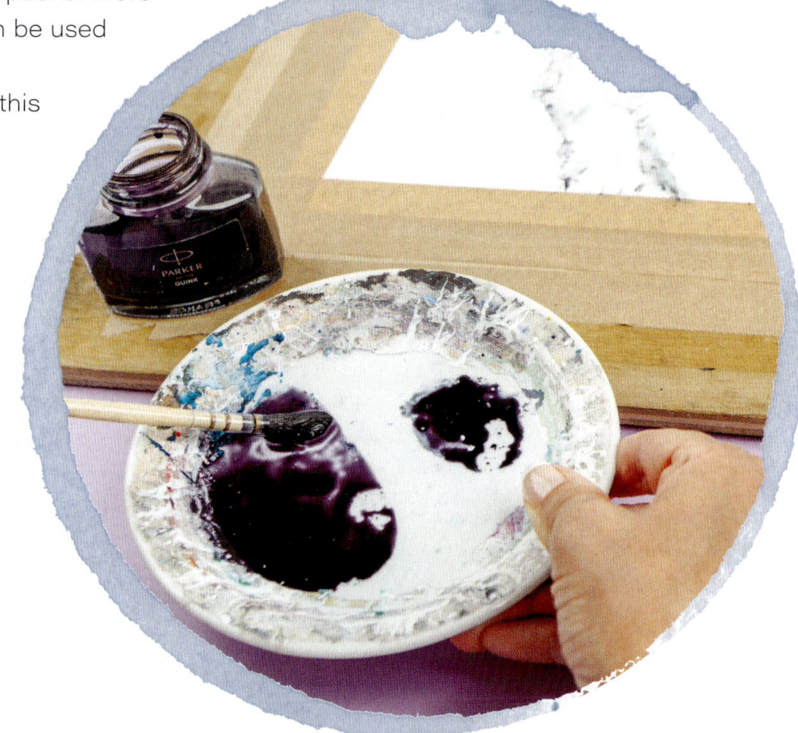

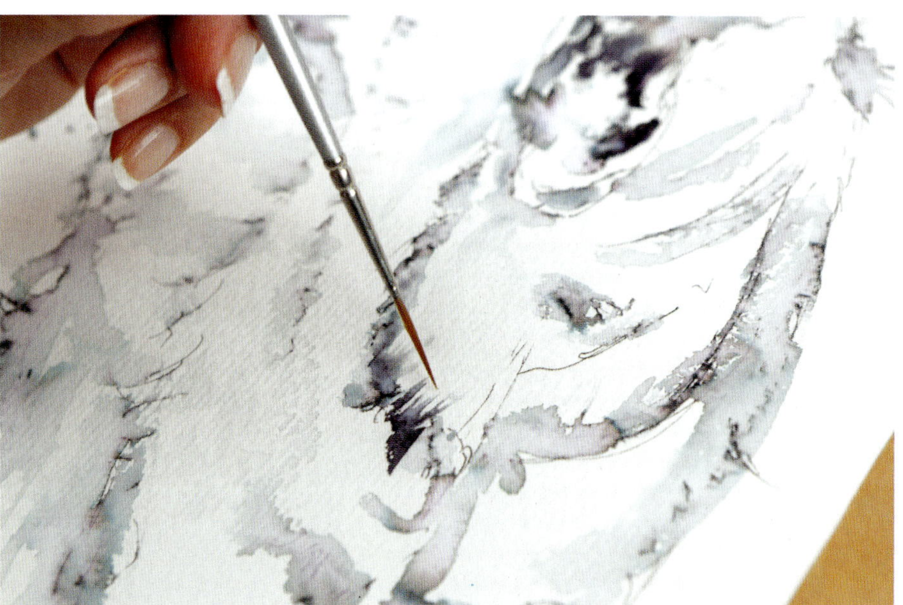

11 Using the diluted Quink ink, use the small brush to add fine, considered marks within the stripes and dark areas. Apply small amounts of Quink wet in wet, then feather them out.

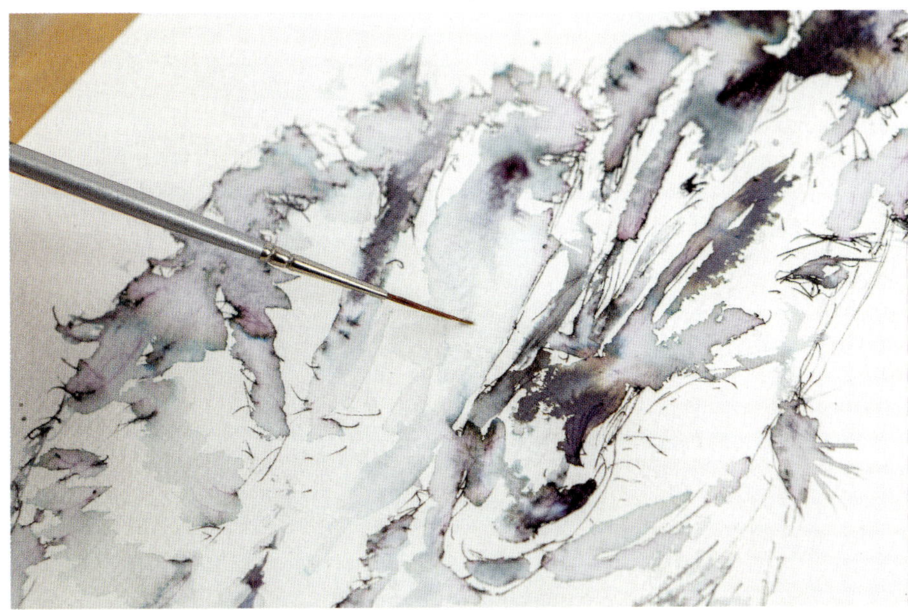

12 Still using the diluted Quink ink, and swapping between the small and medium brushes, continue to develop the markings on the zebra – pay attention to the reference photograph to guide you, but don't feel constrained by it.

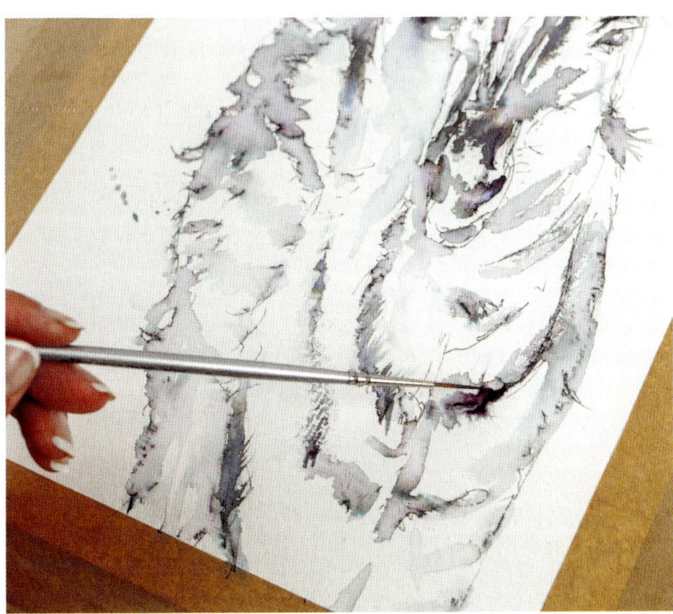

13 If you see marks that have appeared that you like, don't work over them. Instead, work around them and incorporate them into your picture.

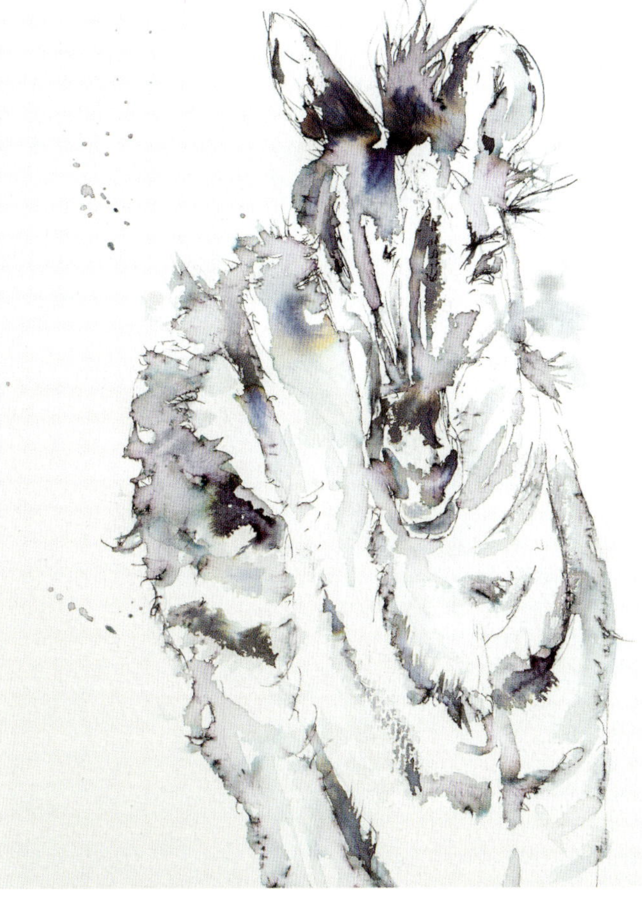

14 Still swapping between the small and medium brushes, use the undiluted Quink ink on the plate to tweak and add some darker or stronger areas in the same way. Once you're happy with the results, leave the painting to dry completely.

Making the painting yours

This final stage is all about working carefully. The effects you've created with the ink can easily be spoiled, so consider what you'll add carefully before getting stuck in.

The pink 'hot spot' on the nose draws the viewer's eye and works as an anchorpoint for the whole painting. It may be a small touch, but it's a crucial one that helps to lift the whole painting.

Finishing the painting

I used the small brush with undiluted Quink ink to add a few marks on the zebra's stomach to help reinstate the curve of his belly. To finish, I added a little rose madder to draw a little more attention to the face.

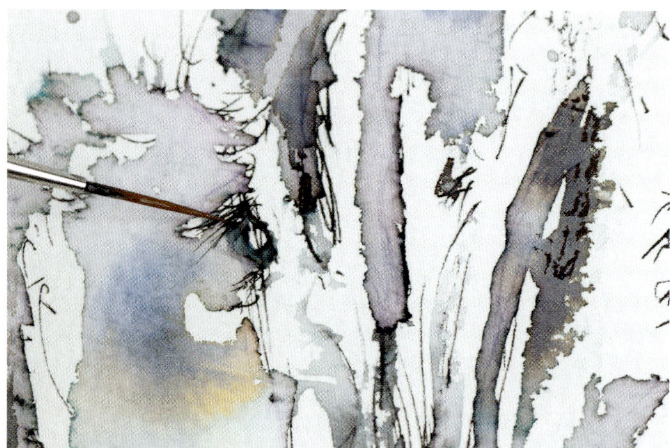

Bringing the eyes to life

Once completely dry, use the permanent fineliner to add detail, including the eyelashes, around the zebra's eyes. Leave it for a moment to dry, then use the damp tip of the small brush to pick out the eye itself, using the ink from the initial sketch.

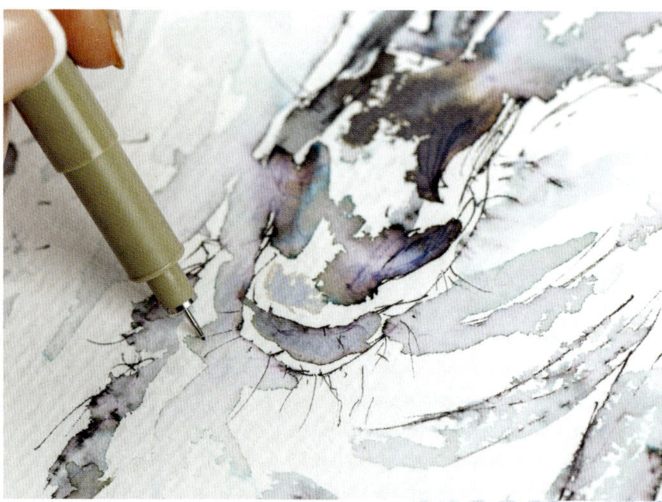
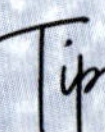

Whiskers

Using the fineliner, add some whiskers around the zebra's muzzle. I really liked the area to the left of the muzzle, so I didn't add any here, to avoid spoiling it.

Tip

While acrylic inks sits on top of dark watercolours, Quink soaks through, making the paper surface dirty and less pure. Don't worry, though – if you need to add white details, like whiskers or other highlights, you can use the tip of a sharp knife to scratch out these details, as described on page 20.

Opposite:
Zahara
25.5 x 35.5cm (10 x 14in)

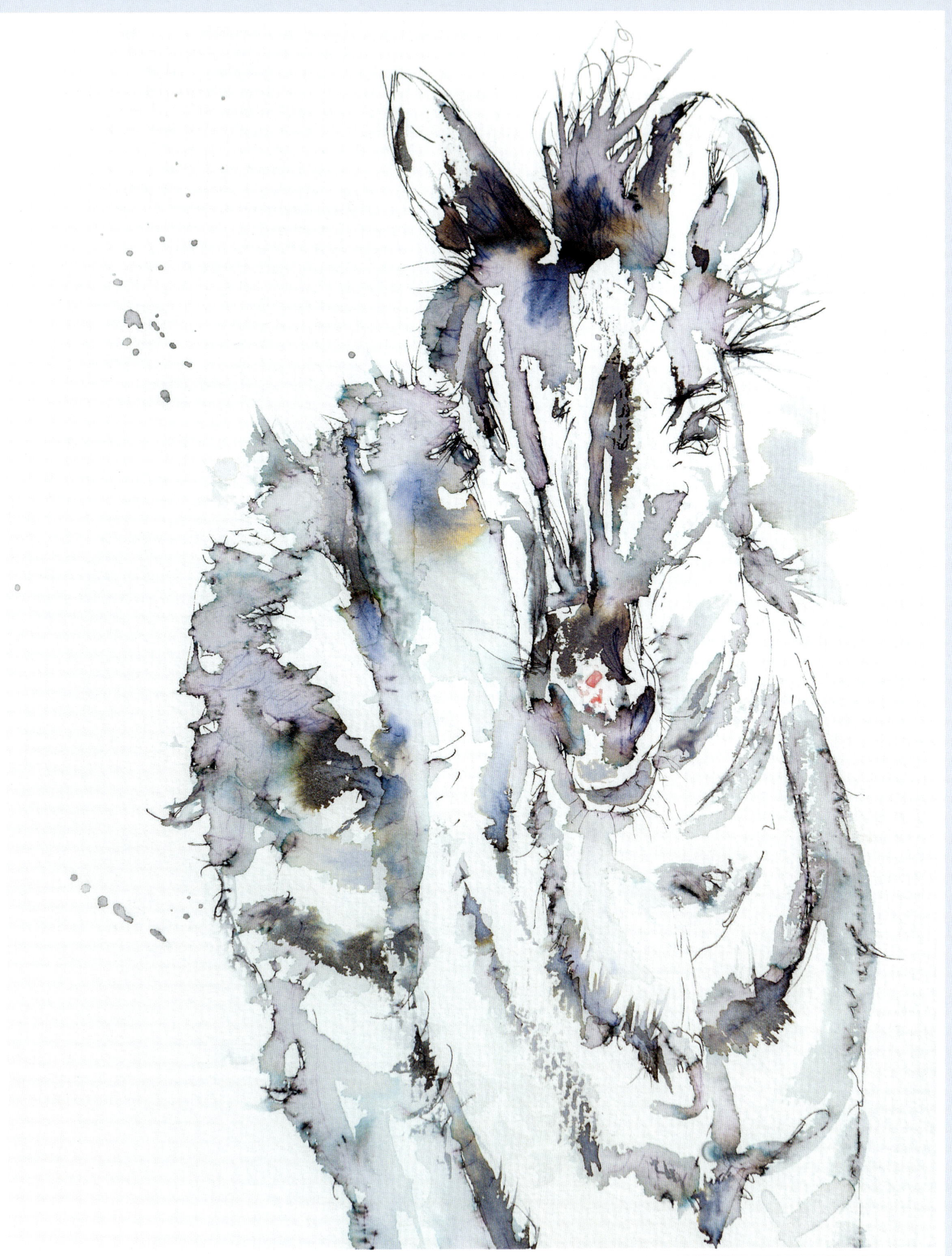

Exploring negative painting

I almost always begin my painting with the positive subject – the animal itself. On rare occasions, I find it easier to instead identify the negative space (background) around them.

Simple shapes like ovals, squares and rectangles are easier to identify than more complex shapes. When painting difficult subjects, like a trotting horse, look for the gaps around the legs and break the space down into simpler shapes.

Another way to use negative painting is to sketch the animal quite simply, then paint into the subject to suggest more complex details. For example, the hedgehog below is a simple oval shape, if you ignore the spines. The mass of details is instead suggested by painting into the basic shape.

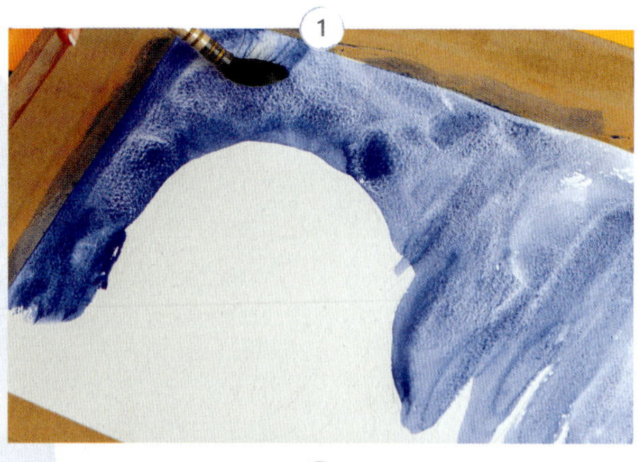

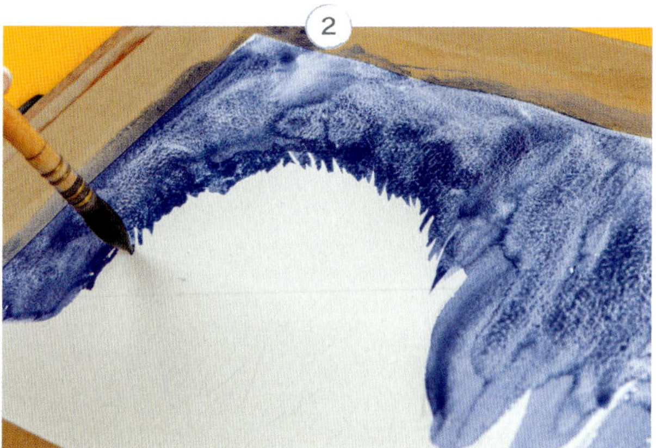

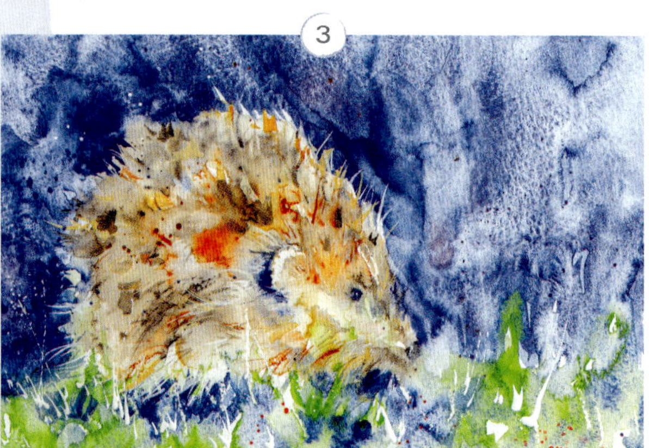

1 Paint boldly around the simple shape of the animal using a dark tone, ignoring the spines for now. You can work quite quickly with this technique.

2 While the paint remains wet, use the tip of the brush to pull the background wash into the animal shape to create the spines (or the animal's fur or feathers, for example). You'll get finer results than you would if painting the positive shapes directly.

3 As you continue painting your animal, try to leave some of the initial marks showing – but feel free to add to them or enhance them with some additional flicks.

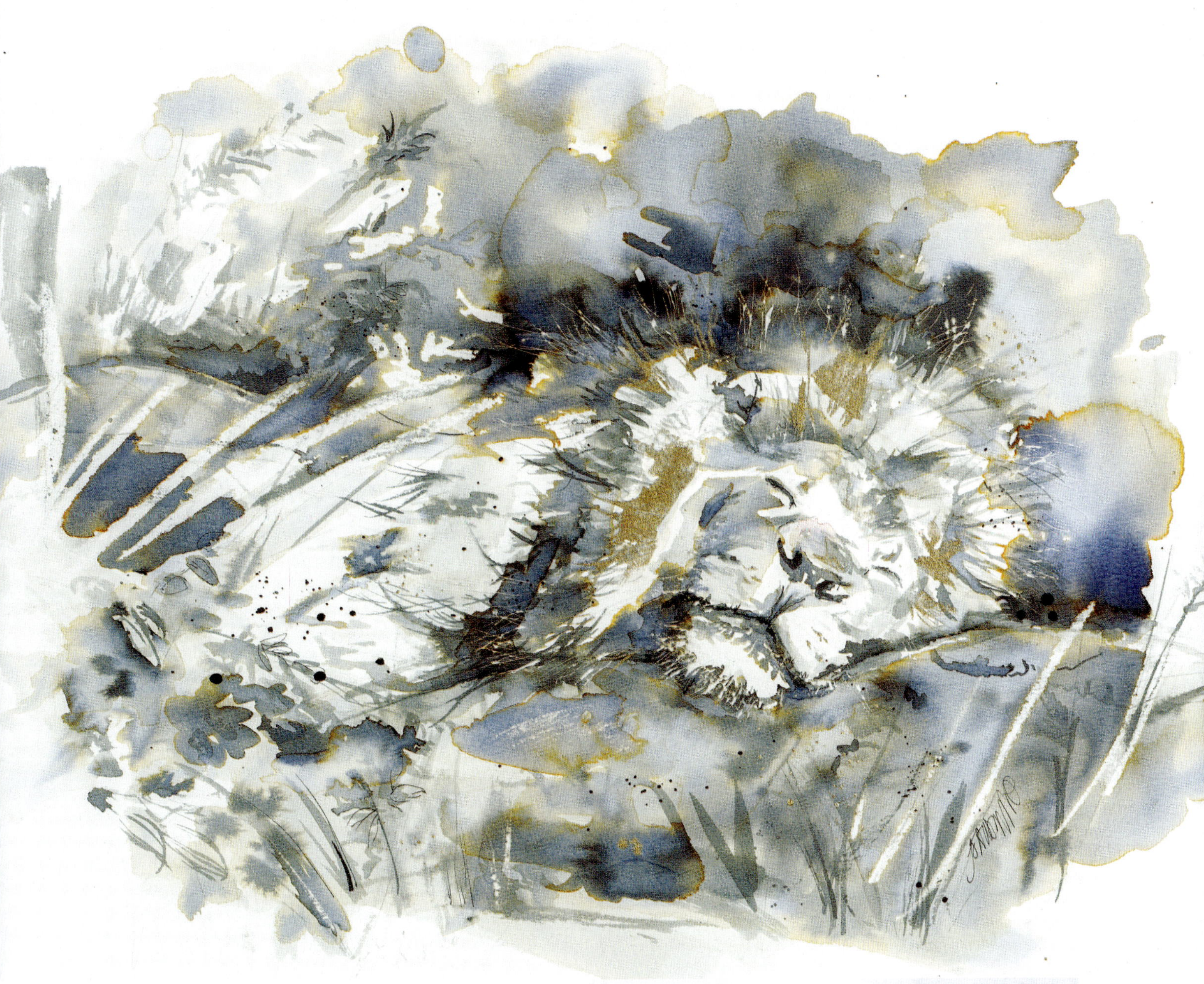

Regal Rest

31 x 23cm (12¼ x 9in)

Whilst this sleeping lion looks peaceful, I wanted to also demonstrate
his majesty and strength. This determined my approach, which was to
use a combination of different techniques and media for a dramatic finish.
Negative painting was at the heart of this approach, with the body, head and
surrounding grass all initially left as clean paper.

For texture, I used a combination of wax resist (see page 115) and then the
tip of a scalpel to gently scratch away and reveal paper highlights for his
unkempt hair. I added sparkle at the end with bronzing powder (see page 113)
here and there, which has similar warm elements to the yellow-browns that
separate out of the black Quink ink.

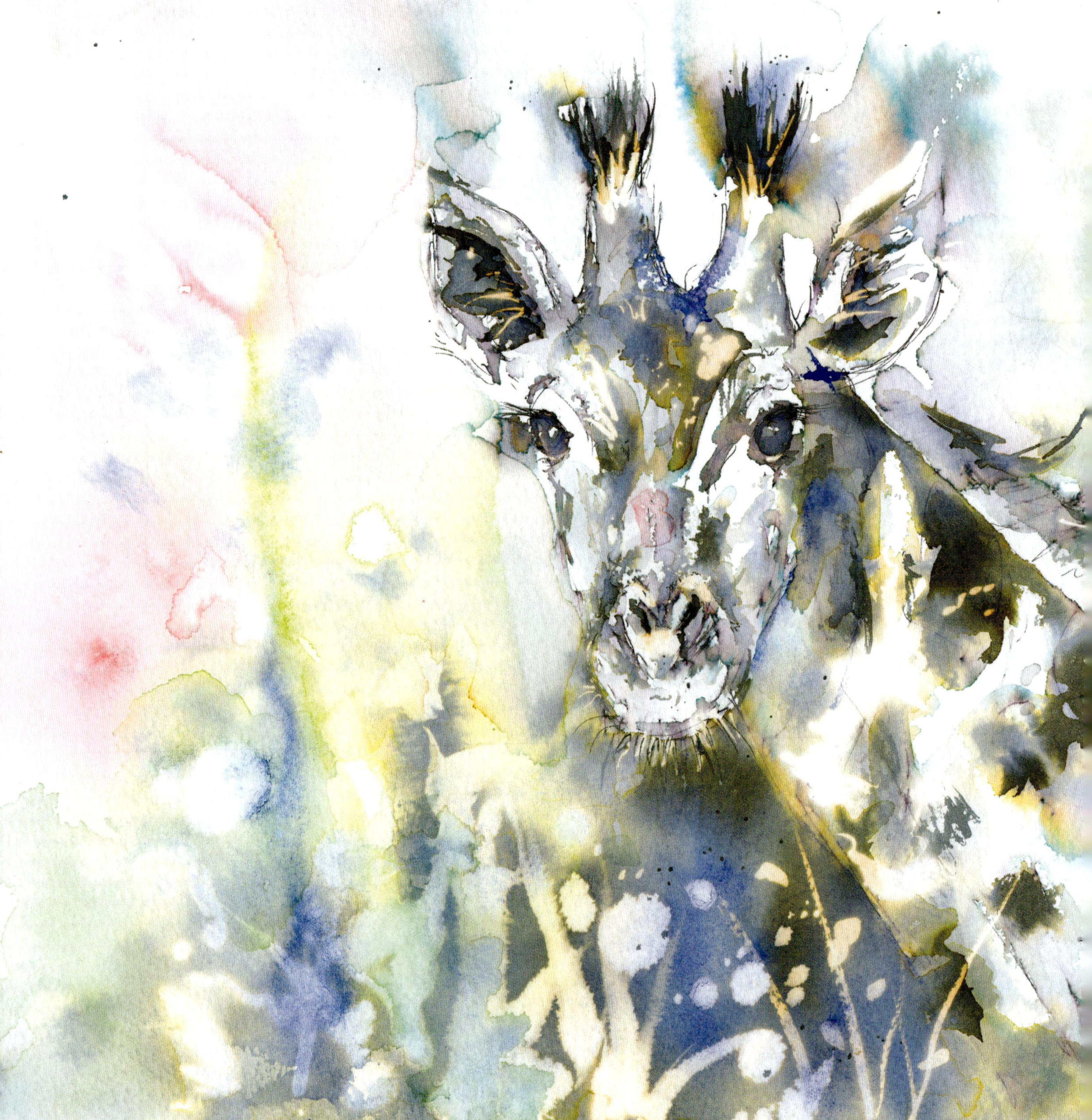

Gigi

39 x 28.5cm (15½ x 11¼in)

For a different approach to the monochromatic giraffe, I did add a little green and red watercolour here and there this time. Once I had built up at least six values (see pages 128–129) on my giraffe, near the end, I stroked some neat bleach through some areas that were still wet and some of the already dry areas too. In hardly any time at all, there was evidence of where I had made the marks using a brush for some strokes, a cotton bud for the foliage and even a cocktail stick for other areas too.

Exploring bleach

Bleach can be a surprisingly useful addition to your mixed media work, as explained on page 90. Applied like a watercolour paint, bleach will add light marks to both paint and ink. The results aren't a stark white, but instead a warmer value.

Be careful when using bleach, as it is corrosive. Don't worry, however, it's not going to burn a hole in your paper. Similarly, there's no need to use gloves – just take the same precautions as you might when washing the floors: keep it away from your skin and eyes, and rinse it off with plenty of cold water if you do get it on your skin.

Likewise, you don't need special brushes. I use my best brushes for applying bleach, and simply make sure to rinse them out thoroughly afterwards.

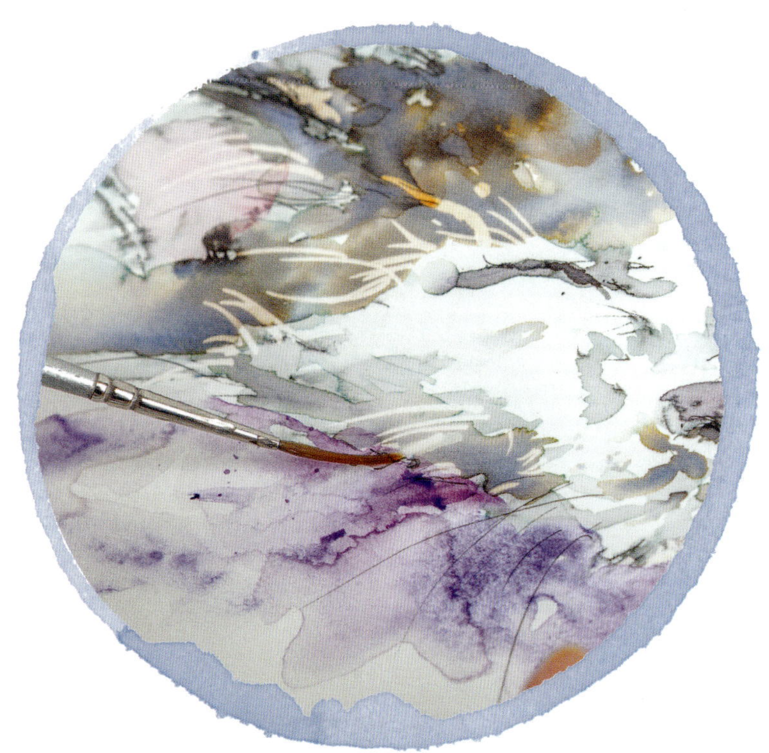

Using bleach
Here, I've used my rigger brush to draw some fine details on this cat. Bleach is fantastic for adding whiskers, as the marks it makes aren't as stark as white ink.

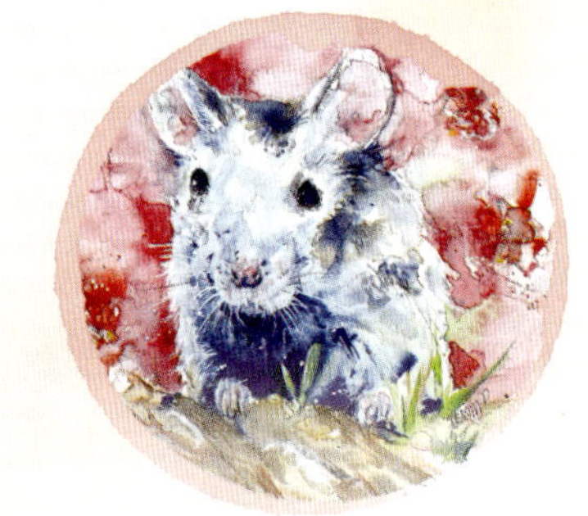

Afterword

While writing this book, I've kept in mind my main objective: to inspire
and motivate anyone who wishes to loosen up their artwork. I have
almost twenty-five years of experience in painting, illustration and
teaching, and the common thread has always been my passion to
pass on any knowledge and skills I have acquired to assist others
in their own artistic journeys.

I hope that reading my book has given you plenty of ideas to
think about, new techniques to explore, and has helped to build your
confidence in producing fresh paintings of which you are proud. Most of
all, I hope that *Loose and Lively Animals* has inspired you to really let go
of any inhibitions or worries about your painting, and that you can have
fun painting in a carefree, non-contrived way. I wish you all the very best
as you carry on exploring.

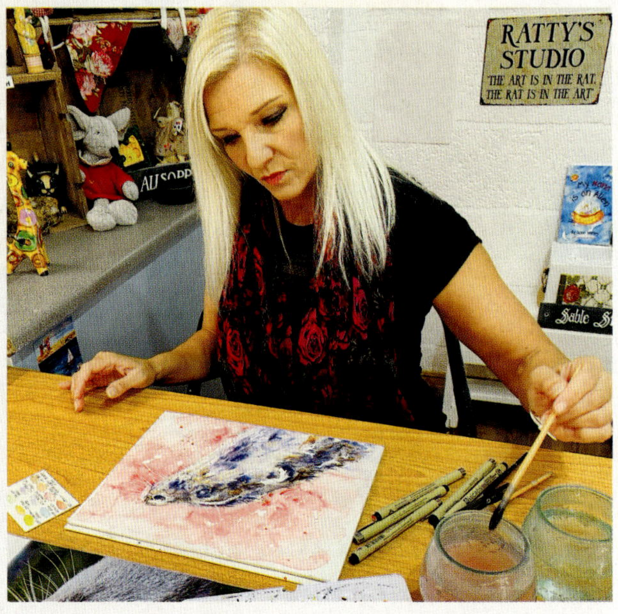

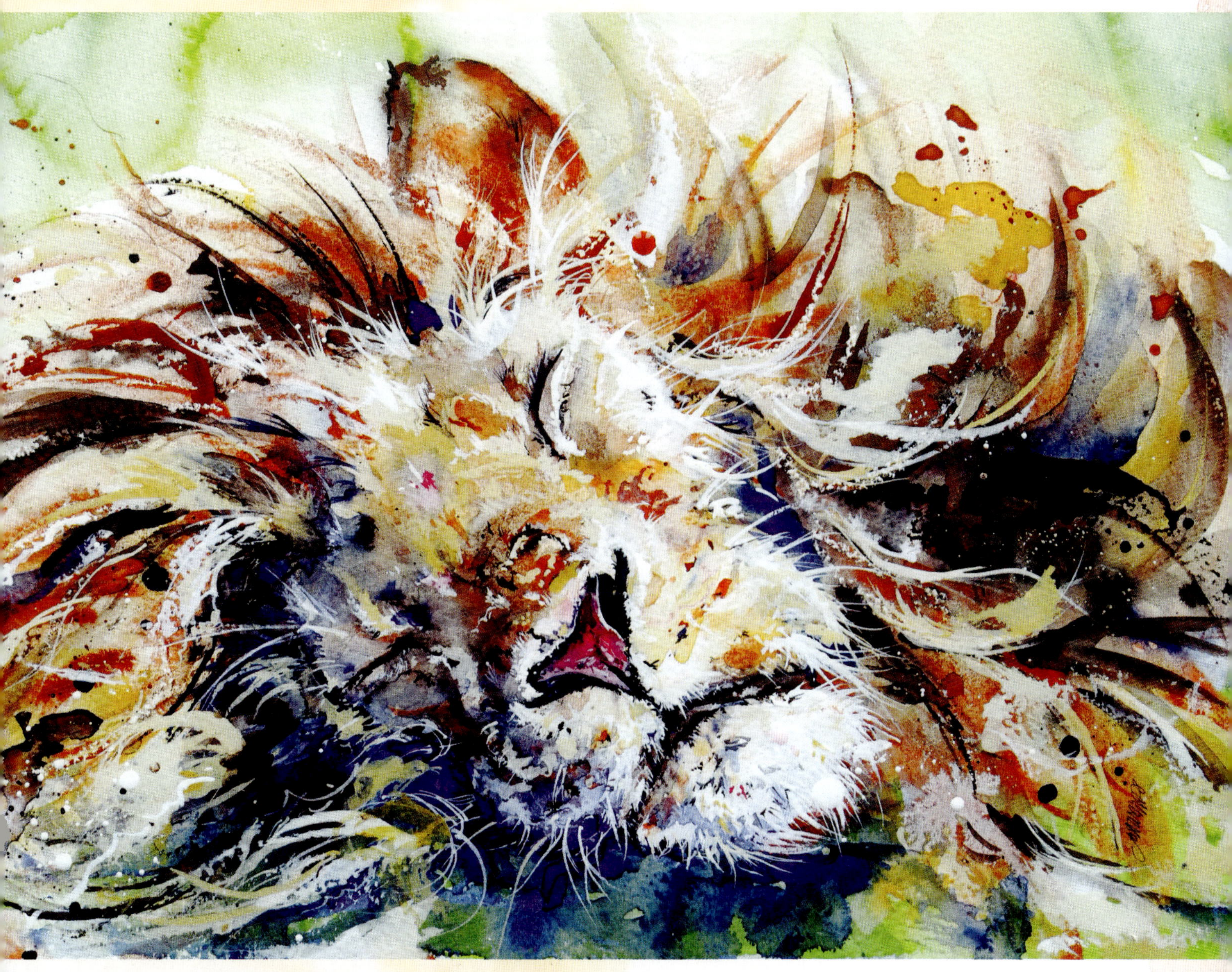

A Sleeping Lion

This big cat appeared on BBC television's *Home is Where the Art Is* programme, and won many admirers. It represents a big step forward on my own journey.

Index

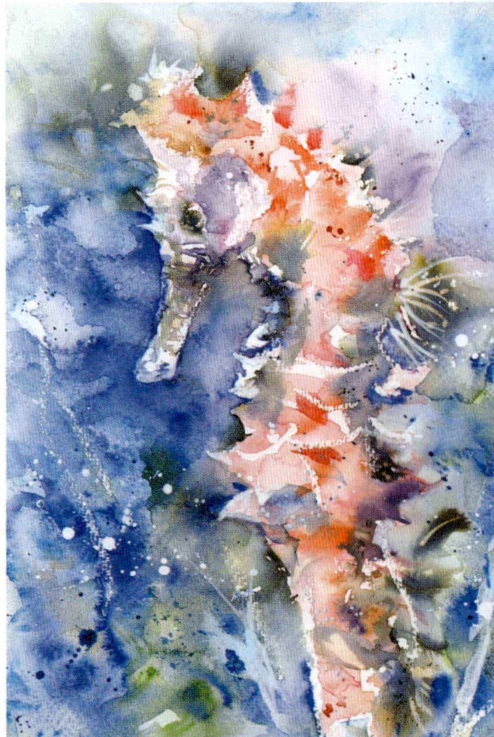